THE BOOK OF THOMAS THE CONTENDER

FROM CODEX II OF THE CAIRO GNOSTIC

LIBRARY FROM NAG HAMMADI (CG II,7)

SOCIETY OF BIBLICAL LITERATURE

DISSERTATION SERIES

Edited by

Howard C. Kee

and

Douglas A. Knight

Number 23

THE BOOK OF THOMAS THE CONTENDER

FROM CODEX II OF THE CAIRO GNOSTIC

LIBRARY FROM NAG HAMMADI   (CG II,7)

by

John Douglas Turner

_____

SCHOLARS PRESS
Missoula, Montana

THE BOOK OF THOMAS THE CONTENDER

FROM CODEX II OF THE CAIRO GNOSTIC

LIBRARY FROM NAG HAMMADI   (CG II,7):

The Coptic Text with Translation

Introduction and Commentary

by

John Douglas Turner

Published by

SCHOLARS PRESS

and

The Society of Biblical Literature

Distributed by

SCHOLARS PRESS
University of Montana
Missoula, Montana 59801

THE BOOK OF THOMAS THE CONTENDER

FROM CODEX II OF THE CAIRO GNOSTIC

LIBRARY FROM NAG HAMMADI (CG II,7):

The Coptic Text with Translation
Introduction and Commentary

by

John Douglas Turner
Department of Religious Studies
University of Montana
Missoula, Montana 59801

Ph.D., 1970   Advisor:
Duke University   Orval Wintermuth

Library of Congress Cataloging in Publication Data

Turner, John Douglas
    The Book of Thomas the Contender, from Codex II of
the Cairo gnostic library from Nag Hammadi   (CG II, 7)

    (Dissertation series ; no. 23)
    Thesis - Duke University, 1970.
    Bibliography: p.
    Includes index.
    1. Book of Thomas the Contender. 2. Gnosticism--
History--Sources. 3. Coptic language--Texts. I. Book
of Thomas the Contender. English & Coptic. 1975.
II. Chenoboskion manuscripts. III. Series: Society
of Biblical Literature. Dissertation series ; no. 18.
BS2970.T8   273'.1   75-22446
ISBN 0-89130-017-1

Printed in the United States of America
1 2 3 4 5 6
Printing Department
University of Montana
Missoula, Montana 59801

PREFACE

The Coptic text, English translation and word indices of
this dissertation were revised in 1975 according to the photo-
graphic facsimiles of Codex II in *The Facsimile Edition of the
Nag Hammadi Codices*, Published under the Auspices of The Department of Antiquities of the Arab Republic of Egypt in Conjunction
with the United Nations Educational, Scientific and Cultural
Organization: Codex II (Leiden: E. J. Brill, 1974). See also
M. Krause and P. Labib, *Gnostische und hermetische Schriften
aus Codex II und Codex VII*, Abhandlungen des Deutschen Archao-
logischen Instituts Kairo, Koptische Reihe, Band 2 (Gluckstadt,
Verlag J. J. Augustin, 1971 [appeared 1972]), pp. 88-106, for
Coptic text and German translation by M. Krause, and review by
H.-M. Schenke, "Sprachliche und exegetische Probleme in den
beiden letzten Schriften des Codex II von Nag Hammadi," *Oriental-
ische Literaturzeitung* LXX 1, (1975), 6-14. The textual revi-
sion necessarily creates some minor discrepancies between the
text and the remainder of the dissertation which is unaltered
in accordance with the wishes of the editors of this series;
for these the author begs the indulgence of the reader.

Addenda et Corrigenda:

Delete entry ⲘⲚⲦⲈⲓϥ from Index, p. 42, and add ⲘⲚⲦⲰⲚϨ 141:29
"vitality" to Index, p. 54, s.v. ⲰⲚϨ .

TABLE OF CONTENTS

THE BOOK OF THOMAS THE CONTENDER

FROM CODEX II OF THE CAIRO GNOSTIC

LIBRARY FROM NAG HAMMADI (CG II,7):

The Coptic Text with Translation

Introductions and Commentary

The *Book of Thomas the Contender*, or as we shall refer to it, *Thomas the Contender*, is the seventh and last tractate of Codex II of the Coptic Gnostic Corpus discovered in 1945/6 at Nag Hammadi, Egypt. Because of its unavailability, this short 318 line document has not received much attention. H.-C. Puech and Jean Doresse have published surveys of the entire Nag Hammadi discovery which included a few pages relative to this document.[1] Outside of a few illustrative passages from the tractate published in the Works Cited, there exists no rendering of the treatise into a modern language.[2]

The purpose of this dissertation is to place before the scholarly world new material contributary to the study of the history of religions. The aim is to provide a translation, indices, grammatical analysis, and commentary on *Thomas the Contender*. This material is offered as a contribution to what will hopefully be an ongoing discussion of this document, and no claim to finality in interpretation is intended.

Restorations of the text have been offered wherever justifiable on the basis of the clues provided by fragments of words together with the context of the portion of text where these word-fragments appear. Since *Thomas the Contender* is likely to be of interest primarily to scholars the translation will be kept as literal as possible without being wooden.

The chapter on the grammatical analysis of the tractate is divided into sections, one dealing with the dialect, and the other with the syntax, of the Coptic text. The analysis is presented in virtually tabular form, with a view to providing ease of access to the main features of the Coptic text. It represents only one among many possible ways of presenting the grammatical profile of *Thomas the Contender* and is offered primarily as an aid to readers who are neither beginners nor experts in the language, but whose linguistic skills are average. No attempt is made either at finality or exhaustiveness; rather we offer a "bird's eye view." To this end various kinds of anomalies or obscurities are left to be treated in the commentary.

3

The commentary is divided into sections whose extent is basically governed by the form of the tractate. Where the tractate is dialogue, that is, the first three-fifths of the text which, for reasons which will be explained, we designate "section A," the division corresponds to the changes in speaker. Each response by Thomas or the Savior will be treated in a separate section, except in cases where individual speeches are best treated by subdividing them according to subject matter. Where the tractate is monologue, that is, the last two-fifths of the text which we designate "section B," the division corresponds to the form of the discourse; accordingly, a section apiece is devoted to the apocalyptic introduction (142:26-143:7), the chain of woes (143:8-145:1), the beatitudes (145:1-8) and the conclusion (145:8-end). In the commentary, reference is made to the text by the Coptic page number within Codex II, and the line number counting from the top of the page. References to other tractates in the Nag Hammadi Corpus are designated by library (CG, "Cairo Gnostic" library), codex number in Roman numerals, tractate number in underlined "Arabic" numerals, plus codex page and line number (e.g. *Thomas the Contender* would be CG II, 7,138,1-145,19).

Paleographical matters are not dealt with, since they have been treated *in extenso* by Søren Giversen and Martin Krause.[3] Giversen dated Codex II around the middle of the fourth century, although it is possible that the date may extend before this time, even to the second half of the third century.[4] The actual content of *Thomas the Contender*, however, and especially the content of section B, is probably older than the earliest of these dates, perhaps much older.

Section A, the dialogue, teaches that if one wants to be perfect, that is free from the cumbersome passions that weigh down the soul, one must be aware that he inhabits a lust-ridden bestial body whose ultimate fate is dissolution. The cardinal passion is described under the metaphor of the fire of lust; he who submits to the body's fire of lust will likewise be destroyed by the fire of Hell. Thomas, the twin of the Savior, receives this teaching just prior to the Savior's ascension, that is while the Savior is in his resurrected state, thus revealing his true nature as the light that is about to withdraw back to the heavenly essence of light. As the light, he serves to illumine the secrets of darkness, to reveal the truth about existence in the body. By acting on his teaching, one becomes perfect.

On the other hand, section B, the homily, is shown to represent a very late stage in the "sayings of Jesus" tradition, which contains little more than speech-formulae traditionally attributed to Jesus, while the body of the saying consists of little else than contemporary ascetic teaching placed in Jesus' mouth.

In an attempt to provide a more creative vehicle for the ascetic teaching of section B than the limited scope of its character as a sayings-collection could provide, it is suggested that a redactor combined section B with section A to form the current *Book of Thomas the Contender*. Such creative potential was achieved by construing the entire tractate as a scribal record of the most authoritative last-minute revelations of the resurrected Savior to a revered apostle. It is speculated that sections A and B were composed in Greek in the first half of the third century, and translated into Coptic and then combined in the second half of the third century.

NOTES

[1]Henry-Charles Puech, "Les nouveaux écrits gnostiques découverts en Haute-Égypte: premier inventaire et essai d'identification," *Coptic Studies in Honor of Walter Ewing Crum* (Bulletin of the Byzantine Institute, ed. W. Schneemelcher. No. 2; Boston: Byzantine Institute, 1950), pp. 105, 117-120; *id.* "The Book of Thomas the Athlete" in E. Hennecke, *New Testament Apocrypha*, (2 vols. 1; Philadelphia: Westminster, 1963), Vol. 2, pp. 307-313. Jean Doresse, "Nouveaux écrits coptes," *Vigiliae Christianae* III (1949), 34; *id. The Secret Books of the Egyptian Gnostics*, trans. Philip Mairet (New York: Viking, 1960), p. 225f. See also C.D.G. Müller "Buch von Thomas dem Athleten," *Kindlers Literatur Lexikon*, I (Zürich: Kindler Verlag, 1965), p. 1936f.

[2]I have given an account of the content and provenance of the tractate to the national meeting of the Society of Biblical Literature meeting in December 1968 at Berkeley, California. The tractate is due to be published by Martin Krause and Pahor Labib, *Gnostische und hermetische Schriften aus Codex II und VI* (Abhandlungen des Deutschen Archäologischen Instituts Abteilung Kairo, Koptische Reihe 2, to appear in 1970 (appeared 1972).

[3]Søren Giversen, *Apocryphon Johannis: the Coptic Text of the Apocryphon Johannis in the Nag Hammadi Codex II with Translation, Introduction and Commentary* (Acta Theologica Danica, vol. V; Copenhagen: Munksgaard, 1963), pp. 19-45; Martin Krause *Die drei Versionen des Apokryphon des Johannes im Koptischen Museum zu Alt-Kairo*, Mitteilungen des Deutschen Archäologischen Institutes Abteilung Kairo, XIX, 1963), pp. 106-113. Cf. Doresse, *Secret Books*, pp. 138-145.

ⲛ̄ϣⲁϫⲉ ⲉⲑⲏⲡ` ⲛⲁⲓ̈ ⲉⲛⲧⲁϥϣⲁϫⲉ ⲙ̄ⲙⲟⲟⲩ ⲛ̄ϭⲓ ⲡⲥⲱⲣ ⲛ̄

2 ⲓ̈ⲟⲩⲇⲁⲥ ⲑⲱⲙⲁⲥ ⲛⲁⲓ̈ ⲉⲛⲧⲁⲓ̈ⲥⲁⲍⲟⲩ· ⲁⲛⲟⲕ ϩⲱⲱⲧ` ⲙⲁ

ⲑⲁⲓⲁⲥ ⲛⲉⲉⲓⲙⲟⲟϣⲉ ⲉⲉⲓⲥⲱⲧⲙ̄ ⲉⲣⲟⲟⲩ ⲉⲩϣⲁϫⲉ ⲙⲛ̄

4 ⲛⲟⲩⲉⲣⲏⲩ ⲡⲁϫⲉϥ ⲛ̄ϭⲓ ⲡⲥⲱⲣ ϫⲉ ⲡⲥⲁⲛ` ⲑⲱⲙⲁⲥ ϩⲱⲥ

ⲉⲩⲛ̄ⲧⲁⲕ` ⲙ̄ⲙⲁⲛ ⲛ̄ⲟⲩⲟⲉⲓϣ ϩⲙ̄ ⲡⲕⲟⲥⲙⲟⲥ ⲥⲱⲧⲙ̄ ⲉⲣⲟⲓ̈

6 ⲛ̄ⲧⲁϭⲱⲗⲡ` ⲛⲁⲕ` ⲉⲃⲟⲗ ⲉⲧⲃⲉ ⲛⲉⲛⲧⲁⲕ`ⲙⲉⲉⲩⲉ ⲉⲣⲟⲟⲩ

ϩⲣⲁⲓ̈ ϩⲙ̄ ⲡⲉⲕ`ϩⲏⲧ` ⲉⲡⲉⲓⲇⲏϩ ⲁⲩϫⲟⲟⲥ ϫⲉ ⲛ̄ⲧⲟⲕ` ⲡⲁ

8 ⲥⲟⲉⲓϣ` ⲁⲩⲱ ⲡⲁϣⲃⲣ̄ⲙ̄ⲙⲏⲉ· ϩⲉⲧϩⲱⲧⲕ̄ ⲛ̄ⲕⲙ̄ⲙⲉ

ϫⲉ ⲛ̄ⲧⲕ ⲛⲓⲙ` ⲁⲩⲱ ⲁⲕϣⲟⲟⲡ` ⲛ̄ⲁϣ ⲛ̄ϩⲉ ⲏ ⲉⲕⲛⲁϣⲱ

10 ⲡⲉ ⲛ̄ⲛⲁϣ ⲛ̄ⲣⲏⲧⲉ ⲉⲡⲉⲓⲇⲏ ⲥⲉⲙⲟⲩⲧⲉ ⲉⲣⲟⲕ` ϫⲉ ⲡⲁⲥⲟⲛ̄

ⲡⲉⲧⲉⲥϣⲉ ⲁⲛ ⲡⲉ· ⲉⲧⲣⲉⲕ`ϣⲱⲡⲉ ⲉⲕⲟ ⲛ̄ⲁⲧⲥⲟⲟⲩⲛ`ⲉ·

12 ⲉⲣⲟⲕ` ⲙ̄ⲙⲓⲛ` ⲙ̄ⲙⲟⲕ` ⲁⲩⲱ †ⲥⲟⲟⲩⲛⲉ ϫⲉ ⲁⲕⲙ̄ⲙⲉ ⲁⲕⲟⲩ

ⲱ ⲅⲁⲣ ⲉⲕⲙ̄ⲙⲉ ⲙ̄ⲙⲟⲉⲓ ϫⲉ ⲁⲛⲟⲕ ⲡⲉ ⲡⲥⲟⲟⲩⲛ ⲛ̄ⲧⲙⲏⲉ

14 ϩⲱⲥ ⲉⲕⲙⲟⲟϣⲉ ϭⲉ ⲛⲙ̄ⲙⲁⲉⲓ ⲕⲁⲛ ⲛ̄ⲧⲁⲕ` ⲟⲩⲁⲧ`ⲥⲟⲟⲩⲛ`

* ⲁⲕⲟⲩⲱ ⲉⲕⲥⲟⲟⲩⲛⲉ ⲁⲩⲱ ⲥⲉⲛⲁⲙⲟⲩⲧⲉ ⲉⲣⲟⲕ` ϫⲉ ⲡⲣⲉϥ`

16 ⲥⲟⲟⲩⲛ`ⲉ ⲉⲣⲟϥ` ⲙ̄ⲙⲓⲛ ⲙ̄ⲙⲟϥ` ϫⲉ ⲡⲉⲧⲉ ⲙ̄ⲡϥ̄ⲥⲟⲩ

ⲱⲛϥ ⲅⲁⲣ` ⲙ̄ⲡϥ̄ⲥⲟⲩⲱⲛ ⲗⲁⲁⲩ` ⲡⲉⲛⲧⲁϥⲥⲟⲩⲱⲛϥ ⲇⲉ ⲟⲩ

18 ⲁⲁⲧϥ` ⲁϥⲟⲩⲱ ⲟⲛ` ⲉϥϫⲓ ⲥⲟⲟⲩⲛⲉ· ⲁⲡⲃⲁⲑⲟⲥ ⲙ̄ⲡⲧⲏⲣϥ

ⲉⲧⲃⲉ ⲡⲁⲓ̈ ϭⲉ ⲛ̄ⲧⲟⲕ` ⲡⲁⲥⲟⲛ̄ ⲑⲱⲙⲁⲥ` ⲁⲕⲛⲁⲩ ⲁⲡⲡⲉⲑⲏⲡ`

20 ⲉⲃⲟⲗ ϩⲛ̄ ⲣⲣⲱⲙⲉ ⲉⲧⲉ ⲡⲁⲓ̈ ⲡⲉ ⲉⲧⲟⲩϫⲓ ϫⲣⲟⲡ` ⲉⲣⲟϥ` ⲉⲛ`

ⲥⲉⲥⲟⲟⲩⲛ ⲁⲛ` ⲡⲁϫⲉϥ ⲇⲉ ⲛ̄ϭⲓ ⲑⲱⲙⲁⲥ ⲙ̄ⲡϫⲟⲉⲓⲥ ϫⲉ

138:7 ⲉⲡⲉⲓⲇⲉ   for ⲉⲡⲉⲓⲇⲏ ; perhaps ⲉⲡⲉⲓ ⲇⲉ , "Now since..."
138:18   ⲃ in ⲃⲁⲑⲟⲥ written over original ⲡ for ⲡⲁⲑⲟⲥ.

The secret words which the Savior (σωτήρ) spoke to

2   Judas Thomas, the ones which I wrote down, even I, Mathaias.

I was walking, listening to them speak with

4   one another. The Savior (σωτήρ) said: "Brother Thomas, while (ὡς)

you (sg) have time in the world (κόσμος), listen to me

6   that I may reveal to you (sg) the things you have pondered

in your (sg) mind. <Since (ἐπειδή)> it has been said that you (sg) are my

8   twin and my true companion, inquire that you (sg) may understand

who you (sg) are, and in what way you (sg) exist, or (ἤ)

10   in what manner you (sg) will come to be. Since (ἐπειδή) you (sg) are

called my brother

it is not fitting that you (sg) should be ignorant

12   of yourself. And I know that you (sg) have understood,

because (γάρ) you (sg) had already understood that I am the knowledge of

the truth.

14   Now while (ὡς) you (sg) walk with me, even though (κἄν) you (sg) are

unknowing,

you (sg) have come to know, and you (sg) will be called 'the one who

16   knows himself.' For (γάρ) he who has not known

himself has known nothing, but (δέ) he who has known himself

18   has also already obtained knowledge about the depth (βάθος) of the All.

So, therefore, you (sg) are my brother, Thomas. You (sg) have beheld

what is hidden

20   from men; that is, that on which they stumble without

knowing." And (δέ) Thomas said to the Lord:

138:19 or: "the one who is hidden"
Note: "(sg)" denotes the use of the second person masculine
         singular pronoun.

22 ⲉⲧⲃⲉ ⲡⲁⲉⲓ ϭⲉ ϯⲥⲟⲡⲥ̄ ⲙ̄ⲙⲟⲕ ϫⲉⲕⲁⲁⲥ ⲉⲕⲛⲁϫⲱ ⲛⲁⲓ
    [ⲛ̄ⲛ]ⲉⲧϣⲓⲛⲉ ⲙ̄ⲙⲟⲕ‘ ⲉⲣⲟⲟⲩ· ϩⲁⲑⲏ ⲛ̄ⲧⲉⲕ‘ ⲁⲛⲁⲗⲏⲙⲯⲓⲥ
24 [ⲁⲩ]ⲱ ϩⲟⲧⲁⲛ‘ ⲉⲉⲓϣⲁⲛⲥⲱⲧⲙ̄ ⲉⲃⲟⲗ ϩⲓⲧⲟⲟⲧⲕ‘ ϩⲁⲡⲣⲁ
    ⲛⲛⲉⲑⲏⲡ‘ ⲧⲟⲧⲉ ⲟⲩⲛ̄ϭⲟⲙ ⲙ̄ⲙⲟⲉⲓ ⲉϣⲁϫⲉ ⲉⲧⲃⲏ‘
26 ⲧ[ⲟ]ⲩ ⲁⲩⲱ ⲥⲟⲩⲟⲛϩ ⲉⲃⲟⲗ ⲛⲁⲉⲓ ϫⲉ ⲧⲙⲏⲉ ⲥⲙⲟⲕϩ ⲁ‘
    ⲁ[ⲥ] ⲛ̄ⲛⲁϩⲣⲛ̄ ⲛ̄ⲣⲱⲙⲉ ⲁϥⲟⲩⲱϣⲃ̄ ⲛ̄ϭⲓ ⲡⲥⲱⲣ ⲉϥϫⲱ ⲙ̄
28 ⲙ̣[ⲟ]ⲥ ϫⲉ ⲉϣⲡⲉ ⲛⲉⲧⲟⲩⲟⲛϩ ⲉⲃⲟⲗ ⲛⲏⲧⲛ̄ ⲥⲉϩⲏⲡ‘
    ⲛ̄[ⲛ̣]ⲁϩⲣⲛ̄ ⲧⲏⲛⲉ ⲛ̄ⲁϣ ⲛ̄ϩⲉ· ⲉⲩⲛ̄ϭⲁⲙ ⲙ̄ⲙⲱⲧⲛ̄ ⲁⲥⲱⲧⲙ̄
30 ⲁⲛⲉⲧⲉ ⲛ̄ⲥⲉⲟⲩⲟⲛϩ ⲉⲃⲟⲗ ⲁⲛ‘ ⲉϣⲡⲉ ⲛ̄ϩⲃⲏⲩⲉ ⲛ̄ⲧⲙⲏⲉ
    ⲉⲧⲟⲩⲟⲛϩ ⲉⲃⲟⲗ ϩⲙ̄ ⲡⲕⲟⲥⲙⲟⲥ ⲥⲉⲙⲟⲕϩ ⲁⲧⲣⲉⲧⲛ̄ⲁ‘
32 ⲁⲩ ⲉⲉⲓⲉ ⲡⲱⲥ ϭⲉ ⲉⲧⲉⲧⲛⲁⲉⲓⲣⲉ ⲛ̄ⲛⲁⲡⲙⲉⲅⲉⲑⲟⲥ ⲉⲧ‘
    ϫⲟⲥⲉ· ⲁⲩⲱ ⲛⲁⲡⲡⲗⲏⲣⲱⲙⲁ ⲉⲧⲉ ⲛ̄ⲥⲉⲟⲩⲟⲛϩ ⲉⲃⲟⲗ
34 ⲁⲛ· ⲛ̄ⲛⲁϣ ϭⲉ ⲛ̄ϩⲉ ⲉⲩⲛⲁⲙⲟⲩⲧⲉ ⲉⲣⲱⲧⲛ̄ ϫⲉ ⲉⲣⲅⲁⲧⲏⲥ
    ⲉⲧⲃⲉ ⲡⲁⲓ̈ ⲛ̄ⲧⲱⲧⲛ̄ ϩⲉⲛⲥⲃⲟⲩⲉⲓ ⲁⲩⲱ ⲙ̄ⲡⲁⲧⲉⲧⲛⲁⲓ ⲙ̄
36 ⲡⲙⲉⲅⲉⲑⲟⲥ ⲛ̄ⲧⲙ̄ⲛ̄ⲧⲧⲉⲗⲉⲓⲟⲥ ⲁϥⲟⲩⲱϣⲃ̄ ⲇⲉ ⲛ̄ϭⲓ
    ⲑⲱⲙⲁⲥ ⲡⲉϫⲁϥ ⲙ̄ⲡⲥⲱⲣ ϫⲉ ϫⲟⲥ ⲛⲁⲛ‘ ⲉⲧⲃⲉ [ⲛ̣]ⲁⲉⲓ
38 ⲉⲧⲕϫⲱ ⲙ̄ⲙⲟⲟⲩ ϫⲉ ⲥⲉⲟⲩⲟⲛϩ ⲉⲃⲟⲗ ⲁⲛ‘ ⲁ[ⲗⲗ]ⲁ ⲥⲉ̣ϩⲏⲡ‘
    ⲉⲣⲟⲛ· ⲡⲁϫⲉ ⲡⲥⲱⲣ ϫⲉ ⲥⲱⲙⲁ [ⲛⲓ]ⲙ̣‘ [ⲛ̄ⲧⲉ ⲛ̄ⲣⲱⲙⲉ ⲙ̣ⲛ̄
40 ⲛ̄ⲧⲃⲛⲟⲟⲩⲉ ⲉⲩϫⲡⲟ ⲙ̄ⲙⲟⲟⲩ ⲟ[ⲩⲛ̄ϣ ⲗⲟⲅ]ⲟⲥ [ⲉⲉⲓ]ⲉ
    ⲥⲉ[ⲟⲩ]ⲟⲛϩ ⲉ[ⲃ]ⲟⲗ ⲙ̄ⲡⲓⲣⲏⲧⲉ ⲛ̄ⲑⲉ ⲛ̄̄[ⲟⲩⲥⲱⲛⲧ‘ ⲉϥϣⲡ
42 [ⲙ̄ⲙⲟϥ ⲛ̄ⲟⲩⲗⲟⲅⲓ]ⲕ̣[ⲟⲛ] ⲛⲁⲓ ϩⲱⲱϥ ⲛⲉⲧⲙ̄ⲡⲥⲁⲛ‘ⲧⲡⲉ
    [ⲥⲉⲟⲩⲟⲛϩ ⲉⲃⲟⲗ ⲁⲛ ϩⲛ̄] ⲛⲉⲧⲟⲩⲟⲛϩ ⲉⲃⲟⲗ ⲁⲗⲗⲁ ⲉ[ⲩ]

138:25   may read ⲛⲡⲉⲑⲏⲡ
138,43-139,1   ⲉ[ⲩ]/ⲟⲛϩ ⲉⲃⲟⲗ for ⲉⲟⲩⲟⲛϩ ⲉⲃⲟⲗ

22 "Therefore I beg you (sg) to tell me

[the things] about which I ask you before your Ascension (ἀνάλημψις).

24 And whenever (ὅταν) I hear from you (sg) about

the hidden things, then (τότε) I can speak about

26 them. And it is obvious to me that the truth is difficult to

perform before men." The Savior (σωτήρ) answered, saying:

28 "If the things that are visible to you are hidden

before you, how is it possible for you to hear

30 about the things that are not visible? If the deeds of the truth

which are visible in the world are difficult for you to perform,

32 how (πῶς) indeed, then, will you perform those (deeds) of the

exalted Majesty (μέγεθος) and those (deeds) of the Pleroma (πλήρωμα)

which are not visible?

34 And how will you be called 'Laborers' (ἐργάτης)?

Therefore you are disciples, and have not yet received

36 the Majesty (μέγεθος) of the Perfection (-τέλειος)." And (δέ) Thomas

answered

and said to the Savior (σωτήρ): "Tell us about these things

38 which you (sg) say are not visible, [but are] hidden

from us." The Savior (σωτήρ) said: "[All] bodies (σῶμα) [of men and]

40 beasts are begotten [irrational (-λόγος). Surely]

they appear just like [a creature] who reckons

42 [himself rational (λογικόν)]. Those, however, that are above

[do not appear in] visible things. Rather (ἀλλά) they

```
    ⲟ̣ⲛϩ ⲉⲃⲟⲗ ϩⲛ ⲧⲟⲩⲛⲟⲩⲛⲉ ⲟⲩⲁⲁⲧⲟⲩ ⲁⲩⲱ ⲛⲉⲩⲕⲁⲣ
2   ⲡⲟⲥ ⲡⲉⲧˋⲥⲁⲁⲛ ϣ ⲙⲙⲟⲟⲩ ⲛⲉⲉⲓⲥⲱⲙⲁ ⲛⲧⲟⲟⲩ ⲉⲧⲟⲩ
    ⲟⲛϩ ⲉⲃⲟⲗ ⲉⲩⲱⲙ ⲉⲃⲟⲗ ϩⲛ ⲛⲥⲱⲛⲧ ⲉ†ⲛⲉ ⲙⲙⲟⲟⲩ
4   ⲉⲧⲃⲉ ⲡⲁⲓ̈ ϭⲉ ⲛⲥⲱⲙⲁ ⲥⲉϣⲓⲃⲉ  ⲡⲉⲧϣⲓⲃⲉ ⲇⲉ ⲩⲛⲁⲧⲉ
    ⲕⲟ ⲛ̅ϥⲱϫⲛ̅ ⲁⲩⲱ ⲙⲛ̅ⲧⲉϥ ϩⲉⲗⲡⲓⲥ ⲛ̅ⲱⲛϩ ϩⲙ ⲡⲓⲛⲁⲩ
6   ⲇⲉ ⲡⲓⲥⲱⲙⲁ ⲅⲁⲣˋ ⲟⲩⲧⲃⲛⲏ ⲡⲉ ⲛ̅ⲛ̅ⲑⲉ ϭⲉ ⲛ̅ⲛ̅ⲧⲃⲛⲟⲟⲩⲉ
    ⲉⲩϣⲁⲣⲉⲡⲟⲩⲥⲱⲙⲁ ⲧⲉⲕⲟ ⲧⲉⲉⲓ ⲧⲉ ⲑⲉ ⲛⲛⲉⲉⲓⲡⲗⲁⲥⲙⲁ
8   ⲥⲉⲛⲁⲧⲉⲕⲟˉ ⲙⲏⲧⲓ ⲟⲩⲉⲃⲟⲗ ⲁⲛ ⲡⲉ ϩⲛ ⲧⲥⲩⲛⲟⲩⲥⲓⲁ ⲛ
    ⲑⲉ ⲙ̅ⲡⲁⲛ̅ⲧⲃⲛⲟⲟⲩⲉˉ ⲉϣϫⲉ ⲟⲩⲉⲃⲟⲗ ⲛ̅ϩⲏⲧⲥ̅ ϩⲱ
10  ⲱϥ ⲡⲉ ⲛ̅ⲁϣ ⲛ̅ϩⲉ ⲉϥⲛⲁϫⲡⲟ ⲛⲟⲩⲇⲓⲁⲫⲟⲣⲁ ⲛϩⲟⲩⲟ
    ⲉⲣⲟⲟⲩ ⲉⲧⲃⲉ ⲡⲁⲓ̈ ϭⲉ ⲛ̅ⲧⲱⲧⲛ̅ ϩⲉⲛⲕⲟⲩⲉⲓ ϣⲁⲛⲧⲉ
12  ⲧⲛ̅ⲣ̅ⲧⲉⲗⲉⲓⲟⲥˉ ⲁϥⲟⲩⲱⲏⳠ ⲇⲉ ⲛ̅ϭⲓ ⲑⲱⲙⲁⲥ ϫⲉ ⲉ
    ⲧⲃⲉ ⲡⲁⲓ̈ †ϫⲱ ⲙⲙⲟⲥ ⲛⲁⲕˋ ⲡϫⲟⲉⲓⲥ ϫⲉ ⲛⲉⲧϣⲁϫⲉ
14  ⲉⲧⲃⲉ ⲛⲉⲧⲉ ⲛⲥⲉⲟⲩⲟⲛϩ ⲉⲃⲟⲗ ⲁⲛˋ ⲁⲩⲱ ⲛⲉⲧⲙⲟⲕϩ
    ⲛ̅ⲃⲟⲗⲟⲩ ⲉⲩⲧⲛ̅ⲧⲱⲛ ⲁⲛⲉⲧϫⲱⲗⲕˋ ⲛ̅ⲛⲉⲩⲥⲁⲧⲉ ⲁⲩ
16  ⲙⲏⲓ̈ⲛⲉ ϩⲛ ⲧⲟⲩϣⲏ ⲥⲉϫⲱⲗⲕˋ ⲙⲉⲛ ⲛ̅ⲉⲩⲥⲟⲧⲉ ⲛ̅ⲑⲉ
    ⲛ̅ϩⲟⲉⲓⲛⲉ ϫⲉ ⲉⲩϫⲱⲗⲕˋ ⲁⲡⲙⲁⲓ̈ⲛⲉˉ ⲁⲗⲗⲁ ϥⲟⲩⲟⲛϩ
18  ⲉⲃⲟⲗ ⲁⲛˋ ϩⲟⲧⲁⲛ ⲇⲉ ⲉⲣϣⲁⲛⲡⲟⲩⲟⲉⲓⲛ ⲉⲓ ⲉⲃⲟⲗ ⲛϥˋ
    ϩⲱⲡ ⲙ̅ⲡⲕⲁⲕⲉ ⲧⲟⲧⲉ ⲡϩⲱⲃ ⲙ̅ⲡⲟⲩⲁ ⲡⲟⲩⲁ ⲛⲁⲟⲩⲱⲛϩ
20  ⲉⲃⲟⲗˋ ⲛ̅ⲧⲟⲕˋ ⲇⲉ ⲡⲛ̅ⲟⲩⲟⲉⲓⲛˋ ⲉⲕⲣ̅ⲟⲩⲟⲉⲓⲛ ⲡϫⲟⲉⲓⲥˋ
    ⲡⲁϫⲉϥ ⲛ̅ϭⲓ ⲓ̅ⲥ̅ ϫⲉ ⲡⲟⲩⲟⲉⲓⲛ ⲉϥϣⲟⲟⲡˋ ϩⲙ ⲡⲟⲩ[ⲟ]
```

139:3   ⲉⲩⲱⲙ   for   ⲉⲩⲟⲩⲱⲙ

appear from their own root, and it is their fruit (καρπός)

2   that nourishes them. But these bodies (σῶμα) that are visible

eat of creatures similar to them;

4   so, therefore, the bodies (σῶμα) change. But (δέ) that which changes will

be destroyed and perish, and has no hope (ἐλπίς) of life from now on,

6   for (γάρ) that body is bestial. So just as the body (σῶμα) of the beasts

perishes, so also will these bodies (πλάσμα)

8   perish. Does it (the body) not (μήτι) derive from intercourse (συνουσία)

like that (body) of the beasts? If it too derives from it (intercourse),

10   how will it (the body) beget anything different (διαφορά) from

them (beasts)? So, therefore, you are babes until

12   you become perfect (τέλειος)." And Thomas answered:

"Therefore I say to you, Lord, that those who speak

14   about things that are not visible and difficult

to explain are like those who shoot their arrows at a

16   target at night. To be sure (μέν), they shoot their arrows as

anyone would, since they shoot at the target; however, (ἀλλά) it is

        not visible.

18   But (δέ) when (ὅταν) the light comes forth and

hides the darkness, then (τότε) the work of each will appear.

20   And (δέ) you (sg) are our light, because you enlighten, Lord!"

Jesus said: "It is in light that light exists."

22 ειν· παχεϥ· ῏Νϭι θωμαϲ· εϥχω ῀μμοϲ· χε παο[ειϲ]
    ετβε ου πιουοειν· ετουονϩ εβολ ετρ̅ουοειν
24 ετβε ῏νρωμε· ϣαϥπρ̅ριε αυω ϣαϥϩωτπ· παχεϥ·
    ῏νϭι πϲω̅ρ̅ χε ω πμακαριοϲ· θωμαϲ πιουοειν [ϥ]ω
26 ετουονϩ εβολ αϥρ̅ουοεινε ετβε τηνε χεκα[αϲ]
    αν ετετναϭω ῀μπιμα αλλα χε ετετναει εβ[ολ]
28 ῏νϩητϥ· ϩοταν δε ερεϣανϲωτπ· τηρου κω [ε]ϩ
    ραϊ ῏ν̅τ̅μ̅ντ̅τβ̅νη· τοτε πιουοειν ϥναρανα
30 χωρει εϩραϊ ετεϥ·ουϲια αυω τεϥ·ουϲια ναϣοπϥ·
    εροϲ χε ουϩυπηρετηϲ εναανουϥ· πε   τοτε
32 αϥουωϩ ετοοτϥ· ῏νϭι πϲω̅ρ̅ παχεϥ· χε ω̅ τετε
    μαυϣ῀νρατε̅ ταγαπη ῀μπουοειν· ω̅ πϲιϣε ῀μ
34 πκωϩτ· ετχερο ϩραϊ ϩ̅ν ῏νϲωμα ῏ννρωμε μ̅ν̅
    νευατκαϲ· εϥχερο ϩραϊ ῏νϩητου ῏ντουϣη μ̅ν̅
36 φ[οου] αυω ετρωχ ϩ̅ν ῀μμελοϲ ῏ννρωμε· αυω
    ε[τρεν]ευϩητ ⳁϩε αυω νευⲯυχη εϥ[ϭ]τρουπωϩ̅ϲ̅
38 α[υω ετκιμ·] ερ̅[ο]ου ϩραϊ ϩ̅ν ῏νϩουτ· μ̅ν ῏νϲϩιομε
    [῀μ]πεϩοο[υ] μ̅ν το[υ]νϣη αυω ετκιμ· εροου [ϩ̅ν] ου
40 [κι]μ· εϥ[κιμ· ϩ]̅ν ουϩωπ· μ̅ν ουωνϩ εβο[λ· ϲε]
    [κι]μ γαρ· ῏νϩοουτ· ϲ[ε]κιμ· εϩραϊ αχ̅ν ῏νϲϩιο[μ]
42 με· αυω ῏νϲϩιομε· αχ[̅ν ῏νϩοουτ· ετβε παϊ ϲε]

22   Thomas spoke, saying: "Lord,

     why does this visible light that shines

24   on behalf of men rise and set?" The Saviour (σωτήρ)

     said: "O (ὦ) blessed (μακάριος) Thomas, this same visible light

26   shone for your sakes, not in order that

     you might remain here, but rather (ἀλλά) that you might come

28   forth; and (δέ) whenever (ὅταν) all the elect abandon

     bestiality, then (τότε) this light will withdraw (ἀναχωρεῖν)

30   up to its essence (οὐσία), and its essence (οὐσία) will welcome it,

     since it is a good servant (ὑπηρέτης)." Then (τότε)

32   the Saviour (σωτήρ) continued and said: "Oh (ὦ)

     unsearchable love (ἀγάπη) of the light! Oh (ὦ) bitterness of

34   the fire that burns in the bodies (σῶμα) of men, and (in)

     their marrow, burning in them night and

36   day, burning in the limbs (μέλος) of men and

     making their minds drunk and their souls (ψυχή) deranged

38   [and moving them] within males and females

     [by day and] night and moving them [with] a

40   [movement that moves] secretly and visibly.

     For (γάρ) the males [move. They move upon the females]

42   and the females [move] upon [the males. Therefore it is]

ϫⲱ ⲙ̄ⲙⲟⲥ ϫⲉ ⲟⲩⲟⲛ ⲛⲓⲙˋ ⲉⲧϣⲓⲛⲉ ⲛ̄ⲥⲁ ⲧⲙⲏⲉ ⲉⲃⲟⲗ

2 ϩⲛ̄ ⲧⲥⲁⲃⲏ ⲙ̄ⲙⲏⲉ ϥⲛⲁⲥⲙⲓⲛⲉ ⲛⲁϥˋ ⲛ̄ϩⲉⲛⲧⲛ̄ϩ ⲁⲧⲣⲉϥˋ

ϩⲱⲗˋ ⲉϥⲡⲏⲧˋ ϩⲏⲧⲉ̄ ⲛ̄ⲧⲉⲡⲓⲑⲩⲙⲓⲁ ⲉⲧⲣⲱⲕ ⲛ̄ⲙ̄ⲡⲛ̄ⲁ̄

4 ⲛ̄ⲛ̄ⲣⲱⲙⲉˋ ⲁⲩⲱ ϥⲛⲁⲥⲙⲓⲛⲉ ⲛⲁϥˋ ⲛ̄ϩⲉⲛⲧⲛ̄ϩ ⲉϥⲡⲱⲧ

ϩⲏⲧϥˋ ⲙ̄ⲡⲛ̄ⲁ̄ ⲛⲓⲙˋ ⲉⲧⲟⲩⲟⲛϩ ⲉⲃⲟⲗˑ ⲁⲩⲟⲩⲱϣ̄ⲃ ⲛ̄ϭⲓ

6 ⲑⲱⲙⲁⲥˋ ⲉϥϫⲱ ⲙ̄ⲙⲟⲥ ϫⲉ ⲡϫⲟⲉⲓⲥˋ ⲡⲁⲓ̈ ⲣⲱ ⲡⲉϯϣⲓ

ⲛⲉ ⲙ̄ⲙⲟⲕˋ ⲉⲧⲃⲏⲧϥˋ ϩⲱⲥ ⲉⲡⲓⲇⲏ ⲁⲉⲓⲙ̄ⲙⲉ ϫⲉ ⲛ̄ⲧⲟⲕˋ

8 ⲡⲉⲧⲣ̄ⲛⲟⲩⲣⲉ ⲛⲁⲛˋ ⲕⲁⲧⲁ ⲑⲉ ⲉⲧⲕϫⲱ ⲙ̄ⲙⲟⲥ ⲡⲁⲗⲓⲛ ⲁϥˋ

ⲟⲩⲱϣ̄ⲃ ⲛ̄ϭⲓ ⲡⲥⲱ̄ⲣ ⲡⲉϫⲁϥ ϫⲉ ⲉⲧⲃⲉ ⲡⲁⲓ̈ ⲟⲩⲁⲛⲁⲅⲕⲏ

10 ⲉⲣⲟⲛ ⲧⲉˑ ⲁϫⲟⲟⲥ ⲛⲏⲧⲛ̄ ϫⲉ ⲧⲁⲉⲓ ⲅⲁⲣ ⲧⲉ ⲧⲉⲥⲃⲱ ⲛ̄ⲛ̄ⲧⲉ

ⲗⲉⲓⲟⲥ ⲉϣⲡⲉ ⲧⲉⲧⲛ̄ⲟⲩⲱϣⲉ ϭⲉˑ ⲁⲣ̄ⲧⲉⲗⲉⲓⲟⲥˋ ⲧⲉⲧⲛⲁ

12 ⲁⲣⲉϩ ⲉⲛⲁⲉⲓˋ ⲉϣⲱⲡⲉ ⲙ̄ⲙⲟⲛˋ ⲡⲉⲧⲛ̄ⲣⲁⲛ ⲡⲉ ⲁⲧⲥⲃⲱˋ

ⲉⲡⲓⲇⲏ ⲙⲛ̄ϣϭⲟⲙ ⲛ̄ⲧⲉⲟⲩⲣⲙⲛ̄ϩⲏⲧˋ ⲟⲩⲱϩ ⲙⲛ̄ ⲟⲩˋ

14 ⲥⲟϭ ⲡⲣⲙⲛ̄ϩⲏⲧˋ ⲅⲁⲣˋ ϥϫⲏⲕˋ ⲉⲃⲟⲗ ⲛ̄ⲥⲟⲫⲓⲁ ⲛⲓⲙˋ

ⲡⲥⲟϭ ⲛ̄ⲧⲟϥˋ ⲡⲡⲉⲧⲛⲁⲛⲟⲩϥ ⲡⲡⲉⲑⲟⲟⲩ ⲡⲓϣϣ

16 ⲛ̄ⲟⲩⲱⲧˋ ⲛⲁϥˋ ⲡⲉ ϫⲉ ⲡⲥⲟⲫⲟⲥ ⲅⲁⲣˋ ϥⲛⲁⲥⲁⲁⲛϣ ϩⲛ̄

ⲧⲙⲏⲉ ⲁⲩⲱ ϥⲛⲁϣⲱⲡⲉ ⲛ̄ⲑⲉ ⲙ̄ⲡⲓϣⲏⲛ ⲉⲧⲣⲏⲧˋ ϩⲓ

18 ϫⲛ̄ ⲡⲙⲟⲩ ⲛ̄ⲥⲱⲣⲙˋ ⲉⲡⲓⲇⲏ ⲟⲩⲛ̄ϩⲟⲉⲓⲛⲉ ⲉⲩⲛ̄ⲧⲛ̄ϩ

ⲙ̄ⲙⲟⲟⲩ ⲉⲩⲡⲱⲧˋ ϩⲓϫⲛ̄ ⲛⲉⲧⲟⲩⲟⲛϩ ⲉⲃⲟⲗ ⲛⲁⲉⲓ ⲉ

20 ⲧⲟⲩⲏⲩ ⲉⲃⲟⲗ ϩⲛ̄ ⲧⲙⲏⲉˋ ⲡⲉⲥⲧϫⲓ ⲙⲟⲉⲓⲧˋ ⲅⲁⲣ ϩⲏⲧⲟⲩˋ

ⲉ[ⲧ]ⲉ ⲡⲕⲱϩⲧ ⲡⲉˋ ϥⲛⲁϯ ⲛⲁⲩ ⲛ̄ⲟⲩⲫⲁⲛⲧⲁⲥⲓⲁ ⲙ̄ⲙⲏⲉ

140:13   or: ⲟⲩⲱϩⲙ ⲛ̄ˋ
140:20   ⲡⲉϯϫⲓ for ⲡⲉⲧϫⲓ

said: 'Everyone who seeks the truth from

2   the truly wise One will make himself wings so as to

fly, fleeing the lust (ἐπιθυμία) that scorches the spirits (πνεῦμα)

4   of men.' And he will make himself wings to flee

every visible spirit (πνεῦμα)." And Thomas answered

6   saying: "Lord this indeed is what I am asking

you (sg) about, since (ὡς ἐπειδή) I have understood that you (sg)

8   are the one who is good for us, as (κατά-) you (sg) say." Again (πάλιν)

the Savior (σωτήρ) answered and said: "Therefore it is necessary (ἀνάγκη)

10 for us to speak to you, for (γάρ) this is the doctrine for the perfect

(τέλειος).

If, now, you desire to become perfect (τέλειος) you shall

12 observe these things; if not, your name is 'Ignorant,'

since (ἐπειδή) it is impossible that a wise man dwell with a

14 fool, for (γάρ) the wise man (σοφός) is perfect in all wisdom (σοφία).

To the fool, however, the good and the bad are the

16 same. For (γάρ) the wise man (σοφός) will be nourished by

the truth and will become like a tree growing by

18 the meandering stream. When (ἐπειδή) others have wings,

it is upon the visible things that they rush, things that

20 are far from the truth. For (γάρ) that which guides them,

the fire, will give them an illusion (φαντασία) of truth,

140:13 or: "answer" a fool

22   [ⲁⲩ]ⲱ ϥⲛⲁϯⲟⲩⲟⲉⲓⲛ ⲉⲣⲟⲟⲩ ϨⲚ ⲟⲩⲥⲁⲉⲓⲉ ⲉⲩⲛⲁⲧⲉ

      [ⲕⲟ] ⲁⲩⲱ ϥⲛⲁⲣⲁⲓⲭⲙⲁⲗⲱⲧⲓⲍⲉ ⲘⲘⲟⲟⲩ· ϨⲚ ⲟⲩϨⲁ̄

24   ϬⲈ ⲚⲔⲀⲔⲈ· Ⲛϥⲧⲟⲣⲡⲟⲩ ϨⲚ ⲟⲩϨⲏⲆⲟⲛⲏ ⲉϥϯ ⲥⲧⲟⲉⲓ

      ⲁⲩⲱ ϥⲛⲁⲁⲩ Ⲛ̄ⲂⲖⲖⲈ Ϩⲣⲁ̈ⲓ ϨⲚ ⲧⲉⲡⲓⲑⲩⲙⲓⲁ Ⲛⲁⲧⲥⲉⲓ

26   ⲁⲩⲱ ϥⲛⲁⲭⲁϥⲭⲏ̄ ⲚⲚⲉⲩ̄ⲯⲩⲭⲟⲟⲩⲉ· ⲁⲩⲱ Ⲛ̄ϥϣ ϣ

      [ⲡⲉ] ⲛⲁⲩ Ⲛ̄ⲑⲉ Ⲛ̄ⲛⲟⲩϣ ⲙ ⲟⲩⲉ· ⲉⲥⲧⲁⲕⲥ̄ ϨⲘ ⲡⲟⲩϨⲏⲧ·

28   ⲉ[Ⲙ]Ⲛ̄ϣϬⲟⲙ· ⲘⲘⲟⲟⲩ Ⲛ̄ⲛⲁⲥⲥ̄ ⲉⲛⲉϨ ⲁⲩⲱ Ⲛ̄ⲑⲉ Ⲛ̄

      ⲟⲩⲭⲁⲗⲓⲛⲟⲥ ϨⲚ· ⲟⲩⲧⲁⲡⲣⲟ ⲉⲩⲥⲱⲕ· ⲘⲘⲟⲟⲩ ⲁⲡⲉⲩ·

30   ⲟⲩⲱϣⲉ· ⲘⲘⲓⲛ· Ⲙⲙⲟϥ· ⲁⲩⲱ ⲁϥⲙⲟⲣⲟⲩ ϨⲚ ⲛⲉⲩ·

      ⲁⲗⲩⲥⲓⲥ· ⲁⲩⲱ ⲛⲉⲩⲙⲉⲗⲟⲥ ⲧⲏⲣⲟⲩ ⲁϥⲥⲟⲛϨⲟⲩ Ⲛ̄

32   Ϩⲣⲁ̈ⲓ ϨⲘ ⲡⲥⲓϣⲉ· Ⲛ̄ⲧⲘ̄ⲣⲣⲉ Ⲛ̄ⲧⲉⲡⲓⲑⲩⲙⲉⲓⲁ· Ⲛ̄ⲛⲁⲉⲓ

      ⲉⲧⲟⲩⲟⲛϨ ⲉⲃⲟⲗ ⲉⲧⲛⲁⲧⲉⲕⲟ ⲁⲩⲱ ⲉⲧⲛⲁϣⲓⲃⲉ·

34   ⲁⲩⲱ ⲉⲧⲛⲁⲡⲱⲛⲉ ⲕⲁⲧⲁ ⲡⲥⲱⲕ· Ⲛ̄ⲧⲁⲩⲥⲟⲕⲟⲩ·

      Ⲛ̄ⲧⲡⲉ ⲁⲡⲓⲧⲚ̄ Ⲛ̄ⲟⲩⲟⲉⲓⲩ ⲛⲓⲙ· ⲉⲩϨⲱⲧⲃ̄ ⲘⲘⲟⲟⲩ

36   ⲉⲩⲥⲱⲕ ⲘⲘⲟⲟⲩ ϨⲓⲭⲚ̄ Ⲛ̄ⲦⲂⲛⲟⲟⲩⲉ· ⲧⲏⲣⲟⲩ Ⲙ̄ⲡ

      ⲭⲱϨⲘ̄ ⲁϥ·ⲟⲩⲱϣϬ̄ⲃ̄ Ⲛ̄Ϭⲓ ⲐⲰⲘⲀⲤ ⲡⲁϫ[ⲉϥ ϫⲉ] ϥ·

38   ⲟⲩⲟⲛϨ ⲉⲃⲟⲗ· ⲁⲩⲱ ⲁⲩϫⲟⲟⲥⲥⲩ ϫⲉ Ϩ[ⲁϨ] ⲛ[ⲉⲧϬⲱⲗⲡ·

      ⲉ[ⲃⲟⲗ] Ⲛ̄ⲛⲉⲧⲉ Ⲛ̄ⲥⲉⲥⲟⲟⲩⲛ ⲁ[ⲛ ϫⲉ ⲥⲉⲛⲁ]ϯ [ⲟⲥⲉ Ⲛ̄]

40   [ⲧⲟⲩ]ⲯⲩⲭⲏ ⲁⲩⲟⲩⲱϣϬ̄ⲃ̄ ⲆⲈ Ⲛ̄Ϭ[ⲓ ⲡⲥⲱ̄ⲣ] ⲉϥϫⲱ

      [ⲘⲘⲟⲥ ϫⲉ ⲛⲁⲉⲓⲁⲧϥ· Ⲙ̄]ⲡⲥⲁⲃⲉ Ⲛ̄ⲣⲱⲙⲉ Ⲛ̄ⲧⲁϥ[ϣⲓ]

42   [ⲛⲉ Ⲛ̄ⲥⲁ ⲧⲙⲏⲉ ⲁⲩⲱ Ⲛ̄ⲧ]ⲁⲣⲉϥϬⲚ̄ⲧⲥ̄ ⲁϥⲘ̄ⲧⲟⲛ· Ⲙ̄

141:38   Ms. has ⲁⲩϫⲟⲟⲩ

22 and will shine on them with a beauty that will perish
    and will imprison (αἰχμαλωτίζειν) them in a dark
24 sweetness and captivate them with fragrant pleasure (ἡδονή).
    And it will blind them with insatiable lust (ἐπιθυμία)
26 and it will burn their souls (ψυχή) and it will be
    for them like a stake stuck in their heart
28 which they can never dislodge. And like
    a bit (χαλινός) in a mouth it leads them according to its
30 own desire. It fettered them with its
    chains (ἄλυσις), and bound all their limbs (μέλος)
32 in the bitterness of the bond of lust (ἐπιθυμία) for these
    visible things that will decay and change
34 and swerve by (κατά) impulse. They have
    always been attracted from heaven to earth: as they are killed,
36 they are drawn upon all the beasts of
    corruption." Thomas answered and said: "It
38 is obvious and has been said: ['Many are the things revealed]
    to those who do not know [that they will forfeit]
40 [their] soul (ψυχή).'" And (δέ) [the Savior (σωτήρ)] answered, saying:
    ["Blessed is] the wise man who [sought]
42 [after the truth, and] when he found it, he rested

ⲙⲟⲩ· ⲉϩⲣⲁⲓ ⲉϫⲱⲥ ϣⲁⲉⲛⲉϩ ⲁⲩⲱ ⲙ̄ⲡⲩⲣ̄ϩⲟⲧⲉ ϩⲏⲧⲟⲩ

2 ⲛ̄ⲛⲉⲧⲟⲩⲱϣⲉ ⲁϣⲧⲣ̄ⲧⲱⲣϥ· ⲁⲩⲟⲩⲱϣ̄ⲃ̄ ⲛ̄ϭⲓ ⲑⲱⲙⲁⲥ

ⲡⲁϫⲉϥ· ϫⲉ ⲥ̄ⲣ̄ⲛⲟⲩⲣⲉ ⲛⲁⲛ· ⲡϫⲟⲉⲓⲥ· ⲁⲙ̄ⲧⲟⲛ ⲙ̄ⲙⲟⲛ

4 ϩⲛ̄ ⲛⲉⲧⲉ ⲛⲱⲛ ⲛⲉ ⲡⲁϫⲉϥ ⲛ̄ϭⲓ ⲡⲥⲱⲣ ⲇⲉ ⲡⲉⲧⲣ̄ϣⲁⲩ

ⲅⲁⲣ ⲡⲉ· ⲁⲩⲱ ⲛⲁⲛⲟⲩⲥ ⲛⲏⲧⲛ̄ ⲉⲡⲓⲇⲏ ⲛⲉⲧⲟⲩⲟⲛϩ

6 ⲉⲃⲟⲗ ϩⲛ̄ ⲣ̄ⲣⲱⲙⲉ· ⲥⲉⲛⲁⲃⲱⲗ ⲉⲃⲟⲗ ⲡⲥⲕⲉⲩⲟⲥ ⲅⲁⲣ ⲛ̄

ⲧⲟⲩⲥⲁⲣⲝ̄· ⲛⲁⲃⲱⲗ ⲉⲃⲟⲗ ⲁⲩⲱ ⲉϥϣⲁⲛϫⲱⲣⲉ ⲉⲃⲟⲗ

8 ϥⲛⲁϣⲱⲡⲉ· ϩⲛ̄ ⲛⲉⲧⲟⲩⲟⲛϩ ⲉⲃⲟⲗ ϩⲛ̄ ⲛⲉⲧⲟⲩⲛⲁⲩ ⲉ

ⲣⲟⲟⲩ ⲁⲩⲱ ⲧⲟⲧⲉ ⲡⲕⲱϩⲧ· ⲉⲧⲟⲩⲛⲁⲩ ⲉⲣⲟϥ· ⲉϥϯ ⲧⲕⲁⲥ ⲛⲁⲩ

10 ⲉⲧⲃⲉ ⲧⲁⲅⲁⲡⲏ ⲛ̄ⲧⲡⲓⲥⲧⲓⲥ· ⲉⲧⲉ ⲟⲩⲛ̄ⲧⲁⲩⲥ· ϩⲁⲑⲏ ⲙ̄ⲡⲓ

ⲟⲩⲟⲉⲓϣ ⲡⲁⲗⲓⲛ· ⲥⲉⲛⲁⲥⲟⲟⲩϩⲟⲩ ⲁⲡⲉⲧⲟⲩⲟⲛϩ ⲉⲃⲟⲗ

12 ⲛⲉⲧⲛⲁⲩ ⲇⲉ ⲉⲃⲟⲗ ϩⲛ̄ ⲛⲉⲧⲟⲩⲟⲛϩ ⲉⲃⲟⲗ ⲁⲛ· ⲁϫⲛ̄

ⲧϣⲟⲣⲡ· ⲛ̄ⲁⲅⲁⲡⲏ ⲥⲉⲛⲁⲧⲁⲕⲟ ϩⲙ̄ ⲡⲣ[ⲟ]ⲟⲩϣ ⲙ̄ⲡⲃⲓⲟⲥ

14 ⲙⲛ̄ ⲡⲣⲱⲭ ϩⲙ̄ ⲡⲕⲱϩⲧ· ⲛ̄ⲟⲩⲕⲟⲩⲓ̈ ⲛ̄ⲟⲩⲟⲉⲓϣ ϣⲁⲛ

ⲧⲉⲩⲃⲱⲗ ⲉⲃⲟⲗ· ⲛ̄ϭⲓ ⲡⲉⲧⲟⲩⲟⲛϩ ⲉⲃⲟⲗ ⲧⲟⲧⲉ ⲥⲉⲛⲁ

16 ϣⲱⲡⲉ ⲛ̄ϭⲓ ϩⲉⲛ·ⲉⲓⲇⲱⲗⲟⲛ ⲉⲙⲛ̄ⲧⲉⲩ ⲙⲟⲣⲫⲏ ⲁⲩⲱ

ⲛ̄ⲧⲙⲏⲧⲉ ⲛ̄ⲛ̄ⲧⲁⲫⲟⲥ ⲛ̄ⲥⲉϣⲱⲡⲉ ϩⲓϫⲛ̄ ⲛ̄ⲕⲱⲥ ⲛ̄ϣⲁ

18 ⲉⲛⲉϩ ϩⲛ̄ ⲟⲩϯ ⲧⲕⲁⲥ ⲙⲛ̄ ⲟⲩⲧⲁⲕⲟ ⲙ̄ⲯⲩⲭⲏ ⲁⲩⲟⲩⲱ

ϣⲃ ⲇⲉ ⲛ̄ϭⲓ ⲑⲱⲙⲁⲥ ⲡⲁϫⲉϥ ϫⲉ ⲟⲩ ⲡⲉⲧⲉ ⲟⲩⲛ̄ⲧⲁⲛⲩ·

20 ⲁϫⲟⲟⲩ· ⲛ̄ⲛⲁϩⲣⲛ̄ ⲛⲁⲉⲓ ⲏ ⲟⲩ ⲡⲉⲧⲛ̄ⲛⲁϫⲟⲟⲩ· ⲛ̄ⲃⲗⲉ

ⲉⲩⲉ ⲛ̄ⲣⲱⲙⲉ ⲏ ⲁϣ ⲛ̄ⲥⲃⲱ ⲧⲉⲧⲛ̄ⲛⲁϫⲟⲟⲥ ⲛ̄ⲛⲓⲧ[ⲁⲗⲁ]ⲓ

141:9   Ms. inserts ⲧⲟⲧⲉ above the line
141:14 Ms. reads ⲡⲣⲱⲭϩ· ⲙ̄ⲛ ⲡⲕⲱϩⲧ·

upon it forever and was not afraid of those

2   who wanted to disturb him." Thomas answered

and said: "Is it good for us, Lord, to rest

4   among our own?" The Savior (σωτήρ) said: "Yes (γάρ) it is useful.

And it is good for you since (ἐπειδή) things visible

6   among men will dissolve; for (γάρ) the vessel (σκεῦος) of

their flesh (σάρξ) will dissolve and when it is brought to naught

8   it will come to be among visible things, among things that are seen.

And then (τότε) the fire which they see gives them pain

10   on account of the love (ἀγάπη) of the faith (πίστις) which they

formerly possessed. They will be gathered back (πάλιν) to that which

is visible.

12   But (δέ) as for those who see among things that are not visible, without

the first love (ἀγάπη) they will be destroyed by the concern for this

14   life (βίος) and the scorching in the fire. Only a little time

until that which is visible dissolves; then (τότε)

16   formless (-μορφή) phantoms (εἴδωλον) will arise and,

in the midst of the tombs (τάφος), they will dwell upon the corpses

18   forever in pain and corruption of soul (ψυχή)."

Thomas answered and said: "What have we

20   to say in the face of these things, or (ἤ) what shall we say to

blind men, or (ἤ) what teaching should we express to these

141:15 or: "the one who is visible"

22 ⲡⲱⲣⲟⲥ ⲛ̄ⲑⲏⲧⲟⲥ ⲛⲉⲧⲝⲱ ⲙ̄ⲙⲟⲥˋ ϫⲉ ⲁⲛⲉⲓ ⲁ[ⲡ̄ⲡⲉ]
    ⲧⲛⲁⲛⲟⲩϥˋ ⲁⲩⲱ ⲁⲩⲥⲁϩⲟⲩ ⲁⲛˋ ⲡⲁⲗⲓⲛ ⲇⲉ ⲥⲉⲛⲁϫ[ⲟⲟⲥ]ˋ
24 ϫⲉ ⲉⲛⲉ ⲙ̄ⲡⲟⲩϫⲡⲟⲛ ϩⲛ̄ ⲧⲥⲁⲣⲝ̄ ⲛⲉⲛⲛⲁⲥⲟⲩⲱⲛ [ⲧⲥ]ⲁ
    ⲧⲉ ⲁⲛ ⲡⲉ ⲡⲁϫⲉϥ ⲛ̄ϭⲓ ⲡⲥⲱ̄ⲣ̄ ϫⲉ ϩⲛ̄ ⲟⲩⲙⲏⲉ ⲛ[ⲁ̈ⲓ] ⲉ
26 ⲧⲙ̄ⲙⲁⲩ ⲙ̄ⲡⲣ̄ⲕⲁⲁⲩ ⲛⲁⲕˋ ⲛ̄ⲣⲱⲙⲉ ⲁⲗⲗⲁ ⲟⲡⲟⲩ ϩ[ⲱⲥ ⲛ̄ⲧⲃ̄]
    ⲛⲟⲟⲩⲉˋ ⲛ̄ⲑⲉ ⲅⲁⲣ ⲛ̄ⲛ̄ⲧⲃ̄ⲛⲟⲟⲩⲉ ⲉⲩⲟⲩⲱⲙ ⲛ̄ⲛ[ⲉⲩⲉ]
28 ⲣⲏⲩ ⲧⲁⲉⲓ ⲧⲉ ⲑⲉ ϩⲱⲟⲩ ⲛ̄ⲛⲉⲉⲓⲣⲱⲙⲉ ⲛ̄ⲧⲉⲉⲓⲙⲓⲛ[ⲉ ⲥⲉ]
    ⲟⲩⲱⲙˋ ⲛ̄ⲛⲉⲩⲉⲣⲏⲩ ⲁⲗⲗⲁ ⲥⲉϩⲟⲩⲣⲟⲉⲓⲧˋ ⲛ̄ⲧⲙⲛ̄ⲧ̄[ⲱⲛϩ]
30 ⲉⲡⲓⲇⲏ ⲥⲉⲙⲁⲉⲓⲉ ⲛ̄ⲧϩⲁⲃⲉ ⲙ̄ⲡⲕⲱϩⲧ ⲁⲩⲱ ⲥⲉⲟ ⲛ
    ϩⲙ̄ϩⲁⲗ ⲙ̄ⲡⲙⲟⲩ ⲁⲩⲱ ⲥⲉⲡⲏⲧˋ ⲁⲛϩⲃⲏⲩⲉ ⲙ̄ⲡϫⲱϩⲙⲉ
32 ⲥⲉϫⲱⲕ ⲉⲃⲟⲗ ⲛ̄ⲧⲉⲡⲓⲑⲩⲙⲉⲓⲁ ⲛ̄ⲛⲉⲩⲉⲓⲟⲧⲉ ⲥⲉⲛⲁ
    ⲛⲟϫⲟⲩ ⲉϩⲣⲁ̈ⲓ ⲁⲡⲛⲟⲩⲛˋ ⲛ̄ⲥⲉⲣ̄ⲙⲁⲥⲧⲓⲅⲟⲩ ⲙ̄ⲙⲟⲟⲩ
34 ⲉⲃⲟⲗ ϩⲓⲧⲛ̄ ⲧⲁⲛⲁⲅⲕⲏ ⲙ̄ⲡⲥⲓϣⲉ ⲛ̄ⲧⲟⲩⲫⲩⲥⲓⲥ ⲉⲑⲟ
    ⲟⲩ ⲥⲉⲛⲁⲫⲣⲁⲅⲉⲗⲗⲟⲩ ⲅⲁⲣˋ ⲙ̄ⲙⲟⲟⲩ ⲁⲩⲣⲟⲩⲡⲱⲧ ⲛ̄
36 ⲥⲁϫⲱⲟⲩ ⲁⲡⲙⲁ ⲉⲧⲉ ⲛ̄ⲥⲉⲥⲟⲟⲩⲛ ⲙ̄ⲙⲟⲩ ⲁⲛˋ ⲁⲩⲱ
    ⲥⲉⲛ[ⲁⲗ]ⲟ ⲛ̄ⲛⲉⲩⲙⲉⲗⲟⲥˋ ϩⲛ̄ ⲟⲩϩⲩⲡⲟⲙⲟⲛⲏ ⲁⲛ ⲁⲗ
38 ⲗⲁ [ϩⲛ̄ ⲟⲩ]ⲕⲁ ⲧⲟⲟⲧ⟨ⲥ⟩ˋ ⲉⲃⲟⲗˋ ⲁⲩⲱ ⲥⲉⲣⲁϣⲉ ⲉϫ[ⲙ̄ ⲡ]
    ⲣ̄[ⲟⲟⲩϣ ⲙ̄ⲡⲓⲃⲓⲟⲥ ϩⲙ̄] ⲡⲁⲓⲃⲉ ⲙⲛ̄ ⲡⲡⲱϣⲉ̄ ⲉⲛϩ̄[ⲟⲉⲓ]
40 [ⲛⲉ] ⲡⲏⲧ ⲛ̄[ⲥⲁ ⲡⲓ]ⲡⲱϣⲉ̄ ⲛ̄ϩⲏⲧˋ ⲉⲛ[ⲥ]ⲉⲙ̄ⲙⲉ ⲁ[ⲛ ⲙ̄ⲡⲟⲩ]
    [ⲗⲓ]ⲃⲉˋ ⲉⲩ[ⲙⲉⲉ]ⲩⲉ ϫⲉ ϩⲛ̄ⲥⲁⲃⲉⲉⲩ ⲛ[ⲉ] ⲉⲩⲥⲱⲕ ϩⲓⲧⲙ̄]
42 [ⲡⲥ]ⲁⲉⲓⲉ ⲙ̄ⲡⲟⲩⲥⲱⲙⲁ ϩⲱ[ⲥ ⲉⲩⲛⲁⲧⲁⲕⲟ ⲁⲛˋ ⲁⲩⲱ]

141:38   Ms. reads ⲕⲁ ⲧⲟⲟⲧⲕ
141:42   or [ⲡⲙ]ⲁⲉⲓⲉ , "the love of their body"

22   miserable (ταλαίπωρος) mortals who say: 'We came to [do]

      good and not to curse' and yet (πάλιν) claim:

24   'Had we not been begotten in the flesh (σάρξ) we would not have

      known the fire.'" The Savior (σωτήρ) said: "Truly, as for

26   those, do not esteem (sg) them as men, but regard (sg) them [as (ὡς)]

      beasts, for (γάρ) just as beasts devour one another,

28   so also men of this sort

      devour one another. Rather (ἀλλά) they are deprived of [vitality],

30   since (ἐπειδή) they love the sweetness of the fire, and are

      servants of death and are rushing to the works of corruption.

32   They complete the lust (ἐπιθυμία) of their fathers. They will

      be thrown down to the abyss and be afflicted (μαστιγοῦν)

34   by the torment (ἀνάγκη) of the bitterness of their evil nature (φύσις).

      For (γάρ) they will be scourged (φραγελλοῦν) so as to make them

36   rush headlong to the place that they do not know, and

      they [will not abandon] their members (μέλος) patiently, but (ἀλλά)

38   [with] despair. And they rejoice over [the]

      [concern for this life (βίος) with] madness and derangement.   [Some]

40   pursue [this] derangement without realizing [their]

      madness, thinking that they are wise.   [They are beguiled by]

42   [the] beauty of their body (σῶμα) [as if (ὡς) it would not perish.   And]

ЄΡЄΠΟΥϨΗΤˋ ΠΟΟΝЄ ЄΡΟΟΥˋ ЄΡЄΠΟΥΜЄЄΥЄ ϨΙ

2 ΝЄΥΠΡΑϪΙСˋ ΤСΑΤЄ ΔЄ ΤЄΤΝΑΡѠΚϨ ΜΜΟΟΥˋ ΑΥˋ

ΟΥѠϢΒ ΔЄ Ñ6Ι ѲѠΜΑСˋ ΠΑϪЄϥˋ ϪЄ ΠϪΟЄΙСˋ ΠЄΝ

4 ΤΑΥΝΟϪΥˋ ЄϨΡΑΪ ЄΡΟΟΥ ЄϥΝΑΡΟΥ †ϮΜЄΡΙΜΝΑ

ΓΑΡ ΜΠϢΑˋ ЄΤΒΗΤΟΥ ϨΑϨ ΓΑΡˋ ΝЄΤϮ ΟΥΒΗΥ ΑΥˋΟΥ

6 ѠϢΒ Ñ6Ι ΠСѠΡ ΠΑϪЄϥˋ ϪЄ ЄΥÑΤΑΚˋ ΠЄΤΟΥΟΝϨ

ЄΒΟΛ ΝΑΚˋ ΠΑϪЄϥ Ñ6Ι ΪΟΥΔΑСˋ ΠΑΙ ЄΤΟΥΜΟΥΤЄ Є

8 ΡΟϥ ϪЄ ѲѠΜΑС ϪЄ ÑΤΟΚ ΠϪΟЄΙСˋ ΠЄΤСˋΡΠΡЄΠЄΙˋ

ΝΑΚˋ ΑϢЄϪЄˋ ΑΝΟΚ ΔЄ ÑΤΑСѠΤΜ ЄΡΟΚˋ ΑΥˋΟΥˋ

10 ѠϢΒ Ñ6Ι ΠСѠΡ ϪЄ СѠΤΜ ΑΠЄϮΝΑϪΟΟΥ ΝΑΚˋ

ÑΚΡΠΙСΤЄΥЄ ϨÑ ΤΜΗЄ ΠЄΤˋϪΟ ΜÑ ΠЄΤΟΥΛΟ ΜΜΟΥˋ

12 СЄΝΑΒѠΛ ЄΒΟΛ ϨΜ ΠΟΥΚѠϨΤ ϨΡΑΪ ϨΜ ΠΚѠϨΤˋ

ΜÑ ΠΜΟΟΥ [Α]ΥѠ ÑСЄϨѠΠˋ ϨÑ ÑΤΑΦΟСˋ ΜΠΚΑΚЄ

14 ΑΥѠ ΜÑÑСΑ ϨΑϨ ÑΟΥΟЄΙϢ СЄΝΑΟΥѠΝϨ ЄΒΟΛ Ñ

ÑΚΑΡΠΟС ÑÑϢΗΝˋ ЄѲΟΟΥ ЄΥΡΚΟΛΑϪЄ ΜΜΟΟΥ ЄΥ

16 ϨѠΤΒЄ ΜΜΟΟΥ ϨÑ ΤˋΤΑΠΡΟˋ ÑÑΤΒΝΟΟΥЄ ΜÑ ÑΡѠ

ΜЄˋ ϨÑ ΤΑΦΟΡΜΗˋ ÑÑϨΟΟΥ ΜÑ ÑΤΗΥ ΜÑ ΠΑΗΡˋ

18 ΜÑ ΠΟΥΟЄΙΝˋ ЄΤΡΟΥΟЄΙΝˋ ΜΠСΑϨΡЄ ΑϤΟΥѠϢΒ

ΔЄ Ñ6Ι ѲѠΜΑСˋ ϪЄ ΑΚΡΠΙѲЄ ΜЄΝˋ ΜΜΟΝˋ ΠϪΟЄΙСˋ

20 ΑΝΡΝΟЄΙ ϨΜ ΠÑϨΗΤˋ ΑΥѠ СΟΥΟΝϨ ЄΒΟΛ ϪЄ ΤΑΙ

[ΤЄ Ѳ]Є ΑΥѠ ΠЄΚϢΑϪЄ Ο ÑΑΤΦѲΟΝΟС ΑΛΛΑ ΝΙϢΑ

142:21   Ms. inserts Ο above the Є of ϢΑϪЄ.

they are frenetic; their thought is occupied

2   with their deeds (πρᾶξις). But it is the fire that will burn them!"
    And (δέ) Thomas answered and said: "Lord, what will the one

4   thrown down to them do? For (γάρ) I am most anxious (μεριμνᾶν)
    about them, for (γάρ) many are those who fight them."

6   The Savior (σωτήρ) answered and said: "Do you (sg) possess that which is
    visible?" Judas said - the one called

8   Thomas - "It is you (sg), Lord, whom it befits (πρέπειν)
    to speak, and (δέ) I to listen."

10 The Savior (σωτήρ) replied: "Listen to what I am going to tell you (sg)
    and believe (πιστεύειν) in the truth. That which sows and that which
            is sown

12 will dissolve in the fire - within the fire
    and the water - and they will hide in tombs (τάφος) of darkness.

14 And after a long time there shall be revealed
    the fruits (καρπός) of the evil trees, being punished (κολάζειν),

16 being slain in the mouth of beasts and men
    at the instigation (ἀφορμή) of the rains and winds and air (ἀήρ)

18 and the light that shines above." Thomas
    replied: "You (sg) have indeed (μέν) persuaded (πείθειν) us, Lord.

20 We realized (νοεῖν) in our heart and it is obvious that this
    [is] so, and that your (sg) word is sufficient (-φθόνος). But (ἀλλά)

142:6 or: "the one who is visible"

22 [ⲭⲉ ⲉ]ⲧⲕⲁⲱ ⲙ̄ⲙⲟⲟⲩ ⲛⲁⲛ· ⲍⲉⲛⲥⲱⲃⲉ ⲛⲉ ⲙ̄ⲡⲕⲟⲥ

[ⲙⲟ]ⲥ· ⲁⲩⲱ ⲍⲛ̄ⲗ̄ⲕⲱⲁⲉⲓ ⲛ̄ⲥⲱⲟⲩ ⲛⲉ· ⲉⲡⲓⲇⲏ ⲥⲉⲥⲟ

24 [ⲟⲩ]ⲛⲉ ⲙ̄ⲙⲟⲟⲩ ⲁⲛ· ⲛ̄ⲁⲱ ϭⲉ ⲛ̄ⲣⲏⲧⲉ ⲉⲛⲛⲁⲩⲃⲱⲕ· ⲁ̄

[ⲧⲁ]ⲱϣⲉ ⲟⲉⲓⲱ ⲙ̄ⲙⲟⲟⲩ ⲉⲡⲓⲇⲏ ⲇⲉ ⲥⲉⲱⲡ· ⲙ̄ⲙⲟⲛ·

26 [ⲉⲛⲍ]ⲙ̄ ⲡⲕⲟⲥⲙⲟⲥ· ⲁⲩⲟⲩⲱϣⲃ̄ ⲛ̄ϭⲓ ⲡⲥⲱ̄ⲣ ⲡⲁⲭⲉⲩ ⲭⲉ

[ⲍⲁⲙ]ⲏⲛ· ϯⲭⲱ ⲙ̄ⲙⲟⲥ ⲛⲏⲧⲛ̄ ⲭⲉ ⲡⲉⲧⲛⲁⲥⲱⲧⲙ̄ ⲁⲡⲉ

28 [ⲧⲛ̄ⲱ]ⲁⲭⲉ· ⲁⲩⲱ ⲛ̄ⲩⲕⲧⲟ ⲙ̄ⲡⲉⲩⲍⲟ ⲉⲃⲟⲗ· ⲏ ⲛ̄ⲩⲗⲕⲱϣⲉ

[ⲉ] ⲛ̄ⲥⲱⲩ· ⲏ ⲛ̄ⲩⲥⲱⲧⲣ̄ ⲛ̄ⲛⲉⲩ·ⲥⲡⲟⲧⲟⲩ ϩⲓ ⲛⲁⲉ[ⲓ] ϩⲁ

30 ⲙⲏⲛ· ϯⲭⲱ ⲙ̄ⲙⲟⲥ ⲛⲏⲧⲛ̄ ⲭⲉ ⲥⲉⲛⲁⲧⲁⲁⲩ· ⲁⲧⲟⲟⲧⲩ·

ⲙ̄ⲡⲁⲣⲭⲱⲛ ⲉⲧⲙ̄ⲡⲥⲁⲛⲧⲡⲉ· ⲡⲁⲓ ⲉⲧⲁⲣⲭⲉⲓ ⲉⲍⲣⲁⲓ̈ ⲉ

32 ⲭⲛ̄ ⲛ̄ⲉⲍⲟⲩⲥⲓⲁ ⲧⲏⲣⲟⲩ ⲉⲩⲟ ⲛ̄ⲣⲣⲟ ⲉⲭⲱⲟⲩ ⲛ̄ⲩⲕⲧⲟ

ⲙ̄ⲡⲁⲉⲓ ⲉⲧⲙ̄ⲙⲁⲩ ⲛ̄ⲩⲛⲟⲭϥ̄ ⲭⲛ̄ ⲛ̄ⲧⲡⲉ· ϣⲁⲡⲓⲧⲛ̄ ⲁ·

34 ⲡⲛⲟⲩⲛ· ⲛ̄ⲥⲉⲱⲣⲉⲭ· ⲁⲣⲱⲩ· ϩⲛ̄ ⲟⲩⲙⲁ ⲉⲩϭⲏⲩ ⲉⲩⲟ

ⲛ̄ⲕⲁⲕⲉ· ⲙⲁⲩϣϭⲛ̄ϭⲱⲙ ϭⲉ ⲙ̄ⲡⲟⲛⲉⲩ· ⲏ ⲁⲕⲓⲙ· ⲉⲧⲃⲉ

36 ⲡⲓⲛⲟϭ ⲛ̄ⲃⲁⲑⲟⲥ· ⲛ̄ⲧⲉ ⲡⲧⲁⲣⲧⲁⲣⲟⲥ ⲙⲛ̄ ⲡⲓ[ϣⲟⲓ]ⲉ ⲉ

[ⲧⲡⲟⲣ]ϣ ⲛ̄ⲧⲉ ⲁⲙⲛ̄ⲧⲉ ⲡⲁⲓ̈ ⲉⲧ·ⲧⲁⲭⲣⲏⲩ ⲁ[ⲣⲱⲩ ⲉ]ⲩ

38 [ⲱⲧⲡ̄] ⲙ̄ⲙⲟⲟⲩ ⲉⲍⲟⲩⲛ ⲉⲣⲟⲩ ⲭⲉ[ⲕⲁⲁⲥ ⲛ̄ⲛⲉⲩ ⲣ̄]

[ⲡⲃⲟⲗ]· ⲛ̄ⲥⲉⲛ[ⲁ]ⲕⲱ ⲁⲛ· ⲉⲃⲟⲗ ⲙ̄[ⲡⲟⲩⲗⲓ]ⲃⲉ [ⲁⲩⲱ]

40 [ⲛⲓⲁⲣⲭⲱⲛ ⲉⲧⲛ̄]ⲁⲡⲱⲧ· ⲛ̄ⲥⲁ ⲧⲏⲛⲉ ⲥ[ⲉⲛⲁⲡ]ⲁⲣⲁⲇⲓⲇ[ⲟⲩ]

[ⲙ̄ⲙⲟⲟⲩ ⲉⲍⲣⲁⲓ̈ ⲉⲡⲁⲅ]ⲅⲉⲗⲟⲥ· ⲡⲧⲁⲣⲧⲁⲣⲟⲩⲭ[ⲟ]ⲥ

42 [ⲛ̄ⲩⲭⲓ ⲛ̄ⲍⲉⲛⲙⲁⲥⲧⲓϫ ⲛ̄ⲥ]ⲁⲧⲉ ⲉⲩⲡⲏⲧ· ⲛ̄ⲥⲱⲟⲩ

142:29 Ms. reads ⲛⲥⲱⲩ· ⲇ̄ ⲏ ⲛ̄·

22 these words that you (sg) speak to us are laughing-stocks to the
    world (κόσμος) and derided, since (ἐπειδή) they are not
24 understood. So how can we go
    preach them since we are reckoned
26 as in the world (κόσμος)?" The Savior (σωτήρ) answered and said:
    "Truly (ἀμήν) I tell you that he who will listen to
28 your word and turn away his face or (ἤ) sneer
    at it or (ἤ) smirk at these things, truly (ἀμήν)
30 I tell you that he will be handed over to
    the Archon (ἄρχων) who is above, he who rules (ἄρχειν) over
32 all the powers (ἐξουσία) as their king, and he will turn
    that one around and cast him from heaven down to
34 the abyss, and he will be imprisoned in a narrow
    dark place. Moreover, he can neither turn nor move on account of
36 the great depth (βάθος) of Tartaros and the [wide wall]
    of Hades that is set [against him. They are]
38 [imprisoned] in it in [order that they might not]
    [escape]. Their [madness] will not be forgiven. [And]
40 [the archons (ἄρχων)] who will pursue you [will] deliver (παραδιδόναι)
    [them over to the] angel (ἄγγελος) Tartarouchos
42 [and he will take whips (μάστιξ) of] fire, pursuing them

[Ñ]ϩενⲫⲣⲁⲅⲉⲗⲗⲟⲩ ⲛ̄ⲥⲁⲧⲉ· ⲉⲩⲛⲉϫ ϯⲕ̄ ϯⲕ̄ ⲉⲃⲟⲗ· ⲉϩⲟⲩ̄

2   ⲉⲫⲟ ⲙ̄ⲡⲉⲧⲟⲩⲡⲏⲧ ⲛ̄ⲥⲱϥ· ⲉⲩⲡⲏⲧ· ⲁⲡⲁⲙⲛⲧⲉ ⲉⲩϭⲓ

[ⲛ̄]ⲉ ⲛ̄ⲧⲥⲁⲧⲉ· ⲉⲩϣⲁⲛⲕⲧⲟⲩ· ⲁⲣⲏⲥ ⲉⲩϭⲛ̄ⲧⲉ̄ ⲟⲛ̄ ⲙ̄ⲙⲁⲩ

4   ⲉⲩϣⲁⲛⲕⲧⲟⲩ ⲁϩⲏⲧ· ϣⲁⲥⲧⲱⲙⲧ ⲉⲣⲟϥ ⲁⲛ· ⲛ̄ϭⲓ ⲧⲁⲡⲓⲗⲏ

ⲛ̄ⲥⲁⲧⲉ· ⲉⲥⲃⲣ̄ⲃⲣ̄ ⲙⲁⲩϭⲓⲛⲉ ⲇⲉ ⲛ̄ⲧⲟⲩ ⲛ̄ⲑⲓⲏ ⲙ̄ⲡⲁⲉⲓⲃⲧⲉ

6   ⲁⲡⲱⲧ· ⲉⲙⲁⲩ ⲛ̄ϩⲟⲩϫⲁⲉⲓ ⲙ̄ⲡⲉϥϭⲛ̄ⲧⲉ̄ ⲅⲁⲣ ⲙ̄ⲫⲟⲟⲩ ⲉϥ

ϩⲛ̄ ⲥⲱⲙ[ⲁ] ϫⲉⲕⲁⲁⲥ ⲉϥⲛⲁϭⲛ̄ⲧⲉ̄ ⲙ̄ⲫⲟⲟⲩ ⲛ̄ⲧⲕⲣⲓⲥⲓⲥ·

8   ⲧⲟⲧⲉ ⲁϥ·ⲟⲩⲱϩ ⲁⲧⲟⲟⲧϥ· ⲛ̄ϭⲓ ⲡⲥⲱ̄ⲣ ⲉϥϫⲱ ⲙ̄ⲙⲟⲥ

ϫⲉ ⲟⲩⲟⲉⲓ ⲛⲏⲧⲛ̄ ⲛ̄ⲁⲧⲛⲟⲩⲧⲉ· ⲉⲧⲉ ⲙⲛ̄ⲧⲉⲩ ϩⲉⲗⲡⲓⲥ·

10   ⲉⲧ·ⲧⲁϩⲣⲁⲓ̈ⲧ· ⲉϩⲣⲁⲓ̈ ⲉϫⲛ̄ ⲛⲉⲧⲛⲁϣⲱⲡⲉ ⲁⲛ ⲟⲩⲟⲓ̈ ⲛⲏⲧⲛ̄

ⲛⲉⲧⲣ̄ϩⲉⲗⲡⲓⲍⲉ ⲁⲧⲥⲁⲣⲝ̄ ⲁⲩⲱ ⲡⲓϣⲧⲉⲕⲟ ⲉⲧⲛⲁⲧⲉⲕⲟ ϣⲁ̄

12   ⲧⲉⲟⲩϣⲱⲡⲉ ⲉⲧⲉⲧⲛ̄ⲟⲃⲩ̄ ⲁⲩⲱ ⲛ̄ⲁⲧ·ⲧⲉⲕⲟ ⲉⲧⲉⲧⲛ̄ⲙⲉ

ⲉⲩⲉ ⲉⲣⲟⲟⲩ ϫⲉ ⲥⲉⲛⲁⲧⲁⲕⲟ ⲁⲛ· ⲉⲧⲉ[ⲧⲛ̄]ϩⲉⲗⲡⲓⲥ ⲧⲁϫⲣⲏⲩ

14   ⲁϫⲛ̄ ⲡⲕⲟⲥⲙⲟⲥ ⲁⲩⲱ ⲡⲉⲧⲛ̄ⲛⲟⲩⲧⲉ ⲡⲉ ⲡⲉⲉⲓⲃⲓⲟⲥ

ⲉⲧⲉⲧⲛ̄ⲧⲁⲕⲟ ⲛ̄ⲛⲉⲧⲛ̄ⲯⲩⲭⲟⲟⲩⲉ· ⲟⲩⲟⲉⲓ ⲛⲏⲧⲛ̄ ϩⲣⲁⲓ̈

16   ϩⲙ̄ ⲡⲕⲱϩⲧ· ⲉⲧⲣⲱⲕϩ ϩⲣⲁⲓ̈ ϩⲛ̄ ⲧⲏⲛⲉ ϫⲉ ⲟⲩⲁⲧⲥⲓ ⲡⲉ

ⲟⲩⲟⲉⲓ ⲛⲏⲧⲛ̄ ⲉⲃⲟⲗ ϩⲓⲧⲟⲟⲧⲟⲩ ⲙ̄ⲡⲕⲁⲧ· ⲉⲧⲕⲱⲧⲉ ϩⲛ̄

18   ⲛⲉⲧⲛ̄ⲙⲉⲉⲩⲉ ⲟⲩⲟⲉⲓ ⲛⲏⲧⲛ̄ ⲛ̄ⲧⲟⲟⲧⲟⲩ̄ ⲙ̄ⲡⲙⲟⲩ[ϩ]

ⲉⲧϩ[ⲛ̄] ⲧⲏⲛⲉ ϫⲉ ϥⲛⲁⲟⲩⲱⲙ ⲛ̄ⲛⲉⲧⲛ̄ⲥⲁⲣⲝ̄ ϩⲛ̄ ⲟⲩⲱⲛϩ

20   ⲉⲃⲟⲗ· ⲁⲩⲱ ϥⲛⲁⲟⲩⲱϩ ⲛ̄ⲛⲉⲧⲛ̄ⲯⲩⲭⲟⲟⲩⲉ ϩⲛ̄ ⲟⲩ

ϩⲱⲡ ⲛ̄ⲩⲥⲃ̄ⲧⲉ ⲧⲏⲛⲉ ϩⲣⲁⲓ̈ ϩⲛ̄ ⲛⲉⲧⲛ̄ⲉⲣⲏⲩ· ⲟⲩⲟ[ⲓ̈ ⲛ̄]ⲏ

[with] fiery scourges (φραγγελοῦν) that cast a shower of sparks into

2 the face of the one who is pursued. If he flees westward, he

finds the fire. If he turns southward, he finds it also there.

4 If he turns northward, the threat (ἀπειλή)

of seething fire meets him again. Nor (δέ) does he find the way to

the East

6 so as to flee there and be saved, for (γάρ) he did not find it in the day

he was in the body (σῶμα), so that he will find it in the day of

8 Judgment (κρίσις)." Then (τότε) the Savior (σωτήρ) continued, saying:

"Woe to you, godless ones, who have no hope (ἐλπίς),

10 who rely on things that will not happen! Woe to you

who hope (ἐλπίζειν) in the flesh (σάρξ) and in the prison that will

12 perish! How long will you be oblivious? And the imperishables, do you

think that they also will perish? Your hope (ἐλπίς) is set

14 upon the world (κόσμος) and your god is this life (βίος)!

You are corrupting your souls (ψυχή)! Woe to you for

16 the fire that burns in you, for it is insatiable!

Woe to you because of the wheel that turns in

18 your minds! Woe to you because of the burning

that is in you, for it will devour your flesh (σάρξ) openly

20 and rend your souls (ψυχή) secretly,

and prepare you for your companions! Woe to you,

22 ⲧⲛ̄ ⲛ̄ⲁⲓⲭⲙⲁⲗⲱⲧⲟⲥ ⲇⲉ ⲧⲉⲧⲛ̄ⲙⲏⲣ· ⳉⲛ̄ ⲛ̄ⲥⲡⲏⲗ[ⲁⲓ]
    ⲟⲛ· ⲧⲉⲧⲛ̄ⲥⲱⲃⲉ ⲉⲧⲉⲧⲛ̄ⲣ̄ⲟϣⲉ ⳉⲣⲁⲓ̈ ⳉⲛ̄ ⲛ̄ⲥⲱⲃ[ⲉ]

24 ⲛ̄ⲗⲓⲃⲉ ⲧⲉⲧⲛ̄ⲣ̄ⲛⲟⲉⲓ ⲁⲛ ⲙ̄ⲡⲉⲧⲛ̄ⲧⲁⲕⲟ ⲟⲩⲧⲉ ⲧ[ⲉ]
    ⲧⲛ̄ⲣⲛⲟⲉⲓ ⲁⲛ· ⳉⲛ̄ ⲛⲉⲧⲉⲧⲉⲧⲛ̄ⳉⲏⲧⲟⲩ ⲟⲩⲧⲉ ⲙ̄ⲡ[ⲉⲧ]ⲛ̄

26 ⲙ̄ⲙⲉ ϫⲉ ⲧⲉⲧⲛ̄ϣⲟⲟⲡ· ⳉⲙ̄ ⲡⲕⲁⲕⲉ· ⲙⲛ̄ ⲡⲙⲟ[ⲩ]
    ⲁⲗⲗⲁ ⲉⲧⲉⲧⲛ̄ⲧⲁⳉⲉ ⳉⲙ̄ ⲡⲕⲱⳉⲧ· ⲁⲩⲱ ⲧⲉⲧⲛ̄[ⲙⲉⳉ]

28 ⲛ̄ⲥⲓϣⲉ ⲉⲣⲉⲡⲉⲧⲛ̄ⳉⲏⲧ· ⲡⲟϣⳅ ⲉⲣⲱⲧⲛ̄ ⲉⲧⲃⲉ ⲡ[ⲙ]ⲟⲩⳉ
    ⲉ[ⲧ]ⳉⲛ̄ ⲧⲏⲛⲉ· ⲁⲩⲱ ⲩ̄ⳉⲟⲗϭ ⲛⲏⲧⲛ̄ ⲛ̄ϭⲓ ⲡⲕⲗⲟⲙ ⲛ̄

30 ⲧⲡⲗⲏⲅⲏ ⲛ̄ⲛⲉⲧⲛ̄ϫⲁϫⲉ· ⲁⲩⲱ ⲡⲕⲁⲕⲉ ⲁⲩϣⲁⲉ ⲛⲏ
    ⲧⲛ̄ ⲛ̄ⲑⲉ ⲙ̄ⲡⲟⲩⲟⲉⲓⲛ· ⲧⲉⲧⲛ̄ⲙⲛ̄ⲧⲣⲙ̄ⳉⲉ ⲅⲁⲣ· ⲁⲧⲉⲧⲛ̄

32 ⲧⲁⲁⲥ ⲛ̄ⲧⲙⲛ̄ⲧⳉⲙ̄ⳃⲁⲗ ⲁⲧⲉⲧⲛ̄ⲉⲓⲣⲉ ⲛ̄ⲛⲉⲧⲛ̄ⳉⲏⲧ· ⲛ̄
    ⳉⲏⲧ· ⲛ̄ⲕⲁⲕⲉ· ⲁⲩⲱ ⲛⲉⲧⲛ̄ⲙⲉⲉⲩⲉ· ⲁⲧⲉⲧⲛ̄ⲧⲁⲁⲩ

34 ⲛ̄ⲧⲙⲛ̄ⲧⲥⲉⲃⲉ· ⲁⲩⲱ ⲁⲧⲉⲧⲛ̄ⲙⲟⲩⳉ ⲛ̄ⲛⲉⲧⲛ̄ⲙⲉ
    ⲉ[ⲩⲉ] ⳉⲛ̄ ⲡⲕⲁⲡⲛⲟⲥ· ⲙ̄ⲡⲕⲱⳉⲧ· ⲉⲧⳉⲛ̄ ⲧⲏⲛⲉ ⲁⲩ

36 ⲱ [ⲁⲩⳉ]ⲱⲡ· ⲛ̄ϭⲓ ⲡⲉⲧⲛ̄ⲟⲩⲟⲉⲓⲛⲉ· ⳉⲛ̄ ⲧⲕⲗⲟⲟⲗⲉ
    [ⲛ̄ⲕⲁⲕⲉ ⲁ]ⲩⲱ ⲧ̄ⳉⲃⲥⲱ ⲉⲧ·ⲧⲟ ⳉⲓ ⲧⲏⲛⲉ ⲁⲧⲉⲧⲛ̄ⲡ[ⲟⳉⳅ]

38 [ⲁⲩⲱ ⲁⲧⲉⲧⲛ̄ⲱ]ⲃϣ· ⲁⲩⲱ ⲁⲩⲣ̄ⲕⲁⲧⲉⲭⲉ ⲙ̄ⲙⲱ[ⲧⲛ̄ ⳉⲓ]
    [ⲧⲛ̄] ⲑⲉⲗ[ⲡⲓⲥ ⲉⲧ]ϣⲟⲟⲡ· ⲁⲛ ⲁⲩⲱ ⲛⲓ̈ⲙ ⲡⲉⲛⲧ[ⲁⲧⲉ]

40 [ⲧⲛ̄]ⲡⲓⲥⲧ[ⲉⲩⲉ] ⲉⲣⲟ· ⲧⲉⲧⲛ̄ⲥⲟⲟ[ⲩⲛ ⲁⲛ ϫⲉ ⲧⲉⲧⲛ̄]
    [ϣ]ⲟⲟⲡ ⲧⲏⲣⲧⲛ̄ ⳉⲛ̄ ⲛⲉⲧ[ⲟⲩⲱϣⲉ ⲉⲧⲣⲉⲧⲛ̄ⲥⲁ]

42 ⳉⲟⲩ ⲙ̄ⲙⲱⲧⲛ̄ ⳉⲱⲥ ⲉⲣ[ⲉⲧⲉⲧⲛ̄ⳉⲉⲗⲡⲓⲥ ϣⲟⲟⲡ ⲁⲛ]

22 captives (αἰχμάλωτος), for you are bound in caverns (σπήλαιον)!
    You laugh! In mad laughter you rejoice!

24 You neither recognize (νοεῖν) your perdition, nor (οὔτε)
    do you reflect (νοεῖν) on your circumstances, nor (οὔτε) have [you]

26 understood that you dwell in darkness and death!
    On the contrary (ἀλλά), you are drunk with the fire and [full]

28 of bitterness! Your mind is deranged on account of the [burning]
    that [is in] you, and sweet to you is the victory of

30 smiting (πληγή) your enemies! And the darkness rose for
    you like the light, for (γάρ) you surrendered your freedom

32 for servitude! You darkened your hearts
    and you surrendered your minds

34 to folly, and you filled your thoughts
    with the smoke of the fire that is in you! And

36 your light has hidden in the cloud
    [of darkness] and the garment that is put on you, you [rent].

38 [And you have forgotten] and you were seized (κατέχειν) [by]
    [the hope (ἐλπίς) that] does not exist. And whom is it [you]

40 [have believed (πιστεύειν)]? Do you [not] know that [you]
    all dwell among those [who want you to curse]

42 yourselves as if (ὡς) [your hope (ἐλπίς) is non-existent]?

143:39 literally: "crown of the smiting"

ⲁⲧⲉⲧⲛ̅ⲱⲙⲥ̅ ⲛ̅ⲛⲉⲧⲛ̅ⲯⲩⲭⲏ ϩⲙ̅ ⲡⲙⲟⲟⲩ ⲙ̅ⲡⲕⲁⲕ[ⲉ]

2 ⲁⲧⲉⲧⲛ̅ⲡⲱⲧ` ϩⲛ̅ ⲛⲉⲧⲛ̅ⲟⲩⲱϣⲉ ⲙ̅ⲙⲓⲛ ⲙⲙⲱⲧⲛ̅ ⲟ[ⲩ]

ⲟⲉⲓ ⲛⲏⲧⲛ̅ ⲛⲉⲧ`ϣⲟⲟⲡ` ϩⲙ̅ ⲡⲥⲱⲣⲙ̅ ⲉⲧⲉⲧⲛ̅ϭⲁϣⲧ

4 ⲁⲛ ⲁⲡⲟⲩⲟⲉⲓⲛ ⲙ̅ⲡⲣⲏ· ⲡⲉⲧⲕⲣⲓⲛⲉ ⲙ̅ⲡⲧⲏⲣϥ` ⲉⲧ

ϭⲁϣⲧ` ⲁϫⲛ̅ ⲡⲧⲏⲣϥ` ϫⲉ ϥⲛⲁⲕⲱⲧⲉ ⲁϫⲛ̅ ⲛ̅ϩⲃⲏⲩⲉ

6 ⲧⲏⲣⲟⲩ ⲁⲧⲣⲉⲛ̅ϫⲁϫⲉ ⲣ̅ϩⲙ̅ϩⲁⲗ ⲁⲩⲱ ⲟⲛ ⲧⲉⲧⲛ̅ⲣⲛⲟⲉⲓ

ⲁⲛ ⲙ̅ⲡⲟⲟϩ ϫⲉ ⲛ̅ⲁϣ ⲛ̅ϩⲉ ⲛ̅ⲧⲟⲩϣⲏ ⲙⲛ̅ ⲫⲟⲟⲩ ⲉϥ

8 ϭⲁϣⲧ` ⲉϩⲣⲁⲓ̈ ⲉϥⲛⲁⲩ ⲁⲛⲥⲱⲙⲁ ⲛ̅ⲛⲉⲧ[ⲛ̅]ϩⲉⲧⲃⲉ ⲟⲩⲟⲓ̈

ⲛⲏⲧⲛ̅ ⲛⲉⲧⲙⲁⲉⲓⲉ ⲛ̅ⲧⲥⲩⲛⲏⲑⲉⲓⲁ ⲛ̅ⲧⲙ̅ⲛ̅ⲧⲥϩⲓⲙⲉ

10 ⲙⲛ̅ ⲡⲉⲥϣⲱⲡⲉ ⲛⲙ̅ⲙⲁⲥ ⲉⲧⲥⲟⲟϥ` ⲁⲩⲱ ⲟⲩⲟⲉⲓ·

ⲛⲏⲧⲛ̅ ⲛ̅ⲧⲟⲟⲧⲟⲩ ⲛ̅ⲛⲉϩⲟⲩⲥⲓⲁ ⲙ̅ⲡⲉⲧⲛ̅ⲥⲱⲙⲁ ϫⲉ

12 ⲛⲉⲧⲙ̅ⲙⲟ ⲅⲁⲣ` ⲥⲉⲛⲁⲑⲙ̅ⲕⲉ ⲧⲏⲛⲉ· ⲟⲩⲟⲓ̈ ⲛⲏⲧⲛ̅ ⲛ̅ⲧⲟ

ⲟⲧⲟⲩ· ⲛ̅ⲛⲉⲛⲉⲣⲅⲉⲓⲁ ⲛ̅ⲛ̅ⲇⲁⲓⲙⲱⲛ` ⲙ̅ⲡⲟⲛⲏⲣⲟⲛ`

14 ⲟⲩⲟⲓ̈ ⲛⲏⲧⲛ̅ ⲛⲉⲧ`ⲥⲱⲕ` ⲛ̅ⲛⲉⲩⲙⲉⲗⲟⲥ` ϩⲙ̅ ⲡⲕⲱϩⲧ`

ⲛⲓⲙ` ⲡⲉⲧⲛⲁϩⲱⲟⲩ ⲛⲏⲧⲛ̅ ⲛⲟⲩⲉⲓⲱⲧⲉ ⲙ̅ⲙⲧⲟⲛ`

16 ϫⲉⲕⲁⲁⲥ ⲉⲥⲛⲁϩⲱⲧⲙ̅ ⲛ̅ϩⲁϩ ⲛ̅ⲕⲱϩⲧ` ⲉⲃⲟⲗ ϩⲛ̅ ⲧⲏⲛⲉ

ⲙⲛ̅ ⲡⲉⲧⲛ̅ⲣⲱⲕϩ` ⲛⲓⲙ ⲡⲉⲧⲛⲁϯ ⲛⲏⲧⲛ̅ ⲙ̅ⲡⲣⲏ ⲁⲡⲣ

18 ⲣⲓⲉ ⲁϫⲛ̅ ⲧⲏⲛⲉ· ⲁⲃⲱⲗ ⲉⲃⲟⲗ ⲙ̅ⲡⲕⲁⲕⲉ· ⲉⲧϩⲛ̅ ⲧⲏⲛⲉ

ⲁⲩⲱ ⲁϩⲱⲡ· ⲙ̅ⲡⲕⲁⲕⲉ ⲙⲛ̅ ⲡⲙⲟⲟⲩ ⲉⲧⲥⲟⲟ[ϥ] ⲡⲣⲏ

20 ⲙⲛ̅ ⲡⲟⲟϩ ⲛⲁϯ ⲥⲧⲛⲟⲩϥⲉ ⲛⲏⲧⲛ̅· ⲙⲛ̅ ⲡⲁⲏ[ⲣ] ⲙⲛ̅

ⲡⲡ̅ⲛ̅ⲁ̅ ⲙⲛ̅ ⲡⲕⲁϩ ⲙⲛ̅ ⲡⲙⲟⲟⲩ ⲡⲣⲏ ⲅⲁⲣ` ⲉϥⲧⲙ̅

You baptized your souls (ψυχή) in the water of darkness!

2 You walked in your own desires! Woe

to you who dwell in error, not looking at

4 the light of the sun that judges the All, that

looks down upon the All, for it will circle around all things

6 to enslave the enemies. You do not even notice (νοεῖν)

the moon, how by night and day it

8 looks down, looking at the bodies (σῶμα) of your corpses! Woe

to you who love intimacy (συνήθεια) with womankind

10 and polluted intercourse with it! And woe

to you because of the powers (ἐξουσία) of your body (σῶμα),

12 for (γάρ) those will afflict you! Woe to you because of

the forces (ἐνέργεια) of the evil (πονηρόν) demons (δαίμων)!

14 Woe to you who beguile your limbs (μέλος) with the fire!

Who is it that will rain a refreshing dew on you

16 in order that it might extinguish a multitude of fire from you

together with your burning? Who is it that will give you the sun to

18 shine upon you to disperse the darkness in you

and hide the darkness and the polluted water? The sun

20 and the moon will give a fragrance to you, together with the air (ἀήρ) and

the spirit (πνεῦμα) and the earth and the water. For (γάρ) if the sun

[does not]

ⲡⲣ̄ⲣⲓⲉ ⲁϫⲛ̄ ⲛⲓⲥⲱⲙⲁ ⲥⲉⲛⲁⲗⲟⲩⲗⲉϥ` ⲛ̄ⲥⲉ[ⲧ]ⲁⲕⲟ̣
[ⲙ̄]ⲡⲣⲏⲧⲉ ϩⲱⲱϥ` ⲛ̄ⲟⲩⲛ̄ⲧⲏϭ ⲏ ⲟⲩⲭⲟⲣⲧⲟⲥ` ⲉϣⲱⲡⲉ
[ⲙ]ⲉⲛ ⲉⲡⲣⲏ ⲡⲣ̄ⲣⲓⲉ ⲁϫⲱϥ` ϣⲁϥϭⲛ̄ϭⲁⲙ` ⲛ̄ϥⲱϭⲧ`
[ⲛ̄]ⲧ̣ⲃⲱ ⲛ̄ⲉⲗⲟⲟⲗⲉ· ⲉϣⲱⲡⲉ ⲇⲉ ⲉ̣ⲥϣⲁⲛϭⲛ̄ϭⲟⲙ·
[ⲛ̄]ϭ̣ⲓ̣ ⲧⲃⲱ ⲛ̄ⲉⲗⲟⲟⲗⲉ· ⲛ̄ⲥⲣ̄ϩⲁ̈ⲓ̈ⲃⲉⲥ ⲁϫⲛ̄ ⲛⲓⲛ̄ⲧⲏϭ`
[ⲙⲛ̄] ⲛⲓⲕⲉϣⲛⲁ ⲧⲏⲣⲟⲩ ⲉⲧⲣⲏⲧ` ⲉϩⲣⲁ̈ⲓ̈ ⲛ̄ⲙ̄ⲙⲁⲥ` ⲛ̄[ⲥ]
[ⲡⲱⲣ]ϣ` ⲉⲃⲟⲗ` ⲁⲩⲱ ⲛ̄ⲥⲟⲩⲟⲥⲧⲛ̄ ⲉⲃⲟⲗ ϣⲁⲥⲣ̄ⲕⲗⲏ
[ⲣⲟⲛⲟ]ⲙⲉⲓ ⲙ̄ⲡⲕⲁϩ ⲟⲩⲁⲁⲧⲥ̄ ⲡⲁ̈ⲓ̈ ⲉⲧⲥⲣⲏⲧ` ϩⲣⲁ̈ⲓ̈ ⲛ̄ϩⲏⲧϥ`
ⲁ̣ⲩ̣ⲱ <ϣ>ⲁⲥⲣ̄ⲛⲁⲡ ⲁⲙⲁ ⲛⲓⲙ` ⲉⲧⲁⲥⲣ̄ϩⲁⲉⲓⲃⲉⲥ` ⲁϫⲱϥ`
ⲧⲟⲧⲉ ϭⲉ ⲉⲥϣⲁⲛⲁⲩⲝⲁⲛⲉ ϣⲁⲥⲣ̄ⲛⲉⲡ ⲁⲡⲕⲁ̣ϩ̣ ⲧ̣ⲏ̣ⲣ̣ϥ̄
ⲁⲩⲱ ϣⲁⲥⲣ̄ϩⲉⲛⲟⲩϥⲉ· ⲙ̄ⲡⲉⲥϫⲟⲉⲓⲥ ⲛ̄ⲥⲣ̄ⲁⲛⲁϥ·
ⲛ̄ϩⲟⲩⲟ ⲇⲉ ⲛⲉϥⲛⲁϣⲱⲡ` ⲅⲁⲣ` ⲛ̄ϩⲉⲛⲛⲟϭ ⲛ̄ϩⲓⲥⲉ
ⲡⲉ· ⲉⲧⲃⲉ ⲛⲓⲛ̄ⲧⲏϭ ϣⲁⲛⲧϥ̄ⲡⲟⲣⲕⲟⲩ ⲁⲗⲗⲁ ⲧⲃⲱ
ⲛ̄ⲉⲗⲟⲟⲗⲉ ⲟⲩⲁⲁⲧⲥ̄ ⲁⲥϥⲓⲧⲟⲩ ⲙ̄ⲙⲁⲩ ⲁⲩⲱ ⲁⲥⲱϭⲧ ⲙ̄
ⲙⲟⲟⲩ ⲁⲩⲙⲟⲩ· ⲁⲩϣⲱⲡⲉ ⲛ̄ⲑⲉ ⲙ̄ⲡⲕⲁϩ ⲧⲟⲧⲉ̣ [ⲁϥ]
ⲟ̣ⲩⲱϩ ⲉⲧⲟⲟⲧϥ` ⲛ̄ϭⲓ ⲓ̅ⲥ̅ ⲡⲁϫⲉϥ ⲛⲁⲩ ϫⲉ ⲟⲩ[ⲟⲉⲓ ⲛ]ⲏ
[ⲧⲛ̄] ϫⲉ ⲙ̄ⲡⲉⲧⲛ̄ϫⲓ ⲛ̄ⲧⲥⲃⲱ· ⲁⲩⲱ ⲛⲉⲧⲟ̣ [ⲛ̄ⲁⲧⲥⲟ]
[ⲟⲩⲛ] ⲥⲉⲛⲁϩⲓⲥⲉ ⲉⲩⲧⲁϣⲉ ⲟⲉⲓ̣ϣ̣ [ⲉⲡⲙⲁ ⲛ̄ⲧⲉ ⲧⲏ]
[ⲛⲉ] ⲁ̣ⲩⲱ ⲧ̣ⲉ[ⲧⲛ̄]ⲡ̣ⲏⲧ ⲁϩⲟⲩⲛ ⲁ[ⲧⲙⲛ̄]ⲧ̣ϣⲛ[ⲁ]
[ⲟⲩⲛ̄ϩⲟⲉⲓⲛⲉ ⲇⲉ] ⲉ̣ⲁ̣ⲩ̣ⲧⲛ̄ⲛⲟⲟⲩⲟ[ⲩ ⲁⲡ]ⲓⲧⲛ̄ ⲛ̄ⲛⲁ
[ϩⲙ̄ ⲛⲁⲉⲓ ⲧⲏⲣⲟⲩ ⲛ̄ⲧⲁⲧⲉ]ⲧ̣ⲛⲙⲟⲟⲩⲧⲟⲩ ⲙ̄ⲙⲏⲛ̣[ⲉ]

144:35 Ms. inserts ⲥ above ⲁϥⲓⲧⲟⲩ to read ⲁⲥϥⲓⲧⲟⲩ.

22 shine upon these bodies they will wither and perish

just like weeds or (ἤ) grass (χόρτος). If,

24 now (μέν), the sun shines on it (the weed), it prevails and chokes

the grapevine; if, however (δέ), the grapevine

26 prevails and shades those weeds

[and] all that other brush growing up with it, and

28 spreads and broadens out, it alone

inherits (κληρονομεῖν) the land in which it grows

30 and it dominates every place it shaded.

So then (τότε) when it grows up (αὐξάνειν), it dominates all the land,

32 and it is bountiful for its master, and it pleases him

even more, for (γάρ) he would have suffered great pains

34 on account of these plants until he uprooted them. But (ἀλλά) the

grapevine alone removed them and choked

36 them, and they died and became like the land."

Then (τότε) Jesus continued, and said: "[Woe to]

38 [you], for you did not receive the doctrine, and those who are [ignorant]

will labor at preaching [instead of you].

40 And [you] are rushing into [debauchery].

[Yet (δέ) there are some who have been] sent down to [rescue]

42 [those whom you] killed daily

ⲇⲉⲕⲁⲁⲥ ⲉⲩⲛⲁⲧⲱⲟⲩⲛ ⲍⲙ̄ ⲡⲙⲟⲩ ⲛⲁⲉⲓⲁⲧ' ⲧⲏⲛⲉ

2   ⲛⲉⲧⲣ̄ϣⲣⲡ̄ ⲛⲙ̄ⲙⲉ· ⲁⲛⲥⲕⲁⲛⲇⲁⲗⲟⲛ' ⲁⲩⲱ ⲉⲧⲡⲱⲧ'

ⲍⲏⲧϥ̄ ⲛ̄ⲛ̄ⲁⲗⲗⲟⲧⲣⲓⲟⲛ' ⲛⲁⲉⲓⲁⲧ' ⲧⲏⲛⲉ ⲛⲉⲧⲟⲩⲛⲟϭ

4   ⲛⲉϭ ⲙ̄ⲙⲟⲟⲩ ⲁⲩⲱ ⲉⲩⲱⲡ ⲙ̄ⲙⲟⲟⲩ ⲁⲛ· ⲉⲧⲃⲉ ⲡⲙⲁⲉⲓⲉ

ⲉⲧⲉⲩⲛ̄ⲧⲁϥϥ' ⲉⲍⲟⲩⲛ ⲉⲣⲟⲟⲩ ⲛ̄ϭⲓ ⲡⲟⲩⲇⲟⲉⲓⲥ ⲛⲁⲉⲓⲁⲧ'

6   ⲧⲏⲛⲉ ⲛⲉⲧⲣⲓⲙⲉ· ⲁⲩⲱ ⲉⲧⲟⲩⲣ̄ⲑⲗⲓⲃⲉ ⲙ̄ⲙⲟⲟⲩ ⲍⲓⲧⲛ̄

ⲛⲉⲧⲉⲙ[ⲛ̄ⲧⲉ]ⲩ ⲍⲉⲗⲡⲓⲥ ⲇⲉ ⲥⲉⲛⲁⲃⲱⲗ ⲧⲏⲛⲉ ⲍⲓⲧⲙ̄ ⲙ̄ⲣ̄

8   ⲣⲉ ⲛⲓⲙ· ⲣⲟⲉⲓⲥ ⲉⲧⲉⲧⲛ̄ⲥⲟⲡⲥ̄ ϫⲉ ⲉⲧⲉⲧⲛⲁϣⲱⲡⲉ ⲁⲛ·

ⲍⲛ̄ ⲧⲥⲁⲣⲝ' ⲁⲗⲗⲁ ϫⲉ ⲉⲧⲉⲧⲛⲁⲉⲓ ⲉⲃⲟⲗ ⲍⲛ̄ ⲧⲙⲣ̄ⲣⲉ ⲙ̄ⲡⲥⲓ

10   ϣⲉ ⲛ̄ⲧⲉ ⲡⲃⲓⲟⲥ ⲁⲩⲱ ⲉⲧⲉⲧⲛ̄ⲥⲟⲡⲥ̄ ⲧⲉⲧⲛ̄ⲛⲁϭⲓⲛⲉ

ⲛ̄ⲟⲩⲙ̄ⲧⲟⲛ ϫⲉ ⲁⲧⲉⲧⲛ̄ⲕⲱ ⲛ̄ⲥⲱⲧⲛ̄ ⲙ̄ⲡϩⲓⲥⲉ ⲙ̄ⲛ ⲡⲛⲟϭ

12   ⲛⲉϭ ⲛ̄ϩⲏⲧ' ⲉⲧⲉⲧⲛ̄ϣⲁⲛⲉⲓ ⲅⲁⲣ ⲉⲃⲟⲗ ⲍⲛ̄ ⲛ̄ϩⲓⲥⲉ ⲙ̄ⲛ

ⲙ̄ⲡⲁⲑⲟⲥ ⲛ̄ⲧⲉ ⲡⲥⲱⲙⲁ· ⲧⲉⲧⲛⲁϫⲓ [ⲛ̄ⲟ]ⲩⲁⲛⲁⲡⲁⲩⲥⲓⲥ

14   ⲛ̄ⲧⲟⲟⲧϥ̄ ⲙ̄ⲡⲁⲅⲁⲑⲟⲥ ⲁⲩⲱ ⲧⲉⲧⲛⲁⲣ̄ⲣ̄ⲣⲟ ⲙ̄ⲛ ⲡⲣ̄ⲣⲟ ⲉ

ⲧⲉⲧⲛ̄ⲧⲏⲧ' ⲛⲙ̄ⲙⲁⲩ' ⲉⲩⲧⲏⲧ ⲛ̄ⲙ̄ⲙⲏⲧⲛ̄ ϫⲓⲛ ⲧⲉⲛⲟⲩ ϣⲁ

16   ⲉⲛⲉϩ ⲛ̄ⲁⲛⲉϩ ϩⲁⲙⲏⲛ:

        ⲡϫⲱⲙⲉ   ⲛ̄ⲑⲱⲙⲁⲥ

18   ⲡⲁⲑⲗⲏⲧⲏⲥ   ⲉϥⲥϩⲁⲓ̈

        ⲛ̄ⲛⲧⲉⲗⲉⲓⲟⲥ

20   ⲁⲣⲓ ⲡⲁⲙⲉⲉⲩⲉ ⲍⲱ ⲛⲁⲥⲛⲏⲩ

       ⲍ[ⲛ̄] ⲛⲉⲧⲛ̄ⲡⲣⲟⲥⲉⲩⲭⲏ'

22   ⲉⲓⲣⲏⲛⲏ ⲧⲟⲓⲥ ⲁⲅⲓⲟⲓⲥ

       ⲙ̄ⲛ ⲛⲓⲡⲛⲉⲩⲙⲁⲧⲓⲕⲟⲥ

in order that they might rise from death. Blessed are you

2   who have prior knowledge of the stumbling blocks (σκάνδαλον) and who

   flee alien things (ἀλλότριον). Blessed are you who are reviled

4   and not esteemed on account of the love

   their Lord has toward them. Blessed are

6   you who weep and are oppressed (θλίβειν) by

   those without hope (ἐλπίς), for you will be released from

8   every bondage. Watch and pray that you will not come to be

   in the flesh (σάρξ), but rather (ἀλλά) that you will come forth from the

      bondage of the bitterness

10 of this life (βίος). And as you pray, you will find

   rest, for you have left behind the suffering and the

12 disgrace. For (γάρ) when you come forth from the sufferings and

   passions (πάθος) of the body (σῶμα), you will receive rest (ἀνάπαυσις)

14 from the Good One (ἀγαθός), and you will reign with the King,

   you joined with him and he with you, from now on,

16 forever and ever. Amen."

                    The Book of Thomas

18   the Contender (ἀθλητής), writing

                 to the Perfect (τέλειος).

20   Remember me also, my brethren,

                in your prayers (προσευχή):

22   Peace to the Saints (εἰρήνη τοῖς ἁγίοις)

             and the Spiritual (πνευματικός)

THE BOOK OF THOMAS THE CONTENDER

CG II,7, 138:1-145:23

INDEX TO THE TRANSCRIPTION

Coptic Index[1]

ⲁⲁⲧⲕⲁⲥ n.m.   "marrow" (6b)
          139:35

ⲁⲙⲛ̄ⲧⲉ n.m.   "Hades," "the West" (8b)
     142:37 "Hades"
     143:2   "the West"

ⲁⲛ   negative part. (10b)
     138:11,21,30,34; 139:8,14,17,26; [140:39]; 141:12,23,25,36,
     37,[42]; 142:23,39; 143:10,24,25,39,[40]; 144:4,7; 145:4,8

ⲁⲛⲁⲓ "be pleasing" (11a)
     ⲡ̄ ⲁⲛⲁⲥ   144:32   "to please"

ⲁⲛⲟⲕ   first pers. indep. prn. "I" (11b)
     138:2,13; 142:9

ⲁⲩⲱ   coord. conj. "and" (19b)
     138:8,9,12,15,24,26,33,35,38; 139:1,5,14,24,35,36,36,37,39,
     42; 140:4,17,[22],23,25,26,26,28,31,33,34,38; 141:1,5,7,9,
     16,23,30,31,36,38; 142:13,14,20,21,23,28; 143:11,12,14,20,
     27,29,30,33,35,37,38,[38],39; 144:6,10,19,[27],28,30,32,35,
     38,40; 145:2,4,6,10,14

ⲁⲩ   interrogative "who," "what" (22a)
     ⲛ̄ⲁⲩ ⲛ̄ⲍⲉ   138:9,29,34; 139:10; 144:7 "how"
     ⲛ̄ⲁⲩ ⲛ̄ⲣⲏⲧⲉ   138:10; 142:24 "in what manner"
     ⲁⲩ ⲛ̄   141:21 "what"

---

[1]Each Coptic word is followed by: 1) the "part of speech" it
functions as, except for verbs, for which no "part of speech" is
listed; 2) its English definition; 3) a reference, enclosed in
parentheses, to the page and column of its entry in W.E. Crum:
A Coptic Dictionary (Oxford: Clarendon Press, 1962); 4) alternate
forms, if any, of the main entry as they appear in the text; and
5) the location of the Coptic word in the text, cited by page and
line number of Codex II of Nag Hammadi. The listing of alternate
forms, which includes different states of the verb, dialectal variants, and distinguishable syntactic applications, are followed
by their respective English translations, if they differ from the
main entry. Any instance of (3) in which the reference is preceded by "K" (e.g. K103), refers to a word entered in R. Kasser,
Compléments au dictionnaire Copte de Crum (Le Caire: Inst.
Français, 1964).

ⲁϪⲚ̄´ prep.   "without"   (25b)
    141:12

Ⲃⲱ   n.f.   "tree"   (28a)
    Ⲃⲱ Ⲛ̄ⲉⲗⲟⲟⲗⲉ   144:25,26,34   "grapevine"

Ⲃⲱⲕ   "go," "depart"   (29a)
    Ⲃⲱⲕ ⲉ´   142:24

Ⲃⲱⲗ   "loosen," "dissolve"   (32a)
    Ⲃⲱⲗ ⲉⲃⲟⲗ   141:6,7,15; 142:12; 144:18   "dissolve"
    Ⲃⲟⲗ⸗   139:15   "explain"
    Ⲃⲱⲗ ϩⲓⲧⲚ̄´   145:7   "be released from"
    ⲡ̄ Ⲃⲟⲗ   142:[39]   "escape"

Ⲃⲗ̄ⲗⲉ   n.m.   "blind person"   (38a)
    ⲁⲁ° Ⲛ̄Ⲃⲗⲗⲉ   140:25   to "blind"
    n.m.pl. Ⲃⲗ̄ⲗⲉⲉⲩⲉ Ⲛ̄ⲣⲱⲙⲉ   141:20   "blind men"

Ⲃⲡ̄Ⲃⲡ̄   "boil," "seethe"   (42b)
    143:5

Ⲉⲗⲟⲟⲗⲉ   n.m.   "grape"   (54b)
    Ⲃⲱ Ⲛ̄ⲉⲗⲟⲟⲗⲉ   144:25,26,35   "grapevine"

Ⲉⲛⲉ´   prefix of unfulfilled condition   (56b)
    with neg. first perf.   141:24

Ⲉⲛⲉϩ   n.m.   "eternity"   (57a)
    adv. abs.   140:28   "ever"
    ⳡⲁⲉⲛⲉϩ   141:1; 145:16   "forever"
    Ⲛ̄ⳡⲁⲉⲛⲉϩ   141:17f   "forever"
    ⳡⲁⲉⲛⲉϩ Ⲛ̄ⲁⲛⲉϩ   145:16   "forever and ever"

Ⲉⲣⲏⲩ   n.m.f.   "fellow"   (59a)
    w. poss. adj.   138:4; 141:[27],]9; 143:21   "one another"

Ⲉⲧⲃⲉ´   prep.   "because of," "concerning," "in behalf of"   (61a)
    138:6,25,37; 139:14,24,26,[42]; 140:7; 141:10; 142:5,35;
    143:28; 144:34; 145:4
    ⲉⲧⲃⲉ ⲡⲁⲓ   138:19,22,35; 139:4,11,12,[42]; 140:9   "therefore"
    ⲉⲧⲃⲉ ⲟⲩ   139:23   "why"

ⲈⳡϪⲉ   conj.   "if," "as if"   (63b)
    139:9

Ⲉⲓ   "come"   (70a)
    ⲉⲓ ⲉⲃⲟⲗ   139:18   "come forth"
    ⲉⲓ ⲉⲃⲟⲗ ϩⲛ̄´   139:27; 145:9,12   "come forth from"
    ⲉⲓ ⲁ´   141:22   "come (in order) to do"

Ⲉⲓⲁ   n.   "eye" (and its sight)   (73b)
    n.f. Ⲙⲛ̄ⲧ[ⲉⲓⲁ]   141:29   "sight"
    nom. vb. Ⲛⲁⲉⲓⲁⲧ⸗   140[41]; 145:1,3,5   "blessed is"

Ⲉⲓⲉ   "surely," "then"   (74a)
    ⲉⲉⲓⲉ   138:32,[40]

(Ⲉ)ⲉⲓⲉⲃⲧ   n.m.   "East"   (76b)
    ⲁⲉⲓⲃⲧⲉ   143:5

ⲉⲓⲙⲉ   "know," "recognize"   (77b)
     ⲘⲘⲉ   138:8,12; 140:7; 141:40; 143:26
     ⲘⲘⲉ ⲘⲘⲟⲉⲓ Ⲇⲉ ⲀⲚⲟⲕ ⲡⲉ...   138:13
     ⲘⲘⲉ ⲀⲨ   145:2

ⲉⲓⲛⲉ   be "like"   (80b)
     ⲓⲛⲉ ⲘⲙⲟⲨ   139:3

ⲉⲓⲣⲉ   "do," "make"   (83a)
     ⲉⲓⲣⲉ ⲚⲨ   138:32; 143:32
     Ⲣ̄Ⲩ   (often w/ Gk. inf.) 139:12,20,23,26,29; 140:22,23;
     141:1,[22],33; 142:4,8,11,15,18,19,20,[38]; 143:11,24,25,
     38; 144:6,6,26,28,30,30,31,32; 145:2,6
     ⲀⲨ   138:27f,31f; 140:25
     ⲞⲨ ⲚⲨ   138:11; 141:30; 142:21,32,34; 144:38
     imper. ⲀⲣⲓⲨ   145:20

ⲉⲓⲱⲧ   n.m. "father"   (86b)
     n. pl. ⲉⲓⲟⲧⲉ   141:32

ⲉⲓⲱⲧⲉ   n.f. "dew"   (87b)
     144:15

ⲉⲓⲧⲚ̄   n.m. "ground"   (87b)
     ⲀⲡⲓⲧⲚ̄Ⲩ   144:[41] "down"
     Ⲛ̄ⲧⲡⲉ ⲀⲡⲓⲧⲚ̄   140:35 "from heaven to earth"
     ⲀⲚ Ⲛ̄ⲧⲡⲉ ⲨϣⲀⲡⲓⲧⲚ̄ ⲀⲨ   142:33 "from heaven to the bottom of"

ⲕⲉ   n. "other," "also"   (90b)
     144:27

ⲕⲟⲨⲓ̈   n. "young person"   (92b)
     n.m.pl. ⲕⲟⲨⲉⲓ   139:11 "babes"
     adj. ⲕⲟⲨⲓ̈ Ⲛ̄Ⲩ   141:14 "short"

ⲕⲱ   "place," "appoint," "make"   (94b)
     ⲕⲀⲀⲨ ⲚⲀⲨ Ⲛ̄Ⲩ   141:26 "esteem as"
     ⲕⲱ ⲉⲂⲟⲗ Ⲛ̄Ⲩ   142:39 "release"
     ⲕⲱ ⲉⲌⲣⲀⲓ̈ Ⲛ̄Ⲩ   139:28 "abandon"
     ⲕⲱ Ⲛ̄ⲥⲱⲨ Ⲛ̄Ⲩ   145:11 "leave behind"
     ⲕⲀⲧⲟⲟⲧⲨ ⲉⲂⲟⲗ   141:38 "despair"

ⲕⲀⲕⲉ   n.m. "darkness"   (101b)
     139:19; 142:13; 143:26,30; 144:1,18,19
     adj. Ⲛ̄ⲕⲀⲕⲉ   140:24; 142:35; 143:33,[37] "dark"

ⲕⲗⲟⲟⲗⲉ   n.f. "cloud"   (104a)
     143:36

ⲕⲗⲟⲙ   n.m. "crown"   (104b)
     143:29

ⲕⲓⲙ   "move"   (108a)
     138:[40],[41],[41]; 139:39
     n.m. 139:40 "movement"

ⲕⲱⲱⲥ   "bury"   (120a)
     n.f. ⲕⲱⲥ   141:17 "corpse"

ⲔⲰⲦⲈ   "turn," "go around" (124a)
   143:17
   ⲔⲰⲦⲈ ⲀⲬⲚ́ 144:5 "circle around"
   n.m. ⲔⲀⲦ 143:17 "wheel"

ⲔⲦⲞ   "turn," "surround"   (127b)
   ⲔⲦⲞ ⲘⲡϨⲟ ⲈⲂⲞⲖ   142:28 "turn face away," "reject"
   ⲔⲦⲞ Ⲛ́   142:32 "turn around" (trans.)
   ⲔⲦⲞⸯ Ⲁ́   143:3,4 "turn (self) toward"

ⲔⲀϨ   n.m. "land" (131a)
   144:21,29,31,36

ⲔⲰϨⲦ   n.m.   "fire"   (133b)
   139:34; 140:21; 141:9,14,30; 142:12,12; 143:16,27; 144:14,16

ⲖⲞ   "abandon"   (135a)
   141:[37]

ⲖⲒⲂⲈ   n.m.   "madness"   (136b)
   141:39,[41]; 142:39; 143:24

ⲖⲀⲀⲨ   "anything"   (146a)
   138:17

ⲖⲞⲨⲖϤ̄   "perish"   (148b)
   ⲖⲞⲨⲖⲈϤ   144:22 "wither"

ⲘⲀ   n.m. "place"   (153a)
   139:27; 141:36; 142:34; 144:30,[39]

ⲘⲈ   to "love"   (156a)
   ⲘⲀⲈⲒⲈ   141:30; 144:9
   n.m. ⲘⲀⲈⲒⲈ   145:4

ⲘⲈ   n.f. "truth"   (156b)
   ⲘⲎⲈ   138:13,26,30; 140:1,17,20,[42]; 142:11
   adj. Ⲙ̄ⲘⲎⲈ   138:8; 140:2,21 "true"
   adv. ϨⲚ̄ ⲞⲨⲘⲎⲈ   141:25 "truly"

ⲘⲞⲨ   "die" (159a)
   144:36
   n.m. 141:31; 143:26; 145:1 "death"

ⲘⲔⲀϨ "be painful," "be difficult" (163a)
   ⲘⲞⲔϨ̄ Ⲁ́ 138:26,31
   ⲘⲞⲔϨ̄ Ⲛ́ 139:14

Ⲙ̄ⲘⲚ́ "not be" (166b)
   Ⲙ̄ⲚⲦⲈⸯ 139:5; 141:16; 143:9; [145:7] "not have"
   Ⲙ̄Ⲛ̄ϢϬⲞⲘ Ⲛ̄ⲦⲈ́ (conjunctive) 140:13
   Ⲙ̄Ⲛ̄ϢϬⲞⲘ Ⲙ̄ⲘⲞⸯ Ⲛ̄́ (plus inf.) 140:28
   particle (ⲈϢⲰⲡⲈ) Ⲙ̄ⲘⲞⲚ   140:12 "(if) not"

Ⲙ̄ⲘⲒⲚ   "own," "proper" (168b)
   Ⲙ̄ⲘⲒⲚ Ⲙ̄ⲘⲞⸯ 138:12,16; 140:30; 144:2

ⲘⲚ̄, Ⲛ̄Ⲙ̄ⲘⲀⸯ   prep. "with" (169b)
   138:3,14; 144:10,27; 145:14,15,15
   as coord. conj. 139:34,35,38,40; 141:14,18,39; 142:11,13,
   16,17,17,18,36; 143:26; 144:7,10,17,19,20,20,21,21,[27];

145:11,12,23 "and"
prep. ⲙ̄ⲛ̄ⲛ̄ⲥⲁ   142:14 "after"

ⲙⲁⲉⲓⲛ   n.m. "sign," "mark" (170b)
n.m. ⲙⲁⲓⲛⲉ   139:17 "target"
n.m. ⲙⲏⲓ̈ⲛⲉ   139:16 "target"

ⲙⲏⲛⲉ adv. "daily" (172a)
ⲙⲏ[ⲛⲉ]   144:42

ⲙⲓⲛⲉ n.f. "sort," "quality" (172b)
adj. ⲛ̄ⲧⲉⲉⲓⲙⲓⲛⲉ   141:28 "such," "of this sort"

ⲙ̄ⲡⲱⲁ adv. "very" (180a)
142:5

ⲙⲟⲩⲣ   "bind" (180a)
ⲙⲟⲣ⸗ ⳓⲛ̄⸗   140:30 "bind with"
ⲙⲏⲣ† ⳓⲛ̄⸗   143:22 "bound in"
n.f. ⲙ̄ⲣⲣⲉ 140:32; 145:7f,9 "bond," "bondage"

ⲙⲟⲉⲓⲧ   n.m. "road," "path" (188a)
ⲝⲓ ⲙⲟⲉⲓⲧ ⳓⲏⲧ⸗   140:20 to "lead," "guide"

ⲙⲏⲧⲉ n.f. "middle" (190b)
ⲛ̄ⲧⲙⲏⲧⲉ ⲛ̄⸗   141:17 "in the midst of"

ⲙⲟⲩⲧⲉ   "call," "speak" (191b)
ⲙⲟⲩⲧⲉ ⲉⲣⲟ⸗ ⲭⲉ⸗   138:10,15,34; 142:7 (passive) "be called"

ⲙⲧⲟⲛ   "rest," "be relieved" (193b)
ⲙⲧⲟⲛ ⲙⲙⲟ⸗   140:42; 141:3 (reflex.) "rest oneself"
n.m. 145:11 "rest"
adj. ⲛ̄ⲙⲧⲟⲛ   144:15 "refreshing"

ⲙⲁⲩ (place) "there" (196b)
adj. ⲉⲧⲙ̄ⲙⲁⲩ   141:26; 142:33 "that," "those"
subst. ⲛⲉⲧⲙ̄ⲙⲟ   144:12 "those"
adv. ⲙ̄ⲙⲁⲩ   138:5; 143:3; 144:35 "there"
adv. ⲉⲙⲁⲩ   143:6 "away"

ⲙⲟⲟⲩ n.m. "water" (197b)
142:13; 144:1,19,21
ⲙⲟⲩ ⲛⲥⲱⲣⲙ   140:18 "meandering stream"

ⲙⲉⲉⲩⲉ   "think" (199a)
ⲙⲉⲉⲩⲉ ⲉ⸗   138:6
ⲙⲉⲉⲩⲉ ⲁⲉ⸗   141:41
ⲙⲉⲉⲩⲉ ⲉⲣⲟ⸗ ⲭⲉ⸗   143:12f
n.m. 142:1; 143:18,33,34f "thought"
ⲁⲣⲓ (ⲛⲁ)ⲙⲉⲉⲩⲉ   145:20 "remember"

ⲙⲟⲩⲟⲩⲧ   "kill" (201a)
ⲙⲟⲟⲩⲧ⸗ 144:42

ⲙⲟⲟⲩⲱⲉ   "walk" (203b)
138:3
ⲙⲟⲟⲩⲱⲉ ⲛ̄ⲙ̄ⲙⲁ⸗ 138:14

ⲘⲞⲨⳞ   "fill"   (208a)
   ⲘⲞⲨⳞ ⳞⲚ̄⸌   143:34   "fill with"
   [ⲘⲉⳞ] ⳞⲚ̄⸌   143:27   "full of"

ⲘⲞⲨⳞ   "burn"   (210a)
   n.m.   143:[18],[28]

Ⲛ̄; Ⲛⲁ°   prep. "to," "for"   (216b)
   138:6,22,26,28,37; 139:13; 140:2,4,8,10,16,21,27; 141:3,5,9,
   26; 142:7,9,10,22,27,30; 143:9,10,17,18,[21],29,30; 144:3,
   9,11,12,14,17,20,37,37

Ⲛⲁⳉ   "be great"   (218b)
   Ⲛⲁⲉⲓⲁⲧ⸍   145:1,3,5   "blessed is (one)"

ⲚⲎⲂ   n.m.   "lord"   (221a)
   ⲣ̄ⲚⲀⲡ ⲁ⸍   144:30   "dominate"
   ⲣ̄Ⲛⲉⲡ ⲁ⸍   144:31   "dominate"

ⲚⲓⲘ   adj. "every"   (225b)
   adj. 138:[39]; 140:5,35; 144:30; 145:8
   n. indef. ⲞⲨⲞⲚ ⲚⲓⲘ   140:1   "everyone"
   interrog. pron.   ⲚⲓⲘ   138:9; 143:39; 144:15,17   "who?"

ⲚⲞⲨⲚ   n.m.   "abyss"   (226b)
   141:33; 142:34

ⲚⲀⲚⲞⲨ⸍   "be good"   (227a)
   139:31; 141:5
   subst. ⲡⲉⲧⲚⲀⲚⲞⲨⳡ   140:15; 141:22f   "the good"

ⲚⲞⲨⲚⲉ   n.f.   "root"   (227b)
   139:1

ⲚⲞⲨⲧⲉ   n.m.   "god"   (230b)
   143:14
   adj. ⲁⲧⲚⲞⲨⲧⲉ 143:9   "godless"

Ⲛ̄ⲧⲞⲔ   second pers. indep. prn. sg.   "thou"
   138:7,19; 139:20; 140:7; 142:8
   Ⲛ̄ⲧⲔ⸍   138:9
   Ⲛ̄ⲧⲁⲔ   138:14

Ⲛ̄ⲧⲱⲧⲚ̄   second pers. indep. prn. pl. "you"
   138:35; 139:11
   dep. prn. ⲧⲎⲚⲉ   138:29; 139:26; 142:40; 143:16,19,21,29,
   35,37; 144:12,16,18,18,[39]; 145:1,3,6,7

Ⲛ̄ⲧⲞⲞⲨ   third pers. indep. prn. pl.   "they"
   as intensifier   139:2   "but," "however"

Ⲛ̄ⲧⲞⳡ   third pers. indep. prn. sg.   "he"
   as intensifier   140:15; 143:5   "but," "however"

Ⲛ̄ⲧⲎ6   n.m. "plant," "weed"   (233a)
   144:23,26,34

ⲚⲀⲨ   "look," "behold," "see"   (233b)
   ⲚⲀⲨ ⲉ⸍   138:19; 141:8,0; 144:8
   ⲚⲀⲨ ⲉⲂⲞⲗ   141:12

ⲚⲀⲨ   n.m. "time," "moment" (234b)
      ⲬⲘ ⲠⲒⲚⲀⲨ 139:5 "from now on"

ⲚⲞⲨⲨⲢ̄ "be good" (239b)
      Ⲣ̄ⲚⲞⲨⲢⲉ ⲚⲀ⸗   140:8; 141:3 "be profitable for (one)"
      n.m. ⲤϮⲚⲞⲨⲨⲉ 144:20 "good smell (ⲤⲦⲞⲒ̈)," "fragrance"
      Ⲣ̄ⲌⲉⲚⲞⲨⲨⲉ Ⲛ̄⸗   144:32 "be good season (Ⲍⲉ)," "be
      plentiful for (one)"

ⲚⲞⲨⲌⲉ "shake Off" (241b)
      ⲚⲀⲌ⸗ 140:28 "dislodge"

ⲚⲞⲨⲌⲘ̄ "rescue" (243b)
      ⲚⲀⲌⲘ⸗ 144:[41]

ⲚⲞⲨϪⲉ "throw," "cast" (247a)
      ⲚⲞϪ⸗ ⲈⲌⲢⲀⲒ̈ Ⲁ⸗   141:33; 142:4 "cast down"
      ⲚⲞϪ⸗ Ⲁ̄Ⲛ Ⲛ̄ⲦⲠⲉ ⲰⲀⲠⲒⲦⲚ̄ Ⲁ⸗   142:33 "cast from heaven down to"
      ⲚⲈϪ⸗ ⲈⲂⲞⲖ ⲈⲌⲞⲨⲚ Ⲉ⸗   143:1 "cast into"

ⲚⲞϬ adj. "great," "large" (250a)
      ⲚⲞϬ Ⲛ̄⸗ 142:36; 144:33

Ⲛ̄ϬⲒ   particle of extra position "namely" (252a)
      138:1,4,21,27,36; 139:12,21,22,25,32,41; 140:5,9,37,40;
      141:2,4,15,16,19,25; 142:3,6,7,10,19,26; 143:4,8,29,36;
      144:[26],37; 145:5

ⲚⲞϬⲚⲈϬ "reproach," "revile" (252b)
      145:3
      n.m. ⲚⲞϬⲚⲈϬ Ⲛ̄ⲌⲎⲦ 145:11 "mocking"

ⲞⲚ adv. "also," "again," "still" (255b)
      138:18; 143:3
      Ⲁ̄Ⲛ 143:4
      ⲀⲨⲱ ⲞⲚ 144:6 (with neg.) "not even"

ⲞⲤⲈ n.m. "loss" (256b)
      Ϯ ⲞⲤⲈ 140:[39] "forfeit"

ⲞⲈⲒⲰ n. "cry" (257b)
      ⲦⲀⲨϬ ⲞⲈⲒⲰ 142:25; 144:39 "proclaim," "preach"

ⲞⲞⲌ n.m. "moon" (257b)
      144:7
      ⲞⲌ 144:20

Ⲡ̄Ⲁ̄; Ⲧ̄Ⲁ̄, ⲚⲀ⸗   poss. adj. (258b)
      passim

Ⲡ̄Ⲁ̄; Ⲧ̄Ⲁ̄; ⲚⲀ⸗   poss. art. "the one belonging to" (259a)
      138:32,33; 139:9

ⲠⲈ n.f. "heaven" (259a)
      Ⲛ̄ⲦⲠⲉ Ⲁ̄ⲠⲒⲦⲚ̄   140:35 "downwards"
      Ⲁ̄Ⲛ Ⲛ̄ⲦⲠⲉ ⲰⲀⲠⲒⲦⲚ̄ Ⲁ⸗   142:33 "all the way down to"
      subst. ⲚⲈⲦⲘ̄ⲠⲤⲀ Ⲛ̄ⲦⲠⲉ   138:42; 142:31 "the things above"

παϊ, ταϊ, ναϊ demon. "this" (259a)
παϊ, παει, πεει- ; ταει, τεει- ; ναϊ, ναει, νεει- *passim*
ετε παϊ πε 138:20 "that is," "i.e."
ταει τε θε 139:7; 141:28; 142:20f "so also"
ετβε παϊ (δε) 138:19,22,35; 139:4,11,13; 140:9 "therefore"
παει ετμ̄μαυ 142:33 "that one"
ναει ετμ̄μαυ 141:25 "those"

πω=, τω=, νω= poss. prn. (260b)
νετε νων νε 141:4 "our own"

πωωνε "turn," "change" (264a)
πωνε 140:34
πονε= 142:35
π=...ϩητ ποονε† ερο= (refl.) "be frenetic" 142:1

πειρε "shine," "come forth" (267a)
πρ̄ριε 139:24; 144:7,22,24

πωρκ̄ "uproot" (268b)
πορκ= 144:34

πωρϣ "be spread out" (269b)
[πωρ]ϣ εβολ 144:28
ε[τ πο]ρϣ† 142:37

πωτ "run," "flee," "go" (274a)
πωτ ε- 141:31; 143:2,6
πωτ αϩουν α- 144:40 "rush to"
πωτ ν̄cαϫω= α- 141:35 "rush headlong to"
πωτ ν̄cα- 141:40; 142:40,42; 143:2 "pursue"
πωτ ϩν̄- 144:2 "walk in," "behave according to"
πωτ ϩητ= ν̄- 140:3,4; 145:2 "flee"
πωτ ϩιϫν̄- 140:19 "rush upon"

πωϣc̄ "be beside oneself," "turn aside" (279b)
πωϣc̄ ε- 139:[37]; 143:28 (refl.) "be deranged"
n.m. πωϣc̄ 141:39 "dernagement"
n.m. πωϣc̄ ν̄ϩητ 141:40 "derangement"

πωϩ "burst," "rend" (280a)
143:20
ποϩ= 143:[37]

πεϫε- "say" (285a)
παϫε- 138:39
παϫε= 138:4,21; 139:21,22,24,32; 140:37; 141:3,4,19,25;
142:3,6,7,26; 144:37
πεϫα= 138:37; 140:9

ρα n.m. "state," "condition" (287a)
prep. ϩαπρα 138:24 "concerning"

ρη n.m. "sun" (287b)
144:4,17,19,21,24

ρο n.m. "mouth" (288a)
αρω= 142:34,[37] "against"

ⲣⲱ part. "same," "again" (290a)
139:[25]; 140:6

ⲣⲱⲕϩ "burn," "scorch" (293a)
ⲣⲱⲕϩ, ⲣⲱϫ 139:36; 141:14; 142:2; 143:16
ⲣⲱⲕ 140:3
n.m. ⲣⲱⲕϩ 144:17 "burning"

ⲣⲓⲙⲉ "weep" (294a)
145:6

ⲣⲱⲙⲉ n.m. "man" (294b)
138:20,27,[39]; 139:24,34,36; 140:4,41; 141:6,21,26,28;
142:16
n.m. ⲣⲙⲛ̄ϩⲏⲧ 140:13,14 "wise man"

ⲣⲙ̄ϩⲉ n.m.f. "free person" (297a)
n.f. ⲙⲛ̄ⲧⲣⲙ̄ϩⲉ 143:31 "freedom"

ⲣⲁⲛ n.m. "name" (297b)
140:12

ⲣ̄ⲣⲟ n.m. "king" (299a)
145:14
ⲣ̄ⲣ̄ⲣⲟ ⲙⲛ̄- 145:14 "reign with"
ⲣ̄ ⲛ̄ⲣ̄ⲣⲟ ⲉϫⲛ̄- 142:32 "be king over"

ⲣⲏⲥ n.m. "south" (299b)
143:3

ⲣⲟⲉⲓⲥ "watch," "be awake" (300b)
145:8

ⲣⲁⲧ n.m. "foot" (302b)
ⲉⲧⲉ ⲙⲁⲩϣⲛⲣⲁⲧⲥ̄ adj. 139:33 "unsearchable"

ⲣⲱⲧ "grow" (303b)
ⲣⲏⲧ† ⲉϩⲣⲁï ⲙⲛ̄- 144:27 "grow up with"
ⲣⲏⲧ† ϩⲣⲁï ϩⲛ̄- 144:29 "grow up in"
ⲣⲏⲧ† ϩⲓϫⲛ̄- 140:17 "grow beside"

ⲣⲏⲧⲉ n.m. "manner," "fashion," "likeness" (304b)
ⲙ̄ⲡⲣⲏⲧⲉ ϩⲱⲱϥ ⲛ̄- 144:23 "the same way as"
ⲙ̄ⲡⲓⲣⲏⲧⲉ ⲛ̄ⲑⲉ ⲛ̄- 138:41
ⲛ̄ⲁϣ ⲛ̄ⲣⲏⲧⲉ 138:10; 142:24 "in what way," "how"

ⲣⲟⲟⲩϣ "have care for" (306b)
n.m. 141:13,[39] "concern"

ⲣⲁϣⲉ "rejoice" (308b)
ⲣⲁϣⲉ ⲉϫⲛ̄- 141:38
ⲣⲁϣⲉ ϩⲣⲁï ϩⲛ̄- 143:23

ⲥⲁ n.m. "side," "part"
prep. ⲛ̄ⲥⲁ- 140:1,42; 141:[40]; 142:23,29,40,42; 143:2;
145:11 "after"
adv. ⲛ̄ⲥⲁϫⲱ⸗ 141:35 "headlong"
adv. ⲙ̄ⲡⲥⲁ ⲛⲧⲡⲉ 138:42; 142:31 "above"
adv. ⲙ̄ⲡⲥⲁ ⲛϩⲣⲉ 142:14 "above"
prep. ⲙⲛ̄ⲛⲥⲁ- 142:14 "after" (temporal)

ⲥⲁ   "be beautiful" (315a)
    n.m. ⲥⲁⲉⲓⲉ   140:22; 141:[42] "beauty"

ⲥⲉⲓ   "be satisfied" (316a)
    adj. ⲁⲧⲥ(ⲉ)ⲓ   140:25; 143:16 "insatiable"

ⲥⲁⲃⲉ   n.m. "wise person" (319a)
    n.m. ⲥⲁⲃⲉ ⲛ̄ⲣⲱⲙⲉ   140:41 "wise man"
    n.f. ⲥⲁⲃⲏ ⲙ̄ⲙⲏⲉ   140:2 "wise One"
    n.pl. ⲥⲁⲃⲉⲉⲩ   141:41 "wise ones"
    n.m. ⲥⲃⲟⲩⲉⲓ   138:35 "disciple"
    n.f. ⲥⲃⲱ   140:10; 141:21; 144:38 "doctrine," "teaching"
    adj. ⲁⲧⲥⲃⲱ   140:12 "ignorant"

ⲥⲱⲃⲉ   "laugh" (320b)
    143:23
    n.m. 142:22; 143:23 "laughter," "laughingstock"

ⲥⲟⲃⲧⲉ   "prepare," "set in order" (323a)
    ⲥⲃ̄ⲧⲉ ⲧⲏⲛⲉ ⲍⲣⲁⲓ̈ ⲍⲛ̄ ⲛⲉⲧⲛⲉⲣⲏⲩ   "prepare you for one
    another"(?)
    143:21

ⲥⲱⲕ   "draw," "beguile," "impel," "gather" (325a)
    140:29,34; 141:[41] "drag," "lead"
    ⲥⲱⲕ ⲍⲛ̄´ 144:14 "beguile with"
    ⲥⲱⲕ ⲍⲓⲝⲛ̄´ 140:36 "drag upon"
    n.m. 140:34 "impulse"

ⲥⲙⲓⲛⲉ   "establish," "construct" (337a)
    ⲥⲙⲓⲛⲉ ⲛⲁ⸗ 140:2,4 "make (for oneself)"

ⲥⲟⲛ   n.m. "brother" (342b)
    138:10,19
    n.m. ⲥⲁⲛ 138:4
    n.pl. ⲥⲛⲏⲩ 145:20

ⲥⲱⲛⲧ   n.f. "creature" (345a)
    138:[41]; 139:3

ⲥⲁⲁⲛⲟⲩ̄ⲩ̄   "nourish" (347b)
    139:2; 140:16

ⲥⲱⲛⲍ   "be bound," "be fettered" (348b)
    ⲥⲟⲛⲍ⸗ ⲛ̄ⲍⲣⲁⲓ̈ ⲍⲛ̄´ 140:31 "bind with"

ⲥⲟⲡⲥ̄   "pray," "entreat" (352a)
    138:22; 145:8,10

ⲥⲡⲟⲧⲟⲩ   n.m. "lips" (353a)
    142:29

ⲥⲱⲣⲙ   "wander," "err" (355a)
    n.m. 144:3 "error"
    adj. ⲙⲟⲩ ⲛⲥⲱⲣⲙ 140:18 "meandering stream"

ⲥⲁⲧⲉ   n.f. "fire" (360a)
    141,[24]; 142:2,[42]; 143:1,3,5

ϭⲓⲧⲉ   "throw" (360b)
    n.f. ϭⲟⲧⲉ   139:16 "arrow"
    n.f. ϭⲁⲧⲉ   139:15 "arrow"

ⲥⲧⲟⲓ̈   "smell" (362b)
    † ⲥⲧⲟⲉⲓ   140:24 to "be fragrant"
    † ⲥ†ⲛⲟⲩϥⲉ   144:20 "give a fragrance"

ⲥⲱⲧⲙ̅   "hear," "listen" (363b)
    ⲥⲱⲧⲙ̅ ⲉ⸍ 138:3,5,29; 142:9,10,27 "listen to"
    ⲥⲱⲧⲙ̅ ⲉⲃⲟⲗ ϩⲓⲧⲟⲟⲧ⸍ ϫⲁ⸍   138:24 "hear from (s.one) about"

ⲥⲱⲧⲡ   "choose" (365a)
    n.m. 139:28 "elect"

ⲥⲱⲧⲡ̅   "turn," "twist" (366a)
    ⲥⲱⲧⲡ̅ ⲛ̅...ⲥⲡⲟⲧⲟⲩ 142:29 "sneer"

ⲥⲟⲟⲩⲛ   "know" (369b)
    ⲥⲟⲟⲩⲛ 138:21; 140:39; 141:36; 143:40
    ⲥⲟⲟⲩⲛⲉ 138:12,15; 142:23
    ⲥⲟⲩⲱⲛ⸍ 138:17; 141:24
    ⲥⲟⲩⲱⲛ⸗ 138:16,17
    ϫⲓ ⲥⲟⲟⲩⲛ ⲁ⸍   138:18 "obtain knowledge about"
    n.m. ⲥⲟⲟⲩⲛ 138:13 "knowledge"
    adj. ⲁⲧⲥⲟⲟⲩⲛ 138:14; 144:[38] "ignorant"
    adj. ⲁⲧⲥⲟⲟⲩⲛⲉ 138:11 "ignorant"
    n.m. ⲣⲉϥⲥⲟⲟⲩⲛⲉ ⲉⲣⲟ⸗ 138:15 (refl.) "self-knower"

ⲥⲱⲟⲩϩ   "gather" (372b)
    ⲥⲟⲟⲩϩ⸗   141:11

ⲥⲟⲉⲓϣ   n.m. "pair," "twin" (374b)
    138:8

ⲥⲓϣⲉ   "be bitter" (376b)
    n.m. 139:33; 140:32; 141:34; 143:28; 145:9 "bitterness"

ⲥⲱⲱϥ   "be polluted" (378b)
    ⲥⲟⲟϥ† 144:10,[19]

ⲥϩⲁⲓ   "write" (381b)
    145:18
    ⲥϩⲁ⸗ 138:2

ⲥϩⲓⲙⲉ   n.f. "woman" (385a)
    n.pl. ⲥϩⲓⲟⲙⲉ   139:38,[41],42 "women"
    n.f. ⲙⲛ̅ⲧⲥϩⲓⲙⲉ 144:9 "womanhood," "womankind"

ⲥϩⲟⲩⲟⲩ   "curse" (387a)
    143:[41]
    subst. inf. ⲁⲩⲥϩⲟⲩⲟⲩ ⲁⲛ   141:23 "not for (a) cursing"

ⲥⲟϭ   n.m. "fool" (388a)
    140:14,15
    n.f. ⲙⲛ̅ⲧⲥⲟϭⲉ 143:34 "folly"

† "give" (392a)
    † ⲛⲁ⸗ 140:21; 144:17 "give to"
    ⲧⲁⲁ⸗ ⲉⲧⲟⲟⲧ⸍ 142:30 "hand over"

ⲦⲀⲀϤ ⲛ̄ⲁ̄   143:32,33 "exchange for," "surrender (smg) to"
ϯ ⲤⲦⲞⲈⲒ   140:24 "be fragrant"
ϯ ⲤⲦⲚⲞⲨϤⲈ   144:20 "give fragrance to"
ϯ ⲦⲔⲀⲤ   141:9,18 "give pain"
ϯ ⲞⲤⲈ 140:[39] "forfeit"
ϯ ⲞⲨⲂⲎⲤ   142:5 "fight against"
Ⲧⲟϯ ϩⲓⲁ̄   143:37 "wear," "be put on"

Ⲧⲃ̄ⲚⲎ n.m. "beast" (400b)
    n.pl. ⲦⲂⲚⲞⲞⲨⲈ   138:40; 139:6,9; 140:36; 141:[26],27; 142:16
    n.f. ⲘⲚ̄ⲦⲦⲂ̄ⲚⲎ   138:29 "bestiality"

ⲦⲰⲔ "kindle," "burn" (404a)
    ϯⲔ ϯⲔ   143:1 "(shower of) sparks"

ⲦⲀⲔⲞ "destroy," "perish" (405a)
    139:8; 141:13,[42]; 143:13,15; 144:[22]
    ⲦⲈⲔⲞ   139:4,7; 140:22,33; 143:11
    n.m. ⲦⲀⲔⲞ   141:18; 143:24 "destruction"
    adj. ⲀⲦⲦⲈⲔⲞ   143:12 "imperishable"

ⲦⲰⲔⲤ̄ "be pierced," "be stuck" (406b)
    ⲦⲀⲔⲤ̄ ϩⲚ̄ⲁ   140:27

ⲦⲔⲀⲤ n.m. "pain" (407b)
    ϯ ⲦⲔⲀⲤ ⲚⲀⲤ   141:9 "give pain to"
    ϩⲚ̄ ⲞⲨϯ ⲦⲔⲀⲤ   141:18 "in pain"

ⲦⲰⲘⲦ "meet" (416b)
    143:4

ⲦⲘ̄ⲁ neg. inf. 144:[21]

ⲦⲚ̄ⲚⲞⲞⲨ   "send" (419b)
    ⲦⲚⲚⲞⲞⲨⲥ   144:41

ⲦⲞⲚⲦⲚ̄ "be like," "resemble" (420a)
    ⲦⲚⲦⲰⲚⲧ   139:15

ⲦⲚϩ̄ n.m. "wing" (421a)
    140:2,18; 144:4

ⲦⲀⲠⲢⲞ n.f. "mouth" (423a)
    140:29; 142:16

ⲐⲎⲢⲥ adj. "all," "whole," "every" (424a)
    139:28; 140:31,36; 142:32; 143:41; 144:6,27,31
    n.m. ⲠⲦⲎⲢϤ   138:18; 144:4,5 "the All," "the "universe"

ⲦⲰⲢⲈ n.f. "hand" (425a)
    ⲔⲀ ⲦⲞⲞⲦⲥ ⲈⲂⲞⲖ   141:38 to "despair"
    prep. ⲚⲦⲞⲞⲦⲥ   143:18; 144:11,12; 145:14 "on account of,"
    (instrum) "with"
    prep. (ⲈⲂⲞⲖ) ϩⲓⲦⲚ̄ⲁ, ϩⲓⲦⲞⲞⲦⲥ   138:24; 141:34,[41]; 143:17,[38];
    145:6,7 "by," "through"
    ⲦⲀⲀϤ ⲈⲦⲞⲞⲦⲥ   142:30 "hand over"
    ⲞⲨⲰϩ ⲈⲦⲞⲞⲦⲥ   139:32; 143:8; 144:37 "continue"

ⲦⲰⲢⲠ "seize," "rob" (430b)
    ⲦⲞⲢⲠⲥ   140:24

ⲦⲰⲦ "join," "unite" (437b)
    ⲦⲎⲦ⁺ ⲚⲘ̄ⲘⲀⲤ 145:15,15 "be united with"

ⲦⲎⲨ n.m. "wind" (439b)
    142:17

ⲦⲰⲞⲨⲚ "arise" (445a)
    145:1

ⲦⲀⲨⲞ "increase" (452b)
    ⲦⲀⲨⲈ ⲞⲈⲒⲨ 142:25; 144:39 "proclaim"

†ϨⲈ "be drunk" (456b)
    139:37
    ⲦⲀϨⲈ⁺ ϨⲚ̄ 143:27 "be drunk with"

ⲐⲘ̄ⲔⲞ "afflict," "humiliate" (459b)
    ⲐⲘ̄ⲔⲈ 144:12

ⲦⲀⲨⲢⲞ "make strong" (462b)
    ⲦⲀⲨⲢⲎⲨ⁺ (Ⲉ·) 142:37; 143:13 "be fixed," "make fast against"
    ⲦⲀⲨⲢⲀⲒⲦ⁺ ⲈϨⲢⲀⲒ ⲈⲬⲚ̄ 143:10 "rely upon"

ⲞⲨ interr. prn. "who," "what" (467b)
    139:23; 141:19,20; 142:4; 143:12

ⲞⲨⲀ n.m. "one," "someone" (469b)
    indef. art. 139:8,9,31; 141:14
    ⲠⲞⲨⲀ ⲠⲞⲨⲀ 139:19 "each one"

ⲞⲨⲀⲀ part. "alone," "self" (470a)
    138:17; 139:1; 144:29,35

ⲞⲨⲈ "be distant" (470b)
    ⲞⲨⲎⲨ⁺ ⲈⲂⲞⲖ ϨⲚ̄ 140:20

ⲞⲨⲞⲈⲒ interj. "woe" (472b)
    143:9,15,17,18; 144:2,10,37
    ⲞⲨⲞ'Ï 143:10,[21]; 144:8,12,14

ⲞⲨⲰ "cease" (473b)
    ⲞⲨⲰ + circum. 138:12,15,18 "to have already (done, etc.)"

ⲞⲨⲂⲈ·, ⲞⲨⲂⲎ "against," "opposite" (476a)
    † ⲞⲨⲂⲎ 142:5 "fight against"

ⲞⲨⲰⲘ "eat," "bite" (478a)
    141:27,29; 143:19
    ⲞⲨⲰⲘ ⲈⲂⲞⲖ ϨⲚ̄ 139:3 "eat of"

ⲞⲨⲞⲈⲒⲚ n.m. "light" (480a)
    139:18,20,21,21,23,25,29,33; 142:18; 143:31,36; 144:4
    Ⲣ̄ⲞⲨⲞⲈⲒⲚ 139:20,23,26; 140:22; 142:18 "enlighten,"
    "illumine"

ⲞⲨⲞⲚ "be" (481a)
    ⲞⲨⲚ̄ 140:18; 141:39; 144:[41]
    ⲞⲨⲚ̄ + noun ⲘⲘⲞ 140:18 "have"
    ⲞⲨⲚ̄ⲦⲀ 138:5; 141:10,19; 142:6 "have"
    ⲞⲨⲚ̄ⲦⲀ ⲈϨⲞⲨⲚ Ⲉ 145:5 "have (an affection) towards"
    ⲞⲨⲚ̄ϬⲞⲘ Ⲙ̄ⲘⲞ Ⲉ 138:25 "be able"

ⲞⲨⲞⲚ   prn. "someone," "something" (482a)
    ⲞⲨⲞⲚ ⲚⲓⲘ   140:1   "everyone"

ⲞⲨⲚⲞⲨ   n.f. "hour" (484b)
    ⲜⲓⲚ ⲦⲈⲚⲞⲨ   145:15   "from now on"

ⲞⲨⲱⲚⳤ   "appear," "reveal," "be visible" (486a)
    ⲞⲨⲱⲚⳤ ⲈⲂⲞⲗ   139:19; 142:14
    ⲞⲨⲞⲚⳤ† ⲈⲂⲞⲗ   138:26,28,30,31,33,38,41,[43],43,[43]; 139:2,
    14,17,23,26; 140:5,19,33,38; 141:5,8,11,12,15; 142:6,20
    n.m. ⳍⲚ ⲞⲨⲱⲚⳤ ⲈⲂⲞⲗ   139:40; 143:19 "openly"

ⲞⲨⲞⳌⲦⲚ̄   "broaden" (492b)
    ⲞⲨⲞⳌⲦⲚ̄ ⲈⲂⲞⲗ   144:28

ⲞⲨⲱⲦ adj. "single," "alone" (494a)
    ⲩⳙⲱⳙ Ⲛ̄ⲞⲨⲱⲦ   140:16 "one and the same"

ⲞⲨⲞⲈⲓⳙ   n.m. "time" (499b)
    138:5; 141:14; 142:14
    Ⲙ̄ⲠⲓⲞⲨⲞⲈⲓⳙ   141:11 "now"
    Ⲛ̄ⲞⲨⲞⲈⲓⳙ ⲚⲓⲘ   140:35 "always"

ⲞⲨⲱⳙⲈ   "to desire" (500a)
    140:11; 141:2; 143:[41]
    n.m. 140:30; 144:2 "desire"

ⲞⲨⲱⳙ   n.m. "gap" (501a)
    ⲞⲨⳙⲚ̄   138:[40] "without"

ⲞⲨⳙⲎ   n.f. "night" (502a)
    139:16,35,39; 144:7

ⲞⲨⲱⳙⲂ̄   "answer" (502b)
    138:27,36; 139:12; 140:5,8,37,40; 141:2,18; 142:3,5,9,18,26

ⲞⲨⲱⳤ   "put," "set" (505b)
    ⲞⲨⲱⳤ ⲈⲦⲞⲞⲦ⸲   139:32; 143:8; 144:37 "continue"
    ⲞⲨⲱⳤ ⲘⲚ̄   140:13 (?) "dwell with"

ⲞⲨⲱⳤⲘ̄   "repeat," "answer" (509a)
    ⲞⲨⲱⳤⲘ Ⲛ̄   140:13 (?)

ⲞⲨⲬⳉⲓ   "be safe" (511b)
    ⲞⲨⲬⳉⲈⲓ   143:6 "be saved"

ⲱⲂⳙ̄ "forget" (518b)
    143:38
    ⲞⲂⳙ̄†   143:12 "be oblivious"

ⲱⲗⲕ̄   "be bent" (522a)
    ⲗ̄ⲕ ⳙⳉⲈⲓ Ⲛ̄Ⲥⳉ   142:23   "sneer at"
    ⲗ̄ⲕ ⳙⲈⲉ Ⲛ̄Ⲥⳉ   142:28   "sneer at"

ⲱⲘⲥ̄   "plunge," "submerge" (523a)
    144:1 "baptize"

ⲱⲚⳤ   "live" (525a)
    n.m. ⲱⲚⳤ   139:5 "life"

ⲱⲡ   "count," "esteem" (526a)
    ⲱⲡ   138:41; 145:4

ωπ + circum. 142:25 "reckon as"
οπ⸱ ϩⲱⲥ 141:26 "reckon as"

ⲱⲣⲝ̄ "be firm," "imprison" (530a)
ⲱⲣⲉⲝ ⲁⲣⲱ⸱ 142:34 "imprison"

ⲱⲧⲡ "imprison" (531b)
ⲱⲧⲡ ⲉϩⲟⲩⲛ ⲉ⸍ 142:38

ⲱⲝⲛ̄ "cease," "perish" (539a)
139:5

ⲱϭⲧ "choke" (540b)
144:24,35

ϣ "be able" (541a)
139:33; 142:24
ϣϭⲛ̄ϭⲟⲙ 142:35 "can"
ⲙⲛ̄ϣϭⲟⲙ ⲙ̄ⲙⲟ⸱ ⲛ̄⸍ (+ inf.) 140:28 "can not"
ⲙⲛ̄ϣϭⲟⲙ (+ conj.) 140:13 "can not"

ϣⲁ⸍ prep. "toward" (541b)
adv. ϣⲁⲉⲛⲉϩ 141:1; 145:15 "forever"
adv. ⲛ̄ϣⲁⲉⲛⲉϩ 141:17 "forever"
prep. ϣⲁⲡⲓⲧⲛ ⲇ⸍ 142:33 "down to"

ϣⲁ "rise" (542b)
143:30

ϣⲁ n.m. "nose" (543b)
ⲗ̄ⲕ ϣⲁⲉⲓ ⲛ̄ϭⲁ⸍ 142:23 "sneer at"
ⲗ̄ⲕ ϣⲉ[ⲉ] ⲛ̄ϭⲁ⸍ 142:28 "sneer at"

ϣⲓⲃⲉ "change" (551a)
139:4,4; 140:33

ϣⲃⲏⲣ n.m. "companion" (553a)
138:8

ϣⲙⲟⲩ n.f. "stake" (565a)
ϣⲙⲟⲩⲉ 140:27

ϣⲏⲛ n.m. "tree" (568b)
140:17; 142:15

ϣⲓⲛⲉ "seek," "ask" (569a)
ϣⲓⲛⲉ ⲉ⸍ 138:23 "ask about"
ϣⲓⲛⲉ ⲉⲧⲃⲉ⸍ 140:6 "ask about"
ϣⲓⲛⲉ ⲛⲥⲁ 140:1,[41] "seek after"

ϣⲛⲁ "be waste," "be dried up" (571b)
n.m. 144:27 "stubble," "brush"
ⲙⲛ̄ⲧϣⲛⲁ n.f. 144:[40] "debauchery"

ϣⲁⲛⲧⲉ⸍ pref. "until" (573a)
ϣⲁⲛⲧⲉⲟⲩ ϣⲱⲡⲉ 143:12 "how long" (ἕως πότε)

ϣⲱⲡ "receive," "suffer" (575a)
ϣⲟⲡ ⲉⲣⲟ⸱ 139:30 "welcome"
ϣⲱⲡ... ϩⲓⲥⲉ ⲉⲧⲃⲉ⸍ 144:33 "take pains with"

56

ϣⲱⲡⲉ "become," "happen," "dwell" (577b)
 138:9,11; 140:17; 141:8,16,17; 143:10; 145:8
 ϣⲟⲟⲡ⁺ 138:9; 139:21; 143:26,39,[41],[42]; 144:3 "exist,"
 "dwell"
 ϣⲱⲡⲉ ⲛ̄ⲑⲉ ⲛ̄⸌ 140:26; 144:36 "be like"
 n.m. ϣⲱⲡⲉ ⲙⲛ̄⸌ 144:10 "(sexual) intercourse"
 conj. ⲉϣⲱⲡⲉ 144:23,25 "if"
 conj. ⲉϣⲱⲡⲉ 138:28,30; 140:11
 conj. ⲉϣⲱⲡⲉ ⲙ̄ⲙⲟⲛ 140:12 "if not"
 ϣⲁⲛⲧⲉⲟⲩ ϣⲱⲡⲉ 143:12 "how long"

ϣⲱⲣⲡ̄ "be first" (586b)
 ⲣ̄ϣⲱⲣⲡ̄ ⲛ̄⸌ (+ inf.) 145:2 "be first to"
 adj. ϣⲟⲣⲡ̄ 141:13 "first"

ϣⲧⲉⲕⲟ n.m. "prison" (595b)
 143:11

ϣⲧⲟⲣⲧⲣ̄ "disturb," "trouble" (597b)
 ϣⲧⲣ̄ⲧⲱⲣ⸍ 141:2

ϣⲁⲩ n.m. "use," "value" (599a)
 ⲡⲉⲧⲣ̄ϣⲁⲩ ⲡⲉ 141:4 "it is useful"

ϣⲱϣ "make equal" (606a)
 n.m. ϣⲱϣ ⲛ̄ⲟⲩⲱⲧ 140:15 "one and the same (thing)"

ϣϣⲉ "be fitting" (607b)
 verbal subst. ⲡⲉⲧⲉϣϣⲉ ⲁⲛ ⲡⲉ ⲉⲧⲣⲉ⸍ 138:11 "it is not
 fitting to"

ϣⲁϫⲉ "speak" (613a)
 138:1
 ϣⲉϫⲉ 142:9
 ϣⲁϫⲉ ⲉⲧⲃⲉ⸍ 138:25; 139:13 "speak about"
 ϣⲁϫⲉ ⲙⲛ̄⸌ 138:3 "speak with"
 n.m. 138:1; 142:21,21,[28] "word"

ϥⲓ "bear," "carry," "take" (620a)
 ϥⲓⲧ⸍ ⲙ̄ⲙⲁⲩ 144:35 "remove"

ϩⲁ prep. "under," "in," "at" (632a)
 prep. ϩⲁⲑⲏ ⲛ̄⸌ 138:23; 141:10 "before"
 prep. ϩⲁⲡⲣⲁ 138:24 "concerning"

ϩⲉ n.f. "way" (638b)
 conj. ⲧⲁⲉⲓ ⲧⲉ ⲑⲉ 139:7; 141:28; 142:[21] "so also"
 prep. ⲕⲁⲧⲁ ⲑⲉ 140:8 "just as"
 prep. ⲛ̄ⲑⲉ 138:[39],41; 139:6,9,16; 140:17,27,28; 141:27;
 143:31; 144:36 "like," "as"
 adv. ⲛ̄ⲁϣ ⲛ̄ϩⲉ 138:9,10,29,34; 144:7 "how"

ϩⲏ n.f. "forepart" (640b)
 prep. ϩⲁⲑⲏ ⲛ̄⸌ 138:23; 141:10 "before"
 verb complement ϩⲏⲧ⸌ 140:3,5,20; 141:1; 145:3

ϩⲏ n.m. "season" (643a)
 ⲣ̄ϩⲉ ⲛⲟⲩϥⲉ 144:32 "be plentiful"

ϩⲓ, ϩⲓⲱⲱ⸗   prep. "on," "at," "in" (643b)
    142:1,29; 143:[38]
    prep. ϩⲓⲧⲛ̅⸗   141:[41]; 143:[38] "through," "by"
    prep. ⲉⲃⲟⲗ ϩⲓⲧⲛ̅⸗, ϩⲓⲧⲟⲟⲧ⸗ 138:24; 141:34; 143:17; 145:6
    prep. ϩⲓⲭⲛ̅⸗ 140:17,19,36; 141:17 "upon," "over"
    ⲧⲟ† ϩⲓ⸗   143:37 "be put on"

ϩⲓⲏ   n.f. 143:5 "way"

ϩⲟ   n.m. "face"
    142:28; 143:2
    prep. ⲛ̅ⲛⲁϩⲣⲛ̅⸗   138:27,29; 141:20 "before," "in presence of"

ϩⲱⲱ⸗   part. "for (my) part," "too," "also" (651b)
    138:2,42; 139:9; 141:28; 144:23; 145:20

ϩⲱⲃ   n.m. "thing," "work," "event" (653a)
    139:19
    n.pl. ϩⲃⲏⲩⲉ   138:30; 141:31; 144:5

ϩⲁⲓⲃⲉⲥ   n.f. "shade," "shadow" (657b)
    ⲣ̅ ϩⲁⲉⲓⲃⲉⲥ ⲁⲭⲛ̅⸗ 144:26,30 "to shade"

ϩⲱⲃⲥ̄   "cover" (658b)
    n.f. ϩⲃⲥⲱ 143:37 "garment"

ϩⲁⲗ   n. "servant," "slave" (665a)
    n.m. ϩⲙ̅ϩⲁⲗ   141:31 "servant"
    n.f. ⲙⲛ̅ⲧϩⲙ̅ϩⲁⲗ   143:32 "slavery"
    ⲣ̅ ϩⲙ̅ϩⲁⲗ   144:6 "enslave"

ϩⲱⲗ   "fly" (665b)
    140:3

ϩⲗⲟϭ   "be sweet" (673a)
    ϩⲟⲗϭ†   143:29
    n.f. ϩⲗϭⲉ   140:23; 141:30 "sweetness"

ϩⲛ̅⸗, ⲛ̅ϩⲏⲧ⸗   prep. "in," "by"(agency), "with"(agency) (683a)
    138:5,31; 139:16,21,36,[39],40; 140:16,22,23,27,29,30;
    141:4,6,8,8,12,13,18,24,25,37,[39]; 142:11,12,13,16,17,20,
    [26],34; 143:7,17,19,20,22,25,26,27,29,35,36,41; 144:1,2,
    14,18; 145:1,9,[21]
    ⲉⲃⲟⲗ ϩⲛ̅⸗   138:20; 139:1,3,8,9,28; 140:2,20; 144:16; 145:9,
    12 "from"
    ϩⲣⲁⲓ̈ ϩⲛ̅⸗   138:7; 139:34,35,38; 140:25; 143:16,16,21,23;
    144:29 "within"
    ⲛ̅ϩⲣⲁⲓ̈ ϩⲛ̅⸗ 140:32; 142:12 "in," "within"

ϩⲟⲩⲛ   n.m. "inward part" (685b)
    prep. ⲉϩⲟⲩⲛ ⲉ⸗, ⲉⲣⲟ⸗   142:38; 144:40; 145:5 "into,"
    "towards"

ϩⲟⲉⲓⲛⲉ   n.pl. "some," "certain," "others" (689b)
    139:17; 140:18; 141:[39]; 144:[41]
    indef. art. pl. ϩⲉⲛ⸗, ϩⲛ̅⸗ 138:35; 139:11; 140:2,4; 141:41;
    143:1

ϩⲱⲡ "hide" (695a)
139:19; 142:13; 143:[36]; 144:19
ϩⲏⲡ† 138:1,19,25
ϩⲏⲡ† ⲉ- 138:38 "hidden from"
ϩⲏⲡ† ⲛ̄ⲛⲁϩⲣⲛ̄- 138:28 "hidden before"
ϩⲛ̄ ⲟⲩϩⲱⲡ 139:40; 143:21 "secretly"

ϩⲣⲁï "upper part;" ϩⲣⲁï "lower part" (698a; 700a)
prep. ϩⲣⲁï ϩⲛ̄- 138:7; 139:34,35,38; 140:25; 143:15,16,23; 144:29 "within"
prep. ⲛ̄ϩⲣⲁï ϩⲛ̄- 140:31f; 142:12 "in," "within"
adv. ⲉϩⲣⲁï 139:28; 144:8,27
prep. ⲉϩⲣⲁï ⲉ- 139:30; 141:33; 142:4,[41] "up to/down to"
prep. ⲉϩⲣⲁï ⲉϫⲛ̄- 139:41; 141:1; 142:31; 143:10 "upon"
adv. ⲙ̄ⲡⲥⲁ ⲛϩⲣⲉ 142:18 "above"

ϩⲁⲣⲉϩ "keep," "guard" (707b)
ⲁⲣⲉϩ ⲉ- 140:12 "observe," "pay attention to"

ϩⲓⲥⲉ "labor," "be difficult" (710b)
144:39
n.m. 144:33; 145:11,12 "pain," "suffering"

ϩⲏⲧ n.m. "heart," "mind" (714a)
138:7; 139:37; 140:27; 141:40; 142:1,20; 143:28,32,33; 145:12
n.m. ⲣⲙⲛ̄ϩⲏⲧ 140:13,14 "wise man"

ϩⲏⲧ n.m. "North" (717b)
143:4

ϩⲟⲧⲉ n.f. "fear" (720b)
ⲣ̄ϩⲟⲧⲉ ϩⲏⲧ⸗ 141:1 "be afraid of"

ϩⲱⲧⲃ̄ "kill," "slaughter" (723b)
140:35; 142:16
n.f. ϩⲉⲧⲃⲉ 144:8 "corpse"

ϩⲱⲧⲙ̄ "extinguish" (K103)
144:16

ϩⲱⲧⲡ "join," "sink"(sun) (724b)
139:24 "set"(light)

ϩⲱⲧϩⲧ "inquire" (728a)
ϩⲉⲧϩⲱⲧ⸗ 138:8 (refl.)

ϩⲟⲟⲩ n.m. "day" (730a)
139:36,[39]; 143:6,7; 144:7

ϩⲟⲟⲩ "be bad" (731a)
adj. ⲉⲑⲟⲟⲩ 141:34; 142:15
subst. ⲡⲉⲑⲟⲟⲩ 140:15 "the bad"

ϩⲱⲟⲩ to "rain" (732a)
144:15
n.m. ϩⲟⲟⲩ 142:17

ϩⲟⲩⲟ n.m. "greater part" (735a)
adv. ⲛ̄ϩⲟⲩⲟ 139:10; 144:33 "more"

ϩⲟⲟⲩⲣ(ⲉ)   "deprive" (737b)
   ϩⲟⲩⲣⲟⲉⲓⲧ⳿ ⲛ⳿ 141:29 (first attestation) "deprived of"

ϩⲟⲟⲩⲧ n.m. "male" (738b)
   ϩⲟⲩⲧ 139:38
   ϩⲟⲟⲩⲧ 139:41,[42]

ϩⲁϩ adj. "much," "many" (741b)
   140:[38]; 142:5,14; 144:16

ϫⲉ⳿ conj. (746b)
   introd. direct/indirect speech 138:4,7,9,10,13,15,21,26,
   28,34,37,38,39; 139:12,13,21,25,32; 140:1,6,7,9,10,[37];
   141:3,4,19,22,24,25,41; 142:3,6,8,8,10,19,20,25,27,30;
   143:9,13,[40]; 144:37
   conj. 138:16; 139:6,17,31; 143:16,17,22; 144:5,7,11,33,38;
   145:7,11 "because"
   final 139:27; 145:8,9 "in order that"

ϫⲓ "receive," "take" (747b)
   138:35; 142,[42]; 144:38; 145:13
   ϫⲓ ⲥⲟⲟⲩⲛⲉ ⲁ⳿   138:18 "obtain knowledge about"
   ϫⲓ ϫⲣⲟⲡ ⲉⲣⲟ⳿   138:20 "stumble on"
   ϫⲓ ⲙⲟⲉⲓⲧ ϩⲏⲧ⳿   140:20 "guide," "lead"

ϫⲟ "sow" (752a)
   142:11,11

ϫⲟⲉ n.m. "wall" (753b)
   [ϫⲟⲓ]ⲉ   142:[36]

ϫⲱ "speak," "say," "tell" (754a)
   138:7,22,27,38; 139:13,22; 140:1,6,8,10,38,40; 141:20,20,21,
   22,23; 142:10,22,27,30; 143:8
   imper. ϫⲟⲟ⳿ 138:37 "tell"

ϫⲱ n.m. "head" (756a)
   ⲉϫⲛ⳿, ⲁϫⲛ⳿, ⲉϫⲱ⳿ 139:[41],42; 141:1,38; 142:32; 143:10,14;
   144:5,5,18,22,24,26,30 "upon"
   ⲛⲥⲁϫⲱ⳿ 141:36 "headlong"
   ϩⲓϫⲛ⳿ 140:17,19,36; 141:17 "upon," "over"

ϫⲱⲕ "complete," "finish," "perfect" (761a)
   ϫⲱⲕ ⲉⲃⲟⲗ   141:32 "complete"
   ϫⲏⲕⲧ ⲉⲃⲟⲗ ⲛ⳿ 140:14 "be perfect in (respect of)"

ϫⲉⲕⲁⲁⲥ conj. "in order that" (764a)
   w/second fut. 138:22; 143:7; 144:16; 145:1
   ϫⲉⲕⲁⲁⲥ ⲁⲛ + second fut. 139:26 "not in order that"

ϫⲱⲁⲕ "tension," "stretch" (766b)
   ϫⲱⲁⲕ ... ⲥⲟⲧⲉ 139:15,16 "shoot," "aim"(arrow)
   ϫⲱⲁⲕ ⲁ⳿ 139:17 "shoot," "aim at"

ϫⲱⲱⲙⲉ n.m. "book" (770b)
   ϫⲱⲙⲉ 145:17

60

ϫⲓⲛ; ϫⲛ̅ prep. "from" (772b)
    139:5
    prep. ϫⲛ̅ ⲛ̅ⲧⲡⲉ ϣⲁⲡⲓⲧⲛ̅ ⲁ⁄ 142:33 "from heaven down to"
    adv. ϫⲓⲛ ⲧⲉⲛⲟⲩ 145:15 "from now on"

ϫⲡⲟ "beget," "bring forth," "acquire" (779a)
    138:40; 139:10; 141:24

ϫⲉⲣⲟ "blaze," "burn" (781b)
    139:34,35

ϫⲱⲱⲣⲉ "scatter," "disperse" (782b)
    ϫⲱⲣⲉ ⲉⲃⲟⲗ 141:7 "bring to naught"

ϫⲱⲣⲡ "stumble" (786a)
    ϫⲓ ϫⲣⲟⲡ ⲉ⁄ 138:20 "stumble on"

ϫⲟⲉⲓⲥ n.m. "lord," "master" (787b)
    138:21; 139:13,20,[22]; 140:6; 141:3; 142:3,8,19; 144:32;
    145:5

ϫⲓⲥⲉ "be high" (788b)
    adj. ⲉⲧϫⲟⲥⲉ⁺ 138:33 "exalted"

ϫⲟⲩϫⲁⲩ̄ "burn," "cook" (796b)
    ϫⲁⲩϫⲁⲩ̄ 140:26

ϫⲱ̄ⲙ "be defiled" (797b)
    n.m. ϫⲱ̄ⲙ(ⲉ) 140:37; 141:31 "corruption"

ϫⲁϫⲉ n.m. "enemy" (799b)
    143:30; 144:6

ϭⲉ part. "then," "therefore," "now" (802a)
    138:14,19,22,32,34; 139:4,6,11; 142:24,35; 144:31

ϭⲱ "remain" (803a)
    139:27

ϭⲱⲗⲡ "reveal" (812a)
    ϭⲱⲗⲡ ⲉⲃⲟⲗ 138:6; 140:[38]

ϭⲟⲙ n.f. "power," "strength" (815b)
    ⲟⲩⲛ̄ϭⲟⲙ ⲙ̄ⲙⲟ⁼ + inf. 138:25,29 "be able to," "can"
    ϭⲛ̄ϭⲟⲙ + conj. 144:24,25 "be able to," "can"
    ⲙⲛ̄ϭϭⲟⲙ + conj. 140:13 "not be able to"
    ⲙⲛ̄ϣϭⲟⲙ ⲙ̄ⲙⲟ⁼ ⲛ̄⁄ + inf. 140:28 "not be able to"
    ϣϭⲛϭⲟⲙ ⲛ̄⁄ + inf. 142:35 "be possible"

ϭⲓⲛⲉ "find" (820a)
    140:42; 143:2,3,5,6,7; 145:10
    ϭⲛ̄ϭⲟⲙ + conj. 144:24,25 "be able," "can"
    ϣϭⲛ̄ϭⲟⲙ ⲛ̄⁄ + inf. 142:35 "be able," "can"

ϭⲱⲟⲩ "be narrow" (835a)
    ϭⲏⲩ⁺ 142:34

ϭⲱϣⲧ "look, see" (837a)
    ϭⲁϣⲧ ⲁ⁄ 144:3 "look at"
    ϭⲁϣⲧ ⲁϫⲛ̄⁄ 144:5 "look upon"
    ϭⲁϣⲧ ⲉϩⲣⲁⲓ̈ 144:8 "look down"

Greek Index

ἀγαθός   adj.   "good"   145:14

ἀγάπη   n.f.   "love"   139:33; 141:10,13

ἄγγελος   n.m.   "angel"   142:[41]

ἅγιος   adj. as n.   "saint"   145:22

ἀήρ   n.m.   "air"   142:17; 144:[20]

ἀθλητής   n.m.   "contender"   145:18

αἰχμαλωτίζειν   "imprison"   140:23

αἰχμάλωτος   n.m.   "captive"   143:22

ἄλυσις   n.f.   "chain"   140:31

ἀλλά   conj.   "but," "rather"   138:43; 139:17,27; 141:26,29,37; 142:21; 143:27; 144:34; 145:9

ἀλλότριον   n.n.   "alien"   145:3

ἀμήν (ⲁⲙⲏⲛ)   interj.   "amen"   142:[27],]9; 145:16

ἀνάγκη   n.f.   "necessity," "torment"   140:9; 141:34

ἀνάλημψις   n.f.   "ascension"   138:23

ἀνάπαυσις   n.f.   "rest"   145:13

ἀναχωρεῖν   "revert"   139:29

ἀπειλή (ⲁⲡⲓⲗⲏ)   n.f.   "threat"   143:4

ἀρχεῖν   to "rule"   142:31

ἄρχων   n.m.   "Archon," (spiritual) "ruler"   142:31,[40]

αὐξάνειν   "grow"   144:31

ἄφθονος (ⲁⲧ + φθόνος)   adj.   "sufficient"   142:21

ἀφορμή   n.f.   "instigation"   142:17

βάθος   n.m.   "depth"   138:18; 142:36

βίος   n.m.   (this)"life"   141:13,[39]; 143:14; 145:10

γάρ   conj.   "for," "since"   138:13,17; 139:6,41; 140:10,14,16, 20; 141:6,27,35; 142:5,5; 143:6; 144:12,21,33; 145:12
        interj.   "yes"   141:5

δαίμων   n.m.   "demon"   144:13

δέ   conj.   "and," "but"   138:17,21,36; 139:4,12,18,20,28; 140:40; 141:12,19,23; 142:2,3,9,19; 143:5; 144:25,[41]

διαφορά   n.n.   "different sort"   139:10

εἴδωλον   n.n.   "phantom"   141:16

εἰρήνη   n.f.   "peace"   145:22

ἐλπίζειν (ϩⲉⲗⲡⲓⲍⲉ)   "to hope"   143:11

ἐλπίς (ϩⲉⲗⲡⲓⲥ)   n.f.   "hope"   139:5; 143:9,13,[39],[42]; 145:7

ἐνέργεια   n.f.   "force"   144:13

ἐξουσία   n.f.   "authority," "power"   142:32; 144:11

ἐπειδή   conj.   "since," "because"   138:7,10; 140:7,13,18;
141:5,30; 142:2,25

ἐπιθυμία   n.f.   "lust"   140:3,25,32; 141:32

ἐργάτης   n.m.   "laborer"   138:34

ἤ   conj.   "or"   138:9; 141:20,21; 142:28,29,35; 144:23

ἡδονή   n.f.   "pleasure"   140:24

θλίβειν   "be oppressed"   145:6

θνητός   adj. as n.   "mortal"   141:22

κἄν   conj.   "although"   138:14

καπνός   n.m.   "smoke"   143:35

καρπός   n.m.   "fruit"   139:1; 142:15

κατά   prep.   "as," "according to"   140:8,34

κατέχειν   "restrain"   143:38

κληρονομεῖν   "inherit"   144:28

κολάζειν   "punish"   142:15

κόσμος   n.m.   "world"   138:5,31; 142:22,26; 143:14

κρίνειν   to "judge"   144:4

κρίσις   n.f.   "judgement"   143:7

λόγος   n.m.   "reason"   138:[40]

λογικόν   adj.   "rational"   138:[42]

μακάριος   adj.   "blessed"   139:25

μαστιγοῦν   "afflict," "whip"   141:33

μάστιξ   n.f.   "whip"   142:[42]

μέγεθος   n.n.   "majesty"   138:32,36

63

μέλος   n.n.   "limb," "member"   139:36; 140:31; 141:37; 144:14

μέν   conj.   "indeed," "on the one hand"   139:16; 142:19;
144:[24]

μεριμνᾶν   "be anxious"   142:4

μήτι   interrog. part. in neg. question   "is not?"   139:8

μορφή   n.f.   "form"   141:16

νοεῖν   "recognize," "notice"   142:20; 143:24,25; 144:6

ὅταν   conj.   "when"   138:24; 139:18,28

οὐσία   n.f.   "essence"   139:30,30

οὔτε   conj.   "nor," "neither"   143:24,25

πάθος   n.m.   "passion"   145:13

πάλιν   adv.   "yet," "again," "back"   140:8; 141:11; 141:23

παραδιδόναι   "hand over"   142:40

πείθειν   "persuade"   142:19

πιστεύειν   "believe"   142:11; 143:[40]

πίστις   n.f.   "faith"   141:10

πλάσμα   n.n.   "body"   139:7

πληγή   n.f.   "smiting"   143:30

πλήρωμα   n.n.   "Pleroma," (divine world)   138:33

πνεῦμα   n.n.   "spirit"   140:3,5; 144:21

πνευματικός   adj.   "spiritual" (one)   145:23

πονηρόν   adj.   "evil"   144:13

πρᾶξις   n.f.   "deed"   142:2

πρέπει   (impers)   "it befits"   142:8

προσευχή   n.f.   "prayer"   145:21

πῶς   interrog.   "how"   138:32

σάρξ   n.f.   "flesh"   141:7,24; 143:11,19; 145:9

σκάνδολον   n.n.   "stumbling-block"   145:2

σκεῦος   n.n.   "vessel"   141:6

σοφία   n.f.   "wisdom"   140:14

σοφός   adj.   "wise (man)"   140:16

64

σπήλαιον   n.n.   "cavern"   143:22

συνήθεια   n.f.   "intimacy"   144:9

συνουσία   n.f.   "(sexual) intercourse"   139:8

σῶμα   n.n.   "body"   138:39; 139:2,4,6,7,34; 141:42; 143:7;
    144:8,11,22; 145:13

σωτήρ   (c̄ω̄ρ̄)   n.m.   "Savior"   138:1,4,27,37,39; 139:25,32;
    140:9,[40]; 141:4,25; 142:6,10,26; 143:8

ταλαίπωρος   adj.   "miserable"   141:21

τάρταρος   n.m.   "Tartaros" (netherworld of punishment)   142:36

ταρταροῦχος   n.m.   "Tartarouchos," "Chief of Tartarow"   141:41

τάφος   n.m.   "tomb"   141:17; 142:13

τέλειος   adj.   "perfect"   140:10; 145:19
    p̄τελειος   to "perfect"   139:12; 140:11
    м̄ν̄ττελειος   "perfection"   138:36

τότε   adv.   "then"   138:25; 139:19,29,31; 141:9,15; 143:8;
    144:31,36

ὑπηρέτης   n.m.   "servant"   139:31

ὑπομονή   n.f.   "patience"   141:37

φαντασία   n.f.   "appearance"   140:21

φθόνος   n.m.   "jealousy"
    adj. ⲁⲧφⲑⲟⲛⲟⲥ   142:21   "sufficient"

φραγελλοῦν   to "scourge"   141:35; [φ̄ⲣⲁ̄ⲅⲉ̄ⲗⲗⲟ̄ⲩ   (for φραγέλ-
                λιον?)]   n.m.   "whip"   143:1

φύσις   n.f.   "nature"   141:34

χαλινός   n.m.   "bit"   140:29

χόρτος   n.m.   "grass"   144:23

ψυχή   n.f.   "soul"   139:37; 140:40; 141:18; 144:1; pl.
    ⲯⲩⲭⲟⲟⲩⲉ   140:26; 143:15,20

ⲱ̄   vocative part.   "O"   139:25

ⲱ̄   interj.   "O!"   139:32,33

ὡς   (ⲍⲱⲥ)   conj.   "while"   138:4,14; 140:7; 141:42; 143:42

Proper Names

θωμᾶς   Thomas   138:2,4,19,21,37; 139:12,22,25; 140:6,37;
    141:2,19; 142:3,8,19; 145:17

'Ιησοῦς   (ιϲ̄)   Jesus   139:21; 144:37

'Ιούδας   Judas   138:2; 142:7

Μαθαῖας   Mathaias   138:2

ὁ Σωτήρ   (πϲⲱⲣ)   "Savior"   138:1,4,27,37,39; 139:25,32;
         140:9,[40]; 141:4,25; 142:6,10,26; 143:8

Ταρταροῦχος   "Chief of Tartaros"   141:41

CHAPTER I

THE LANGUAGE OF THE BOOK OF THOMAS THE CONTENDER

The following linguistic analysis, given in quasi-tabular
form, concerns the text of Codex II from page 138 to the end of
the Codex. While the author has had opportunity to examine the
linguistic features of many of the tractates of Codex II, the
current aim is to restrict the analysis of the tractate at hand,
only rarely referring to these features of other tractates in
the Codex. However, it can be broadly stated at the outset that
the Nag Hammadi Corpus appears to contain three main types of
Coptic dialects: Subachmimic (the Jung Codex, Codex X and the
first part of XI); a quasi-Sahidic dialect whose syntax and, to
a lesser extent, orthography display features mostly attested in
lower Egyptian dialects, e.g. Bohairic and Fayyumic ("The Three
Steles of Seth" [CG VII,5], "Zostrianos" [CG VIII,1], "Allogenes"
[CG XI,1]); and a type of Sahidic whose orthography displays many
features attested mostly in Subachmimic texts, of which Codex II
is a very good example. Codex II, though representative of one
of the main dialect-types found in the Nag Hammadi Corpus, does
not possess within itself complete linguistic unity, since it
contains tractates probably taken from a number of other Coptic
manuscripts of various milieux. For this reason we limit our-
selves to a consideration of the linguistic features of the
single tractate, *Thomas the Contender*.

The linguistic analysis will be divided into two sections:
syntax and dialect.

Syntax

Though the syntax of *Thomas the Contender* could be laid
out in a number of ways, we have adopted the form of a tabular
presentation divided according to the types of clauses, both
main and subordinate, used to create meaning units. As such,
the analysis is entirely restricted to the way in which, gram-
matically speaking, a given topic (or "subject") is commented
upon (receives a "predicate"). This means that we shall be
discussing the two main types of Coptic sentences, non-verbal

70

and verbal, rather than discussing questions of morphology,
phonetics and the use of particles and prepositions. The presentation will be from a synchronic (descriptive) rather than
a diachronic (historical) perspective, except where, in a few
cases, a comment from the latter perspective seems apt.

Accordingly we will treat: I) non-verbal clauses, both
nominal and adverbial, and II) verbal clauses. The verbal
clauses will be discussed under five heads:[1] A. Basic tenses,
which comprise seven tenses, including three pairs of affirmative
and negative forms plus one long negative form; B. Satellites of
the basic tenses, of two kinds: 1) the second tense, which has
the effect of making the verb to which the second tense morpheme
is prefixed into the logical subject of an adverbial sentence
whose adverbial element becomes the logical predicate, and 2) the
sentence converters which (a) in the case of the particle Ⲛⲉⳉ
converts the sentence into its corresponding preterit,[2] and (b)
in the case of the circumstantial particle Ⲉⳉ and of the relative particles Ⲉⲧⳉ, Ⲉⲧⲉ, Ⲉⳉ and (Ⲉ)ⲛⲧⲁⳉ convert the tense from
a main sentence into a subordinate clause; C. Clause conjugations
which comprise 1) three subordinate clause equivalents which tem-
porally or conditionally qualify a main sentence, and 2) two con-
junctives which serve to continue a preceding sentence or clause
conjugation. Clause conjugations are earmarked by a unique negative, Ⲧⲙⳉ ; D. The imperatives are set apart from sentence conjugations since only the causative imperative is really a conjugation. E. Infinitive constructions which, while they neither
form sentences nor conjugations, can be elements of sentences,
e.g., the actor or complementary (direct, oblique) object expression.

It is hoped that such an arrangement will not only possess
a logical structure but also provide a framework within which
certain striking features of the syntax of *Thomas the Contender*
can be set in relief against an orderly pattern. Not every
detail, normal or abnormal, will be treated here; irregular
features crucial to the interpretation of the tractate which are
not covered in the grammatical analysis will be dealt with in
the commentary.

I. *Non Verbal Clauses.*

    A. The Nominal Sentence. In *Thomas the Contender*, nominal
       sentences are used to state an identity between two or

more subjects expressed as substantives, and to assign
properties to one or more subjects expressed as substantives. Identity statements consist in three patterns:
1) The immediate juxtaposition of the absolute independent pronoun of the first or second person with a
definite substantive (138:7; 139:20; cf. 138:9) which
uses the construction reduced pronoun plus substantive;
2) the mediate juxtaposition of one or more definite
substantives with another definite substantive by means
of the (demonstrative) particle ⲡⲉ, ⲧⲉ, ⲛⲉ functioning
as copula in the pattern: substantive or independent
pronoun plus ⲡⲉ plus substantive (138:13; 143:14; most
often ⲧⲁⲉⲓ ⲧⲉ ⲑⲉ , 139:7; 141:28; 142:20), or in the
pattern: substantive plus substantive plus ⲡⲉ (140:15f);
and 3) the juxtaposition of a substantive or pronoun
(independent, demonstrative or interrogative) with the
demonstrative (or interrogative) with the demonstrative
particle ⲡⲉ, ⲧⲉ, ⲛⲉ, functioning as "subject," and often
followed by a complement, either a relative adjective or
an infinitive phrase: ⲡⲉ etc. plus relative (139:1f;
140:6,7f; 141:19f; 142:2f,8; 143:39; 144:15,17); ⲡⲡⲉ
followed by infinitive phrase (138:11); ⲡⲉ alone (141:4).

Attributive statements assigning properties to a
subject expressed by a substantive have much the same
pattern as identity statements, except that the topic
of the sentence ("subject") is a definite substantive
or pronoun (independent or demonstrative) and the comment ("predicate") is an indefinite expression. The
patterns are 1) immediate juxtaposition of a first or
second person independent pronoun with an indefinite
expression (138:14,35; 139:11); 2) the mediate juxtaposition of a definite subject expression with an indefinite expression by means of the (demonstrative) particle ⲡⲉ, ⲧⲉ, ⲛⲉ functioning as copula and following the
indefinite expression (139:6; 142:22); and 3) the juxtaposition of an indefinite expression with the (demonstrative) particle ⲡⲉ, ⲧⲉ, ⲛⲉ functioning as "subject" which
always follows the indefinite expression (141:41; 142:5;
143:16). The pattern can contain an adverbial or adnomi-
nal complement which immediately follows the indefinite

expression (139:9f,31; 140:9). The demonstrative particle can also occur within the indefinite expression
(139:8). Should the "subject," expressed by the demonstrative particle, be defined by a relative adjective,
the latter is immediately joined to the demonstrative
particle, e.g. ϩⲁϩ ⲅⲁⲣ ⲛⲉⲧϯ ⲟⲩⲃⲏⲩ (142:5). Finally,
the attributive statement, like the identity statement
can take a complementary infinitive (140:9).

A peculiarity related to the non-verbal sentence
deserves mention. In 142:20f we read: ⲁⲩⲱ ⲥⲟⲩⲟⲛϩ
ⲉⲃⲟⲗ ⲭⲉ ⲧⲁⲉⲓ [ⲧⲉ ⲉ]ⲉ ⲁⲩⲱ ⲡⲉⲕϣⲁⲭⲉ ⲟ ⲛ̄ⲁⲧⲫⲑⲟⲛⲟⲥ .
The qualitative ⲟ is clearly inserted above the line
over the ⲉ of ϣⲁⲭⲉ . Assuming the restoration ⲧⲁⲉⲓ ⲧⲉ
ⲑⲉ is correct, the insertion of ⲟ in the sentence coordinate with it is very peculiar. The scribe ought to
have crossed out the ⲛ̄ of ⲛ̄ⲁⲧⲫⲑⲟⲛⲟⲥ and written ⲟⲩ
above it and inserted a ⲡⲉ after the emendation to
ⲟⲩⲁⲧⲫⲑⲟⲛⲟⲥ . What must have happened is that the
scribe executed the correction requiring the least emendation. ⲡⲉⲕϣⲁⲭⲉ ⲛ̄ⲁⲧⲫⲑⲟⲛⲟⲥ is not a sentence, as it
lacks a copula, and the easiest way to create a sentence
is to insert the qualitative ⲟ before the ⲛ̄ in ⲛ̄ⲁⲧⲫⲑⲟⲛⲟⲥ,
yielding a sentence usually reserved for the attribution
of accidents (properties contingent on time, etc.) rather
than of enduring properties.

B. The Adverbial Sentence. There are six pure adverbial
sentences in *Thomas the Contender* (143:6f,19,25,29,35;
144:18), occurring in adjectival phrases employing the
preposition ϩⲛ̄ⲿ preceded either by a relative or circumstantial particle, and a seventh also preceded by the
circumstantial: ⲉⲣⲉⲡⲟⲩⲙⲉⲉⲩⲉ ϩⲓ ⲛⲉⲩⲡⲣⲁϩⲓⲥ (142:1).

II. *Verbal Clauses.* Verbal clauses in *Thomas the Contender* can
be treated under five heads: Basic Tenses, Satellites of the
Basic Tenses, Clause Conjugations, Imperatives, and Infinitive
Constructions. The First Present will be discussed as a basic
tense, in spite of the fact that diachronically it belongs to
the class of adverbial sentences.

A. Basic Tenses.
1) Bipartite Basic Tenses.
a. First Present. Morphologically the First Present

appears as described in the standard manuals, with
no anomalous forms. Syntactically, the First Present is used in *Thomas the Contender* in four main
ways. As an independent statement of fact in present time it is used with verbs of knowing, per-
ceiving and saying as these occur in direct discourse (138:12,22,38; 139:13; 142:4,27,30) as well
as in the indirect statements created by them
(138:26,38), and finally in the course of a narrative (139:16). Unquestionably in *Thomas the
Contender*, the First Present is used preponderantly
in the formation of substantives (relative substantive, fifty times), of adjectives (relative
adjective with definite antecedent, forty times,
circumstantial with indefinite nouns, pronouns,
and relative adjectives, ten times) and, as cir-
cumstantials, of adverbs (forty times).

A second use of the First Present is found in
phrases with an impersonal subject (138:26; 140:37;
141:3; 142:20), cast in the third feminine singular. The third use is found in causal clauses
introduced by ⲉⲡⲓⲆⲏ (138:10; 141:30f; 142:23,25),
ⲅⲁⲣ (140:14; 142:4), and once by Ⲇⲉ′ (143:22).
Lastly, the First Present is used in the protasis
of present general conditional clauses, introduced
by ⲉⲩⲡⲉ′ (138:28,30; 140:11).

In *Thomas the Contender* the First Present often occurs with an anticipatory subject which is
recapitulated by a proclitic pronoun. The First
Present is, finally, negated by ⲁⲛ alone except
where it occurs in a relative substantive or adjective, where it is negated by ⲛ̄ .... ⲁⲛ. An
exception is 141:12: ⲛⲉⲧⲛⲁⲩ Ⲇⲉ ⲉⲃⲟⲗ ⲍ̄ⲛ
ⲛⲉⲧⲟⲩⲟⲛⲍ̄ ⲉⲃⲟⲗ ⲁⲛ.

Finally, there seems to be a preference for
the use of the qualitative ⲡⲏⲧ wherever the verb
ⲡⲱⲧ could be used in the First Present. This is
good Sahidic style for verbs of motion in the
present tense.

b. First Future. Morphologically, the First Future

presents no anomalous forms, except in the assimilation of Ñ in the second person plural proclitic
pronoun ⲦⲈⲦⲚ´ with the Ⲛ of ⲚⲀ´ producing ⲦⲈⲦⲚⲀ
instead of ⲦⲈⲦⲚ̄ⲚⲀ´ . There is, however, one case
(145:10) where we have ⲦⲈⲦⲚ̄ⲚⲀ´ without assimilation. In the case of the first person plural,
where the First Future is preceded by a tense
converter such as a relative (ⲈⲦ´) or preterit
(ⲚⲈ´), necessitating the replacement of the proclitic pronoun ⲦⲚ̄´ by the suffix pronoun Ñ, there
are no cases of the assimilation of Ñ with ⲚⲀ´ to
produce ⲚⲀ´ alone (cf. ⲦⲈⲦⲚ̄ⲚⲀ , 141:20,21).

Syntactically, the First Future is used in
Thomas the Contender mainly in narrative (twenty-
four times). It is occasionally used in relative
forms: relative substantive: 141:20; 142:27; 143:
10; 144:15,17); and relative adjective: (140:33
[three times]; 143:11). It is frequently used
in the apodosis of temporal result clauses, mostly
accompanied by ⲦⲟⲦⲈ : (139:19,29f [two times];
141:8,15; 142:14; 145:13,14f), and in the apodosis of conditional clauses: (140:11f; 141:24 [im-
perfect future]; 144:22). In causal clauses, except for 144:5,33, it is used mostly in the woe
(ⲟⲩⲟⲓ̈ ⲚⲀ´ ...ⲬⲈ´, 143:19,20; 144:12) and macarism
(ⲚⲀⲈⲓⲀⲦ´ ... ⲬⲈ´, 145:7) formulas. Finally, it
occurs in phrases better rendered by the habitude
(cf. 139:4; 140:16 etc.).

In *Thomas the Contender* the First Future is
accompanied by an anticipatory subject recapitulated by a proclitic pronoun almost twice as often (thirteen out of forty-seven times) as is the
First Present (six of thirty-seven instances).
In narrative, it is continued almost as often by
another First Future (five times) as it is by the
conjunctive (seven times) (an interesting sequence
occurs at 140:21ff: future + ⲀⲨⲱ + future + ⲀⲨⲱ +
future + conjunctive + ⲀⲨⲱ + future + ⲀⲨⲱ + future
+ ⲀⲨⲱ + conjunctive). Finally, we should note two
occurrences of the First Future with the preterit

satellite ⲚⲈˊ, forming the imperfect future, which
is used once as the apodosis of an unreal condition ("would have been" 141:24) and once in a
causal clause ("for he will have been" 144:33).
In both cases it is followed by the enclitic ⲡⲉ.

2) The Old Conjugation and its Descendants.

a. ⲞⲨⲚˊ, ⲘⲚˊ Clauses. The only morphological peculiarity of ⲞⲨⲚˊ phrases is a variation in the way
it combines with a relative converter. Twice
(141:10,19) the relative of ⲞⲨⲚˊ plus the preposition ⲚⲦⲀˁ (ⲞⲨⲚⲦⲀˁ, "to have") occurs as is expected in Sahidic, i.e. ⲈⲦⲈ ⲞⲨⲚⲦⲀˁ , but in a
third occurrence ⲉ contracts with ⲞⲨⲚ to produce
ⲈⲦⲈⲨⲚⲦⲀˁ (145:5).

Syntactically, in *Thomas the Contender* ⲞⲨⲚˊ
and ⲘⲚˊ are used in two basic ways: to express
existence/non-existence, and, in combination with
the preposition ⲚⲦⲀˋ ("with"), to form the verb
to "have"/"not to have" ⲞⲨⲚⲦⲀˋ /ⲘⲚⲦⲈˋ . The ex-
istential ⲞⲨⲚˊ, ⲘⲚˊ often occurs in *Thomas the
Contender* in assertions of possibility and impossibility in the combination of ⲘⲚˊ plus ϬⲞⲘ
followed by Ⲛˊ, ⲘⲘⲞˁ preceding a complementary infinitive introduced by Ⲉˊ, and in the combination
ⲘⲚˊ plus ⲩϬⲞⲘ ("power knows," "possibility")
followed by Ⲛˊ, ⲘⲘⲞˋ , all of which precedes a
complementary infinitive introduced by Ⲛˊ, or
else in the combination ⲘⲚⲩϬⲞⲘ followed by the
actor expression in the conjunctive. Thus we
have the three possibilities: ⲞⲨⲚϬⲞⲘ ⲘⲘⲞˋ Ⲛˊ
(plus infinitive; 138:25,29), ⲘⲚⲩϬⲞⲘ ⲘⲘⲞˋ Ⲛˊ
(plus infinitive; 140:28); and ⲘⲚⲩϬⲞⲘ ⲚⲦⲈˊ (plus
actor expression plus infinitive; 140:13). The
last possibility occurs frequently in the writings
of Nag Hammadi, particularly in Codex II, where
it takes the following forms: ⲞⲨⲚϬⲞⲘ ⲚⲦⲈˊ (CG
II,3,81:24), ⲞⲨⲚϬⲞⲘ ⲘⲘⲞˋ ⲚⲦⲈˊ (CG II,3,74:5),
ⲘⲚϬⲞⲘ ⲚⲦⲈˊ (CG II,2,41:13,14; 3,53:16; 81:23),
and ⲘⲚϬⲞⲘ ⲘⲘⲞˁ Ⲉˊ (CG II,3,58:23,24; 80:14), to
which we must now add ⲘⲚⲩϬⲞⲘ ⲚⲦⲈˊ (CG II,7,140:

76

13). This use of the conjunctive after an exis-
tential phrase strengthens the observation often
made that the conjunctive can undertake a subjunctive function in Sahidic, as it does regularly
in Bohairic. Usually in Sahidic the conjunctive
coordinates infinitives, but in a phrase such as
ⲘⲚ̅ⲩϬⲟⲘ Ⲛ̅ⲧⲉⲟⲩⲣⲙⲚ̅ϩⲏⲧ ⲟⲩⲱϩ ⲘⲚ· (or: ⲟⲩⲱϩⲘ Ⲛ̅· ,
140:13), the conjunctive forms a subordinate
clause, since it acts as the syntactic equivalent
of a complementary simple or causative infinitive:
"it is impossible that a wise man answer (a fool),"
or "it is impossible for a wise man to answer (a
fool)."

In the sentence ⲉⲡⲓⲆⲏ ⲟⲩⲚϩⲟⲉⲓⲛⲉ ⲉⲩⲚ̅ⲧⲚ̅ϩ
Ⲙ̅Ⲙⲟⲟⲩ ⲉⲩⲡⲱⲧ ϩⲓⲭⲚ̅ ⲛⲉⲧⲟⲩⲟⲛϩ ⲉⲃⲟⲗ (140:18)
(there is no superlinear stroke over ⲟⲩⲚ) ϩⲟⲉⲓⲛⲉ
is preceded by ⲟⲩⲚ to specify the existence of
the indefinite subject.

In *Thomas the Contender*, besides one instance
in the absolute (139:5), expressions for "have"
(ⲟⲩⲚ̅ⲧⲆ⸗ , or ⲟⲩⲚ̅· ⲘⲘⲟ⸗) and "have not" (ⲘⲚ̅ⲧⲉ⸗)
occur: (1) in the circumstantial, as an adjective
modifying an indefinite antecedent (141:16); as
an adverbial (ϩⲱⲥ ⲉⲩⲚ̅ⲧⲆⲕ Ⲙ̅ⲙⲆⲩ Ⲛ̅ⲟⲩⲟⲉⲓⲩ 138:5;
ⲉⲡⲓⲆⲏ ⲟⲩⲚϩⲟⲉⲓⲛⲉ ⲉⲩⲚ̅ⲧⲚ̅ϩ Ⲙ̅Ⲙⲟⲟⲩ 140:18); and
(2) with the relative converter as an adjective
with a definite antecedent (141:10; 143:9). Only
once is ⲟⲩⲚ̅ⲧⲆ⸗ accompanied by Ⲙ̅ⲙⲆⲩ (138:5) where
it is apparently optional.

b. Old Conjugation Verbs with Definite and Indefinite
Actor Expressions. The only true old conjugation
verb in this category used in *Thomas the Contender*
is ⲡⲉⲭⲉ· . Although Steindorff (*Lehrbuch* ¶295)
considered ⲩ , to "be able" (Egyptian rḫ, to
"know how," "understand"), to belong to the suffix
conjugation, it is best to agree with Till[3] that
in Coptic it is an ordinary infinitive used in a
secondary fashion such that in the second present
negative first perfect, and negative third future
it occurs in the word order: conjugation prefix -

ϣ- n. subject. *Thomas the Contender* provides
additional support for this view in that, not only
is ϣ present in the non-existence phrase ⲙⲛ̄ϣϭⲟⲙ
where its syntactic status is indeed obscure, but
also in the tripartite conjugation pattern, i.e.
the negative habitude: ⲙⲁϥϣϭⲛ̄ϭⲟⲙ ⲁⲡⲟⲛⲉϥ ⲏ ⲁⲕⲓⲙ
(142:35), and ⲧⲉⲧⲉ ⲙⲁⲩϣⲛ̄ⲣⲁⲧⲍ̄ (139:33f). These
examples show that the word order can also be
conjugation prefix - prn. subject - ϣ with complementary infinitive in the construct relationship. That is, ϣ has become a standard infinitive capable of governing construct complementary
infinitives precisely on the analogy of the construct form of ⲉⲓⲣⲉ (ⲣ̄) with a (substantival)
Greek verb.

The constructions with ⲡⲉⲝⲉ′ in *Thomas the
Contender* vary a good deal. The nominal form
only occurs in the Achmimic/Subachmimic form
ⲡⲁⲝⲉ′ (138:39). Most frequently it is used
with a proleptic pronominal subject recapitulated
by the nominal subject in a following ⲛ̄ϭⲓ clause
(138:4,21; 139:21,24; 141:4,25; 142:7). A strange
and indeed redundant instance occurs in the phrase
ⲡⲁⲝⲉϥ ⲛ̄ϭⲓ ⲑⲱⲙⲁⲥ ⲉϥⲝⲱ ⲙ̄ⲙⲟⲥ ⲝⲉ′ (139:22). However, in the course of the dialogue ⲡⲁⲝⲉ′′ (S AA^2)
occurs mainly in combination with ⲟⲩⲱϣⲃ̄ , to
"answer" (140:37; 141:3,19; 142:3,6,26; twice
with the Sahidic form ⲡⲉⲝⲁ′′ , 138:37; 140:9) and
with ⲟⲩⲱϩ ⲉⲧⲟⲟⲧ′′ (139:32; 144:37). Other examples
with ⲟⲩⲱϣⲃ̄ and ⲟⲩⲱϩ ⲉⲧⲟⲟⲧ′′ with the circumstantial of ⲝⲱ following seem to show that ⲡⲉⲝⲉ′
could, in these constructions, have a circumstantial meaning: ⲁϥⲟⲩⲱϣⲃ̄ ⲛ̄ϭⲓ .... ⲡⲁⲝⲉϥ ⲝⲉ′ ....
"answered, saying." However, in the translation
I have reserved this rendition for for ⲁϥⲟⲩⲱϣⲃ̄
ⲛ̄ϭⲓ .... ⲉϥⲝⲱ ⲙ̄ⲙⲟⲥ ⲝⲉ′ , and have translated the
construction with ⲡⲁⲝⲉϥ′′ in consecutive style:
"...answered and said." The fact that all of
the formulas used in the dialogues of *Thomas the
Contender* employ the proleptic sequence "he said,

namely Thomas," "he answered, namely the Savior,
and said" etc. is a good indication of a Greek
Vorlage cast in the biblical style: ἀποκριθεὶς
(δὲ) N.N. εἶπεν or ἀποκρίθη N.N. καὶ εἶπεν.

c. Attributive (adjective) Verbs. The attributive
verbs, characterized by the prefix ⲛⲉ′/ⲛⲁ′ plus
a form of the old adjective verb, is represented
in *Thomas the Contender* by the verb ⲛⲁⲛⲟⲩ⸗.
This form occurs as a relative substantive
ⲡⲉⲧⲛⲁⲛⲟⲩϥ, "the good"; 140:15; 141:22), as a
circumstantial with indefinite antecedent (139:
31), and in the impersonal construction ⲛⲁⲛⲟⲩⲥ
ⲛⲏⲧⲛ̄, "it is good for you" (141:5). The verb
ⲛⲁⲉⲓⲁⲧ⸗ ("great is the eye of," "blessed is,"
[140:41]; 145:1,3,5) has an attributive function
and is similar in appearance to ⲛⲁⲛⲟⲩ⸗ , but it
does not belong to the adjective verb classification because the prefix ⲛⲁ′ derives not from M.E.
wnn·f, but from the Coptic verb ⲛⲁⲁ′ , "to be
great." In addition, the verb always has the
integral nominal subject ⲉⲓⲁ (eye) in the status
pronominalis (ⲉⲓⲁⲧ⸗). In *Thomas the Contender*,
its (virtual) pronominal "subject" is always defined by a relative phrase: "Blessed are you who
..."

3) Tripartite Basic Tenses.

a. First Perfect. In *Thomas the Contender* the First
Perfect occurs mostly in the formulas introducing
the responses in the dialogue (ⲁϥⲟⲩⲱϣⲃ ⲛ̄ϭⲓ ,
etc.; fourteen times) and in expressions of con-
tinuance in the midst of long speeches (ⲁϥⲟⲩⲱⲍ
ⲉⲧⲟⲟⲧ⸗ ⲛ̄ϭⲓ , etc.; three times). The latter expression occurs twice (139:32; 143:8) in the
midst of speeches of the Savior at a point where
the subject of the Savior's discourse changes from
narrative to exclamatory (e.g. "O unsearchable
love of the light!" or "Woe to you!") discourse.
The third occurrence (144:37) is something of a
puzzle, for it seems intended to set apart a
hypothetical set of twelve woes from what follows

them, but it actually succeeds in creating a
break between the eleventh and twelfth woe. This
may have occurred because the very long eleventh
woe caused a twelve woe format to be forgotten,
and the ⲁϥⲟⲩⲱϩ ⲉⲧⲟⲟⲧ" ⲛ̄ϭⲓ formula was used to
pick up the woe format again. This can only be a
guess, however, for what seems to be a twelfth
woe lies in a lacuna.

Other than its use in the dialogue formulas,
the First Perfect is used as a narrative tense,
and, within direct address in reference to the
speaker's or addressee's past. Twice it is used
in passive constructions with an impersonal (virtual) subject: "it was said" (138:7; 140:38).
Furthermore, the First Perfect occurs with both
anticipatory subject ⲁⲩⲱ ⲡⲕⲁⲕⲉ ⲁϥϣⲁⲉ , 143:30)
and anticipatory direct object (143:31,33). There
is a noticeable preference for introducing a nominal actor expression of a First Perfect morpheme
by a third person pronoun defined by a following
ⲛ̄ϭⲓ clause.

An interesting feature of the First Perfect
construction in *Thomas the Contender* is the sig-
nification of an act completed in the past by the
use of the verb ⲟⲩⲱ to "cease" as an auxiliary,
in combination with a present circumstantial:
ⲁⲕⲟⲩⲱ ⲅⲁⲣ ⲉⲕⲙ̄ⲙⲉ ⲙ̄ⲙⲟⲉⲓ (138:12f) "for you
ceased knowing me" = "for you have already known
me." See also 138:15,18.

b. Negative First Perfect. The Negative First Perfect occurs seven times in *Thomas the Contender*
with no morphological or syntactical anomalies.
Worthy of mention is 141:24: ⲉⲛⲉ ⲙ̄ⲡⲟⲩⲭⲡⲟⲛ ϩ̄ⲛ
ⲧⲥⲁⲣⲝ̄ ⲛⲉⲛⲛⲁⲥⲟⲩⲱ[ⲛ ⲧⲥⲁ]ⲧⲉ ⲁⲛ ⲡⲉ , a contrary-to-
fact condition in the past, in which the negative
perfect is converted by the circumstantial preterit into a virtual pluperfect subjunctive.

c. "Not yet." The "not yet" (ⲙ̄ⲡⲁⲧⲉ´) tense occurs
only once in *Thomas the Contender* (138:35). An
affirmative counterpart has already been discussed

under the first perfect tense: ⲁⲕⲟⲩⲱ ⲅⲁⲣ ⲉⲕⲙ̄ⲙⲉ
ⲙ̄ⲙⲟⲉⲓ "for you have already known me."[4]

d. Affirmative Habitude. Out of nine occurrences of
the affirmative habitude, six form the apodosis of
a present general condition (143:4; 144:24,28,30,
31,32) in the context of an extended metaphor.
In one case (139:7) it is converted by a prefixed
ⲉ´ into a second habitude. A careful perusal of
its use in *Thomas the Contender* shows that the
definition of the "habitude" as a tense expressing
customary or repeated action is not strictly ac-
curate. Very often it seems to be a tense expressing a kind of natural or logical necessity. Its
use in the apodosis of conditional sentences shows
that the habitude expresses the logical consequence
deriving from a certain condition: "if" ... "then"
...., rather than "if" ... "is wont to" .... A
non-conditional sentence such as ⲛ̄ⲛⲑⲉ ⳓⲉ ⲛ̄ⲛ̄ⲧⲃⲛⲟⲟⲩⲉ
ⲉⲩϣⲁⲣⲉⲛⲟⲩⲥⲱⲙⲁ ⲧⲉⲕⲟ   (139:6f), "now
just as the body of the beasts perishes" actually
means, "now just as the body of the beasts must
(naturally) perish." Such may be the case in the
sentence ⲉⲧⲃⲉ ⲟⲩ ⲡⲓⲟⲩⲟⲉⲓⲛ ⲉⲧⲟⲩⲟⲛ︤ϩ︥ ⲉⲃⲟⲗ ⲉⲧⲡ̄
ⲟⲩⲟⲉⲓⲛⲉ ⲉⲧⲃⲉ ⲛ̄ⲣⲱⲙⲉ ϣⲁⲩⲡⲣ̄ⲣⲓⲉ ⲁⲩⲱ ϣⲁⲩϩⲱⲧⲡ̄
(139:23): not, "why is this visible light which
shines on men's behalf wont to rise and set?" but
rather, "why must this visible light which shines
on men's behalf rise and set?" Thus the "habitude"
tense expresses not simply "customary or repeated
action," but rather natural necessity in a larger
sense, which includes "necessary consequence" as
well. One might almost call it the "nomological"
tense, as in most cases it can be periphrastically
translated "... as a rule ...": ϣⲁⲩⲙⲟⲩⲧⲉ ⲉⲣⲟϥ
ⲭⲉ´, "it is called, as a rule, ..." or "it is by
nature called."

e. Negative Habitude. Morphologically the negative
habitude consistently takes the AA^2 form ⲙⲁⲩ´,
etc. Its syntactical use is hard to determine,
since, like its affirmative counterpart, sometimes

where one expects it, one finds instead the first
future or first present. Of interest is one construction where it is converted into a relative
substantive in apposition to a following noun
phrase: ⲱ̂ ⲧⲉⲧⲉ ⲙⲁⲩⲱ̄ⲛ̄ⲣⲁⲧⲍ̄ ⲧⲁⲣⲁⲡⲏ ⲙ̄ⲡⲟⲩⲟⲉⲓⲛ
(139:32f), literally: "O that which they are not
wont to (=by nature) be able to bring its foot,
the love of the light," rendered: "O unsearchable
love of the light."

    f. Third Future. There are no examples of either the
positive or negative third future in *Thomas the
Contender*. Wherever we would expect the third
future in final or purpose clauses, *Thomas the
Contender* prefers ⲝⲉⲕⲁⲁⲥ (138:22; 139:26; 143:7;
144:16; 145:1) or ⲝⲉⲁ (139:27; 145:8) plus the
second future.

B.   Satellites of the Basic Tenses.
    1) Second Tenses of the Bipartite and Tripartite Pat-
terns.
        a. Second Present. In *Thomas the Contender*, the
second present is prominently used in comparisons
to stress the *comparandum* which is cast in an adverbial phrase consisting of: 1) the compound preposition ⲛ̄ⲑⲉ ⲛ̄ⲁ plus *comparandum* in combination
with any verb in the second present (138:41; 139:7;
140:29; 141:27) and 2) the preposition ⲉ̓ plus
comparandum in combination with a verb of comparison, such as ⲉⲓⲛⲉ or (the qualitative of) ⲧⲟⲛⲧⲛ̄
(139:15). The second present is used as well in
interrogative phrases introduced by ⲛ̄ⲁⲩ ⲛ̄ⲅⲉ (138:9,
29; 144:7). A most perplexing example of the use
of second tenses in questions occurs in an interrogative sentence apparently employing a second
tense, but without adverbial extension. In 142:5ff
we have the sentence ⲁⲩⲟⲩⲱⲱⲃ̄ ⲛ̄ϭⲓ ⲡⲥⲱⲣ ⲡⲁⲝⲉⲩ ⲝⲉ
ⲉⲩⲛ̄ⲧⲁⲕ ⲡⲉⲧⲟⲩⲟⲛⲅ ⲉⲃⲟⲗ ⲛⲁⲕ . Unless we can admit a case of extreme ellipsis, it is impossible
to construe ⲉⲩⲛ̄ⲧⲁⲕ as a circumstantial. If we
construe it as a second present, we are obliged
to regard the ⲛⲁⲕ as the adverbial complement of

ⲉⲩⲛ̄ⲧⲁⲕ, although in terms of its position in the
sentence it seems to modify ⲡⲉⲧⲟⲩⲟⲛ︮ⲍ︮ ⲉⲃⲟⲗ (that
which appears to you). Another possibility is to
read ⲡⲁϫⲉϥ ϫⲉ ⲉⲩ ⲛ̄ⲧⲁⲕ ⲡⲉⲧⲟⲩⲟⲛ︮ⲍ︮ ⲉⲃⲟⲗ ⲛⲁⲕ (nominal
sentence, ⲉⲩ AA$_2$ for S ⲟⲩ) "what is it that is
visible to you?" The best alternative seems to
be the former, understanding ⲉⲩⲛ̄ⲧⲁⲕ as a second
present with ⲛⲁⲕ as its adverbial complement rendering "Is it for *yourself* that you have that
which is visible?"

The remaining second presents exhibit no peculiar features but are extended by adverbial expressions generated by prepositional phrases: with
ⲉ′ , 143:12f; with ϩⲛ̄′ , 139:21; 143:23,27; with
ⲉ̇ⲭⲛ̄′, 143:13f; and with ⲉⲧⲃⲉ′, 141:9. There is
one occurrence (143:3) where the second present
occurs with the pure adverb phrase ⲙ̄ⲙⲁⲩ.

b. Second Future. As in the case of the second present, the second future is used in interrogative
phrases of manner ("how is it that...") where the
adverbial element is an interrogative phrase, such
as ⲛ̄ⲁⲩ ⲛ̄ϩⲉ (138:34; 139:10), ⲛ̄ⲁⲩ ⲛ̄ⲣⲏⲧⲉ (138:9f;
142:24) and ⲉ̇ⲉⲓⲉ ⲡⲱⲥ (138:32). Particularly often, as is the case in many of the Nag Hammadi
texts, the second future is used, in preference
to the third future, after to generate final
clauses (138:22; 143:7; 144:15; 145:1). An interesting example of the use of second tenses is
145:8f: ⲣⲟⲉⲓⲥ ⲉⲧⲉⲧⲛ̄ⲥⲟⲡ︮ⲥ︮ ϫⲉ ⲉⲧⲉⲧⲛⲁϣⲱⲡⲉ ⲁⲛ
ϩⲛ̄ ⲧⲥⲁⲣⲝ ⲁⲗⲗⲁ ϫⲉ ⲉⲧⲉⲧⲛⲁⲉⲓ ⲉⲃⲟⲗ ϩⲛ̄ ⲧⲙⲣ̄ⲣⲉ ⲙ̄ⲡⲥⲓϣⲉ
ⲛ̄ⲧⲉ ⲡⲃⲓⲟⲥ . This sentence presents a number of
alternative possibilities for translation. Literally: 1) "Watch, it is for saying (ϫⲉ′) 'it is
not in the flesh that you will come to be,' that
you are praying, but for saying (ϫⲉ′) that it is
from the bonds...that you will come forth" (ⲥⲟⲡ︮ⲥ︮ ,
ϣⲱⲡⲉ, and ⲉⲓ as second tenses); 2) "Watch, praying that (ϫⲉ′) it is not in the flesh that you will
come to be, but that (ϫⲉ′) it is from the bonds...
that you will come forth" (ⲥⲟⲡ︮ⲥ︮ as circumstantial,

ⲩⲱⲡⲉ and ⲉⲓ as second futures with adverbial extension; 3) "Watch, while you pray, in order that
(ϫⲉ′ for ϫⲉⲕⲁⲁⲥ) you will not (finally) come to
be in the flesh, but that you will come forth from
the bonds..." (ⲥⲟⲡⲍ̄ as circumstantial, ⲩⲱⲡⲉ and
ⲉⲓ as second futures replacing third futures in
final clauses dependent on ⲣⲟⲉⲓⲥ); and 4) "Watch,
praying in order that (ϫⲉ′ for ϫⲉⲕⲁⲁⲥ) you will
not come to be in the flesh, but in order that you
will come forth from the bonds..." (ⲥⲟⲡⲍ̄ as circumstantial, ⲩⲱⲡⲉ and ⲉⲓ as second futures replacing third futures in final clauses dependent
on ⲥⲟⲡⲍ̄).

All of these alternatives are possible, but
since we might expect third negative futures in
3) and 4), and since it is unlikely that the ϫⲉ′
clause is to be stressed as an adverbial element
(alternative 1), the second alternative is most
likely to be correct.

Finally, we have an apparently inexplicable
emploi abusif of the second future: ⲡⲉⲛⲧⲁⲩⲛⲟϫⲩ̄
ⲉⲍⲣⲁ̈ⲓ ⲉⲣⲟⲟⲩ ⲉⲩⲛⲁⲣⲟⲩ (142:4). Clearly we have an
interrogative phrase with ⲟⲩ serving as direct
object. The possibility of ⲉⲩⲛⲁⲣ′ being a circumstantial is excluded by the presence of the
relative substantive as antecedent, leaving a
second future with no adverbial extension, occurring in an interrogative phrase.

c. Second Habitude: The only instance of the second
habitude in *Thomas the Contender* is 139:7, where
it serves to stress the preceding adverbial phrase
(ⲛ̄ⲑⲉ ⲛ̄′).

2) The Sentence Converters.

a. Preterit. In *Thomas the Contender* the preterit
is prefixed to the first present to produce an
independent sentence in the imperfect "tense"
(138:3).[5] Twice it is prefixed to the future
auxiliary, once in the "unreal" causal clause
"for he would have been taking" (144:33), and
once in the apodosis of the negated unreal

condition, "we would not be knowing" (141:24).
In the last two instances the preterit is followed
by the enclitic ⲡⲉ , but the instance (138:3) of
the simple imperfect lacks the ⲡⲉ . It is also
used in the protasis of the unreal condition, converted by the circumstantial (ⲉⲛⲉ′ , 141:24).

b. Circumstantial. In *Thomas the Contender*, there is
one instance of the circumstantial in an adverbial
sentence (143:6), while all other instances occur
in verbal sentences. The only morphological peculiarity is the inclusion (138:20f; 141:40) or
omission (144:3) of the ⲛ′ in the negation ⲛ′...
ⲁⲛ . Syntactically, the circumstantial is used
in dependent clauses: in adjective clauses, to
modify a pronominal or indefinite nominal (including the proper noun without article, 145:18) antecedent (139:31; 140:24,27; 141:16; 142:34; 143:5;
145:18); in clauses complementing the verb of the
main clause (ⲥⲱⲉ , 138:11; ⲟⲩⲱ , 138:13,15,18;
and perhaps 144:39); and in coordinate clauses to
continue relative clauses (139:35,37 [two times];
142:32; 145:4 [cf. Till *Kopt. Gram.* ¶486]). Frequently the circumstantial is used adverbially in
various types of clauses: in causal clauses (141:
40,41; 142:1; 144:3; with ⲏⲱⲥ , 138:5,14), and in
clauses, mostly with a temporal nuance, of attendant circumstance (138:3 [two times]; 140:3,4,18,
35,36; 142:42; 143:6; 144:8; 145:8,10,14f,15).
Finally there is an instance of the circumstantial
used in place of the conditional: ⲉϥⲡⲏⲧ ⲁⲡⲁⲙⲛⲧⲉ
ⲉϥϭⲓⲛⲉ ⲛ̄ⲧⲥⲁⲧⲉ ⲉϥⲱⲁⲛⲕⲧⲟϥ ⲁⲡⲏⲥ ⲉϥϭⲛⲧⲍ̄ ⲟⲛ̄
ⲙ̄ⲙⲁⲩ   (143:2ff). The sentence at issue,
ⲉϥⲡⲏⲧ ⲁⲡⲁⲙⲛⲧⲉ ⲉϥϭⲓⲛⲉ ⲛ̄ⲧⲥⲁⲧⲉ might be expected to read: ⲉϥⲱⲁⲛⲡⲱⲧ ⲁⲡⲁⲙⲛⲧⲉ ... The
use of the circumstantial ⲉϥⲡⲏⲧ in other than a
concessive ("although he runs") sense is unusual
in this position. However, the parallelism between ⲉϥⲡⲏⲧ ⲁⲡⲁⲙⲛⲧⲉ and the protasis of the
succeeding clause ⲉϥⲱⲁⲛⲕⲧⲟϥ ⲁⲡⲏⲥ is so clear,
that the ⲉϥⲡⲏⲧ, on the analogy of ⲉϥⲱⲁⲛⲕⲧⲟϥ ,

must be rendered as a circumstantial with a conditional nuance: "if he runs" (cf. 144:23f). The
ⲉϥϭⲓⲛⲉ ⲛⲧⲥⲁⲧⲉ is probably an *emploi abusif*
(since no adverbial extension is involved) of the
second tense which may have been formed on analogy
to the ⲉϥϭⲛⲧⲥ̄ ⲟⲛ ⲙ̄ⲙⲁⲩ of the following sentence.
c. Relative. The morphological peculiarities of relative constructions in *Thomas the Contender* are
limited to the following cases: 1) Out of eight
instances of the relative perfect morpheme ⲛ̄ⲧⲁˁ,
there are two instances of the allograph ⲉⲛⲧⲁˁ
(140:34,41) and one instance of the allomorph
ⲉⲧⲁˁ (144:30, a phrase with many AA_2 forms). 2)
The present relative negative is always of the
form ⲛⲉⲧⲉ ⲛ̄ⲥⲉⲟⲩⲟⲛⲅ ⲉⲃⲟⲗ ⲁⲛ , ⲛⲉⲧⲉ ⲛ̄ⲥⲉⲥⲟⲟⲩⲛ
ⲁⲛ etc., except for 141:12: ⲛⲉⲧⲟⲩⲟⲛⲅ ⲉⲃⲟⲗ ⲁⲛ .
3) There occurs, besides the standard form ⲉⲧⲉ
ⲟⲩⲛ̄ⲧⲁˁ (141:10,19), the form ⲉⲧⲉⲩⲛ̄ⲧⲁˁ (145:5).
In the negative counterpart, ⲉⲧⲉ ⲙ̄ⲛ̄ⲧⲉ is always used (138:[41]; 143:9; 145:7).

Syntactically, the use of the relative can be
subdivided into the following categories: A. As
an adjective modifying a definite antecedent, consisting of (1) ⲉⲧ´ plus adverb or prepositional
phrase (six times), (2) (ⲉ)ⲛⲧⲁˁ , ⲉⲧⲁˁ or ⲉⲧ´,
ⲉⲧⲉ (sometimes with conjugation prefix) plus actor expression (which except for the relative perfect can be omitted if the actor is the same as
the antecedent) plus infinitive (thirty-one times),
(3) ⲉⲧ´ , ⲉⲧⲉ plus actor expression (if subject of
relative differs from antecedent) plus qualitative
(eighteen times), and (4) ⲉⲧⲉ plus a descendant
of the old conjugation (four times). B. As a
substantive, consisting of (1) definite article
plus ⲉⲧ´ plus actor expression (when subject of
relative differs from antecedent expressed by
definite article, e.g. ϩⲛ̄ ⲛⲉⲧⲉⲧⲛ̄ϩⲏⲧⲟⲩ 143:25)
plus adverb or prepositional phrase (two times),
(2) definite article plus ⲉⲛⲧⲁˁ or ⲉⲧ´, ⲉⲧⲉ
(sometimes with conjugation prefix) plus actor

expression (which except for the relative perfect
can be omitted if the actor is the same as the
antecedent) plus infinitive (twenty-eight times),
(3) definite article plus ⲉⲧ⸱, ⲉⲧⲉ plus actor
expression (if subject of relative differs from
antecedent expressed by definite article) plus
qualitative; a special case of (3) where actor
and antecedent are identical occurs in negative
phrases (e.g. ⲛⲉⲧⲉ ⲛ̄ⲥⲉⲟⲩⲟⲛⲍ̄ ⲉⲃⲟⲗ ⲁⲛ   138:30;
139:14), and (4) definite article plus ⲉⲧ⸱, ⲉⲧⲉ⸱
plus ⲟⲩⲛⲧⲁ⸲, ⲙⲛ̄ⲧⲉ⸲ plus subject plus direct object (e.g. ⲛⲉⲧⲉ ⲙⲛ̄ⲧⲉⲩ ⲍⲉⲗⲡⲓⲥ , 145:7), or definite article plus adjective verb plus subject (e.g.
ⲡⲉⲧⲛⲁⲛⲟⲩⲩ 140:15; 141:22f); in fact ⲡⲉⲧⲛⲁⲛⲟⲩⲩ
is so "substantivized" that it can in turn be preceded by the definite article (e.g. ⲡⲡⲉⲧⲛⲁⲛⲟⲩⲩ
140:15). C̲. A third category of relative expressions in *Thomas the Contender* is the relative
used in non-verbal sentences: ⲉⲧⲉ plus definite
noun, demonstrative or possessive pronoun plus
copula, e.g. ⲉⲧⲉ ⲡⲁⲓ̈ ⲡⲉ ("which means," "i.e.,"
138:20), ⲉⲧⲉ ⲡⲕⲱⲍⲧ ⲡⲉ (140:21), ⲛⲉⲧⲉ ⲛⲱⲛ ⲛⲉ
("the ones that are ours," "our own," 141:4). The
relative also occurs in impersonal expressions,
such as ⲡⲉⲧⲣ̄ⲱⲁⲩ ⲡⲉ (141:4) and ⲡⲉⲧⲉⲥⲱⲉ ⲁⲛ ⲡⲉ
(138:11).

One stylistic feature of *Thomas the Contender*
is the use of the relative substantive after such
expressions as ⲟⲩⲟⲉⲓ ⲛⲏⲧⲛ̄ (143:11, 144:3,9,14)
and ⲛⲁⲉⲓⲁⲧ ⲑⲏⲛⲉ (145:2,3,6).

C. Clause Conjugations.

1) The "until" conjugation. In *Thomas the Contender*
the "until" conjugation presents no morphological or
syntactical anomalies; it occurs three times (139:11f;
141:14f; 144:34) in subordinate temporal clauses expressing the time at which the action of the main
verb will cease. In the phrase ⲱⲁⲛⲧⲉⲟⲩⲱⲱⲡⲉ
ⲉⲧⲉⲧⲛ̄ⲟⲃⲱ̄ (143:11f), lit. "until what happens are
you forgetful?" i.e. "how long will you be oblivious?", it is difficult to tell whether ⲉⲧⲉⲧⲛ̄ⲟⲃⲱ̄

is a circumstantial adverbial complement of ϢⲀⲚ
ⲦⲈⲞⲨϢⲰⲠⲈ or whether the verb phrase ϢⲀⲚⲦⲈⲞⲨϢⲰⲠⲈ
should be understood as the adverbial complement of
ⲈⲦⲈⲦⲚⲞⲂⲰ̄ taken as a second tense.

2) The Past Temporal. *Thomas the Contender* employs the
past temporal once (140:42) in the Achmimic dialectal form Ⲛ̄ⲦⲀⲣⲈˊ , as is common in the Nag Hammadi
texts. It forms a temporal clause the action of
whose infinitive has been completed before the action of the main verb occurs.

3) The Conditionalis. In *Thomas the Contender* the conditionalis is used to form the protasis of contingent
statements, both conditional and temporal. The former is introduced by the conditionalis alone (141:7;
143:3,4; 144:21f) or ⲈϢⲰⲠⲈ plus circumstantial (144:
24), and the latter mostly by ϨⲞⲦⲀⲚ (138:23f; 139:
18,28) or ⲦⲞⲦⲈ (144:31) plus temporal conditionalis.
A substitute for the conditionalis makes use of the
circumstantial with ⲈϢϢⲰⲠⲈ: ⲈϢϢⲰⲠⲈ [Ⲙ]ⲈⲚ ⲈⲠⲣⲎ ⲠⲢ̄ⲣⲓⲈ
ⲀⲬⲰϤ ϢⲀϤϬⲚ̄ϬⲀⲘ ... (144:24). To be compared with
this is the example already discussed, ⲈϤⲠⲎⲦ
ⲀⲠⲀⲘⲚ̄ⲦⲈ ... (143:2).

Another way of expressing the protasis of a contingent statement used in *Thomas the Contender* is
ⲈϢⲠⲈ plus first present (138:28; 138:30) or ⲈϢⲬⲈ
with the nominal sentence (139:9). The apodosis of
these statements can be expressed by a non-verbal
sentence (140:12f) or by the first future (140:11f)
or, with an interrogative apodosis, in the second
present (138:28), or second future (138:32; 139:10).
Unreal conditions formed by means of the preterit
(141:24; 144:34) have been mentioned above.

4) The Conjunctive. Most frequently in *Thomas the Contender* the conjunctive usually coordinates an infinitive with a preceding infinitive either standing
alone as an imperative, or governed by the future
auxiliary ⲚⲀˊ (138:5f,8; 140:24; 141:17,33; 142:13,
32,33,34; 143:21). It is apparently a stylistic
feature that in long predictions which involve a
list of future events, we find the pattern: two

futures followed by a conjunctive (140:22-26 [two
times]; 143:19-21). The future relative is continued by the conjunctive three times in a series
(142:27-29). Elsewhere, the conjunctive continues
the "habitude" (144:24,28 [two times],32), the imperative (138:5f,8; 142:10), the conditionalis (144:
26), and the complementary infinitive (143:6). An
interesting construction employing a conjunctive
occurs in 142:8f: ⲚⲦⲞⲔ ⲠⲬⲞⲈⲓⲤ ⲠⲈⲦⲤⲢⲠⲢⲈⲠⲈⲓ ⲚⲀⲔ
ⲀⲨⲉⲬⲈ ⲀⲚⲞⲔ Ⲇⲉ ⲚⲦⲀⲤⲰⲦⲘ ⲉⲢⲞⲔ . Perhaps what we
have here is a parallel to the ⲘⲚϢϬⲞⲘ plus conjunctive expression discussed above; that is, the conjunctive does not here coordinate infinitives, but
rather subordinates the infinitive ⲤⲰⲦⲘ to the expression ⲤⲢⲠⲢⲈⲠⲈⲓ in the same way as the complementary infinitive ⲀⲨⲉⲬⲈ is "subordinate" to
ⲤⲢⲠⲢⲈⲠⲈⲓ ⲚⲀⲔ . Thus it may not be entirely accu-
rate to say that the conjunctive here *coordinates*
its infinitive with either the entire nominal sentence or with its complementary infinitive, since,
just as we have the sentence ⲘⲚϢϬⲞⲘ ⲚⲦⲈⲞⲨⲢⲘⲚϨⲎⲦ
ⲞⲨⲰϨ ⲘⲚ (or: ⲞⲨⲰϨⲘ Ⲛ') (140:13), so also we could
have the construction *ⲤⲢⲠⲢⲈⲠⲈⲓ ⲚⲢϢⲀⲬⲈ . That is,
the conjunctive can form a subordinate complementary
clause after impersonal verbs, a feature which is
not limited to Bohairic. In such constructions the
conjunctive may be assuming a mood (the subjunctive)
of its own, even though, strictly speaking, it is
not a "verb" or "tense" at all.

D. Imperatives. In *Thomas the Contender*, the imperatives
occur in the three standard ways: (1) as the simple infinitive understood as the imperative, which occurs in
both the absolute (138:6; 142:10; 145:8) and construct
(138:8,37; 141:26) state; (2) as the old construct form
of the imperative (ⲀⲢⲓ ⲠⲀⲘⲈⲈⲨⲈ , 145:20) and (3) in
the negative, in the construct state of ⲘⲠⲰⲢ (141:26).
E. Infinitive Constructions.
   1) Simple Infinitives. The simple infinitive is most
   commonly used in *Thomas the Contender* as a complementary infinitive, i.e. an infinitive which is the

direct object of a preceding verbal or non-verbal
expression. We have previously mentioned how the
conjunctive is used to complement a preceding main
verb. Most often, however, this is done by means of
the preposition ⲉ⳿ (ⲁ⳿) or ⲛ̄⳿. Examples of such
constructions in impersonal verbs expressing possibility and impossibility are: ⲟⲩⲛ̄ϭⲟⲙ ⲉ⳿ (138:25,29),
ⲙⲛ̄ⲩϭⲟⲙ ⲛ̄⳿ (140:28), ⲙⲁⲩⲩϭⲛ̄ϭⲟⲙ ⲙ̄ⲡⲟⲛⲉⲩ ⲏ ⲁⲕⲓⲙ
(142:35; both ⲛ̄⳿ and ⲁ⳿). The preceding verb may
be impersonal by virtue of a third person feminine
singular pronominal subject, e.g. ⲤⲘⲟⲕⳉ ⲁⲁ[ⲥ] ,
138:26f; cf. 141:3; 142:8f). Examples in which the
preceding impersonal expression is non-verbal are:
ⲟⲩⲁⲛⲁⲅⲕⲏ ⲉⲣⲟⲛ ⲧⲉ ⲁⲭⲟⲟⲥ (140:9f); ⲡⲉⲧⲉⲥⲩⲉ ⲁⲛ ⲡⲉ
ⲉⲧⲣⲉⲕⲩⲱⲡⲉ ⲉⲕⲟ ⲛ̄ⲁⲧⲥⲟⲟⲩⲛⲉ (138:11; cf. 142:8f).
The complementary infinitive also follows verbs of
wishing (139:11) and going (142:24f), as well as the
verbs ⲙ̄ⲕⲁⳉ and ⲩⲱⲣⲡ, e.g. ⲛⲉⲧⲙⲟⲕⳉ ⲛ̄ⲃⲟⲗⲟⲩ (139:
14f), and ⲛⲉⲧⲡ̄ⲩⲣ̄ⲡ̄ ⲛ̄ⲙ̄ⲙⲉ (145:2). A construction
difficult to classify is 141:20: ⲟⲩ ⲡⲉⲧⲉ ⲟⲩⲛ̄ⲧⲁⲛⲅ̄
ⲁⲭⲟⲟⲩ, "what have we to say." Again, the complementary infinitive preceded by ⲉ⳿(ⲁ⳿) is used to express the goal or purpose of the action of the main
verb: ⲙⲁⲩϭⲓⲛⲉ ... ⲁⲡⲱⲧ ⲉⲙⲁⲩ ("he does not find...
so as to flee there," 143:5f); ⲛⲓⲙ ⲡⲉⲧⲛⲁϯ ⲛ́ⲏⲧⲛ̄
ⲙ̄ⲡⲣⲏ ⲁⲡ̄ⲣ̄ⲣⲓⲉ ... ⲁⲃⲱⲗ ... ⲁⳉⲱⲡ (144:17-19).

By prefixing the preposition ⳉⲛ̄⳿ plus the indefinite article ⲟⲩ⳿ to an infinitive, an adverbial phrase
is created (139:40; 141:18; 141:37).

An interesting example of the infinitive and the
infinitive phrase as substantives in non-verbal sentences is supplied in 142:22f: ⲁⲗⲗⲁ ⲛⲓⲩⲁⲭⲉ ⲉⲧⲕⲁⲱ
ⲙ̄ⲙⲟⲟⲩ ⲛⲁⲛ ⳉⲉⲛⲥⲱⲃⲉ ⲛⲉ ⳉⲙ̄ ⲡⲕⲟⲥⲙⲟⲥ ⲁⲩⲱ ⳉⲉⲛⲁ̄ⲕⲩⲁⲉⲓ
ⲛ̄ⲥⲱⲟⲩ ⲛⲉ : "but these words which you speak to us
are 'laughings' in the world and they are 'sneered
ats.'"

In 139:3 we have what appears to be a complementary infinitive after ⲟⲩⲟⲛⳉ ⲉⲃⲟⲗ: ⲛⲓⲥⲱⲙⲁ ⲛ̄ⲧⲟⲟⲩ
ⲉⲧⲟⲩⲟⲛⳉ ⲉⲃⲟⲗ ⲉⲩⲱⲙ ⲉⲃⲟⲗ ⳉⲛ̄ ⲛ̄ⲥⲱⲛⲧ ⲉϯⲛⲉ
ⲙ̄ⲙⲟⲟⲩ. But because ⲟⲩⲟⲛⳉ ⲉⲃⲟⲗ cannot mean "to

seem" (δοκεῖν), ⲉⲩⲱⲙ cannot be the complementary
infinitive ⲉ′ⲟⲩⲱⲙ = ⲉⲩⲱⲙ. Thus, in order to create
a main verb for this sentence we must suppose ⲉⲩⲱⲙ
to be a syncopated orthography for ⲉⲩⲟⲩⲱⲙ, a second
tense whose adverbial complement is ⲉⲃⲟⲗ ⲍ̄ⲛ̄ ⲛ̄ⲥⲱⲛⲧ
ⲉⲧⲛⲉ ⲙ̄ⲙⲟⲟⲩ.

2) Causative Infinitive. In *Thomas the Contender* the
causative infinitive has by and large lost its causative nuance, and is merely used to introduce a
complementary infinitive whose subject differs from
that of the main verb. We have seen above that the
conjunctive (and also the circumstantial) can also
assume such a function. There are, however, two instances out of seven occurrences of the causative
infinitive where there remains the causative nuance:
ⲥⲉⲛⲁⲫⲣⲁⲅⲉⲗⲗⲟⲩ ⲅⲁⲣ ⲙ̄ⲙⲟⲟⲩ ⲁⲧⲣⲟⲩⲡⲱⲧ ⲛ̄ⲥⲁⲝⲱⲟⲩ
(141:35; here the causation takes on a purposive
nuance); and ⲁⲩⲱ ⲉ[ⲧⲣⲉ]ⲛⲉⲩⲍⲏⲧ †ⲍⲉ ⲁⲩⲱ ⲛⲉⲩⲯⲩⲭⲏ
ⲉⲥⲧⲣⲟⲩⲡⲱⲱϣⲍ̄ (139:37; the restoration is uncer-
tain).

Dialect

Martin Krause, who intends to publish the *editio princeps*
of Codices II and VI from Nag Hammadi, has made available for
private circulation his preliminary investigations concerning
the dialect of Codex II, and in particular the dialect of tractate four, *The Hypostasis of the Archons*.[6] He arrives at the
conclusion that the dialectal variations in Codex II are due to
the everyday speech of the translator, who lived in the region
of upper Egypt, at the linguistic border between the Sahidic and
Subachmimic dialects. Thus we should expect to find a moderate
amount of Subachmimic dialectal features in our tractate, an ex-
pectation which is confirmed. There are a number of forms hitherto unattested in Sahidic which are similar to but not always
identical with our attested Subachmimic forms, which may be due
to a respelling of the Subachmimic forms in conformity with the
orthography of a scribe accustomed to the Sahidic dialect.

Our method of investigation will be to list separately linguistic features which depart from Sahidic but which are matched
in the text by their Sahidic counterparts, and then linguistic

features which consistently depart from Sahidic. Each list will
be subdivided into dialects, beginning with southern and ending
with northern dialects. It is to be understood that when we
speak of "dialects" or use the terms "Sahidic," "Subachmimic" or
"Achmimic and Subachmimic," etc., we are speaking of forms attested in texts which have been classified as belonging to these
dialects. Specifically, W. E. Crum's *A Coptic Dictionary*, Oxford, 1929-1939, will be used as our authority for such attestation of the dialectal provenance of the words. Furthermore, we
must often reckon with the fact that many of the forms are merely
orthographical variants of a certain dialect, but because they
are attested by Crum as belonging to another dialect, they shall
be listed according to Crum. We shall in addition provide a
separate listing of those forms which seem obviously to be due
to orthographical peculiarities, including defective and plene
forms, and examples of assimilation of letters. Finally, we
shall conclude these listings with an account of the scribal
corrections and punctuation used in the tractate.

I. First of all, it will be convenient to list features of our
    text which are not classified as standard Sahidic, but which
    are also matched in the text by their Sahidic counterparts.
    A. To be assigned to the upper Egyptian dialects of the
        period:
        1) Achmimic (A).
            a. the form ⲘⲞ for ⲘⲀⲨ in ⲈⲦⲘ̄ⲘⲞ (144:12).
        2) Subachmimic (A$_2$).
            a. the qualitative form ⲦⲀⲬⲢⲀⲓ̈Ⲧ (143:10) beside S
                ⲦⲀⲬⲢⲎⲨ (142:37; 143:13).
            b. Ⲉⲩⲡⲉ (138:28,30; 140:11) beside S Ⲉⲓⲩⲱⲡⲉ (140:
                12; 144:23,25)
            c. ⲈⲨ (142:6) beside S ⲞⲨ (141:19; 142:4)? The
                phrase reads: ⲈⲨⲚ̄ⲦⲀⲔⲡⲉⲦⲞⲨⲞⲚ₂ⲈⲂⲞⲗⲚⲀⲔ (142:6),
                which could be read: ⲈⲨ Ⲛ̄ⲦⲀⲔ ⲡⲉⲦⲞⲨⲞⲚ₂ ⲈⲂⲞⲗ
                ⲚⲀⲔ "what is it that is visible to you?", or:
                ⲈⲨⲚ̄ⲦⲀⲔ ⲡⲉⲦⲞⲨⲞⲚ₂ ⲈⲂⲞⲗ ⲚⲀⲔ This reading could
                yield: "do you have that which is visible to
                you?", or: "is it for yourself that you have
                that which is visible?", which best accounts
                for the second present ⲈⲨⲚ̄ⲦⲀⲔ .

d. The (imperative) pronominal form ϫο⸗ (138:37) beside S ϫοο⸗ (eight times).

e. օⳡ (144:7) beside S ооⳡ (144:20).

f. ϩⲱⲧⲃⲉ (142:16) beside S ϩⲱⲧⲃ̄ (140:35).

g. ϫⲱϩⲙⲉ (141:3) beside S ϫⲱϩⲙ̄ (140:37).

3) Achmimic and Subachmimic (AA₂).

a. ⲥⲁⲧⲉ (139:15) beside S ⲥⲟⲧⲉ ("arrow," 139:16).

b. ⲥⲉⳓⲉ beside S ⲥⲟ6 (140:14,15) in ⲙⲛ̄ⲧⲥⲉⳓⲉ (143:34).

c. ⳽ⲉϫⲉ (142:9) beside S ⳽ⲁϫⲉ (eight times).

d. ϩⲟⲩⲧ (139:38) beside S ϩⲟⲟⲩⲧ (139:41). The form is either a Sahidized versionof AA₂ ϩⲁⲩⲧ, SA ϩⲁⲩⲧ, A₂ ϩⲏⲩⲧ , or is an error in the construction ϩⲟⲩⲧ ⲙⲛ̄ ⲥϩⲓⲙⲉ (139:38) influenced by the common expression ϩⲟⲩⲧⲥϩⲓⲙⲉ , using the status nominalis of ϩⲟⲟⲩⲧ.

e. high incidence of the preposition ⲁ⸗ (in compounds and by itself) beside S ⲉ⸗ (less often).

f. the use of ⲧⲏⲛⲉ (seventeen times) for S ⲧⲏⲩⲧⲛ̄ after the status nominalis of infinitives and prepositions. To be noted is ⲛ̄ⲥⲁ ⲧⲏⲛⲉ (142:40) beside ⲛ̄ⲥⲱⲧⲛ̄ (145:11).

g. the independent pronoun ⲛ̄ⲧⲁⲕ (138:14) beside S ⲛ̄ⲧⲟⲕ (138:7; 139:2) and ⲛ̄ⲧⲕ (138:9).

h. ⲣ̄⸗ is used before the following Greek verbs: αἰχμαλωτίζειν (140:23), ἀναχωρεῖν (139:29), ἐλπίζειν (143:11), θλίβειν (145:6), κατέχειν (143:38), κληρονομεῖν (144:28f), κολάζειν (142:15), μαστιγοῦν (141:33), μεριμνᾶν (142:4), νοεῖν (142:20; 143:24,25; 144:6), πείθειν (142:19), πιστεύειν (142:11), and πρέπειν (142:8), but not before ἀρχεῖν (142:31), αὐξάνειν (144:31), κρίνειν (144:4), παραδιδόναι (142:41f; lies in lacuna, but not enough room for ⲣ̄), and φραγελλοῦν (141:35); omission of ⲣ̄ is normal in Sahidic. Peculiar is the phrase ⲣ̄ⲧⲉⲗⲉⲓⲟⲥ (139:12; 140:11) for ϣⲱⲡⲉ ⲛ̄ⲧⲉⲗⲉⲓⲟⲥ, as is also the infinitive form ⲫⲣⲁⲅⲉⲗⲗⲟⲩ (143:1) for the noun form φραγέλλιον.

4) Achmimic, Subachmimic and Achmimic-influenced
Sahidic (AA_2S^a).

   a. ΠⲀϪⲈˊ (seventeen times) beside S ΠⲈϪⲀˊ (138:37;
140:9); status nominalis is A^2 ΠⲀϪⲈˊ (138:39).

   b. ⲦⲈⲔⲞ (infinitive 139:4f,7; 140:33; 143:11, and
adjective ⲀⲦⲦⲈⲔⲞ, 143:12) beside SB ⲦⲀⲔⲞ (infinitive, 139:8; 141:13; 143:13,15; 144:22, and
noun, 141:18; 143:24).

5) Achmimic-influenced Sahidic (S^a).

   a. ⲤⲞⲞⲨⲚⲈ (infinitive, 138:11,15,16; 142:23f; noun,
138:18, and adjective ⲀⲦⲤⲞⲞⲨⲚⲈ 138:11) beside
S ⲤⲞⲞⲨⲚ (infinitive, 138:21; 140:39; 141:36,
noun 138:13, and adjective ⲀⲦⲤⲞⲞⲨⲚ, 138:14).

   b. Others could be added to this category, which
may equally well be classified as archaic Sahidic, e.g. ⲀⲚⲈϤ (145:16) for ⲈⲚⲈϤ (145:16 etc.)
and possibly ⲀⲦⲤⲈⲓ (140:25) for ⲀⲦⲤⲓ (143:16).

B. To be assigned to both upper (SAA_2) and lower (BF)
Egyptian dialects.

1) Achmimic, Subachmimic and Fayyumic (AA_2F).

   a. ⲀⲚ (143:4) beside S ⲞⲚ (138:18; 144:6; and
ⲞⲚ̄, sic!, 143:3).

   b. ⲞⲨⲚ̄ϬⲀⲙ (138:29), ϬⲚ̄ϬⲀⲙ (144:24) beside S
ⲞⲨⲚϬⲞⲙ (138:25), ϬⲚ̄ϬⲞⲙ (144:25).

   c. ⲤⲀⲚ (138:4) beside S ⲤⲞⲚ (138:10,19).

2) Achmimic, Fayyumic and Bohairic (AFB).

   a. the second present ⲀⲔˊ (138:9) beside S ⲈⲔˊ
(elsewhere).

   b. ⲤⲀⲂⲎ (140:2) beside S ⲤⲀⲂⲈ (140:41).

3) Achmimic, (Subachmimic), Fayyumic and Bohairic
($A(A_2)FB$).

   a. the relative first perfect form ⲈⲦⲀˊ (144:30)
occurs once beside S (Ⲉ)ⲚⲦⲀˊ (seven times).

II. Second, we list forms not classified as standard Sahidic
which occur without their Sahidic counterparts.

A. To be assigned to upper-Egyptian dialects.

1) Achmimic (A).

   a. Πⲣ̄ⲡⲓⲈ (139:24; 144:18,22,24) instead of S ΠⲈⲓⲣⲈ.

2) Subachmimic (A_2).

   a. the pronominal conditionalis ⲈⲣⲈϣⲀˊ (139:28)

      instead of S ⲉⲣϣⲁⲛ‑ , ⲉⲣⲉϣⲁⲛ‑ and ⲉⲣϣⲁ‑ . Crum,
      59a, lists ⲉⲣⲉϣⲁⲛ‑ as archaic, from which all
      the other forms could have derived.

b. ⲙⲁⲉⲓⲉ (141:30; 144:9; 145:2) instead of S ⲙⲉ
     ("love").

c. ⲙⲁⲓⲛⲉ (139:17) instead of S ⲙⲁⲉⲓⲛⲉ (see be-
     low under A₂F).

d. ⲣ̄ ⲛⲉⲡ (144:31; cf. B. ⲉⲣ ⲛⲏⲃ , Crum 221a, Kasser
     36b) instead of S ⲣ̄ ⲭⲟⲉⲓⲥ . Also ⲣ̄ⲛⲁⲡ (144:30),
     which is either a "Sahidizing" of the Sub-
     achmimic ⲛⲉⲡ, or is the actual Sahidic form
     of Bohairic ⲉⲣ ⲛⲏⲃ ("be lord," "dominate").

e. ⲍⲉⲧⲃⲉ (144:8) instead of S ⲍⲁⲧⲃⲉⲥ .

f. ⲟⲁϣⲧ (144:3,5,8; qualitative of ⲟⲱϣⲧ) in-
     stead of S ⲟⲟϣⲧ.

3) Achmimic and Subachmimic (AA₂).

a. ⲙ̄ⲙⲉ (seven times) instead of S ⲉⲓⲙⲉ .

b. ⲙ̄ⲛ̄ⲧⲉ⸗ (139:5; 141:16; 143:9; 145:7) instead
     of S ⲙ̄ⲛ̄ⲧⲁ⸗,   .

c. ⲡⲟⲛⲉ⸗ (142:35; for A₂ ⲡⲁⲛⲉ⸗ ?) instead of S
     ⲡⲟⲛⲥ⸗ ("turn").

d. ⲭⲁⲩⲭⲩ̄ (140:26) instead of S ⲭⲟⲩⲭⲩ̄ (?).

e. the adjectival use of ⲙ̄ⲡϣⲁ (142:5; usually
     AA₂ "much," "very") is noted by Crum as occur-
     ring once in Sahidic.

f. the negative habitude ⲙⲁ⸗ (139:33; 142:35;
     143:5) instead of S ⲙⲉ⸗.

g. the past temporal ⲛ̄ⲧⲁⲣⲉ⸗ (140:42) instead of
     S ⲛ̄ⲧⲉⲣⲉ⸗ .

4) Achmimic influenced Sahidic (Sᵃ).

a. ⲥⲁⲛ (138:4,10,19) instead of S ⲥⲟⲛ (cf.
     also under AA₂F).

b. ϣⲁⲉ (143:30) instead of S ϣⲁ ("rise").

B. To be assigned to upper (AA₂) and lower (BF) Egyptian
    dialects.

    1) Achmimic and Fayyumic (AF).

      a. the demonstrative ⲧⲉⲉⲓ (139:7) instead of
        S ⲧⲁⲓ̈ .

    2) Subachmimic and Fayyumic (A₂F).

      a. ⲙⲏⲓ̈ⲛⲉ (139:16) instead of S ⲙⲁⲉⲓⲛⲉ (see
        above under A₂).

   b. ⲭⲱⲙⲉ (145:17) instead of S ⲭⲱⲱⲙⲉ.

  3) Achmimic, Subachmimic and Bohairic (AA₂B).

   a. the singular possessive article of the third
    person plural is always ⲡⲟⲩⲋ (139:7; 141:42;
    142:1; 145:5), ⲧⲟⲩⲋ (141:34). The plural form
    is S ⲛⲉⲩⲋ (139:1,15,16,37; 140:31; 141:32,37;
    142:2; 143:14) except for the form ⲛⲟⲩⲉⲣⲏⲩ
    (138:5; a secondarily added title).

 C. To be assigned to lower Egyptian dialects (BF).

  1) Bohairic (B).

   a. ⲁⲧⲕⲁⲥ (145:35) instead of S ⲁⲗⲧⲕⲁⲥ ("marrow").

   b. ⲕⲱⲥ (141:17) instead of S ⲕⲱⲱⲥ (n.f. "corpse").

   c. ⲩⲁⲉⲓ ("nose" 142:23), an orthographic variant
    of B. instead of S. ⲩⲁ , ⲩⲉ .

III. Phonological Variations.

 A. The form ϩⲱⲱⲧ (138:2; "I, too") *versus* the form ϩⲱ
  (145:20, "me, too"), a variation which leads one to
  suspect that the *incipit* and the colophon were composed by different authors.

 B. The doubling of consonants.

  1) ⲛ is doubled in the following instances:

   a. before ⲁ in ⲛ̅ⲛⲁⲩ ⲛ̅ϩⲉ (138:10,34).

   b. before ⲟⲩ in ⲛ̅ⲑⲉ ⲛ̅ⲛⲟⲩⲩⲙⲟⲟⲩⲉ (140:27).

   c. before ⲧ(ϩ) in ⲛ̅ⲛⲑⲉ ⲛ̅ⲋ (139:6).

 C. Assimilation of .

  1) ⲛ is always assimilated to ⲙ before ⲡ except in
   ϩⲛ̅ ⲡⲕⲁⲡⲛⲟⲥ 143:33.

  2) ⲛ is assimilated to ⲙ before ⲯ in ⲟⲩⲧⲁⲕⲟ ⲙ̅ⲯⲩⲭⲏ
   (141:18).

  3) ⲛ is usually not assimilated to ⲣ before ⲣ (e.g.
   138:27; 139:24,34,36; 140:4; 141:26; 142:16f) except for two instances: ⲉⲃⲟⲗ ϩⲛ̅ ⲡ̅ⲣⲱⲙⲉ (138:20;
   141:6).

  4) ⲛ is occasionally assimilated to ⲙ before ⲙ in
   ⲉⲧⲣⲱⲭ ϩⲛ̅ ⲙ̅ⲙⲉⲗⲟⲥ ⲛ̅ⲛⲣⲱⲙⲉ (139:36), ⲧⲥⲁⲃⲏ ⲙ̅ⲙⲏⲉ
   (140:2) and ⲟⲩϥⲁⲛⲧⲁⲥⲓⲁ ⲙ̅ⲙⲏⲉ (140:21), but cf.
   ⲛ̅ⲙⲧⲟⲛ (144:15) etc.

  5) doubling of ⲛ is resolved in ϩⲛ̅ ⲛⲉⲧⲉⲧⲛ̅ϩⲏⲧⲟⲩ
   (143:25) and in all first and second futures except ⲧⲉⲧⲛ̅ⲛⲁⲃ̅ϭⲓⲛⲉ (145:10).

6) N apparently is omitted in ⲧⲉⲧⲉ ⲙⲁⲩϣⲛ̄ⲣⲁⲧⲥ̄
( )ⲧⲁⲅⲁⲡ ⲏ (139:33).

IV. Orthographical Variations.

A. Defective and plene-writing.

1) The plural indefinite article ϩⲉⲛ´ (cf. 138:35; 139:11; 140:2,4; 143:1) appears to be written defectively as ϩⲛ´ in 141:41 and 142:23.

2) The first person plural masculine possessive article is written as ⲡⲛ´ (139:20; 142:20) instead of ⲡⲉⲛ´; the other forms are normal.

3) The "until" form (ϣⲁⲛⲧϥ́, 144:34) is also written plene (ϣⲁⲛⲧⲉϥ´ 141:14f).

4) The plene form ⲱⲣⲉⲭ (142:34) occurs for ⲱⲣⲝ̄ .

B. The variation of ⲉⲓ and ⲓ .

1) After vowels: ⲡⲁⲉⲓ (138:22; 142:23) beside ⲡⲁⲓ̈ (eleven times); ⲧⲁⲉⲓ (140:10; 141:28; 142:20f) always, but cf. AA₂F ⲧⲉⲉⲓ (139:7); ⲛⲁⲉⲓ (138:37; 140:19,32; 141:20; 142:29) beside ⲛⲁⲓ̈ (138:1,2,42).

The first person singular pronominal suffix of prepositions is usually ⲉⲓ : ⲙ̄ⲙⲟⲉⲓ , (138:13), ⲛⲁⲉⲓ (138:26), ⲛⲙ̄ⲙⲁⲉⲓ (138:14); but cf. ⲉⲣⲟⲓ̈ (138:5), ⲛⲁⲓ̈ (138:22). The form ⲛⲁⲓ̈ⲁⲧ˂ is always ⲛⲁⲉⲓⲁⲧˀ (145:1,3,5). The verb ⲟⲩⲭⲁⲓ̈ occurs as ⲟⲩⲭⲁⲉⲓ (143:6). The noun ⲥⲧⲟⲓ̈ occurs as ⲥⲧⲟⲉⲓ (140:24). The explicative ⲟⲩⲟⲓ̈ (143:16; 144:12,14) occurs beside ⲟⲩⲟⲉⲓ (143:9,15,17,18,21; 144:2,10,37). Finally, the construct form of the demonstrative is always ⲡⲉⲉⲓ´, ⲧⲉⲉⲓ´, ⲛⲉⲉⲓ´ in preference to ⲡⲉⲓ´, ⲧⲉⲓ´, ⲛⲉⲓ´.

In Greek words, the spelling ⲓ generally occurs more often than ⲉⲓ in *Thomas the Contender*, e.g. ⲁⲡⲓⲗⲏ = ἀπειλή; ⲉⲡⲓⲇⲏ = ἐπειδή, ⲡⲓⲑⲉ = πείθειν. The causal conjunction ἐπειδή, usually ⲉⲡⲓⲇⲏ (140:3,18; 141:5,30; 142:23,25) is also written plene ⲉⲡⲉⲓⲇⲏ (138:10). The form ⲉⲡⲉⲓ ⲇⲉ (138:7) is probably defective for ⲉⲡⲉⲓⲇⲏ . The Greek noun ἐπιθυμία is written ⲉⲡⲓⲑⲩⲙⲓⲁ (140:3,25) as well as ⲉⲡⲓⲑⲩⲙⲉⲓⲁ (140:32; 141:32).

In the verbal system, the first person pronominal suffix is written plene, e.g. circumstantial

ⲉⲉⲓ´ (138:3), preterit ⲛⲉⲉⲓ´ (138:3), conditionalis ⲉⲉⲓϣⲁⲛ´ (138:24), first perfect ⲁⲉⲓ´ (140:7),
except for the relative perfect ⲉⲛⲧⲁⲓ´ (138:2).

   2) After a consonant: ⲁⲧⲥⲓ (143:16) occurs beside
ⲁⲧⲥⲉⲓ (140:25).

C. The author is reluctant to write three vowels in a row
and thus prefers:

   1) ⲥⲙⲟⲕϩ ⲁⲁ[ⲥ] (138:26f) for ⲥⲙⲟⲕϩ ⲁⲁⲁⲥ.

   2) ⲁⲩⲱ ⲩⲛⲁⲁⲩ ⲛ̄ⲃⲁ̄ⲗ̄ⲉ (140:25) for ⲩⲛⲁⲁⲁⲩ ⲛ̄ⲃⲁ̄ⲗ̄ⲉ

D. Internal juncture of ⲧ and ϩ into ⲑ ; and ⲡ and ϩ
into ⲫ .

   1) ⲧ + ϩ mostly, e.g. ⲑⲉ, (ⲡ, ⲛ)ⲉⲑ ⲏⲡ, (ⲡ)ⲉⲑⲟⲟⲩ
("evil"), but not in ⲉⲧ ϩⲛ̄´ (143:19,29,35; 144:18).

   2) ⲡ + ϩ always, i.e. ⲫⲟ (143:2), ⲫⲟⲟⲩ ("day,"
139:36; 143:6,7; 144:7).

V. Scribal Conventions.

A. When ⲛ is the last letter in a line and would have
closed a syllable, it is sometimes replaced by a supralinear stroke over the vowel that would have preceded
it, e.g. ⲥⲟ̄ for ⲥⲟⲛ (138:10, but cf. ⲥⲟⲛ̄ sic! 138:19),
ⲉϩⲟⲩ̃ for ⲉϩⲟⲩⲛ (143:1), ϣⲁ̄ /ⲧⲉⲟⲩϣⲱⲡⲉ for ϣⲁⲛ/ⲧⲉⲟⲩϣⲱⲡⲉ
(143:11f), ⲉⲩϣⲁ̄/ⲛⲡ̄ⲣ̄ⲣⲓⲉ   for ⲉⲩϣⲁⲛ/ⲛⲡ̄ⲣ̄ⲣⲓⲉ (144:21f),
but there are cases where this feature is absent, e.g.
ϣⲁⲛ/ⲧⲉⲩⲃⲱⲗ ⲉⲃⲟⲗ (141:14f), ⲙ̄ⲡⲟⲛⲏⲣⲟⲛ/ (144:13)
and ⲛ̄ⲙⲧⲟⲛ/ (144:15). This scribal device does not
usually apply where the ⲛ would carry the supralinear
stroke, or when it represents the first person plural
pronominal suffix, e.g. ⲙ̄ⲙⲟⲛ`(141:3).

VI. The following scribal corrections made by inserting missing
letters into the text just above the line are to be noted:

A. ⲧⲟⲧⲉ is inserted above the line in 141:9.

B. ⲛ is crossed out in ⲙⲛ̄ⲡⲣⲱⲭϩ⳯̇ⲙ̄ⲡⲕⲱϩⲧ , "the burning
(ⲣⲱⲭϩ) in the fire," to read ⲙⲛ̄ ⲡⲣⲱⲭ ϩⲙ̄ ⲡⲕⲱϩⲧ "the
burning (ⲣⲱⲭ) in (ϩⲙ̄) the fire" (141:14).

C. ⲟ is inserted above the line in ⲡⲉⲕϣⲁⲭⲉ̇ⲛⲁⲧⲫⲑⲟⲛⲟⲥ
"your sufficient word" to read ⲡⲉⲕϣⲁⲭⲉ ⲟ ⲛ̄ⲁⲧⲫⲑⲟⲛⲟⲥ
"your word is sufficient" (142:21).

D. ⲥ is inserted above the line in ⲧⲃⲱ... ⲁ̇ⲩⲓⲧⲟⲩ ⲙ̄ⲙⲁⲩ
to read ⲧⲃⲱ... ⲁⲥⲩⲓⲧⲟⲩ ⲙ̄ⲙⲁⲩ , "the vine...removed
them" (144:35).

VII. Punctuation. The punctuation tends to be irregular, and is missing in many places where it would be expected.

A. The supralinear stroke lacks in: ⲤⲞⲞⲨⲚ (138:20), ⲘⲡⲁⲦⲈⲦⲚⲬⲒ (138:35), Ⲛ̄ⲈⲚⲦⲚⲌ (140:4), ⲨⲤⲁⲁⲚⲰ (140:16), ⲞⲨⲚ (or is this Greek οὖν?; 140:18), ⲣⲱⲕⲌ (142:2), ⲌⲚ⸴ (142:16), ⲌⲒⲦⲞⲞⲦⲨ (143:17), and Ⲛ̄ⲘⲦⲞⲚ (144:15).

B. The supralinear stroke is mistakenly present in ⲤⲞⲚ̄ (138:19) and ⲞⲚ̄ (143:3).

C. The reason for supralineation in ⲬⲰⲘ̄Ⲉ̄ (141:3) and ⲌⲘⲌⲀ̄Ⲗ̄ (141:31; 143:32) eludes me.

D. There is in addition to the supralinear stroke a form of punctuation resembling an apostrophe mark, sometimes so small as to resemble a point, e.g. ⲈⲐⲎⲡ⸲ which is used with some irregularity, in what seem to be the following situations:

1) It occurs at the end of syllables closed by a consonant (except for Ⲍ , Ⲭ and ⳝ) in Coptic and Greek words, as well as proper names, e.g. ⲡⲣⲙⲚ̄ⲌⲎⲦ⸲ ⲄⲀⲣ⸲ ⲈⲨⲬⲎⲕ⸲ ⲈⲂⲞⲗ (140:14), ⲡⲁⲬⲈⲨ⸲ Ⲛ̄ⳝⲒ ⲐⲰⲘⲀⲤ⸲ (139:15).

2) It replaces the supralinear stroke in words such as: ⲌⲱⲦⲡ⸲ (139:24), ⲬⲰⲗⲕ⸲ (139:15), ⲕⲱⲌⲦ⸲ (141:9), and in pronominal forms such as: ⲚⲁⲰⲟⲡⲨ⸲ (139:30, ⲡⲈⲦⲈⲨⲚⲦⲁⲚⲨ⸲ (141:19), ⲰⲦⲣ̄ⲦⲰⲣⲨ⸲ (141:2), ⲈⲦⲞⲞⲦⲨ⸲ (139:32), ⲌⲒⲦⲞⲞⲦⲕ⸲ (138:24), ⲌⲎⲦⲨ⸲ (140:5), ⲈⲦⲂⲎⲦⲨ⸲ (140:7), etc.

3) Occasionally it separates the second and third person masculine singular possessive adjective from its noun, e.g. ⲡⲈⲕ⸲ ⲌⲎⲦ⸲ (138:7), ⲦⲈⲨ⸲ⲞⲨⲤⲒⲁ (139:30), particularly when the noun occurs on the next line, e.g. ⲁⲡⲈⲨ⸲/ⲟⲛⲱⲰⲈ (140:29f), ⲚⲈⲨ⸲ⲁⲀⲨⲤⲒⲤ (140:30f).

4) Occasionally it separates the relative converter from its infinitive, e.g. ⲁⲨ⸲ⲞⲨ/ⲱⲰⲂ̄ (139:14), ⲁⲨ⸲ ⲞⲨ⸲/ⲱⲰⲂ̄ (142:11).

5) It can separate the conjugation prefix from its infinitive, e.g. ⲁⲨ⸲ⲞⲨ/ⲱⲰⲂ̄ (142:5f), ⲁⲨ⸲ⲞⲨ⸲/ⲱⲰⲂ̄ (142:9f).

6) It occurs mostly at the end of lines, separating
   a prefixal element from its noun or infinitive on
   the following line: e.g. ⲁⲧⲣⲉϥˋ ⲍⲱⲗˋ (140:2f),
   ⲛ̄ⲟⲩˋ/ⲥⲟⲃ (140:13f).

7) It can serve to separate the indefinite plural
   article from its noun, e.g. ⲍⲉⲛˋⲉⲓⲇⲱⲗⲟⲛ (141:16).

8) It occurs after vowels as well, but only at the end
   of a line: ⲡⲉⲧⲭⲓ ⲙⲟⲉⲓⲧˋ ⲅⲁⲣ (sic.) ⲍⲏⲧⲟⲩˋ (140:
   20), ⲡⲉⲧⲛ̄ⲡⲁⲛ ⲡⲉ ⲁⲧⲥⲃⲱˋ (140:12).

9) Finally, it does not occur between a word and the
   enclitic ⲡⲉ, or between the proclitic ⲭⲉˊ and
   the following word.

10) In sum, this type of punctuation seems to serve
    sometimes as syllable divider, sometimes as a con-
    tinuation mark at the end of a line, sometimes as
    an *Ersatz* for the supralinear stroke, and sometimes,
    like the stop sign (ˋ), it serves to delimit mean-
    ing units. There is, however, not enough regular-
    ity in its employment in any of these categories
    to reproduce the precise algorithm governing its
    use.

Having collected the linguistic and orthographic peculiarities of the text of *Thomas the Contender*, we may characterize
its language and orthography.

It appears that there are about as many forms departing from
Sahidic but which have Sahidic parallels in the Text (List I) as
there are forms departing from Sahidic without Sahidic parallels
in the Text (List II). However, within the category of forms
which consistently depart from Sahidic, we may rely only on
those forms which are extremely frequent if we are to use them
as a criterion for judging the scribe's *Sprachgebiet*. If *Thomas
the Contender* had attained the length of the *Apocryphon of John*
or the *Gospel of Philip*, both of Codex II, we might have found
that the forms which, in a short tractate like *Thomas the Contender*, depart consistently from Sahidic would not have done so
in a longer tractate. Therefore, we can only use as evidence
the consistently departing forms which occur very often, such
as A ⲡⲣ̄ⲣⲓⲉ for S ⲡⲉⲓⲣⲉ , A$_2$ ⲙⲁⲉⲓⲉ for S ⲙⲉ , AA$_2$ ⲙ̄ⲙⲉ for S
ⲉⲓⲙⲉ , AA$_2$ ⲙ̄ⲛ̄ⲧⲉˤ for S ⲙ̄ⲛ̄ⲧⲁˤ or ⲙ̄ⲛ̄ⲧˤ, the AA$_2$ negative habitude ⲙⲁˤ for S ⲙⲉˤ, the AA$_2$ past temporal ⲛ̄ⲧⲁⲣⲉˤ for S ⲛ̄ⲧⲉⲣⲉˤ ,

and the AA_2B third person plural possessive article ⲡⲟⲩ- and ⲧⲟⲩ- (but cf. ⲛⲉⲩ-) for S ⲡⲉⲩ- and ⲧⲉⲩ-.

The majority of the dialectal variations in both of the foregoing classes are upper-Egyptian, and in particular Subachmimic, or Achmimic-Subachmimic. Only a few are found in both upper and lower Egyptian dialects, and even fewer are specifically lower-Egyptian. A large part of the variations are probably orthographical, such as the occurrence of ⲉ at the end of words (ϩⲱⲧⲃⲉ, ⲥⲟⲟⲩⲛⲉ, etc.).

On the basis of the information here listed, we conclude that the language of *Thomas the Contender* is not the classical Sahidic of the later Bible translations. The language has not been orthographically standardized, to judge from the rather large amount of spellings differing from attested Sahidic forms but which are matched in the texts by spellings that are attested in Sahidic.

In addition, we have two very rare forms: ⲁⲧⲕⲁⲥ (145:35), which to my knowledge is only attested in the Berlin Gnostic papyrus 8502 (49:17) and in the *Apocryphon of John* in Codex II (CG II,1,63:19; 64:19); ⲣ̄ ⲛⲉⲡ, ⲛⲁⲡ (144:31; 144:30); the former is attested only in the Subachmimic Manichean *Psalmbook* and in the *Gospel of Truth* (CG I,2,20:17; 25:3), whereas the latter is entirely unattested (but may be an orthographical variant of the former).

It is possible to characterize the language of the text as a mixed dialect. Although forms occur which are attested in all the dialects (Sahidic, Achmimic, Bohairic, Fayyumic, and Subachmimic) none of the special characteristics of Achmimic (the letter ϩ), Bohairic (spirantization of ⲡ, ⲧ, ⲕ) or Fayyumic (lambdacism) occur, so that we have to do at most with Sahidic and Subachmimic. All of the forms which consistently depart from Sahidic are attested in Subachmimic except for one Achmimic attestation (ⲡⲣ̄ⲣⲓⲉ), which would suggest that the original scribe thought these to be the normal form of the word. The fact that the scribe in many cases vacillated between Subachmimic and Sahidic forms of the same word would suggest that the scribe knew and wrote a mixed dialect lying between the areas where Sahidic and Subachmimic were spoken. Thus the scribe would not have been at home either in the Sahidic of the Bible translations or in the Subachmimic of the Coptic Manichaea, but rather

in a separate dialect. Since this type of dialect found in
Codex II, and in *Thomas the Contender* in particular, becomes increasingly rare as Achmimic, Subachmimic and Sahidic became nor-
malized, it may be a very early dialect. Since it tends to disappear even before Achmimic and Subachmimic eventually gave way
to Sahidic, a process completed sometime in the fifth century,
the dialect of *Thomas the Contender* may have been employed by
a dialectal group which gradually gave way to those who represented more standardized dialects. This would mean that the
dialect of *Thomas the Contender* is of some antiquity, a judgment which tends to be confirmed by the apparent early date of
Codex II, dated paleographically by S. Giversen as being written
slightly before the writing down of the British Museum Manuscript
Oriental (Coptic) 7594, dated in the middle of the fourth century.[7]

We may conclude with the observation of William H. Willis,
Professor of Greek, Duke University, with which I substantially
agree, and to which the evidence adduced here substantially
points:

> I believe the dialect of *Thomas* to be the
> dialect of the region Dishnah-Nag Hammadi in the
> third and early fourth centuries. It is also the
> dialect of the Mississippi Crosby Codex, alleged by
> some to have been found at Dishnah, and which was
> part of the orthodox Christian library most of which
> was acquired by the Bibliothèque Bodmer in Geneva
> (including also the Chester Beatty Joshua). But
> there by the second half of the fourth century we
> find already classical standard Sahidic, e.g. P.
> Bodmer XXII (Jeremiah-Lamentations-Baruch). It
> strikes me as simply Subachmically-influenced early
> Sahidic native to this region.[8]

NOTES

[1]This division represents a slight modification of that employed by H. J. Polotsky, "The Coptic Conjugation System" *Orientalia* (1960), pp. 392-422.

[2]Within Polotsky's system, the designation of the preterit particle as a sentence converter is not altogether apt, because it can lead to confusion. It has the difficulty of obscuring the difference between two traditionally separate conjugation bases, the imperfect "basic" tense and the preterit converter, which in Bohairic, Achmimic and Fayyumic appear to be distinct morphemes. In these dialects the preterit prefix is Nᴀ⁺ , Nᴀρε´ , Nᴀᴧε´ , while there remains the form Nε´ , Nερε´ , Nεᴧε´ , which forms an independent conjugation base, called the imperfect tense. In Sahidic, however, all these morphemes are the same (Nε´, Nε⁺ and Nερε´), so that they can all be considered as preterit converters.

[3]W. C. Till, "Die Satzarten im Koptischen," Deutsche Akademie der Wissenschaften zu Berlin, Institut für Orientforschung, Mitteilungen, Band II, Heft 3, Berlin (1954), p. 382.

[4] ovw appears to be a *Nebenform* of ovwʐ , both from wšḥ which coalesced with the root wḥ‛ > wḥ from which "w" has dropped leaving ʐᴀ⁺ (Steindorff, *Lehrbuch* ¶313). This often occurs as a prefix in upper Egyptian dialects: ʐᴀï´, ʐᴀk´ .... etc. Steindorff (*Lehrbuch* ¶355) calls it third perfect, although Polotsky claims it to be on the one hand (*Etudes* 14A) an element in a negatived second tense: Nεʐᴀ⁺ ....ᴀN , and on the other hand (*Coptic Conjugation System* II,4) to be the original affirmative of M̄nᴀτε⁺ . It is possible that the ᴀʐ´ form of the first perfect (often in the *Gospel of Thomas* as the relative first perfect when no new subject is introduced) is also derived from wšḥ directly, by the dropping of the initial "w". Neither of these forms, ʐᴀ⁺ or ᴀʐ´ occurs in *Thomas the Contender*, and no example of ʐᴀ´ is as yet known to me from Nag Hammadi.

[4a]See now Codex XI,1 and 2 (Subachmimic) where the first perfect conjugation base comprises ᴀy; ᴀʐov´· , ᴀ´ , ʐᴀ´ , ᴀʐᴀ´ and relative N̄τᴀʐᴀ´.

[5]See footnote 2 above.

[6]"Die Sprache der Hypostase der Archonten," durchgeführt auf Wunsch von Professor K. Aland.

[7]S. Giversen, *Apocryphon Johannis* (Copenhagen: Protestant Apud Munksgaard, 1963), pp. 38-40.

[8]Privately communicated in a personal letter dated October 24, 1969.

CHAPTER II

The *incipit* of *Thomas the Contender* constitutes both the
designation of the content of the work and its legitimization.
That the *incipit* is a later addition is proved by its linguistic
features alone. The language is rather good Sahidic and betrays
forms which, by and large, are absent from the remainder of the
work. The plural demonstrative is elsewhere Nλєι (138:37; 140:
19,32; 141:20; 142:29) while the form Nλï occurs only in 138:1,2
and possibly in 138:42 (directly following a lacuna). The two
relative perfect prefixes єNTλ⸗ occur only in 138:1,2, whereas
elsewhere we find the form NTλ⸗ (140:34,41) and єTλ⸗ (144:30).
Furthermore, the third person plural possessive article is always (nine times) Nєγ⸗, except in 138:4 where the form Noγ⸗ occurs in Noγєpнγ . Finally, the form M̄Mλγ for the *nota accusativi* M̄Mooγ is unique in the document.

The designation N̄ωλχє єθнπ immediately recalls the opening lines of the *Gospel According to Thomas* (CG II,2:32:10):[1]

Ev.Th. 32:10-12	Th.C. 138:1-3
Nλєι Nє N̄ωλχє єθнπ	N̄ωλχє єθнπ Nλï
єNTλ ī̄c єToNʒ χooγ	єNTλq ωλχє M̄Mλγ N̄бι πc̄ω̄p
	N̄ιoγλ̄c̄ θωMλc
λγω λγcʒλïcoγ	Nλï єNTλïcλʒoγ
N̄бι λιλγMoc ïoγλλc θωMλc	λNoκ ʒωωT MλθλιλC

In the case of the *Gospel of Thomas*, the *incipit* title
"hidden words" is appropriate for the contents, since the characterization of its contents as λόγοι reappears within the body
of the work:

> Many times have you desired to hear these words (λTєTN̄p̄
> єπιθγMєι єcωTM̄ λNєєιωλχє) which I say to you
> ... (Log. 38)

> If you become disciples to me and hear my words
> (N̄TєTN̄cωTM̄ λNλωλχє) these stones will minister
> to you. (Log. 19)

> Whoever finds the explanation of these words
> (θєpMнNєιλ N̄Nєєιωλχє) will not taste death.
> (Log. 1; cf. John 8:52)

Clearly the *Gospel of Thomas* purports to be a collection of
Jesus' "words" or sayings. On first inspection, this is not

the case with *Thomas the Contender*, even though it is designated in the *incipit* as "hidden words." *Thomas the Contender* purports to be a dialogue, not a loosely connected chain of sayings.

Taken as a whole, however, *Thomas the Contender* cannot be considered a unity. One of the clearest clues to its composite nature is that only three-fifths of the tractate is in dialogue form. The dialogue proper extends from 138:4-142:26. The last words of this block have Thomas saying:

> You have indeed persuaded us, Lord. We realized in our heart and it is obvious that this is so, and your word is sufficient. But these words that you speak to us are laughing-stocks to the world and are sneered at, since they are not understood. So how can we go preach them since we are reckoned as in the world? (142:19-26)

At this point, Thomas disappears altogether from the dialogue.

It looks very much as though this concluding speech of Thomas is composite. That is, the dialogue section of the tractate originally ended with the words: "You have persuaded us, Lord. We knew in our heart and it is obvious that this is so, and your word is sufficient." The following words about the task of preaching mocked words look like an editorial link designed to introduce the next major block of the tractate, which begins with a section that deals with those who mock Jesus' words.

This second major block of the tractate is not a dialogue, but is rather a homily consisting of an introductory apocalypse (142:26-143:7) followed by a collection of woes (143:7-145:1) and beatitudes (145:1-8), concluded by an admonition and promise of salvation (145:8 *ad. fin.*).

The actual dialogue comes to a formal close with Thomas' affirmation: "your word is sufficient." But immediately Thomas continues on by speaking of Jesus' *words* (plural) rather than Jesus' word (singular). The shift from singular to plural suggests a change in either the topic or the referent of the ensuing discourse; the topic shifts from Jesus' λόγος (ⲡⲉⲕϣⲁϫⲉ) to his λόγοι (ⲛⲓϣⲁϫⲉ ⲉⲧⲕϫⲱ ⲙⲙⲟⲟⲩ ⲛⲁⲛ). At the same time reference is made to the task of preaching these λόγοι, which is hindered by the fact that the world mocks them.

Since the topic now shifts to the subject of Jesus' λόγοι, we must attempt to discover the identity of these "words," and it is natural to look for them in the second section of the

tractate. The closest thing resembling λόγοι in this section is
the long series of woes and macarisms, perhaps including the
closing admonition as well. Now these woes and macarisms are
not λόγοι in exactly the same sense as are the λόγοι of the
Gospel of Thomas since their format is not a chain of isolated
sayings, each introduced by "Jesus said" etc. However, their
designation as λόγοι becomes quite clear when we adopt a slightly
different point of reference, in this case, the *Gospel of Matthew*,
where three of the five major discourse sections are denoted as
collections of λόγοι by the concluding formula: (ἐγένετο) ὅτε
ἐτέλεσεν ὁ 'Ιησοῦς τοὺς λόγους τούτους. (Mt. 7:28; 19:1; 26:1;
cf. 11:1; 14:53). Most significant among these is the Sermon
on the Mount, paralleled by the Lucan "Sermon on the Plain."
A significant part of both of these collections of λόγοι consists of beatitudes, and in the Lucan version we find also woes
(Lk. 6:24-26). Another of Matthew's discourse sections, although
not designated as λόγοι by a concluding formula, consists almost
entirely of woes against the scribes and Pharisees (Mt. 23). We
conclude then that in Christian literature the term "words"
(λόγοι, ⲙ̄ⲁⲝⲉ) can be a *terminus technicus* for collections of
sayings of Jesus.[2]

The phrase with which the second section of *Thomas the Contender* is introduced: "but these words which you speak to us,"
is very probably the reflection of a technical designation of
the following series of sayings (woes and blessings) as λόγοι.
If it is only a reflection, is it possible to find a more immediate source for the designation of the second section as λόγοι?
It seems likely that an affirmative answer is suggested by the
incipit of *Thomas the Contender*, which we regard as a later addition to the tractate as a whole. The *incipit* claims that the
material it entitles is "the hidden *words* which the Savior spoke
to Judas Thomas, which I wrote down, even I, Mathaias." Here we
have the designation λόγοι (ἀπόκρυφοι) which designates, not the
ensuing dialogue, but much more the woes and beatitudes of the
second section. Thus, it is natural to suspect that the *incipit*
title was to some extent borrowed from the title of the second
section as it originally existed (without a dialogue prefixed
to it), and that it originally made no mention of Thomas, who
is never mentioned in the homiletic-discourse material of the
second section. If now we designate the dialogue proper

(138:4-142:26) as section A, and the sayings of the remaining
section (certainly the woes, beatitudes, the final admonition,
and perhaps the introductory apocalyptic section) as section B,
we can schematize the process of the composition of *Thomas the
Contender* as follows:

1. There existed an originally independent collection of
sayings (section B) entitled something like "The Hidden Words
which the Savior spoke, which I wrote down, even I, Mathaias."
This collection consisted of the woes and beatitudes which we
presently find in section B, and was perhaps prefixed by the
introductory apocalypse which served to announce urgency in heed-
ing the following woes, beatitudes and final admonition.

2. This collection of sayings (section B) was then prefixed
with the main dialogue between Thomas and the Savior (section A).
It is quite possible that parts of this dialogue, or even all of
it, served as a source document for the current form of section
A. The title of this source document may have been something
like "The Book of Thomas the Contender writing to the Perfect."
That section A originally bore this title is suggested by the
fact that only A makes mention of Thomas, and the motif of perfection (138:36; 139:12; 140:10f). This combination of A and B
could have been suggested by their serial appearance in a written
document, but their current combination is probably intentional.

3. Once combined, the original title of section A was suffixed to the entire combination of A and B such that the whole
work was attributed to Thomas.

4. The original title of section B ("The secret words which
the Savior spoke, which I wrote down, even I, Mathaias") was then
expanded by the addition of Thomas as recipient of the Savior's
words, and the demotion of Mathaias to the scribe, to produce
the present *incipit*: "The hidden words which the Savior spoke to
Judas Thomas, which I wrote down, even I, Mathaias. I was walking, listening to them speak with one another." Since this step
was effected at the cost of contradicting the subscript title
naming Thomas as the scribe, and since the *incipit*, as we have
shown, bears evidence of being composed by an author separate
from that of either section A or B, it is likely that the composition of the *incipit* is the latest stage in the redaction of
Thomas the Contender.

5. Finally, the completed work was copied by yet another
scribe into the contents of Codex II, since the language of the

colophon written by the scribe of Codex II differs from that of the *incipit*: it uses the first person form ϩⲱ (145:20) of the intensifier ϩⲱⲱ⸗ , while the author of the *incipit* uses (138:2).

The main reasons behind this hypothesis are three: the uniqueness of the language of the *incipit* as compared to the rest of the document; the fact that the dialogue ends after the first three-fifths of the document leaving a long monologue of the Savior; and the fact that important motifs in B (the sun and moon, the grapevine and weeds, the description of Tartaros, and the Jesuanic formulae [truly I say to you, woe to you, blessed are you, watch and pray]) are missing in A, and conversely important motifs in A (the Thomas material, visible and invisible, bestiality, "truth," perfection, the wise man, ἐπιθυμία, knowledge, and light) do not appear in B.

On the other hand, important motifs in B are also found in A, such as the fire of passion, the derangement caused by lust, and the mention of preaching. This fact gives some reason to believe that the prefixing of A to B was intentional, and that, while it is likely that much of A existed prior to the time of its redaction with B, it is also likely that A was to some extent harmonized with B by the redactor who combined A with B and who also composed the *incipit*. The intention of the redactor in combining A with B must have been to produce a literary vehicle more suitable to his intended purpose than the original form of either B or A alone would have been. Some rationale for this process will be offered in our concluding section when we come to discuss the literary profile of *Thomas the Contender*.

At this stage, however, we wish to make it clear that while the ascetic message of abstinence from the body and its fiery passions gives a certain homogeneity to the entire tractate, the two sections A and B basically derive from separate authors. Striking confirmation for this is provided by the distribution between A and B of three Coptic words which are among the most frequent in Coptic Gnostic revelation literature: ⲥⲟⲟⲩⲛ ("knowledge," "to know," thirteen times in A, in B once); (ⲣ)ⲟⲩⲟⲉⲓⲛ ("to illumine," "light," fourteen times in A, three rather innocuous occurrences in B); and ⲟⲩⲱⲛϩ ⲉⲃⲟⲗ ("to appear," "be visible," "revelation," twenty-six times in A, one innocuous occurrence in B). The lack of these *termini technici* in B plus

the distribution of motifs mentioned earlier persuade us that
Thomas the Contender is a combination of two originally separate
sources, the first (A) of which has undergone some harmonizing
currently impossible to isolate with certainty. The redactor
who combined them then prefixed the whole by an *incipit* composed
from the original titles of the two sources.

It now remains to deal with the question of the names
"Thomas" and "Mathaias" as they occur in the *incipit*. It is
quite certain that the name "Judas Thomas" is at home in section
A of *Thomas the Contender*, which is a dialogue between the Savior and Thomas, whose name is mentioned sixteen times. But the
name Mathaias is mentioned nowhere else in A or B, save in the
incipit, and thus we are led to conjecture that the most likely
explanation for this is that it originally occurred in the title
to section B, which was then expunged and included in the present
incipit. Since the current subscript title naming Thomas as
scribe contradicts the current *incipit* naming Mathaias as scribe,
it is clear that both titles did not stem from the same author;
one of them is a later addition. Because the language of the
incipit differs from that of the rest of the tractate, it is more
likely that the *incipit* is a recent construction, and the subscript title ("The Book of Thomas the Contender writing to the
Perfect") was the original title to section A, but now displaced
to the end of the tractate as the title of the whole.

Assuming that section B, a collection of the Savior's (secret?) λόγοι, originally bore a title ("The Secret Words which
the Savior spoke to Mathaias") which connected those λόγοι with
the figure of Mathaias, we must now seek to clarify the significance of the name Mathaias *vis-à-vis* the sayings collection
of section B.

To begin with, the name of Mathaias in various spellings
has been used to designate a certain transmitter of the sayings,
both "canonical" and secret, of Jesus. There is the statement
of Papias of Hieropolis ca. 130 A.D.: "So then, Matthaios com-
piled the sayings (τὰ λόγια) in the Hebrew language, but each
interpreted them as he was able."[3] This is traditionally taken
to refer to the composition of the *Gospel of Matthew*, but since
Schleiermacher most scholars have held that the *Gospel of
Matthew* was not written in or translated from a Semitic language, but was originally written in Greek in dependence on the

Greek *Gospel of Mark*. Thus it is always possible that τὰ λόγια refers to some kind of sayings collection which various scholars have attempted to identify with Q or with a primitive Aramaic gospel. Without trying to debate the question as to the precise relation of Papias' statement to either the *Gospel of Matthew*, or Q, it is clear that the name of a certain Matthaios was bound up with some compilation of Jesus' sayings.

Yet another tradition concerning an individual named Matthias (sic.) is found in the *Elenchos* of Hippolytus, where he calls attention to a Basilidean source which he ascribed to Matthias:

> Basilides and Isidore, the true son and disciple of Isidore, say that Matthias spoke to them secret words (λόγοι ἀπόκρυφοι) which he heard from the Savior when he was taught privately. (*Ref.* VII 20.1; cf. 20.5)[4]

In addition, Clement of Alexandria in his *Stromateis* (II 9,45.4; III 4,26.3; VI 6,35.2; VII 13,82.1; cf. VII 17,108.1) mentions and quotes certain *Traditions of Matthias*. While none of the quotes occurs in *Thomas the Contender*, one of them could serve as a virtual *précis* of *Thomas the Contender*:

> They say that Matthias also taught as follows: "To strive with the flesh and abuse it without yielding to it in any way for unbounded lust, but to increase the soul through faith and knowledge." (*Strom.* III 4,26.3)[5]

In spite of the orthographical variants, it is possible that Mathaias, Matthaios, Matthias may together point to a certain individual to whom tradition ascribed the role of recipient and traditioner of the words (λόγοι, λόγια) of Jesus. He is clearly connected by Papias with a tradition of λόγια, and by Hippolytus with a tradition of λόγοι ἀπόκροφοι, while the *incipit* of *Thomas the Contender* designates him as privy to and scribe of these words spoken, not totally privately, but in the company of Thomas. Clement credits him with being an ascetic teacher, as does the *incipit* of *Thomas the Contender* by implication, and Papias. Therefore, if the name Mathaias entered the *incipit* of *Thomas the Contender* by being borrowed from the title of section B of *Thomas the Contender*, it is reasonable to suppose that section B forms a portion of the stream of traditions about a certain Matthew who was a recipient of the Savior's secret words. The variation in the orthography of

Matthew's name would then have arisen through attempts to harmonize this Matthew's name with the names of other Matthews,
e.g. the tax-collector, or Iscariot's replacement, etc. Even
if the name Mathaias had never been connected with the original
form of section B, his reputation as a recipient and a traditioner of the Savior's words may have secondarily attracted his name
into the *incipit* of *Thomas the Contender*. This would have been
done, however, in contradiction to the obvious attempt to designate Thomas as the Savior's partner in dialogue, as well as to
the subscript title's designation of Thomas as scribe of the
entire *Book of Thomas the Contender*. Such a process of attraction seems less likely than that Mathaias' name was originally
part of the title of section B of *Thomas the Contender*; at least
it seems certain that his name was not part of the original title
to section A, since his name is never mentioned in section A.

The fact that the *incipit* designates the tractate as "secret
words" (Ñϣⲁϫⲉ ⲉⲑⲏⲡ , λόγοι ἀπόκρυφοι) could have resulted in
three ways: 1) "secret words" derives from the original title to
section B which named Mathaias as scribe; 2) "secret words" derives from the original title to section A, naming Thomas as
scribe; or 3) "secret words" was added by the redactor of A and
B by analogy with the *Gospel of Thomas*. Alternative (2) is im-
probable owing to the non-λόγοι (dialogue) character of A. Alternative (3) is a good possibility, but does not account for
the inclusion of Mathaias' name in the *incipit*, and alternative
(1), however, has the merit of helping to account for the inclusion of Mathaias' name in the *incipit*, and providing a good
characterization (λόγοι) for the contents of section B, as well
as a reason (authorship by Mathaias, a traditioner of Jesus'
secret words, according to Hippolytus) for describing the λόγοι
as secret (ἀπόκρυφοι).

Therefore, we regard the *incipit* of *Thomas the Contender*
as being composed out of the original title of section B ("The
Hidden Words the Savior spoke, which I wrote down, even I,
Mathaias") which, when A ("The Book of Thomas the Contender")
was prefixed to B was expanded to yield the current *incipit*
title: "The Hidden Words which the Savior spoke to Judas Thomas,
which I wrote down, even I, Mathaias. I was walking as I lis-
tened to them speak with one another."

138:4-7. The first (A) section, the dialogue proper, is introduced by the Savior's offer to reveal (ⲟ̄ⲱⲗⲡ ⲉⲧⲃⲉ) to Thomas
the things about which he has pondered in his mind, while Thomas
has time in the world.

The temporal clause ⳉⲱⲥ ⲉⲩⲛ̄ⲧⲁⲕ ⲛ̄ⲟⲩⲟⲉⲓⳡ ⳉⲙ̄ ⲡⲕⲟⲥⲙⲟⲥ
implies first of all that the Savior's revelation is an activity
that occurs in the world. As the ensuing dialogue shows, the
revelation is imparted by speech, and, as far as we can tell, by
speech taking place between two embodied beings. In 138:1f this
communication must occur before the Savior's Ascension (a subject
to be discussed later). The implication is that the phrase
"while you (Thomas) have time in the world" sets a limit beyond
which revelation cannot occur, and must be interpreted as "while
you (still) have time (left) in the world." Thus, if we ask
for what it is that Thomas has time in the world, we answer first
of all: "for hearing the Savior's revelation."

However, as we read further in the document we shall see
that Thomas requires time not only for hearing the revelation,
but also for preaching it to others (138:25f; 141:19-25; 142:
21-26). Thus the second implication of the opening phrase of
the Savior's speech is that Thomas possesses time (perhaps better: "opportunity") for executing a mission of preaching.

The Savior tells Thomas that he will reveal to him the
things about which Thomas has pondered in his mind (literally,
"heart," ⳉⲏⲧ). As is true in the Synoptic portrayal of Jesus,
apparently the Savior in *Thomas the Contender* also has unusual
powers of perception, and can recognize the state of mind of
those around him (cf. Mk. 2:8 par.; 8:17 par.; 12:15 par.; 14:18
par.). Thomas does not get a chance to state directly what he
is pondering in his mind, so we must assume that the Savior
recognized these questions without asking Thomas. But because
of Thomas' response to the Savior's opening speech ("Therefore
I beg you to tell me about the things I ask you before your
Ascension," 138:22f), which implies that the Savior has not yet
told him the things he wants to know, we cannot be sure whether
the things the Savior is going to say in his opening speech are
the things which Thomas is pondering. Thus at the most we should
expect that the Savior's opening speech is an introduction to
the dialogue, rather than a summary of the things which Thomas
(and the reader) is going to learn about.

138:7-21. Next, there follows the Savior's instruction for Thomas to inquire and become aware of who he is, in what way he exists, and in what way he will come to be, because he is called the Savior's twin and true companion. Having already addressed Thomas as "brother" in the introduction, here the Savior rather than *addressing* Thomas as his twin and true friend, actually seems to refer to a piece of tradition that Thomas is his twin and true friend: ⲉⲡⲉⲓⲇⲏ ⲁⲩⲝⲟⲟⲥ ⲭⲉ ⲛ̄ⲧⲟⲕ ⲡⲁⲥⲟⲉⲓⲱ ⲁⲩⲱ ⲡⲁⲩⲃⲣ̄ ⲙ̄ⲙⲏⲉ "since it has been said that you are my twin and true companion." To be compared is 138:10; ⲉⲡⲉⲓⲇⲏ ⲥⲉⲙⲟⲩⲧⲉ ⲉⲣⲟⲕ ⲭⲉ ⲡⲁⲥⲟⲛ "since you are called my brother." To see the significance of this tradition that Judas Thomas is the twin brother of the Lord, we must briefly trace its history.

We must begin with the actual name Judas Thomas. Nowhere in the New Testament is there any express connection between the names Judas and Thomas. Thomas is mentioned merely as one among the twelve apostles (Mt. 10:3; Mk. 3:18; Lk. 6:5; Acts 1:13). When we come to the *Gospel of John*, we first encounter the redundant name Θωμας ὁ λεγόμενος Δίδυμος (Jn. 11:16; 20:24; 21:2). We say redundant because δίδυμος (twin) is a Greek rendition of the Aramaic אמ‍‍א‍ת (twin) which has been transliterated into Greek as Θωμᾶ(ς). Thus far, all we have is the mention of an individual named "Twin" or "Thomas," but not of *Judas* Thomas.

The only Judas, besides Judas Iscariot, who is expressly connected with the apostles is a shadowy figure of the Lucan tradition called ʼΙούδας ʼΙάκωβος, Judas son of James (Lk. 6:16; Acts 1:13). However, we also have the tradition of a certain Judas who is one of Jesus' brothers (Mt. 13:55; Mk. 6:3). F Finally, we must take into consideration another most significant canonical witness, the Epistle of Jude, written by ʼΙούδας ʼΙησοῦ Χριστοῦ δοῦλος, ἀδελφὸς δὲ ʼΙακώβου.

Taken as a whole, this evidence points to the existence of Judas who is the brother of Jesus (Mt. 13:55; Mk. 6:3), a James who is brother of Jesus (Gal. 1:19; Mt. 13:55; Mk. 6:3), and a Judas who is a brother of James (Mt. 13:55; Mk. 6:3; Jude 1), all in addition to Judas Iscariot. In the face of this evidence it is tempting to suggest that all these Judas figures, with the exception of Iscariot, were the same person, but we have no way of being sure, since the sources themselves may have confused the names. Nevertheless, there seems to be adequate evidence

(Mt. 13:55; Mk. 6:3; Jude 1) of a primitive tradition that there was an apostle Judas who was the brother of Jesus.

But what of the figure Judas Thomas? Here we have rather slim evidence, since the New Testament does not connect these two names, except in Jn. 14:22 where instead of Ἰούδας οὐχ ὁ Ἰσχαριώτης the Curetonian Syriac version witnesses Ἰούδας Θωμᾶς. Perhaps there is little else that can be said here except to sum up this evidence in the words of Helmut Koester, whose suggestions concerning the canonical Thomas and Judas traditions have influenced the above line of argumentation:

> What is lost in the canonical tradition, however, is the actual, original name of the Apostle (Thomas): Judas. That this was his true name is as probable as is the fact that Peter's given name was Simon. Yet, this Judas is also called the (Twin) brother of the Lord, which raises the question whether the canonical tradition did not after all preserve the name of this Apostle elsewhere: in the name of the author of the Epistle of "Judas (Jude), the brother of James," since this James is certainly the brother of the Lord. Though not desiring to indulge any further in the complex problem of *desposynoi* I would like to affirm that the identity of Judas, the brother of the Lord, and the Apostle Thomas is more likely a primitive tradition than a later confusion - a primitive tradition which was, to be sure, suppressed by later orthodox developments; already 2 Peter, by incorporating the Epistle of Jude, takes a second step in this development; the initial step is reflected in the *incipit* of Jude itself, where "brother of the Lord" is avoided in favor of "brother of James." In any case, it is not impossible that the origin of the primitive designation "Judas Thomas, the brother of the Lord" in the *Gospel*[6] *of Thomas* is the actual historical activity of this Apostle in Edessa or in another area of Palestine-Syria from which Edessene Christianity derives its beginnings. The alternative would be that an early Christian group adopted the name of one of the *desposynoi* at a later date. This is quite possible in view of the role of Jesus' family in the early decades of Christianity. But since this group thus would have preserved an original form of his name that has been lost in the canonical tradition, such adoption must have taken place before the composition of the canonical Gospels.[7]

Whether or not the antiquity of this tradition can ever be demonstrated, it is important to note that it must have been very important in the Osrhoëne, especially in Edessa, the traditional resting place of the bones of the Apostle Thomas.[8] This fact is witnessed to not only by the Syr[c] reading of Jn. 14:22 (Ἰούδας Θωμᾶς), but even indirectly by the Abgar Legend

in Eusebius (*H.E.* I, 13,11).[9] At the same time, however, the
Abgar Legend tends to deny Thomas' role in the evangelizing of
Edessa by having him send Thaddeus (=Addai) in his stead after
Jesus' Ascension. However, Walter Bauer has pointed out that
this tradition of Thaddeus as the apostle to Edessa is late and
suspect:

> Of this report, which ostensibly rested for cen-
> turies in the custody of the record office in Edessa,
> there is certainly no trace in the pre-Eusebian period,
> even in Edessa itself. Ephraem (d. 373), who lauds
> the conversion of the city in rhetorical exuberance,
> mentions indeed the apostle Addai, but drops not a
> single hint about the correspondence.[10]

The most extensive work which deals with Judas Thomas and
which connects him with Eastern Syria is the *Acts of Thomas*.
Originally composed in Syriac,[11] the *Acts of Thomas*

> . . . represents the Gnostic Christianity of Syria in
> the third century, which was domiciled in the region
> of Mesopotamia (somewhere between Edessa and Mesene)
> and was only catholicized at a relatively late date
> (in the 4th and 5th centuries; cf. Bauer, *Rechtgläubig-
> keit und Ketzerei*, p. 6ff). Close connections with
> the Bardesanian Gnosis can be seen in the Wedding
> Hymn of Sophia and in the "Mother" epicleses, but
> there is in addition a long free quotation from the
> Bardesanian "Book of the Laws of the Lands" in the
> speech in c. 91 (Bornkamm, *Mythos und Legende*, pp.
> 85ff). That the Bardesanites composed apocryphal
> Acts and put the doctrines into the mouth of the
> Apostles is moreover expressly stated by Ephraem Syrus
> (cf. Bauer, *op. cit.* pp. 40f). All the same, the
> *Acts of Thomas* give the impression of a "vulgar"
> Gnosticism (Lipsius I. 345), and are distinguished
> from Bardesanes himself (not from his school, cf.
> H. H. Schaeder, *Bardesanes von Edessa*, ZKG 51, 1932,
> pp. 21ff) by their radical dualism and their severely
> Encratite tendency. The latter links them all the
> more closely with Manichaeism, which itself took its
> origin from the Bardesanian Gnosis and made its appear-
> ance in the latter's sphere of influence in the cen-
> tury in which the *Acts of Thomas* came into being.
>   This is shown also by the canon of ascetic ethics
> which is expressly formulated at several points in
> the *Acts of Thomas* (cc. 28, 126) - rejection of the
> pleasures of the table, of avarice and of sexual
> intercourse - and which was adopted by the Manichees
> in their precepts for the *Electi* (*tria signacula*).
> This ascetic canon is certainly pre-Manichaean. The
> same holds for the numerous particular ideas and con-
> ceptions, which have their exact parallels indeed in
> Manichaeism but derive in fact from the older Gnosti-
> cism. From this point of view we can understand the
> diffusion and appreciation of these Acts among the

Manichees, and the fact that traces of Manichaean redaction are almost certainly to be found in the dox-
ology to the Wedding Hymn (c. 7), and in the epiclesis (c. 27) and in the Hymn of the Pearl. The acts
as a whole however prove to be a connecting-link between the older Gnosticism and Manichaeism. They
allow us to recognize a pre-Manichaean Syrian Gnosticism, out of whose elements Mani shaped his own doctrine. Possibly, as Schaeder has conjectured (*Gnomon*,
1933, pp. 351f), the very figure of Thomas, the
Apostle of Syria, played an extremely important role
for Mani. According to the Arabian Fihrist he was
called by an angel "*at-taum*." This angelic name is
only the transposition of the Aramaic "*toma*," which
at one and the same time is the proper name and sig-
nifies "twin." This is now confirmed by Mani's own
account (*Keph*. 14f), where in the place of that angel
there appears the "living Paraclete," whom Mani must
have identified with him.[12] The exact counterpart to
the "twin" of the *Acts of Thomas* is formed by the term
"bosom-friend," frequent in the Coptic texts[13]
(Widengren, *The Great Vohu Mana*, pp. 25ff). The new
Manichaean texts also show that the Thomas legend, as
presented in the *Acts of Thomas*, was well known in
Manichaeism. Thomas is the Apostle to India (MPSB
194:13 et. al.), who met his death at the hands of
four soldiers who thrust him through with lances
(*ib*. 142:17ff; cf. *Acts of Thomas* 165, 168). The
Gnostically interpreted figure of the Apostle Thomas
may thus have been considerable for Mani's understanding of himself. It mediated to him the apostolic
connection with Jesus, and appeared in his eyes indeed
his alter ego, just as Mani's missionary journey to
India before his appearance in Babylon corresponds
to that of the Apostle.

The Gnosticism documented in the *Acts of Thomas*
evidently provided the Manichaeism which was soon
thereafter systematically developed with a considerable portion of its mythological material, and
the "vulgar" form probably with its essential content. That in Catholic circles also these Acts could
be widely read and valued, without concern, is not
surprising, since the translation of the Gnostic myths
into legend seems to have made the heretical poison
largely ineffective for uncritical readers. The
period of origin of the *Acts of Thomas* is settled
by their place in the history of religions between
Bardesanes and Mani; they will have been composed
in the first half of the 3rd century.[14]

Having given reason for situating the *Acts of Thomas* within
the tradition of the early third century Gnosis of the Osrhoëne,
we obtain a valuable point of reference for the traditions about
Thomas contained therein. According to the *Acts of Thomas*, Judas
Thomas is the brother of James the Brother of Jesus (c. 1). He
is the twin of Jesus whom he resembles in appearance (c. 11),
and in fact, in order to avoid confusion, Jesus must say: "I am

not Judas who is called Thomas, I am his brother." In c. 31 of
the Greek version Thomas is called "the twin of Christ," and in
c. 39, he is called "the twin of Christ, the apostle of the
Highest and fellow-initiate in the hidden word of Christ, who
receives his secret words." (cf. also cc. 10, 47, 78).[15]

Another key focal point in the Judas Thomas tradition which
we have already mentioned is the *Gospel of Thomas*. Because this
Gospel circulated in Egypt in the form of P. Oxy. 1 "probably
written not much later than the year 200"[16] it has been often
conjectured that it originated in East Syria, around A.D. 150 or
earlier. H.-C. Puech has showed us that the prologue of the
Gospel of Thomas is echoed in the *Acts of Thomas*, since according to both, the ἀπόκρυφα λόγια have been revealed to Thomas by
Jesus the Life giver (A.Th. 39 Syr. ܚܝܐ) or the living Jesus
(G.Th. Log. 1 ⲣⲓ ⲉⲧⲟⲛⲍ):

> It is therefore clear that either the prologue of
> our gospel is echoed in the *Acts of Thomas* or both are
> influenced by the same tradition. Such a relation
> between the *Acts* and the *Gospel of Thomas* is confirmed
> by the only other passage in the Coptic document in
> which the Apostle Thomas appears, to play moreover an
> important part:
> Jesus said to his disciples: "Make a comparison
> to me and tell me whom I am like." Simon Peter said
> to him: "Thou art like a wise man of understanding."
> Thomas said to him: "Master, my mouth will not at
> all be capable of saying whom thou art like." Jesus
> said to him: "I am not thy Master, because thou hast
> drunk, thou hast become drunk from the bubbling spring
> which I have measured out." (cf. A.Th. cc. 37, 39,
> 147). And he took him, he withdrew (cf. Lk. 9:10),
> he spoke three words to him (cf. A.Th. c. 47). Now
> when Thomas came up to his companions, they asked
> him: "What did Jesus say to thee?" Thomas said to
> them: "If I tell you one of the words which he said
> to me, you will take up stones and throw at me; and
> fire will come from the stones and burn you up."
> (CG II,2: 34:25-35:14).
> It would be possible to establish further but
> less distinct connections between the *Acts* and the
> *Gospel of Thomas* (e.g. 136 and Logion 2, c. 147
> and Logion 22, c. 170 and Logion 52). ...On the
> whole we may conclude from all these connections
> that the Acts are dependent on the gospel.[17]

In view of the preceding evidence, it is justifiable to
conclude that there was at home in the Osrhoëne a primitive tradition according to which Judas the brother of James was considered to be the twin (δίδυμος θωμᾶς) brother of the Jesus, to
whom the Lord entrusted secret words. To quote Koester: "the

Thomas tradition was the earliest form of Christianity in Edessa, antedating the beginning of both Marcionite and orthodox Christianity in that area."[18]

It is interesting to see this tradition appearing in *Thomas the Contender*, a writing belonging to the same Codex as the *Gospel of Thomas*, but many of whose features also approximate those of the *Acts of Thomas*. Therefore we begin to suspect that *Thomas the Contender* is in all probability, at least in its present form, a product of this same East Syrian Gnosis in which the tradition of Thomas, twin brother of Jesus and recipient of his secret teaching, appears to be solidly at home. Indeed the highly ascetic character of *Thomas the Contender* tends to confirm this thesis.

Now the Savior has said that since it is well known (ⲁⲩⲭⲟⲟⲥ ⲭⲉ) that Thomas is his twin and true companion, Thomas should seek to become aware of who he is. That is, since Thomas is commonly called (ⲥⲉⲙⲟⲩⲧⲉ ⲉⲣⲟⲕ ⲭⲉ) the Savior's brother, it is not fitting that he be ignorant of himself (138:10-12), otherwise, presumably, he could not really be the twin of the Savior who is himself the knowledge of the truth (138:13). This self-knowledge, according to *Thomas the Contender*, is knowledge of one's identity (ⲛ̄ⲧⲕ ⲛⲓⲙ), knowledge of the circumstances in which one finds himself (ⲁⲕⲩⲟⲟⲡ ⲛ̄ⲁⲩ ⲛ̄ⲅⲉ , second present) and knowledge of one's destiny (ⲉⲕⲛⲁⲩⲱⲡⲉ ⲛ̄ⲁⲩ ⲛ̄ⲣⲏⲧⲉ). One needs only to compare this with the famous formula of the *Excerpta ex Theodoto* 78,2: "the knowledge (of) who we were, what we have become, where we were or where we were placed, whither we hasten, from what we are redeemed, what birth is and what rebirth,"[19] to see that *Thomas the Contender* makes no mention of the knowledge of one's origin, but only of one's present state and future destiny. Here there is involved no elaborate cosmogonic myth which serves to explain the origin of the evil world of matter in which one is imprisoned through bodily existence.[20] If knowledge of one's origin is vital to the author of this passage in *Thomas the Contender*, it is at most presupposed and not vital enough to specify. Bodily existence is rather simply a present fact which needs no explanation; it is dealt with in the present and future tense throughout this text. On the contrary, what we have here is more like the biblical Gnosis of 2 Pet. 1:3:

He has granted us from his divine power all things pertaining to life and godliness through the knowledge of him who called us to his own glory and excellence, by which he has granted us precious and very great promises, so that through these you may become partakers of the divine nature, fleeing the corruption in the world due to passion.

So also Gnosis in *Thomas the Contender*, while close to that described in the *Excerpta*, appears to be rather more concerned with one's destiny than with one's origin, because the question of one's origin seems to be at most presupposed, but not directly posed.

To make a comparison within the Thomas tradition, the parallel to *Thomas the Contender* 138:9 in the *Acts of Thomas* 15 demonstrates by contrast the future orientation of *Thomas the Contender*: "thou hast shown me how to seek myself and to recognize who I was and who and how I now am, that I may again become what I was."[21] In the *Acts of Thomas*, the bridegroom, newly converted to spiritual marriage, is to become what he was, while in *Thomas the Contender* one becomes what he will be.

Not only is Thomas to know himself, but by coming to know himself, he will automatically come to know the depth (βάθος) of the All. The converse of this may be contained in the *Gospel of Thomas*, Log. 67: ⲡⲉⲝⲉ ⲓ̅ⲥ̅ ⲝⲉ ⲡⲉⲧⲥⲟⲟⲩⲛ ⲙ̅ⲡⲧⲏⲣϥ ⲉϥⲣ̅ϭⲣⲱϩ ⲟⲩⲁⲁϥ ϥ̅ⲣ̅ϭⲣⲱϩ ⲙ̅ⲡⲙⲁ ⲧⲏⲣϥ . Unfortunately the grammar is not clear as to what the knower is deficient in: ⲉϥⲣ̅ϭⲣⲱϩ ⲟⲩⲁⲁϥ . Perhaps ⲟⲩⲁⲁϥ is meant to render σεαυτόν, but this gets us no further. Probably the translation of the Jung Codex Committee interprets as well as can be done: "Whoever knows the all but fails (to know) himself lacks everything."[22] It is quite difficult to tell what is meant by "the depth of the All" in *Thomas the Contender*. βάθος is a term often applied to recondite or advanced knowledge[23] while "the All" generally refers to the *Pleroma*, to the universe and its structure. Thus something like the knowledge of inner meaning of the universe becomes the possession of those who know themselves.

The relationship between self-knowledge and the knowledge of the All is a major Hermetic theme:[24]

Let the man who has Mind recognize himself as immortal, and that the cause of death is desire, and know all things that exist....

He who has recognized himself has come into the good above all things, but he who has loved the body

> which derives from the deceit of desire, continues
> wandering in the darkness, suffering in the senses
> the things of death. (C.H. I,19).

Therefore the Hermetic watchword is expressed in the word of
God: "For God said: 'Let the man who has mind recognize himself'
(C.H. I,21; cf. XIII 22: 'by use of the mind, you have come to
know yourself and our Father.'") This is not to say that the
necessity to know oneself is uniquely Hermetic; indeed such a
call goes back at least to the Delphic Oracle. What it does indicate is that the call to self-knowledge is an extremely wide-
spread theme in the Hellenistic world, and that it came to be
regarded as the key to knowing God and the All. In short, it
is salvific knowledge. For those of old who consulted the Delphic Oracle, self-knowledge was a kind of reflective, objective
seeing of one's capabilities and limitations as they really are
so that one could control himself: know that you are a man, not
a god. In hellenistic times, "know thyself" means: know that
you are essentially divine. Generally, this knowledge is rather
obtained by a vision granted from without (often through a sacred
tradition) and whose object is not the unchanging essence of what
is changing, but rather a transcendent being beyond and apart
from what is changing (e.g. in Poimandres, the "*Nous*"); insofar
as knowledge is of the self, it is not reflection on one's capabilities and limitations, but rather of the tragic history of
the soul.[25] Self-knowledge in *Thomas the Contender*, however, is
half-way between these two, since knowledge of the self leads to
knowledge of the All, yet self-knowledge does not involve reflection on the tragic history of the fallen soul. Self-knowledge
in *Thomas the Contender* is awareness of one's present circumstances (cf. 143:24f) and of his future.

The Savior's opening speech comes to an end immediately
after the gnomic proverb concerning knowledge of oneself and of
the All with these words:

> Therefore you are my brother, Thomas, and you
> have beheld the one who is hidden from men; that is,
> the one against whom they stumble without knowing.

It is worth noting at the outset that the first three of
the Savior's speeches end with clauses introduced by "therefore"
(ⲉⲧⲃⲉ ⲡⲁⲓ̈ ⲅⲉ   ..., 138:19,35; 139:11). Thus there is reason
to suspect some redactional or otherwise stylizing activity at

work in the composition of the Savior's speeches. This becomes more apparent when it is noted that none of the concluding "therefore" clauses draws a conclusion which logically or psychologically follows from what was said immediately prior to it. Each of the "therefore" clauses makes an observation about the participants in (or readers of) the dialogue ("you have beheld the hidden one"; "you are disciples and have not yet received the majesty of the Perfection"; "you are babes until you become perfect"). Thus these clauses probably represent the redactor's interpretation of the material immediately preceding them.

When it is said that Thomas is the Savior's brother, *and* has beheld "the one hidden" (or "that which is hidden," ⲡⲡⲉⲑⲏⲡ) from men, upon whom they stumble without realizing it, the speech must be about Thomas' brother, the Savior, whom men stumble upon, but do not recognize. Thomas, however, even though he is ignorant, has at least recognized that the Savior is the knowledge of the truth (138:13); he has recognized the one hidden from men, and thus is on the way to knowing himself (138:15f), and eventually, the All. Now it appears that knowledge of the Savior is the link which holds the material of the Savior's opening speech together. But it does so only with a certain amount of strain, since the passage is full of inconsistencies.

To begin with, the concluding "therefore" clause does not really follow from the proverb that immediately follows it. Again, if we back up a little, we will find that the sentences in 138:12-16 also betray inconsistencies:

138:12f
And I know that you have understood, for you had already understood that I am the knowledge of the truth.

138:14f
While you walk with me, even though you are ignorant you have already known and you will be called "The one who knows himself."

According to these sentences, Thomas has understood who he is because he had already understood that the Savior is the knowledge of the truth (cf. Jn. 14:6); at the same time, while he walks with[26] the Savior, he is "ignorant," yet "he has already known" (what?) and thus will be called the one who knows himself. It is difficult to see how Thomas can be called the one who knew, the one who is ignorant, and the one who will know himself, all at the same time. One explanation may be that we are dealing with a Platonic epistemology according to which knowledge comes about by the recollection of what the immortal

soul has always known (*Meno* 85, etc.). According to this theory,
Thomas *has* indeed known and therefore *now* knows virtually, and
with the help of the Savior's revelation will recollect clearly
what he once knew and thus become one who knows himself. Again,
the inconsistency could be explained even better by assuming that
indeed Thomas does not and never did know himself, but rather
only knew (by tradition?) that the Savior is the knowledge of the
truth, and because of this can be taught by the Savior to know
himself.

A more suitable explanation of this inconsistency is to
assume that there are two basic themes which have been conflated
into the Savior's opening speech: 1) The tradition of Thomas as
the twin brother of Jesus who ponders things in his heart, who
has recognized the Savior as the knowledge of the truth and
therefore has beheld that which is hidden from ignorant men; 2)
the gnostic call to self-knowledge which is the key to the knowledge of the All.

ΠCΔN ΘⲰMⲀC ⳓⲰC ⲈⲨNTⲀK
ⲘⲘⲀⲨ ⲚOⲨOⲈIⲱ ⳓⲘ Π KOCMOC
CⲰTM ⲈⲣOï ⲚTⲀⳓⲰⲗΠ NⲀK
ⲈTBⲈ NⲈNTⲀKMⲈⲈⲨⲈ ⲈⲣOOⲨ
ⳓⲘ ΠⲈKⳓHT ⲈΠⲈIⲀⲥH⳽ ⲀⲨ⳨OOC
ⳆⲈ ⲚTOK ΠⲀCOⲈIⲱ ⲀⲨⲰ ΠⲀⲱⲃⲣⲘHⲈ
ⲈΠⲈIⲀH CⲈMOⲨTⲈ ⲈⲣOK ⳆⲈ ΠⲀCON

> ΠⲈTⲈⲥⲱⲈ ⲀN ΠⲈ ⲈTⲣⲈKⲱⲱΠⲈ
> ⲈKO ⲚⲀTCOOⲨNⲈ ⲈⲣOK ⲘⲘIN
> ⲘMOK ⲀⲨⲰ ϯⲥOOⲨNⲈ ⳆⲈ

> ⲀKⲘⲘⲈ
ⲀKOⲨⲰ ⲅⲀⲣ ⲈKⲘⲘⲈ ⲘⲘOⲈI ⳆⲈ ⲀNOK
ΠⲈ ΠⲥOOⲨN ⲚTMHⲈ ⳓⲰC ⲈKMOOⲱⲈ
ⳓⲈ ⲚⲘⲘⲀⲈI

> KⲀN ⲚTⲀK OⲨⲀTCOOⲨN

ⲀKOⲨⲰ ⲈKⲥOOⲨNⲈ {ⲀⲨⲰ}

> CⲈⲀMOⲨTⲈ ⲈⲣOK ⳆⲈ ΠⲣⲈⲩⲥOOⲨNⲈ
> ⲈⲣOⲩ ⲘⲘIN ⲘⲘOⲩ ⳆⲈ ΠⲈTⲈ ⲘΠⲩⲥOⲨⲰNⲩ ⲅⲀⲣ
> ⲘΠⲩⲥOⲨⲰN ⲗⲀⲀⲨ ΠⲈNTⲀⲩⲥOⲨⲰNⲩ ⲀⲈOⲨⲀⲀⲩ
> ⲀⲩOⲨⲰ ON ⲈⲩⳆI COOⲨNⲈ ⲀΠBⲀⲐOC ⲘΠTHⲣⲩ

ⲈTBⲈ ΠⲀï ⳓⲈ ⲚTOK ΠⲀCON
ΘⲰMⲀC ⲀKNⲀⲨ ⲀΠΠⲈⲐHΠ
ⲈBOⲗ ⳓⲚ ⲡⲣⲰMⲈ ⲈTⲈ ΠⲀï ΠⲈ
ⲈTOⲨⳆI ⲭⲣOΠ ⲈⲣOⲩ
ⲈNⲥⲈⲥOOⲨN ⲀN

Section 1	Section 2
(Thomas is aware)	(Thomas is ignorant)

The preceding analysis of the Savior's opening speech at
least has the merit of eliminating some of the redundancy (ⲁⲩⲱ
ⲧⲥⲟⲟⲩⲛⲉ ⲭⲉ ⲁⲕⲙ̅ⲙⲉ ⲁⲕⲟⲩⲱ ⲅⲁⲣ ⲉⲕⲙ̅ⲙⲉ ⲙ̅ⲙⲟⲉⲓ... ⲁⲕⲟⲩⲱ ⲉⲕⲥⲟⲟⲩⲛⲉ)
and inconsistency (ⲁⲕⲟⲩⲱ ⲅⲁⲣ ⲉⲕⲙ̅ⲙⲉ ⲙ̅ⲙⲟⲉⲓ ⲭⲉ ⲁⲛⲟⲕ ⲡⲉ ⲡⲥⲟⲟⲩⲛ
ⲛ̅ⲧⲙⲏⲉ ⳓⲱⲥ ⲉⲕⲙⲟⲟⳓⲉ ⲃⲉ ⲛⲙⲙⲁⲉⲓ ⲕⲁⲛ ⲛ̅ⲧⲁⲕ ⲟⲩⲁⲧⲥⲟⲟⲩⲛ ⲁⲕⲟⲩⲱ
ⲉⲕⲥⲟⲟⲩⲛⲉ). If it be correct, we have two sections:

1. Brother Thomas, while you have time in the world,
   listen to me and I will reveal to you about the
   things you have pondered in your heart. Since it
   is said that you are my twin and true companion...
   since you are called my brother...you have been
   aware, for you have already been aware in my case
   that I am the knowledge of the truth. Since you
   walk with me...you have already known and...There-
   fore you are my brother, Thomas, and you have seen
   that which is hidden from men, that is, that which
   they stumble upon, since they are ignorant.

2. Inquire and know who you are, in what way you exist
   and in what manner you shall come to be...It is
   not fitting that you should be ignorant of yourself. And I know that...even though you are ignorant...you will be called the one who knows
   himself, for the one who has not known himself
   has known nothing but the one who has known himself has also already obtained knowledge of the
   depth of the All.

On this theory, section 2, perhaps in a form very much like
the one immediately above, would have provided the basic inspiration and source for the Savior's opening speech, around which
the material from section 1 (though not from a source taking the
form immediately above) was added. Such a conflation would have
produced the redundancy and inconsistency noted above; these
were not serious enough, however, for the author to smooth out
any more than they are in their current form.[27] The objection-
able ⲕⲁⲛ ⲛ̅ⲧⲁⲕ ⲟⲩⲁⲧⲥⲟⲟⲩⲛ has been ameliorated by the immediately following ⲁⲕⲟⲩⲱ ⲉⲕⲥⲟⲟⲩⲛⲉ, although a certain amount of
tolerable redundancy has been generated. The isolation of section 2 in the form proposed has the merit not only of a smoother
flow of speech, but also of exhibiting a more periodic structure.
It also contains representative renderings of wide-spread traditions such as that reflected in *Exc. ex Theod.* 78,2 and *A.Th.*
15, as well as the pithy piece of antithetic parallelism: the
one who has not known himself has known nothing, but the one
who has known himself has known everything ("the depth of the
All").

The material gathered into section 1 consists only of the Thomas tradition and was probably not in any source, but derived directly from the author of the first half of the *Book of Thomas the Contender*.

This material would have been inserted in order to authenticate the urgency and truth of the message "know thyself" to the community which accepted the authority of the Apostle Thomas in his capacity as twin brother of the Savior and one privy to his secret words. As twin of the Savior, Thomas was in a unique position to understand the revelation:

> The Savior secretly taught these same things not to all but only to some of his disciples who could comprehend them and understand what was signified by the scenes, enigmas and parables that came from him.[28]

One should compare this with the use of the same type of "brother of Jesus" tradition in the two Apocalypses of James in Codex V. In the first Apocalypse, James is called Jesus' brother: "I have shown you these things, James my brother, for I have not heedlessly called you my brother, even though you are not my brother in the material (sense)" (CG V,2,24:12-15), and in the second Apocalypse, the Mother says to James: "Do not be overawed, my son, that he has called you 'my brother,' for you were nourished with the same milk. Therefore he calls me 'my mother'... He is your milk-brother" (CG V,3,35:15-23). In the first Apocalypse the identification of James as the (spiritual) brother of "the Lord" serves to identify this "Lord" as Jesus (very much like the identification of Thomas as the twin brother of Jesus identifies the "Savior" of *Thomas the Contender* with Jesus), while in the second Apocalypse of James the identification of James as Jesus' milk-brother serves mostly to glorify the figure of James. Thus we have at least two examples of authenticating the teaching of two dialogues as deriving from Jesus by stressing that the other partner of the dialogue is a brother of Jesus.

Finally, we may regard the last sentence (ⲉⲧⲃⲉ ⲡⲁⲓ̈ ⳓⲉ ...) of the Savior's opening speech as an editorial link which not only changes the subject of the Savior's speech from self-knowledge to seeing "that which is hidden from men" but also forms a bridge to Thomas' response, which introduces the next major subject of the tractate.

We must remember, however, that this source theory cannot be *proved*, since we lack surviving *Vorlagen* from which either of the sections derives. It only has the merit of accounting for the redundancy and inconsistency within the Savior's speech.

138:21-27. Thomas' reply to the Savior's opening speech is not a response to the call to self-knowledge. Rather it relates to the conclusion of the Savior's speech, which we regard as an editorial bridge to the next subject of the tractate. That is, the subject of the dialogue changes from self-knowledge to hidden things *versus* visible things.

Thomas' response begins with a reference to the setting of the dialogue: Thomas desires an answer to the things he has been pondering in his heart. It also adds the additional piece of information that the dialogue is to be regarded as occurring prior to the Savior's ascension (ἀνάλημψις). The term ἀνάλημψις first occurs within the Biblical writings in Luke 9:51 at the critical point where Jesus turns towards Jerusalem ("It came to pass when the days approached for him to *be received up*, he turned his face to go to Jerusalem"). There is no doubt that Luke refers to the post-resurrection assumption of Jesus into heaven (Acts 1:9 ὑπολαμβάνω).

But we have no certain idea of what the ἀνάλημψις means in *Thomas the Contender*, since we do not know what place the orthodox traditions of the crucifixion and resurrection held in the scheme of its author. The only hint we receive is that Thomas wants to know the things he seeks *before* the Savior's ascension (ϩⲁⲑⲏ ⲛ̄ⲧⲉⲕⲁⲛⲁⲗⲏⲙ Ψ ⲓⲥ , 138:22f) as a result (ⲉⲧⲃⲉ ⲡⲁⲓ̈ ⲟ ⲉ ... , 138:22) of being told that he has *seen* that which (or: the one who) is hidden (ⲡⲡⲉⲑⲏⲡ) from men while they only stumble on it (or: him) without knowing (138:19f). At this point in the dialogue, all that Thomas could have *seen* is either the Savior as he walked with him (138:14) or perhaps, in a more noetic sense, he has seen what he "already knew" about Jesus, that he is "the knowledge of the truth" (138:12f). If the former alternative be adopted, we might infer that he has seen the Savior as an ordinary man, walking along with him. If the latter be true, then Thomas has seen only some truth independent of the form in which the Savior currently exists. In view of the mention of walking with the Savior (138:14, which may derive from John 12:35 where it means that the disciples are with the φῶς τοῦ κόσμου) we could assume that what Thomas "saw" was the Savior as "the knowledge of the truth," as "our light" (139:20),

which suggests the Savior in an exalted form. We can thus
assume that the Savior's ascension is immediately pending, since
Thomas seems eager to have his questions answered before this
event; apparently he will not get another chance to ask them.

Another clue to the significance of the ascension may be
provided in 139:20-31, where Thomas confesses: "You are our
light, since you enlighten, Lord," to which Jesus responds: "It
is in light that light exists." When Thomas responds to this
with the question as to why this light which shines in men's
behalf rises and sets, the Savior says:

> O blessed Thomas, this same visible light shone
> for your sake, not in order that you might remain in
> this place, but rather that you might come out of it.
> And when all the elect abandon bestiality then this
> light will withdraw (ἀναχωρεῖν) up to its essence
> (οὐσία) and its essence will welcome it, since it is
> a good servant.

Since Jesus is identified with this light, then it is implied that Jesus is a descending and ascending (ἀναλαμβάνειν,
ἀναχωρεῖν) figure. That is, there may be a parallel between
ascension (ἀνάλημψις) and withdrawal or departure (ἀναχώρησις)
which occurs when men abandon bestiality (i.e. receive the message of this tractate). Thus there is no saving work performed
by the Savior such as the crucifixion and the resurrection.[29]
The only significant events in the life of the Savior are a
descent, perhaps an embodiment, a mission of revealing secret
words to his disciples as he does here with Thomas, and an ascension. Hence we can assume that the Savior is a revealer
figure who has descended, has walked with Thomas, revealing to
him secret words, and is soon to ascend back to the Pleroma or
to the light-substance. However, this scheme is so unimportant
to the author of *Thomas the Contender* that none of it is *expressly* mentioned except walking with Thomas, revealing secret
words to him, and the ascension, which provides the limit beyond which this sort of revelation dialogue or question-and-
answer session cannot take place. What is important is that
Thomas received these secret words before this limit was im-
posed, before the ascension occurred.

We see something of the same situation reflected in the
Acts of the Apostles. In order to replace Iscariot and thus
restore the number of twelve apostles, Peter proposes the following criterion:

> Thus, one of the men accompanying us during the
> whole time the Lord Jesus went in and out among us,
> beginning from the baptism of John until the day he
> was taken up from us, one of these must become with
> us a witness of his resurrection. (Acts 1:21f)

While for Luke an apostle had to have been with Jesus the whole
time between baptism and ascension, and have witnessed the resurrection, it is possible that in *Thomas the Contender* only the
fact of having walked with Jesus before the ascension is important. In the case of Acts, we can infer the importance of having
been with Jesus prior to the ascension. In his introduction Luke
says that for forty days Jesus instructed the apostles ἄχρι
ἡμέρας. . . ἀνελήμφθη (Acts 1:2). When they came together and
asked him if he was going to give the Kingdom back to Israel at
the present time he refused to answer the question, but claimed
that the Holy Spirit would come and empower them from then on.
When Jesus ascends, this *angelus interpres* tells them that Jesus
will not return until he returns the same way he ascended; in
effect, that means that the authorized period for didactic revelations from the Resurrected One is over; the apostles already
have all the Gnosis they need and now need only to depend on
the guidance of the Holy Spirit. Consequently a control can be
exercised over claims to secret revelations from appearances of
Jesus; any such revelations since the ascension are out of order.
From this example taken from orthodox Christianity, we can see
why there would be an effort made, such as is done in *Thomas the
Contender*, to insure that any secret Gnosis, if it were to have
any authenticity, had to be referred to an apostle who received
such Gnosis from the Lord before his ascension. This could be
one reason why so many dialogues between the Savior and his
disciples are set after the Resurrection and, presumably, before
his ascension.[30]

However, we cannot be absolutely sure that the author of
Thomas the Contender entertained the same notions about the significance of the ascension as we feel are evident in the Acts.
For example, in the *Pistis Sophia* Jesus is represented as having spoken for eleven years with his disciples (1a) but the
main body of the revelation occurs only after he ascends on the
fifteenth day of Tobe and descends the next morning (4b-8b); the
Gnosis is imparted after the ascension in this case. In *Thomas
the Contender*, Thomas' request to hear the Gnosis before the

ascension may mean no more than that he wanted to hear it before
Jesus (perhaps by levitation) went away to another (unspecified)
place. Again, the ἀνάλημψις of *Thomas the Contender* may even
refer to the final ascent of the revealer at the final time, the
time when all the elect have abandoned bestiality (139:28f), and
Thomas wants the Gnosis so that he can preach to the remaining
elect before the light (=the Savior) reascends to its essence
(=the Pleroma). Such an "end of time" interpretation fits well
the apocalyptic tenor of the rest of the tractate, although we
cannot be sure that elements of both interpretations are not
involved. One the other hand, the fact that a Day of Judgment
(143:7) figures in the scheme of this tractate may imply that
such a time may be still far off. But simply because it seems
to lie far off in much literature (most of which reflects the
problem of the delay of the Parousia) does not mean that it does
so in *Thomas the Contender*. The only passage in *Thomas the Contender* that might have answered our question lies in a lacuna
in section B (144:37-145:1). The most that can be said is that
the final ascent of the Light-Savior will not occur until all
the elect abandon bestiality, and that such an abandoning seems
to depend upon the response of the elect to Thomas' preaching
(141:19-25; 142:19-26). We simply do not know, however, whether
Thomas is to 1) hear the Gnosis before the Savior's ascension
and preach it after his ascension or 2) both hear and preach the
Gnosis before the Savior's (final) ascension. If 1) applies,
we approach the Lukan scheme: conversations with the apostles -
ascension - time of mission - final judgment; if 2) applies, we
have the scheme: conversation with the apostles - time of mission - final judgment (?) - ascension. Because we do not know
the temporal reference of the words ἀνάλημψις (138:23), ἀναχωρεῖν
(139:29f) and ϣοου ⲛ̄ⲧⲕⲣⲓⲥⲓⲥ (143:7), we must be open to either
possibility. Under either alternative, however, we can see why
it is urgent that Thomas receive the answers to his questions
before the Savior's ἀνάλημψις.

The final sentence of Thomas' response to the Savior: "and
it is apparent to me that the truth is difficult to do before
men" is peculiar in that one would expect it to read "difficult
to speak (or proclaim) before men." Rather we have ⲥⲙⲟⲕϩ ⲁⲁ[ⲥ]
ⲛ̄ⲛⲁϩⲣⲛ̄ ⲛ̄ⲣⲱⲙⲉ . It looks as though this sentence has been
inserted at the end of Thomas' reply to form a bridge to the

Savior's next response when he says: "if the works of the truth
which are visible in the world are difficult for you to perform,
how indeed will you perform the things pertaining to the exalted
majesty and the things pertaining to the Pleroma which are not
visible?" The relevant parts in parallel are:

Thomas 138:26f	The Savior 138:30-32
ⲁⲩⲱ ⲟⲩⲟⲛϩ ⲉⲃⲟⲗ ⲛⲁⲉⲓ ϫⲉ ⲧⲙⲏⲉ	ⲉⲱⲡⲉ ⲛϩⲃⲏⲩⲉ ⲛⲧⲙⲏⲉ ⲉⲧⲟⲩⲟⲛϩ ⲉⲃⲟⲗ ϩⲙ ⲡⲕⲟⲥⲙⲟⲥ ⲥⲉⲙⲟⲕϩ ⲁⲧⲣⲉⲧⲛⲁⲁⲩ
ⲥⲙⲟⲕϩ ⲁⲁ[ⲥ] ⲛⲛⲁϩⲣⲛ ⲛⲣⲱⲙⲉ	

To begin with, ⲟⲩⲟⲛϩ ⲉⲃⲟⲗ has a different meaning ('be
apparent, obvious') in Thomas' speech from that which it has in
the Savior's (ⲉⲧⲟⲩⲟⲛϩ ⲉⲃⲟⲗ ϩⲙ ⲡⲕⲟⲥⲙⲟⲥ, "which are apparent,
visible, revealed in the world"). Secondly, if this conclusion
to Thomas' speech were original, why doesn't the Savior simply
say: "if the *truth* is difficult for you to perform..." rather
than: "if the works of the truth which are visible...''? The
only explanation of the Savior's use of the plural expression
"works of the truth which are visible in the world" can be that
the Savior began his response by using the plural expression "if
the things which are visible to you are hidden before you, how
can you hear about the things which are not visible?" Thus the
material in the Savior's speech belongs together by virtue of
the use of the plural, while Thomas' reference to doing the
truth (sg.) does not fit well with the Savior's "works of the
truth." The third and most basic reason that Thomas' reply and
the Savior's next response do not belong together is that, while
up to this point Thomas has been addressed in the second person
singular (thou), all of a sudden and for no apparent reason he
is addressed in the second person plural (you). No new charac-
ters have been introduced, and if the use of the plural is meant
to include Mathaias among those whom the Savior addresses, why
did the dialogue begin as if the Savior were speaking only to
Thomas? Besides, we have had reason to doubt the originality
of the inclusion of Mathaias, the scribe, among the witnesses
to the dialogue. We are therefore dealing with a literary seam,
whose function is to provide a smooth transition to a new section of the Savior's teaching on a new subject (visible *versus*
invisible things).

138:27-139:12. This entire section of the dialogue, as we have just pointed out, is characterized by the use of the plural form of address, as though Thomas has suddenly become the representative of a larger audience. To be noted is the fact that as soon as the subject changes from self-knowledge, pertaining to Thomas, to that of Thomas' task of speaking about the hidden things to men (138:24-27), the plural form of address is employed. We are obviously dealing with a dialogue composed of different sorts of materials. We should at this time list, for convenience' sake, the breakdown of the "thou" and "you" sections of *Thomas the Contender*:

Thomas='I, Thou'	Thomas='We, You'
138:1-138:27	
	138:27-139:12
139:12-139:20 (?)	
	139:20-141:25
141:25-142:18	
	142:18-142:26

(Thomas disappears from the dialogue at 142:26)

The Savior's answer to Thomas' question is a beautiful example of the dialectical method of inquiry into the transcendental realm *via* the use of the principles of understanding applicable to the phenomenal realm, which achieved its greatest exposition in Kantianism. The argument is *a minore ad majus* - if you cannot see the visible, how can you see the invisible; if you cannot do earthly things, how can you do the things of the Pleroma? The obvious parallel to, and perhaps the inspiration for this piece of dialectic is John 3:12: εἰ τὰ ἐπίγεια εἶπον ὑμῖν καὶ οὐ πιστεύετε, πῶς ἐὰν εἶπω ὑμῖν τὰ ἐπουράνια πιστεύετε;[31]

What corresponds to the Johannine τὰ ἐπουράνια is the Pleroma of *Thomas the Contender*. The meaning of this term as it occurs parallel with ⲠⲘⲈⲣⲈⲐⲞⲤ ⲈⲦⲀⲞⲤⲈ , ("the exalted Majesty"), we should assume that we are dealing with a state of being rather than a substance. In most Gnostic systems, the term Pleroma designates "the totality of the aeons,"[32] but we find no doctrine of aeons in *Thomas the Contender*. It is tempting to connect the term Pleroma with the οὐσία of the light (139:29-32), but no such connection is made in the tractate. If the term Pleroma means the same thing as ⲠⲘⲈⲣⲈⲐⲞⲤ ⲈⲦⲀⲞⲤⲈ , we can infer that, as the only other occurrence of this term in

Thomas the Contender implies, ⲠⲘⲈⲅⲉⲐⲟⲤ ⲚⲦⲘⲚⲦⲦⲈⲗⲉⲓⲟⲤ (138:36), the Pleroma means some state of future perfection which is the goal of Thomas' striving. In the second half of the tractate (section B), this goal is described as rest (ἀνάπαυσις, 147:13) and eternal union with the king (145:15) in what appears to be a bodiless existence (145:8ff).

The Savior tells Thomas (and those with him?) that without this ability to understand earthly and visible things, not only will he not attain the understanding of the exalted Majesty and the Pleroma, but also he cannot be called ἐργάτης, laborer. Thus the goal of Thomas' understanding is not for his own future enlightenment alone. It has a much wider implication in terms of Thomas' present life, in which he is to act so as to be worthy of the name ἐργάτης. Paul applied this term to his opponents, both those in Corinth (2 Cor. 11:13) and those in Philippi (Phil. 3:2). Dieter Georgi has observed that this term applies to the missionary as one doing hard work:

> Nicht nur 1 K.3,3-15 und 9,6ff., sondern auch in dem synoptischen Worten (Mt. 9,37f. par.; Mt. 10,10 par.) und in dem johanneischen Passus 4,35-38 sind Vorstellungen und Bilder aus der Arbeitswelt mittelbar oder unmittelbar auf die christliche Missionarbeit übertragen. 1 Tim. 5,18 und Did. 13,2 nehmen das Herrenwort Mt. 10,10 auf. 2 Tim. 2, 15f. dient ἐργάτης ebenfalls als Kennzeichnung des christlichen Verkündigers.[33]

Thus Thomas' goal is not only to understand the things of the Pleroma, but also to preach about this to others (cf. 138: 25f). But as long as Thomas should remain ignorant of these things, and even of visible earthly things, he is no ἐργάτης, but only a disciple (ⲈⲦⲂⲈ ⲡⲁⲓ ⲚⲦⲰⲦⲚ ⲍⲈⲚⲤⲂⲞⲨⲈⲓ) and has no share in the majesty of the perfection (ⲘⲡⲁⲦⲈⲦⲚⲭⲓ ⲘⲡⲘⲈⲅⲉⲐⲞⲤ ⲚⲦⲘⲚⲦⲦⲈⲗⲉⲓⲟⲤ).

It is interesting to note that in *Thomas the Contender* the disciple seems to be a lower order of person, one who is not perfected, and cannot even be called an ἐργάτης. It seems that such an estimation also prevails in the *Gospel of Thomas*, for here the disciples are ignorant of the presence of the ἀνάπαυσις and the new κόσμος (Log. 51), of the presence in their midst of the Living One (=Jesus, Log. 52 and 91), do not know who Jesus is (Log. 43), and do not even bother to seek the things that they will find from the words of Jesus (Log. 92). Elsewhere, it is implied that they have not yet entered the Kingdom (Log. 22 and 37; cf. Log. 21). The theme of the ignorance of Jesus' disciples is thus widespread, occurring not only in the *Gospel of Thomas* and *Thomas the Contender*, but also in the *Gospel of Mark* (Mk. 4:13,41; 6:51f.; 7:17f.; 8:17-21,33; 9:10,32; 10:26).

Taken as a unit, the Savior's reply bears the marks of a conflation, i.e., the material at the end (138:34-36) shifts from the discussion about visible and invisible to that of being missionaries and disciples who have not been perfected. Furthermore, the fact that 138:35 (ⲉⲧⲃⲉ ⲡⲁⲓ̈) draws a conclusion from a set of rhetorical questions produces a case of evident, although unobjectionable, *anacoluthon*. This conclusion is borne out by Thomas' response (138:37-38), which picks up neither the theme of being a missionary, nor that of attaining the perfection, but rather that of visible and invisible. This response, however, continues in the plural, as if Thomas were the representative of a larger group.

The first part of the Savior's answer (138:39-139:12) lies in a lacuna which cannot be restored with any certainty. The thesis of the answer is that visible things are typified by beasts (139:2f) who, because they derive from intercourse, are always embodied, having to nourish themselves from other embodied things. This results in change and thus eventual dissolution. On the other hand, things which are above, which are not visible, have no need to nourish themselves from other visible things, but are self-nourished (ⲉⲃⲟⲗ ⲍ̄ⲛ ⲧⲟⲩⲛⲟⲩⲛⲉ ⲟⲩⲁⲁⲧⲟⲩ), and thus have hope of life. The basic comparison seems to be inspired by Psalm 48:13, 21 (LXX): ἄνθρωπος ἐν τιμῇ ὤν οὐ συνῆκεν παρασυνεβλήθη τοῖς κτήνεσιν τοῖς ἀνοήτοις καὶ ὡμοιώθη αὐτοῖς, (Man, being in honor, does not last; he is to be compared to the unintelligent beasts and is like them.), and Ecclesiastes 3:18-21 (LXX):

> And I said in my heart concerning the babblings of the sons of men that God is testing them to show that they are but beasts. For the banes of the sons of men and the banes of the beasts are the same. As the death of the one, so is the death of the other, and one breath belongs to all. All things tend to the same place, all things come from dust and all things return to dust. And who knows the spirit of man, whether it goes upward, and the spirit of the beasts, whether it descends into the earth?[34]

This motif enjoyed wide currency in heterodox Christianity. On the basis of Clement of Alexandria, *Strom.* III, 18,102 G. Quispel claims that the use of Ps. 48:13 was a favorite text of the Messalians and that its ascetic application goes back to the Encratite Julius Cassianus:[35]

> If birth is evil, the blasphemers are speaking evilly of the Lord who shared in birth, and evilly of the virgin who gave birth to him...Therefore docetism is to be charged to Cassianas and also to Marcion, and even to Valentinus - (Christ's) body is psychic - since they say: "Man is like the beasts" (Ps. 48:13) when he enters upon wedlock. But it is when a man, heated up with lust, really wants to mount a strange woman for intercourse, then in truth such a man has become a wild beast, "Wild horses have they become, each man neighing after his neighbor's wife." (Jer. 5:8). Cf. also III,9,67.

The likening of man to an unreasoning beast is a theme which also occurs independently of Biblical tradition, for example in the Neoplatonism of the Hermetica:

> The sensations of these men are much like those of the irrational animals, and are a mixture of anger and passion; they do not admire the things worthy of contemplation, paying attention only to the pleasures and appetites of the body, and they believe man has come to be for the sake of these things.[36]

Furthermore, the body of man changes not only because it eats of other bodies, but also because it derives from intercourse, which is not able to produce anything else but this same kind of changeable and perishable body.[37]

The idea developed by the Pre-Socratics, that the invisible is always the same while the visible, typified by the body, is always changing and perishes was most fully developed by Plato:

> "Now," said Socrates, "shall we assume two kinds of existences, one visible, the other invisible?" "Let us assume them," said Cebes. "And that the invisible is always the same and the visible constantly changing?" "Let us assume that also," said he. "Well then," said Socrates, "are we not made up of two parts, body and soul?" "Yes," he replied. "Now to which class should we say the body is more similar and more closely akin?" "To the visible," said he; "that is clear to everyone." "And the soul? Is it visible or invisible?" "Invisible, to man, at least, Socrates." (Phaedo, 79 ab; cf. 79e)[38]

Again:

The body is most like the human and mortal and multi-
form and unintellectual and dissoluble and ever-
changing. (Phaedo, 80b)

and:

The body, which lies in the visible world and which
we call the corpse, which is subject to dissolution
and decomposition... (Phaedo, 80c).

We are therefore dealing with ideas which must have been
well-known in Hellenistic thought. But unlike Platonic and Hermetic tradition, which stressed the more ideal and philosophic
implications of the changeable and perishable nature of the body,
Thomas the Contender stresses the minatory implications of it.
While the former are optimistic in their confidence that the
burden of the body can be overcome by contemplation and exercise
of the mind, in *Thomas the Contender* the reader can only watch
and pray that he will come out of the body with all its passions
(145:8ff). The reader cannot save himself; all he can do is to
deny the body and hope that he is included among the elect who
abandon bestiality (139:28).

As we shall see, the biggest obstacle which bodily life
presents to the reader is that it derives from intercourse, which
on two occasions is condemned. In section A of *Thomas the Contender*, it is said that the body will always be bestial because
it derives from intercourse (139:8-11), and in section B the body
is the subject of a woe: "Woe to you who love intimacy (ουνήθεια)
with anything feminine and the polluted intercourse with it"
(144:8-10). Section B simply offers a blanket castigation of
intercourse, while section A offers a more philosophical condemnation. Here it is condemned because a different sort of thing
(διαφορά) from a beastly body cannot be produced from the intercourse of beasts; it only succeeds in propagating bestiality.

Having given this metaphor of the bestiality of the body to
illustrate what is meant by visible things, the Savior concludes
(139:11f) his speech, "So, therefore, you are babes until you
become perfect (τέλειος)," in exactly the same way as he concluded his immediately preceding speech (138:35f): "Therefore
you are disciples and have not yet received the majesty of the
perfection (τέλειος)." Again, because the conclusion (ⲉⲧⲃⲉ
ⲡⲁⲓ Ⳬⲉ) does not follow from the body of the speech, we regard

the conclusion to the present speech, too, as secondary. In view of the antithesis (ϩⲉⲛⲕⲟⲩⲉⲓ = νήπιοι *vs* τέλειοι) the conclusion probably derives from the New Testament, though a precise citation cannot be determined:

> We will come together...so that we shall no longer be babes tossed and blown about by every wave of doctrine, by the cunning of men, by the craftiness that produces deceitful artifices. (Eph. 4:14).

> For everyone partaking of milk is unexperienced in the word of righteousness, for he is a babe. Solid food is for the perfect, for those having senses trained by practice to distinguish between good and evil. (Heb. 5:13f; cf. 1 Cor. 3:1-3; 1 Pt. 2:2).

Before we go on to Thomas' response, which forms a bridge to the next subject, we should review the teaching of the tractate so far. At the same time we should note that *Thomas the Contender* and the *Gospel of Thomas* treat in order the same subjects:

	Ev. Th.	*Th. C.*
1. Secret words spoken to Judas Thomas	Introd.	138:1f
2. Seek and inquire	Log. 2	138:8, (22ff)
3. Know thyself	Log. 3b	138:8-10
4. Hidden and revealed	Log. 5, 6b	138:19-33
5. Beasts and eating	Log. 7	138:39-139:11

This parallelism of sequence may be accidental, but it is striking enough to notice. There is the possibility that the author of section A of *Thomas the Contender* may have begun with the first few of the Logia of the *Gospel of Thomas* in mind. If these two works attributed to Judas Thomas both originate from the Syrian Osrhoëne, it is hard to see how a work so important as the *Gospel of Thomas* could escape the attention of the author of section A of *Thomas the Contender*. Thus the *Gospel of Thomas*, sharing ideas in common with *Thomas the Contender* could easily have served as an inspiration for the latter work, although the latter work in no sense is a duplication of, or demonstrates extensive borrowing from the former.

Up to this point, the dialogue has centered around soteriology from the perspective of epistemology, the need to know oneself as the key to knowing the All and to know what is visible as the prelude to knowing the invisible. This knowledge is basically anthropocentric, concentrating on one's present condition, e.g. as embodied.

139:12-31. In Thomas' response (139:12-20) to the foregoing
speech of the Savior, we encounter a simile whose function is
to change the subject from a primarily anthropocentric epistemological soteriology to one centered on a redeemer myth.

The simile states that people (excluding the Savior) who
try to explain things which are not visible or revealed
(ΝΕΤΕ Ν̄ϹΕΟΥΟΝϨ ΕΒΟΛ) do not know what they are talking
about. They are like archers who aim or shoot their arrows[39]
at night when they cannot see the target. But when the light
comes and hides the darkness, then the "target," indeed the
work of each (ΠϨⲰⲃ Μ̄ⲡⲟⲩⲁ ⲡⲟⲩⲁ , cf. 1 Cor. 3:13), will appear.[40] This light is then confessed to be the Savior:

and you are our light, since you enlighten, Lord! [41]

The comparison of light with one who speaks the truth,
bringing what is hidden to light is found in the Clementine
Recognitions 8,4:

> It seems to me that those who speak the word of
> truth and who illumine the souls of men are like the
> rays of the sun, which when they have come forth and
> appeared to the world, can no longer be concealed
> or hidden, while they are not so much seen by men
> as they afford sight to all.[42]

In the Clementine parallel, the proof-text is Mt. 5:14f:

> You are the light of the world. A city on a hill
> cannot be hidden. Nor do they light a lamp and put
> it under a bushel, but rather on a lampstand and it
> gives light to everyone in the house.

The entire figure thus applies to those whose task it is
to enlighten others, namely preachers or missionaries. But according to *Thomas the Contender*, without the Savior as light,
they only shoot in the dark.

The subject has thus shifted from the rather Platonic discussion concerning the visible and invisible to a confession of
the Savior's identity. To be sure, he is the one who is to
illumine for everyone the things which are invisible in order
that they can be seen, but of even greater importance is the
fact that he is identical with this revealing light. It is he
who enlightens and dissolves the darkness of the world.

The identification of the Savior with the light that enlightens and disperses the darkness is prominent in the Gospel
of John:

1. It was the true light which enlightens every man (1:9)

2. I am the light of the world. He who follows me will not walk in the darkness. (8:12; cf. 9:5; 12:46)

3. Walk while you have the light, lest the darkness engulf you. He who walks in the darkness knows not where he goes. (12:35)

The Savior's response lets us know explicitly for the first time that the Savior is Jesus, by means of a casual introductory formula to his reply: "Jesus said: 'It is in light that light exists.'" (139:21; cf. 144:37). Therefore we can be certain that we are dealing with Christian, or at least Christianized, material in this section.

The phrase ⲠⲞⲨⲞⲈⲒⲚ ⲈⲨϢⲞⲞⲠ ⲞⲚ ⲠⲞⲨⲞⲈⲒⲚ can mean either that Jesus, as the light, exists in a greater light, perhaps the light-world of the Pleroma, or else that light exists in the Savior, the man of light. The latter concept occurs in the *Gospel of Thomas*, Log. 24:

There is light within a man of light, and he illumines the whole cosmos. If he does not give light, it is dark.

The former concept seems to be expressed by Thomas' next question and the Savior's answer to it (139:22-31):

Lord, why does this visible light which shines in behalf of men rise and set?
The Savior said: "O blessed Thomas, this same visible light shone for your sake not in order that you would remain here, but that you might leave it, and whenever all the elect abandon bestiality, then this light will revert upward to its own essence, and its essence will welcome it, since it was a good servant."

The most illustrative parallel to this concept is contained in the Manichean Kephalaia 67:

Again he spoke to his disciples when he was sitting in the midst of the congregation: Just like the sun, the great Phoster, when he comes in his rising at the time when he is about to shine on the world, spreads his beams on the whole earth, and also when it is about to set, his beams disappear and set, not a single beam is left on the earth, just so it is with me, in the image of the flesh in which I established myself and appeared in the cosmos. But all my sons, the Elect, the righteous, who are mine in every land, are like the beams of the sun. And in the time when I am about to go out of the world and go to the house

of my people, I shall gather all the Elect, who have
believed in me, to that place. I will draw each one
of them to myself at the time of his departure. I
will not leave one of them in darkness. (165:27-166:9)

To this should be compared the redemption scheme of the
Valentinian document *De Resurrectione* from the Jung Codex:

We are his (the Savior's) beams and we are encompassed
by him until our setting, that is, our death from this
life. We are drawn into heaven by him like the beams
(are drawn) by the sun since we are not encompassed
by anything. This is the spiritual resurrection.
(CG I,3: 45:31-39)

In these excerpts from two Gnostic systems, the Savior
(Mani and/or Christ) is compared to the sun which withdraws its
beams from the world when it sets: the Savior as the illuminator
of his elect draws his elect out of the world as he ascends, and
gathers them into the world of light: the idea may be derived
from John 12:32 where ὑψωθῶ refers to both the crucifixion and
resurrection: "And I, if I be elevated from the earth, will draw
all men to myself."

It is thus that Clement of Alexandria interprets the hymn
of Ephesians 5:

He (the Lord) awakes from the sleep of darkness and
raises up those who wander in error. "Awake," he
says, "O sleeper and arise from the dead and he
shall give you light, Christ, the Lord," the sun
of the resurrection "who was born before the morning star," who bestows life by means of his beams.
(Protrepticus IX, 84) [43]

The foregoing illustrations show that the identification
of Jesus with light, whose *locus classicus* is the Gospel of
John, was, for orthodox and heterodox alike, illustrated by the
model of the sun which was thought not only to project its rays
(when it rises), but also to receive them back to itself (when
it sets). If, in *Thomas the Contender*, Jesus is being compared
with the light of the sun, as is suggested by Thomas' use of the
terms rise (ⲡⲣ̄ⲣⲓⲉ) and set (ϩⲱⲧⲡ), then its rising and shining
seems to be a metaphor for the message of redemption, and its
setting the signal of the reception of this message of the elect.
The fact that the light is called a good servant (ὑπηρέτης) recalls the "laborer" terminology applied to the preacher-mission-
ary (cf. the term ἐργάτης, 138:34). It seems that the work of
the light is to be viewed "evangelistically" rather than

metaphysically or substantially, as if the light were attracting, as like to like, light particles back to the light-world. To be sure, the light goes back to its οὐσία, but this seems to refer to the Savior, the good servant, rather than to the souls of the elect who have abandoned bestiality because of the shining of the light. It is quite possible that the term ἀνάλημψις (140:23) is to be interpreted by this motif of the reversion of the light-ray back to its source; the Savior's ascension is a return to the world of light, as in the Gospel of John the Son returns to the Father.

Finally, it should be observed that in section B of *Thomas the Contender*, the light performs, not the function of attracting particles of light back to the world of light, but rather the more preliminary and more restricted function of instigating the dissolution of the body in the same way the sun dissolves the seed to produce a plant or withers the weeds to allow the vine to grow (140:10-18; 144:3-6,21-36).

The fully developed metaphysical model of this scheme of redemption is nicely described in the following sketch of the Manichaean system:

> The liberation, separation, and raising up of
> the parts of light is helped by the praise, the
> sanctification, the pure word and the pious works.
> Thereby the parts of the Light (i.e. the souls of
> the dead) mount up by the pillar of dawn to the
> sphere of the moon, and the moon receives them in-
> cessantly from he first to the middle of the month,
> so that it waxes and gets full, and then it guides
> them to the sun until the end of the month, and
> thus effects its waning in that it is lightened
> of its burden. And in this manner the ferry is
> loaded and unloaded again, and the sun transmits
> the Light to the light above it in the world of
> praise, and it goes on in that world until it
> arrives at the highest and pure Light. The Sun
> does not cease to do this until nothing of the parts
> of the Light is left in this world but a small part
> so bound that sun and moon cannot detach it (this
> the final conflagration will free).[44]

While the rising and setting of the light in *Thomas the Contender* is paralleled by that of the moon in the Manichaean system, *Thomas the Contender* does not call the elect "Light" or "sparks of light," nor does it explicitly mention the sun or the moon. While the sun seems to be presupposed as the *tertium comparationis*, the moon has no part at all in the redemption scheme of *Thomas the Contender*.

139:32-140:6. The Savior's speech is now complemented by a formula of continuation (ⲁⲩⲟⲩⲱϩ ⲉⲧⲟⲟⲧⲩ ⲛ̄ϭⲓ ⲡⲥⲱⲣ ⲡⲁⲭⲉⲩ ⲭⲉ·), a device by which new material is introduced with a minimum of editorial bridging. The bridge with what the Savior has just said consists of two antithetically parallel sentences, the first with the catchword "light" which relates to the foregoing, and the second with the catchword "fire" which introduces the new subject of discourse.

O unsearchable love of the light! (139:32f)	O the bitterness of the fire which burns in the bodies of men and in their marrow! (139:33-35)[45]

Here a basic contrast is established between God's love for man and the bitter passion which burns in man. The second member introduces the major theme of the tractate, namely, the fiery sexual passion which is the major characteristic of the tomb-like body which imprisons men's souls and corrupts them.

Thus far, with the exception of the section on the bestiality of the body, the text has had a positive message, centering on the Thomas tradition, the necessity to know oneself, the task of the missionary, and the mission of the light. Now, however, we will notice that the message becomes negative and extremely minatory, a section containing an apocalyptic scene of punishment. Whereas at first the message of the text was to be commended by the Thomas-twin tradition, we shall see that in what follows, it is to be accepted under the threat of a fiery punishment in Hell.

Fire is the common element between men's embodied predicament and the eventual fate to which that predicament leads. The punishment corresponds in kind to the sin punished; one whose body is enflamed with lust will be punished by fire.

This fire which burns inside men's bodies (139:34; in their "limbs and marrow" is hendiadys) makes them crazy with drunkenness and, although the text is damaged at this point, surely represents the passion by which males and females are impelled towards one another in secret as well as openly (139:38-42). That some such relationship between the fire and males and females must have occupied the lacuna is supported by the Manichaean *Kephalaia* which, by similarity of language (ⲥⲉⲧⲉ, ϩⲁⲩⲧ, ⲥϩⲓⲙⲉ, ⲕⲓⲙ), could indeed have used this section of *Thomas*

the Contender as a source: ⲦⲤⲈⲦⲈ ⲘⲚ [Ⲧ ⲈⲀⲇ ⲟ]ⲛⲏ [ⲈⲦ]ⲟⲨⲏⲌ ⲌⲚ ⲚⲌⲀⲨⲦ
ⲘⲚ ⲚⲤⲌⲒⲀⲘⲈ ⲈⲤⲗⲰⲂⲨ ⲘⲘⲀⲨ ⲀⲌⲟⲨⲚ ⲀⲚⲈⲨⲈⲣⲏⲨ (26:15ff - "the fire
and pleasure which dwell in males and females, enflaming them
for one another"); ⲦⲤⲈⲦⲈ ⲘⲚ ⲦⲌⲎⲀⲟⲚⲏ [ⲈⲦⲟ]Ⲩⲏ[Ⲍ] ⲚⲌⲎⲦⲟⲨ ⲈⲦⲕⲒⲘ
ⲀⲣⲀⲨ ⲀⲌⲟⲨⲚ ⲀⲚⲟⲨⲀⲣⲏⲨ (27:3f - "the fire and pleasure which dwells
in them impelling them to one another").

Fire as a metaphor for passion was wide-spread in the an-
cient world. As one of the four elements earth, air, water, and
fire, fire was understood as essential to animal generation:

> It must be understood that this hot and fiery prin-
> ciple is interfused with the whole of nature such
> that it constitutes the male and female generative
> principles, and thus necessarily causes the birth
> and growth of all animals and things whose roots
> are planted in the earth.[46]

While the philosophic tradition gave fire as the generative
element a positive evaluation, the ascetic tradition, both orthodox and heterodox, tended to view it in a derogatory manner.

The Syrian Makarios distinguishes between fire in the good
sense (akin to the Spirit) and fire in the bad sense. Of the
latter he says:

> And there is an unclean fire which inflames the heart
> and thus overruns all the members and goads men into
> licentiousness and countless evils. And so, stimu-
> lated and gratified within the heart, they end up
> in fornication.[47]

In discussing the old and new birth, the Pseudo-Clementines
oppose the fire of sexual passion to the water of baptism:

> regenerated by water, by good works they extinguish
> the fire of their old birth.[48] For our first birth
> descends through the fire of lust, and thus by
> divine dispensation, this second one is introduced
> by water, which extinguishes the nature of fire.[49]

According to Hippolytus, the Naasenes also conceived of
sexual passion or impulse under the metaphor of fire, as their
exegesis of Is. 41:8 shows:

> You, Israel, are my servant; do not fear. If you pass
> through rivers, they will not overwhelm you. If you
> pass through fire, it will not consume you. "Rivers"
> means the moist substance of generation, and "fire"
> the impulse and lust for generation.[50]

The metaphor of fire as lust is found elsewhere in the Nag
Hammadi Corpus, e.g. the *Teachings of Silvanus* (CG VII,4,108:4-6):
"Do not burn yourself, O miserable one, in the fire of lust."

The Hermetica also employ the metaphor of fire, but to express man's appetites in general, rather than simply sexual passion. In the *Poimandres* (Ch I, 23), Poimandres, the *Nous*, says that he is far removed from godless men:

. . . giving way to the avenging demon, who, applying the sharpness of fire impregnates (sic. θρώσκει; read τιτρώσκει, "pierces"?) him in his senses and arms him the more for lawless deeds, such that a greater punishment meets him. And this man does not cease holding onto the desire for boundless appetites, struggling blindly without end. And this torments him and heaps all the more fire upon him.[51]

The Rabbis apparently could conceive of the evil inclination as a fire. In the tractate *Kiddushin* 81a it is probably the evil inclination which R. Amram conjures out of himself: "Then it went out of him in the guise of a pillar of fire. Then he said: 'I perceive that thou art fire, and I am flesh; but I am stronger than thou.'"[52]

The metaphor of fire abounds in later works on chastity and virginity, where we encounter such language as:

Thus the flame of resuscitated lust recalled them into the glowing heats of bygone youth. . . although the blood, still inexperienced, grows hot and stimulates the natural fires and the blind flames that stir in the marrow to seek a remedy.[53]

In the Pseudo-Titus Epistle:

O flames of lust!. . . O exhalations of the flesh! The glowing fire hidden deep in the heart nourishes a conflagration!. . . Thou canst not expect to bind glowing coals on thy garment and not set the robe alight.[54]

In the face of the widespread use of the metaphor of fire for sexual passion, one cannot expect to find a specific source from which this metaphor in *Thomas the Contender* is drawn. Nevertheless, there can be no mistaking that "fire" stands for sexual ἡδονή and ἐπιθυμία in the pejorative sense. This fire has total control over those who succumb to it (140:22-37) and, correspondingly, is the ultimate instrument of punishment[55] used in Hell by the Tartarouchos (142:42-143:4) and founds Hell on three points of the compass (143:2-4). The fire burning in men makes them crazy and drunk (143:27) and blind (140:2-5); it is insatiable (143:16) and inextinguishable (144:15). To judge from what remains of the text in the lacuna, it is the fire which is responsible for agitating men and women (139:38-42).

The Savior concludes this exclamation of the bitterness of the fire with a piece of advice, the first part of which appears to be some sort of wisdom saying: "Everyone who seeks the truth from the truly wise one (ⲧⲥⲁⲃⲏ ⲙⲙⲏⲉ) will make himself wings in order to fly, fleeing from the lust (ἐπιθυμία) which burns the spirits of men. And he will make himself wings to flee from every visible spirit."

The wisdom saying, "Everyone who seeks the truth from the truly wise one will make himself wings to fly," is peculiar in that the expression "the truly wise one" is feminine in gender, reminding us of personified wisdom, Sophia. Yet Sophia never figures elsewhere in the tractate. The Coptic Gnostic tractates almost always use the Greek noun σοφία to describe the heavenly being, pre-existent with the father, who descends to the earth revealing Gnosis to men and making them spiritual before her reascent. The noun σοφία occurs at 140:15, but in the general sense of the wise man being perfect in all σοφία. Elsewhere, we find only such expression as ⲥⲟⲫⲟⲥ and ⲣⲙⲛ̄ϩⲏⲧ ("wise" or "discerning" man) both of which are masculine: "Since it is impossible for a wise man (ⲣⲙⲛ̄ϩⲏⲧ) to dwell with (or: answer)[56] a fool, for the wise man (ⲥⲟⲫⲟⲥ) is perfect in all wisdom (σοφία). To the fool, however, the good and the bad are one and the same, for the wise man (σοφός) will be nourished by the truth..." (140:15f). Thus we are led to understand the term "wise one" in a more general sense, not in that of the gnostic Sophia myth, but probably in that of the Hellenistic-Jewish hypostatization of wisdom such as is found in Proverbs, Sirach, and in the λόγος-wisdom of Philo, etc.

The gnomic style of this sentence (140:1ff) leads us to expect it to derive from a proverb. Unfortunately no such proverb is known to me. The only notable occurrence of the motif of flight from lust I can find is in Philo's tractate *Legum allegoria* III, 14f where Jacob, his name not yet having been changed to Israel, flees from Laban, who symbolizes perceivable material things:

> For instance, if having seen beauty you are captivated by it, and you are about to get tripped up over it, secretly flee from its sight...for in such cases safety consists in secret flight.[57]

Thus, although there can be no case of dependency, the motif of flight from lust and from visible spirits appears to belong to the sphere of paraenesis in general.

The metaphor of wings which are possessed by the one who consults wisdom is more widespread than the motif of flight. In his discussion of immortality and reincarnation in the *Phaedrus* (249c) Plato supposes that it is the mind of a philosopher which becomes winged and so escapes the 10,000-year cycle of reincarnation; by the recollection (μνήμη) of divine things and separation from the merely human, he becomes truly perfect. To be winged is to dwell with the gods, but the soul which loses its wings settles down into an earthly body (246c,d).

For Philo, those souls who are neither attracted to material things nor to mortal life, and who

> observe the great folly of it (mortal life), call the
> body a dungeon, even a tomb, and fleeing as from a
> prison or grave are lifted above on light wings to-
> wards the aether and range the heights forever.[58]

The collocation of wings and flight is apparently a metaphor of Hellenistic paraenesis usually applied to the denial of or abstinence from the material bodily things of life, and may derive ultimately from Plato. But in *Thomas the Contender* the metaphor can be reversed, for there are also "some with wings who rush to visible things, things which are far from the truth" (140:18f). These are the opposite of the man instructed by wisdom. Rather than fleeing lust and material things, they are attracted to them like insects to a candle in the evening: "For that which leads them, the fire, will give them an appearance (φαντασία) of truth" (140:20f). Philo of Alexandria exhibits both applications of the metaphor of flight in his *Questions and Answers in Genesis* (Armenian version, Ralph Marcus, trans., Loeb Library). On Gen. 27:39 he says:

> But let all thanks be given to a gracious and
> beneficent one who does not permit the mind to be
> emptied and bereft of an excellent and most divine
> form when it descends into an earthly body and is
> burned by the necessities and flames of desire, for
> these are a true Tartarus, but he permits it to
> spread its wings sometimes and to behold heaven
> above and taste of that sight. For there are some
> who through gluttony, lechery, or over-indulgence
> are always submerged or sunken, being drowned in
> passion. And these wicked men do not wish to raise
> themselves up. (*Quest. and Ans. Gen.* IV, 234)

140:6-18. These two passages, the one about those who have
wings to flee (140:1-5) and the one about those who have wings
to flee to visible things (140:18f), may have appeared one after
the other in the material from which this tractate has been composed. This supposition is strengthened by Thomas' reply to the
Savior's saying about the man who has wings to flee lust and
visible spirits:

> And Thomas answered, saying: "Lord, this indeed
> is what I am asking you about, since I have under-
> stood that you are the one who is good for us, as
> you say." (140:5-8)

Now the Savior has said nothing of the sort; Thomas'
response does not follow from the Savior's previous speech, nor
from anything he has previously said in the tractate. Nor in
fact does the Savior's ensuing reply to Thomas' statement follow
from what Thomas said, in spite of the ⲉⲧⲃⲉ ⲡⲁⲓ ("therefore"):

> Therefore it is necessary for *us* (sic!) to speak
> to you, for this is the doctrine for the perfect. If,
> then, you desire to be perfect you must observe these
> things; if not, your name is "Ignorant," since it is
> impossible for a wise man to answer (or: "dwell with")
> a fool, for the wise man is perfect in all wisdom
> (σοφία). To the fool, however, the good and the bad
> are the same. For the wise man will be nourished by
> the truth and will become like a tree growing by the
> meandering stream (or "torrent"). (140:8-18)

Besides the fact that this is not a conclusion to Thomas'
affirmation of the Lord's goodness, we are also in the dark as
to the identity of "these things" which Thomas is to observe.
The entire passage appears to be a collocation of two originally
separate themes, that of becoming perfect, and that of the wise
man. It is difficult to see how the theme of perfection has
again crept in (mentioned much earlier in 138:35f), unless
through attraction by the theme of seeking truth from the truly
wise one (140:1f); the theme of the wise man is clearly connected
with that of 140:1f, that of seeking truth from the truly wise
one (Sophia?). It may have been that these themes of perfection
and of the wise man originally followed one another in a source
used by the author of *Thomas the Contender* and that he has lifted
the whole and inserted it within an originally unified passage
employing the metaphor of wings:

```
originally  ⎧ 140:5b-8a  (the Lord is good)⎫   140:1-5 (wings)    ⎫origi-
a unity?    ⎨ 140:8a-12  (perfection)       ⎬        ⎬            ⎬nally a
            ⎩ 140:13-18a (the wise man)     ⎭   140:18b-20 (wings)⎭unity
```

The identity of such a source may not be irrecoverable,
however. While we have observed that the passage in Plato's
Phaedrus (249c) may have been the ultimate source for the metaphor of the wise man who has wings, it may not be too farfetched
that the same passage in the *Phaedrus* may also have been the ultimate source of inspiration in connecting the theme of the wise
man's wings with that of perfection. For, having just said that
only the mind of the philosopher has wings to ascend into com-
munion with God, he continues:

> Now a man who employs such memories rightly is always
> being initiated into perfect mysteries and he alone
> becomes perfect (τέλεος). . . . separating himself from
> human interests and observing the divine. (249c,d)

It is just possible that this continuation inspired the splitting
of the "wings-source" and the insertion of the discussion about
perfection.

The material which we suppose to be inserted consists of
Thomas' response plus the Savior's declaration about the perfect
wise man. Thomas' response, like his declaration that Jesus is
the light, is a confession which the reader of the tractate must
also affirm if he wants to become perfect. When he says "that
indeed is what I am asking you about," the reader is informed
that the central message of the tractate has to do with the
necessity (and wisdom!) of fleeing the fire of sexual lust which
burns in one's body. The ensuing confession, "since I was aware
that you are the one who is good for us, as you said," even
though it does not follow from anything the Savior has said, has
the effect of closely relating the Savior to the "truly wise
one." As Thomas consults the Savior (perhaps he through whom
the truly wise one speaks, concerning the plight of a soul imprisoned in a lustful body) the reader too is directed to the
statements of the Savior for the answer to his own similar
plight.

That Thomas' statement has been placed here in order to
point out the crucial point of the tractate is confirmed by the
Savior's response when he says, "Therefore it is necessary for
us to speak to you, for *this* is the doctrine of the perfect."

That the Savior, who hardly ever refers to himself, and then
only in the first person singular, here refers to himself in
the first person plural, is either an instance of the royal
self-reference "we" (cf. 1 Jn. 1:1), or else a conscious literary device. If it is a literary device, it is possible that 1)
"us" refers to the Savior and to the "truly wise one," 2) "us"
refers to the Savior and to Thomas, or 3) "us" was in a source
copied by the scribe. Thomas' previous declaration that the
Savior is the one who is good for us has, as we said, the effect
of identifying the Savior and the truly wise one, or at least
closely conjoining them, in which case 1) is correct. On the
other hand, in view of Thomas' immediately preceding confession
and commendation of the Savior before the reader of the tractate,
it is attractive to understand the "us" as a literary device
which does not refer to the Savior as addressing Thomas, but
rather collectively refers to both Thomas and the Savior as
addressing the reader of the tractate. This second alternative
becomes even more attractive when we note that we are still in
the section of the tractate in which Thomas is addressed in the
plural "you," as if he were the representative of a larger group.
Only here the sense would be: "Therefore it is necessary for us
(that is, Thomas and the Savior, and indeed the author of the
tractate) to speak to you (the readers of this tractate), for
this is the doctrine of the perfect. If you desire to become
perfect, you (the readers) will observe these things; if not,
your name is 'stupid.'" If this solution is too far-fetched,
then we are reduced to concluding that "us" lay in some source
used by the scribe, and has no particular significance.

At any rate, we have been alerted that the doctrine of the
perfect is to follow the Savior's advice and flee the burning
lust of the body, and in fact every visible (i.e. this-worldly)
entity. If one does not observe these things, he is a stupid
fool, and will not be able to dwell with the wise man perfect
in all wisdom (who presumably is the Savior).

The gnomic sentences about the wise man and the fool are
probably not to be found in any extant collections of words of
the wise, but they certainly conform to the message of the wisdom books of the Septuagint. Whether the reading be "the wise
man cannot dwell with a fool" (ⲟⲩⲱϩ ⲙⲛ̄·) or "cannot answer
(ⲟⲩⲱϣⲙ ⲛ̄·) a fool," there is enough evidence in the Book of

Proverbs to show that the necessity of a wise man to have nothing
to do with a fool was an important notion of the wisdom tradition
(cf. Prov. 14:7; 23:9; 26:4; cf. Philo, *De mut. nom.* 37).

While the wise man is perfect in all wisdom (or: "is per-
fecting all wisdom," ⳓϫⲏⲕ ⲉⲃⲟⲗ ⲛ̄ⲥⲟⲫⲓⲁ ⲛⲓⲙ), the fool doesn't
know the difference between good and evil. According to
Hebrews 5:14, this is the distinction between the perfect and
the immature: "Solid food is for the perfect, who possess facul-
ties trained by habit to distinguish good from bad."

Thus we are in the sphere of Hellenistic Jewish wisdom
morality which thinks of wisdom as the nourishment of the wise.
The theme of the types of nourishment is popular in the New Testament (I Cor. 3:1-3; Heb. 5:12-14; I Pt. 2:2); solid food is
for the perfect. According to *Thomas the Contender* the nourishment of the wise man is "the truth" (ⲧⲙⲏⲉ). That we have to do
with Jewish wisdom tradition is confirmed by the only definite
literal quotation to be found in *Thomas the Contender*, from
Psalm 1:3, a wisdom psalm. The (wise) man who has meditated on
the Lord's law

ἔσται ὡς τὸ ζύλον	ⳓⲛⲁϣⲱⲡⲉ ⲛ̄ⲑⲉ ⲙ̄ⲡϣⲏⲛ
τὸ πεφυτευμένον παρὰ	ⲉⲧⲣⲏⲧ ϩⲓϫⲛ̄
τὰς διεξόδους τῶν ὑδάτων	ⲡⲙⲟⲩ ⲛ̄ⲥⲱⲣⲙ

The section under discussion (140:6-18) appears to be not
only an insertion into a previously unified section dealing with
the fire of lust and the use of wings to escape it (139:23-140:5)
or to submit to it (140:18-37, yet to be treated), but also a
pastiche of motifs from Hellenistic-Jewish wisdom influenced by
the Septuagint (the wisdom books and Psalm 1). The motivation
behind such an assertion would be to provide an interpretation
of the saying about making wings to flee lust; this is the doctrine of the perfect, the way to escape evil, the way to increase
through nourishment by the truth.

140:18-37. According to our analysis, this section is actually
the second half of the Savior's speech begun at 139:33, but which
was interrupted by the section on wisdom and perfection (140:5-
18). The theme is the obverse of the previous application of the
metaphor about wings: While there are some who have wings to flee
the lust burning in their bodies, and flee visible spirits (140:
1-5), there are also those "who have wings to rush upon (ⲡⲱⲧ ϩⲓϫⲛ̄)
the things that are visible, things far from the truth (140:18-20).

The reason that these people, unlike the wise man who is nourished by the truth, rush to things far from the truth is that they are led (ⲬⲓⲘⲟⲉⲓⲧ) by the fire which gives them an "illusion of truth" (ⲫⲁⲛⲧⲁⲥⲓⲁ Ⲙ̄Ⲙⲏⲉ).[59] The reason that the fire attracts men to the visible is that it shines on them with a beauty which will perish (140:22), while the Savior shines as the true light from the substance of the light above (139:20-31). The light given by fire is a material, earthly light which will sooner or later be extinguished, but the light of the Savior comes from the world above. In this metaphor the fire represents not only lustful passions of the body, but all material visible things, including the body. The fire gives the kind of light by which the senses of the body perceive, so that those who are guided by the fire cannot see true reality. Their souls are imprisoned in dark sweetness (140:23f); seized with aromatic ἡδονή (140:24), blinded with insatiable desire (140:25),[60] nailed fast with a stake (140:26-28), jerked about by a bit (χαλινός) in the mouth, (cf. the myth of Timarchus in Plutarch's *De genio Socratis*, 592; also Plato, *Phaedrus* 256), fettered with chains (140:30f), and bound by bitter lust for the perishable things of the earth (140:31-37).

The plight of such men's souls is much like that of philosophy, which, according to Plato (*Phaedo* 82E-83E), when it first takes possession of the soul, is welded (προσκεκολλημένη) to the body and compelled to σκοπεῖσθαι τὰ ὄντα as through prison bars (διὰ εἱργμοῦ) and thus wallows in ignorance. Philosophy sees that the worst thing about this imprisonment is ὅτι δι' ἐπιθυμίας ἐστίν. It is necessary that ἡ τοῦ ὡς φιλοσόφου ψυχὴ οὕτως ἀπέχεται τῶν ἡδονῶν τε καὶ ἐπιθυμιῶν since:

> Each pleasure and pain nails it (the soul) as with a nail to the body and rivets it and makes it corporeal, accepting as true whatever the body says.

And these pleasures and pains compel the soul to believe that visible objects (τὰ ὁρατά) are reality (ἐναργέστατόν τε εἶναι καὶ ἀληθέστατον).

In *Thomas the Contender* this is precisely the function of the fire considered as the passion which burns in men's bodies. It makes men think that visible things are reality, whereas in fact they are only illusions of truth (ⲫⲁⲛⲧⲁⲥⲓⲁ Ⲙ̄Ⲙⲏⲉ). And because of this there is hardly a ray of hope to escape this

predicament since they are caught by it and will *never*[61] escape
it. The passage thus ends by saying that the lust for visible
and changeable things (the body and its lusts) will always drag
them down to earth (the visible realm), which means their death
and corruption (140:32-37).[62] To this should be compared the
following statement of Socrates:

> And, my friend; one must believe it (the corpor-
> eal) to be burdensome and heavy and earthly and visible.
> And such a soul is weighed down and dragged back into
> the visible sphere through fear of the invisible and
> of Hades, and, as it is said, flits about the graves
> and tombs around which shadowy shapes of souls have
> been seen, such souls as produce shades; these were
> not set free in purity, but retain something of the
> visible, and thus they are seen.[63]

It seems an inescapable conclusion that the author of *Thomas
the Contender* is ultimately dependent on Plato at this point in
his discussion of the fiery lust of the body which causes the
soul such grief. While there is no case of literal citation,
and while Plato does not apply the metaphor of fire to the bodily
lusts, the similarity in motif, language ("dragged," "visible,"
"lust," "pleasure") and metaphor (imprisonment, blinding of perception, being nailed fast, movement from above to below, etc.)
is striking enough to conclude that motifs that occur in Plato's
Phaedo have reached the pen of the author of Section A of *Thomas
the Contender*. While it is not likely that he read the *Phaedo*,
it is easily possible that motifs occurring in the *Phaedo* were
passed on to him or to his community *via* the work of the Alex-
andrian Platonists, such as Philo, Clement and Origen.

140:37-141:4. The next section, introduced by Thomas' response
to the Savior's bitter description of the plight of the soul imprisoned in the body with its fiery lust, again seems to be a
transition point changing the subject from the damage which the
fire of ἐπιθυμία does to the soul to that of the soul and its
rest. We are not at liberty to make any firm judgments about
this section since nearly half of it lies in a lacuna, breaking
the train of thought. All that can be deduced is that Thomas
responds by making a common observation (ⲩⲟⲩⲟⲛⲍ ⲉⲃⲟⲗ ⲁⲩⲱ ⲁⲩⲭⲟⲟ⟨ⲥ⟩
ⲭⲉ⁄, "it is apparent and is said that") having to do with the
soul (ψυχή, 140:40) in relation to those who are not aware of
something (ⲛ̄ⲛⲉⲧⲉ ⲛ̄ⲥⲉⲥⲟⲟⲩⲛ ⲁ̣ⲛ̣.. 140:39). The Savior answers
this observation (ⲁⲩⲟⲩⲱⲱ̣ⲃ ⲇⲉ ⲛ̄ϭⲓ must be continued by ⲡⲥⲱⲣ

since there follows material to which Thomas again responds in
141:2) by some kind of proverb or gnomic utterance which may
derive from wisdom tradition (ⲡⲥⲁⲃⲉ ⲛ̄ⲣⲱⲙⲉ ⲛ̄ⲧⲁⲩ·. . . "the
wise man who. . .) The saying concerns a wise man who did something (lies in the lacuna) and then "after he found it he rested
himself on it forever and was unafraid of those who wanted to
disturb him." The mention of "finding" suggests the popular
theme of seeking and finding (e.g. Luke 15, Gospel of Thomas
Log. 2;92;94; Philo, *De fuga et inven.* 120-176, esp. 126-142).
This recalls the theme of the man who has sought the truth from
the truly wise one (140:1f) and then flees all lust and every
visible spirit. Thus the following restoration of 140:41f is
probable:

> ⲛⲁⲉⲓⲁⲧⲩ ⲙ̄ⲡⲥⲁⲃⲉ ⲛ̄ⲣⲱⲙⲉ ⲛ̄ⲧⲁⲩ[ⲩⲓ]
> [ⲛⲉ ⲛ̄ⲥⲁ ⲧⲙⲏⲉ ⲁⲩⲱ ⲛ̄ⲧ]ⲁⲣⲉⲩϭⲛ̄ⲧϥ̄ ⲁ ⲩ ⲙⲧⲟ ⲛ . . .

> [Blessed (?) is] the wise man who [sought after the truth
> and] after he found it he rested on it forever. . .

Whatever it is the wise man seeks and finds and rests upon,
it is named by a feminine noun, is something he can rest upon
forever in security, and as Thomas' ensuing response implies has
something to do with resting "among our own" (people?). It also
has something to do with the soul and "those who do not know"
something about their soul. Taken together, these hints suggest
something like the truth which, once discovered, proves to be an
abiding secure reality. Something like the truth would be guaranteed of lasting into the future, since the Savior's next speech
is highly apocalyptic both literarily and in terms of content,
treating of the future destruction of the body. Whatever it is
that the wise man seeks and finds, it is clear from Thomas'
response that its salient feature has to do with eternal rest
(ⲙ̄ⲧⲟⲛ in the sense of ἀνάπαυσις) among one's fellows.

Our supposition that it is "the truth" which is sought,
found and rested upon also receives partial confirmation from
the Valentinian document *De Resurrectione* from the Jung Codex
(CG I,3, 43:35-44:2). Unlike those who falsely speculate about
the resurrection and who thus:

> seek their own rest, which we have received through
> our Savior, our Lord Christ, we have received it
> (rest) after we had known the truth and rested our-
> selves upon it.

In *Thomas the Contender*, the "truth" (ⲧⲙⲏⲉ) comes from the
"truly wise one" (140:2) and whoever finds it flees from lust.
The opposite of the "truth" is the fire, which only gives men an
"illusion (φαντασία) of the truth" (140:21) and beguiles them
into the life of lust. The "truth" provides a "rest" for the
soul, while the fire provides "disturbance" (ⲱⲧⲟⲣⲧⲣ̄, 141:2).
Nourished by the truth, the wise man is secure, "like the tree
growing by the meandering stream" (140:16f). This "rest" is
apparently a cessation of anxiety about death and the afterlife,
and a present anticipation of a new life.[64] The "rest," according to section B, is conferred by the good One (ⲡⲧⲟⲟⲧⲋ̄ ⲙ̄ⲡⲁⲅⲁⲑⲟⲥ
145:13f), although in section A, it is a state made possible by
finding the "truth." To be compared is Clement of Alexandria,
Stromateis II 9,45.5: ("He who seeks will not cease till he
find, having found he will wonder, having wondered he will reign,
and having reigned he will rest"), and also the *Gospel of Thomas*
Log. 2 ("He who seeks, let him not cease seeking till he find,
and when he finds he will be troubled (ⲱⲧⲟⲣⲧⲣ̄), and being
troubled, he will be amazed, and he will reign over the All.").

Finally, this rest is to take place among "our own," i.e.
kindred souls, who have found the truth, the distinction between
the truly wise one (σοφία) and the fire, between "the good and
the bad" (140:15f) which the fool doesn't recognize. As for
Thomas' response (ⲥⲣ̄ⲛⲟⲩⲣⲉ ⲛⲁⲛ ⲡⲁⲟⲉⲓⲥ ⲁⲙⲧⲟⲛ ⲙ̄ⲙⲟⲛ ⲍ̄ⲛ ⲛⲉⲧⲉ ⲛⲱⲛ ⲛⲉ)
we cannot tell by the grammar whether he is making the statement
"it is good for us, Lord, to rest among our own," or asking the
Savior whether it is good to rest among our own. However, in
view of the vocative ⲡⲁⲟⲉⲓⲥ ("O Lord") and the Savior's response
ⲡⲉⲧⲣ̄ⲱⲁⲩ ⲅⲁⲣ ⲡⲉ , "Yes,[65] it is useful" it seems best to take
Thomas' response as a question. The precise reference of "our
own" is indeterminate; presumably it refers to those wise men,
who like Thomas, have found the truth, and have not been beguiled
by the fire. They will all dwell together in rest among the
fellows while those beguiled by the fire will be gathered back
to that which is visible (141:11); the wise cannot dwell with
the fool (140:13).

141:4-18. Unlike some responses of the Savior to Thomas' questions this particular response constitutes a good response, by
directly answering what is probably a direct question. The response is both minatory and apocalyptic: it is a good thing to

rest eternally among "one's own" because the σκεῦος of the flesh which is visible will dissolve and come to be among the visible things, presumably corpses or the like.

Again, this response of the Savior seems to be a composite of materials; 141:9-14 seems to introduce material of a different kind into the larger block 141:4-18. Indeed the section itself (141:9-14) does not seem to be a unity:

> The Savior said: "Yes (γάρ) it is useful. And it is good for you since things visible among men will dissolve. For the vessel of their flesh will dissolve and when it comes to naught it will come to be among the visible things, among things that are seen. (141:4-9)

> And then the fire that they see will give them pain on account of the love of the faith that they formerly possessed (141:9-11).

> They will be gathered back (πάλιν) to that which (or: the one who) is visible. But as for those who see among the things that are not visible, without the first love they will be destroyed by the concern for this life and (by) the burning of the fire (141:11-14).

> Only a little time until that which (or: the one who) is visible dissolves; then formless εἴδωλα will arise and in the midst of the tombs they will dwell over the corpses forever in pain and destruction of soul. (141:14-18).[66]

This structuring of the content is suggested by the fact that the main topic seems to be the dissolution of the flesh into the corpse (141:4-9, 14-18, apparently a unity) into which intervening material introduces the theme of love - "the love of the faith" and "the first love" (cf. Rev. 2:4) - and reintroduces the theme of the fire. Furthermore, after the first section (141:11-14) is introduced by the phrase "they will be gathered back to that which is manifest" (141:11) in an effort to relate what follows (141:12-14) back to the larger block (141:4-9, 14-18) encompassing the inserted material, and in particular to the phrase "come to be among the visible things, among things that are seen" (141:8).

The use within the inserted material of the term "love of
the faith" (ⲧⲁⲅⲁⲡⲏ ⲛ̄ⲧⲡⲓⲥⲧⲓⲥ) and "first love" (ⲧⲩ̄ⲟⲣⲡ ⲛ̄ⲁⲅⲁⲧⲏ,
cf. Rev. 2:4) tends to give the whole block a Christian flavor,
while the mention of fire tends to relate the whole block to the
"fire" theme of the entire dialogue. That the complete prediction of the dissolution of the body is to be understood in relation to the fire (or lust) as well as in relation to Christian
tradition is demonstrated by the following phrase from the second
section (141:11-14) of the inserted material: "without the first
love they will perish in the concern for this life and (for) the
burning of the fire." The first half of the phrase "without the
first love they will perish in the concern for this life" supplies
through its New Testament terminology (ⲁⲝⲛ̄ ⲧⲩ̄ⲟⲣⲡ ⲛ̄ⲁⲅⲁⲡⲏ; cf. Rev.
2:4 τὴν ἀγάπην σου τὴν πρώτην ἀφῆκες, and ⲥⲉⲛⲁⲧⲁⲕⲟ ϩⲙ̄ ⲡⲣⲟⲟⲩⲩ
ϩ̄ⲡⲃⲓⲟⲥ, cf. the interpretation of the parable of the sower, Mk.
4:19 par., where the seeds sown among the thorns are those who
first hear the word, but αἱ μερίμναι τοῦ αἰῶνος choke the word)
a Christian flavor to the whole. The second half certainly refers to the concern for the body's desires under the metaphor of
fire, and could, by such association, be meant to refer again to
Mk. 4:19, αἱ περὶ τὰ λοιπὰ ἐπιθυμίαι εἰσπορευόμεναι by way of the
fleshly body to corrupt the soul.

Having said that the entire block has a Christian flavor and
that it refers also to the fire of passion, we must ask what sort
of material is it that is placed in such a context? The answer
to this is that the encompassing material (141:4-9, 14-18), which
when placed together reads as a unity, appears, like other material in section A of *Thomas the Contender* ultimately to derive
from or be inspired by Plato's *Phaedo*. For the sake of convenience we repeat part of the passage quoted above in the commentary on *Thomas the Contender* 140:18-37 above, and continue with
the remainder:

> And, my friend, one must believe it (the cor-
> poreal) to be burdensome and heavy and earthly and
> visible. And such a soul is weighed down and is
> dragged back into the visible sphere through fear of
> the invisible and of Hades, and, as it is said, flits
> about the graves and the tombs around which shadowy
> shapes of souls have been seen, such souls as pro-
> duce shades; these were not set free in purity, but
> return something of the visible; and thus they are
> seen. . . and these are not at all the souls of the
> good, but those of the base, which are compelled to

wander around such places to pay the penalty for their
former evil style of life. And they wander about such
a place until through the desire of the hounding cor-
poreal, they are (again) imprisoned in the body.[67]

141:18-25. Thomas' response is one of alarm at the Savior's
description of the fate of the fleshly body. He responds with
a series of questions which center on the theme of his missionary
task (see above). The series is introduced by the diatribe formula such as is used by Paul, e.g. in Romans 3:5; 4:1; 7:7; 8:31;
9:14,30: τί (οὖν) ἐροῦμεν = ον πετε ογῆτληϥ λχοοϥ (141:29f). The
use of a series of questions to introduce a discourse is known in
other dialogues of the Savior with his disciples: e.g. *The Letter
of Peter to Philip* (CG VIII,2, 134:20-135:2, questions by disciples), *The Sophia Jesu Christi* (BG 8502 79:15-18, by the Savior;
117:13-17, by a disciple), *The Thought of Our Great Power* (CG VI,
4, 36:30-37:2, a series of rhetorical questions answered by the
speaker; not a dialogue), *The Apocryphon of James* (CG I,1, 15:
30-34, questions by disciples; this is a dialogue reported in
epistolary form), and the *Dialogue of the Savior* (CG III,5, 126:
6-8, 18-20, by disciples). The examples within this literature
of questions such as "What will we do or say in the face of these
things, etc.?" are very frequent. The questions which Thomas
asks the Savior are designed to heighten the sense of danger in
which those who are unaware of the Savior's teaching exist. As
such they are "blind men," "miserable mortals," who only plead
excuses for the state in which they are. They are bound by the
flesh without realizing that it is a lustful prison within which
blazes the fire of passion. They claim innocence by saying: "We
came to do good and not for cursing," as Paul enjoins the Romans
to act in the face of persecutors: εὐλογεῖτε τους διώκοντας (ὑμᾶς,
ℵ, A, D, etc.), εὐλογεῖτε καὶ μὴ καταρᾶσθε, Rom. 12:14). Yet at
the same time they also betray their lustful predicament by plead-
ing that if they hadn't been born in the flesh, they would never
have experienced the fire. Taken together, these two claims
placed in the mouth of these men tends to equate them with ordinary mortal men; in fact, if their first claim is a reflection of
Romans 12:14, the miserable mortals could be Christians who have
no idea that they are doing anything else than what is good, but
their second claim belies their innocence by revealing their
awareness of the fire of lust. They conform with the Pauline in-
junction by doing good and not cursing, but since they do not admit

157

the reality of their passions, they are not true ascetics who
know that they must avoid the fiery passion of the body. Unfortunately, no more corroborating evidence is available as to the
identity of the miserable mortals, and although the hints of
their identity contained in this passage point to non-ascetic
Christians who do not reject the body, we can only regard this
identification as a guess. If the identification happens to be
correct, the ensuing speech of the Savior shows that their good
intentions are worth nothing, but are rather a cause of blind-
ness to their animal-like existence and eventual consignment to
Hell.

141:25-142:2. The Savior responds to Thomas' series of questions
with a bitter condemnation of those people who are unaware of the
plight of embodiment. He does so in language which refers the
reader to the discussion about the bestiality of the visible body
(139:5-11). At the same time the reader finds that Thomas is
suddenly addressed again in the second person singular ("thou"):

> The Savior said: "Truly as for those (men) do not
> esteem them for thyself as men, but regard them as
> beasts. For just as the beasts devour one another,
> so also men of this sort devour one another." (141:25-29)

The meaning of this simile is unclear, since it is hard to
imagine what sort of men would devour one another, unless we
take this as an (unlikely) reference to cannibalism. We are re-
minded of the similar statement of 139:2f about bodies which are
visible: "but these bodies which are visible eat from creatures
which are like them." If it is fair to interpret our current
text in the light of this previous statement, to say that men
"devour one another" is another way of saying that they are like
beasts who devour one another (in the sense that these men eat
other bodies, bodies of beasts). This may mean as little as the
modern "dog eat dog" as a metaphor for baseness, but it is also
worth wondering whether, beside the condemnation of sex, we may
possibly have the condemnation of eating meat, presumably because
by eating meat these men think that their existence derives from
their bodily nourishment. In the earlier discussion of bestiality, it was said that "those who are above live from their own
root and it is their fruit which nourishes them," while the
visible bodies eat from other creatures. Thus it seems that
Thomas the Contender is written, among other things, to counsel

not only abstinence from sex, but also from meats, since these only serve to enslave man to his body and blind him to the nourishment brought by the light which shines until "the elect (the abstinent) abandon bestiality" (139:28f) and come out of "this place," the world of embodied life (139:25-27).

A hint of a similar polemic lies in the Latin Hermetic tractate *Asclepius* (a portion of which was found in the Nag Hammadi Corpus, CG VI,8, 65:15-78:43):

> When God, the Father and Lord, after he had made the gods, made man from the divine and from more corrupt portions of matter, weighed out in equal measure, evils inherent in matter were mixed with the body permanently, and other evils entered in because of food, which we necessarily require in common with all animals; from these factors it necessarily follows that lustful passions and the remaining evil inclinations find place in the human soul.[68]

Although we have what seems to be reference to abstention from meats, it is clear that the central thrust of the Savior's speech is not bestiality in relation to either cannibalism or abstention from meats, but bestiality in the sense of possessing a lustful body which is deprived of sight.[69] At this point the metaphors of bestiality and fire are explicitly brought together. These men are beasts, who devour one another in a blind (?) fashion since they love the sweetness of the fire, are servants of death and rush to the works of corruption. Bestiality and lust are similarly connected in the *Teachings of Silvanus*, another Nag Hammadi tractate:

> For it is better not to live than to acquire the life of a beast. Watch yourself lest you are burned with the fire (ⲥⲟⲧⲉ) of fornication. For there are many archers (ⲛ̄ⲣⲉϥⲭⲁⲗⲕ̄ ⲥⲟⲧⲉ) who are its servants.[70]

The fact is, that the fire of lust enslaves men, and entraps them in the same chain of sexual procreation within which they were also begotten. Therefore, these innocent men who are unaware of the danger of the flesh succeed only in "fulfilling the lust of their fathers" (141:32). Such an idea is known in the Manichaean *Kephalaia*, where the chain of the lust which fills the world is traced back to Adam and Eve:

> They formed Adam and Eve, and they begot in order that they might rule the cosmos through them. They completed all the works of lust upon the earth, and the whole cosmos was filled with their lust.[71]

Because of this endless cycle of lust, the fate of such men is to be "thrown down to the abyss," to be "afflicted (μαστιγοῦν) by the torment (or: compulsion, ἀνάγκη) of the bitterness of their evil nature (φύσις). Since the speech is about those who intended to do good, but who must admit that, because they have come to be in the flesh, they have succumbed to the fire (141:23-25), we must conclude that being caught in fiery lust is not a matter of voluntary choice, but rather one of compulsion (ἀνάγκη) due to one's nature (φύσις), which is evil. Men love the sweetness of the fire, are servants of death and pursue works of corruption because they are determined to do so by their basic nature.

Their fate, then, is to be thrown down to the abyss, where they will be scourged till they run headlong to "the place which they do not know," presumably Hell (141:33f). What happens thereafter is not clear, since the text is again defective at this point. They can no longer patiently dispose of the parts of their body.[72] The picture of their punishment is one of utterly mindless abandon, since we encounter such phrases as ⲡⲗⲓⲃⲉ ⲙⲛ ⲡⲱϣⲍ̄, "madness and derangement," "rejoicing over" something, "thinking that they are wise," being "frenetic" and "occupied with their actions" (ⲉⲣⲉⲡⲟⲩⲍⲏⲧ ⲡⲟⲟⲛⲉ ⲉⲣⲟⲟⲩ ⲉⲣⲉⲡⲟⲩⲙⲉⲉⲩⲉ ⲍⲓ ⲛⲉⲩⲡⲣⲁⲍⲓⲥ). And, what is more, we read that "it is the fire that will burn them" (142:2); i.e. that by which one sins, by that shall one be punished. Taken as a whole, this passage is a description of punishment of Hell, and thus is a prelude to the far more elaborate description of punishment in Hell which we shall encounter in section B. However, as each description occurs in section A and B respectively, we shall see that the two do not form a unity.

142:2-9. Thomas responds to the Savior's grave pronouncement with great anxiety over those who fall under it: "O Lord, what will the one thrown down to them do (to whom "them" refers cannot be determined; perhaps the demons of Hell), for many are those who fight against them." At this point, the Savior responds with what must be a question "Is it for yourself that you possess that which is visible (or: the one who appears, ⲡⲉⲧ ⲟⲩⲟⲛⲍ ⲉⲃⲟⲗ)?", since Thomas answers, "It is you, Lord, for whom it is fitting to speak, and I, to listen to you." The Savior's question is obscure, not only because it seems to have nothing to do with Thomas' question about the fate of those in Hell (since it concerns Thomas himself), but also because the grammar itself is puzzling.

The phrase ⲡⲉⲧⲟⲩⲟⲛ︺ ⲉⲃⲟⲗ can read either "he who is
visible" or "that which is visible." If we take it in the personal sense, it seems that it is only the Savior who can be referred to as "he who is visible," and thus the Savior is asking
Thomas if he really possesses the Savior. If, however, we take
the phrase in the impersonal sense, "that which is visible," then
we are talking about visible things. To judge from the section
138:27-139:12, "that which is visible" refers to the material
realities of this world, and in particular to the body (139:2f),
as opposed to the invisible things of the Pleroma. This consideration, plus the fact that after Thomas' answer (actually refusal
to answer), the Savior offers an extended metaphor which apparently concerns the body, tends to drive us to the conclusion that
the Savior answers Thomas' anxiety over the miserable mortals who
are to be punished in Hell by directly asking Thomas if he has a
body.

If Thomas admits that he really does have a body (which seems
to be the force of the second tense with the ethical dative, "is
it for yourself that you possess" (i.e. "do you really have"),
then he has reason to be anxious over the punishment of the bestial body in Hell. But Thomas indicates that only the Savior can
answer this question.

142:9-18. Assuming that the question which Thomas refuses to
answer is whether he possesses "that which is visible," that is,
a body, then the Savior's response should probably be construed
as an answer to this question.

The response takes the form of a conceit, or extended metaphor which typified "that which is visible" (the body) as a sexual
entity (in the pejorative sense) whose process of procreation by
the male sperm can be likened to the germination of a seed. Just
as the seed ("that which is sown"), in the process of germination,
dissolves under the action of rain ("water") and sunlight ("fire")[23]
and lies under the soil ("in tombs of darkness") and after a long
time the fruit is revealed which is then pruned (κολάζειν), and
eaten by man and beast, so also the male sperm ("that which sows"
and "is sown") dissolves in the fire (the male and female generative principles, cf. Cicero *De. nat. deor.* II, 28) and water (the
moisture of the vagina) and hides in the womb (tombs of darkness),
and after a long time another fleshly body is revealed (the fruit
of the evil tree of the flesh) which is then punished (κολάζειν;

as one having been begotten in the flesh, cf. above) and killed
in the mouth of beasts and men (cf. men who like beasts devour
one another), all at the instigation of the rains, winds, air
and the light above. Again, the metaphor can be applied not
only to the reproduction of the body, but also to the history of
the body's life: it both sows and is sown, and because of the
fire of lust will be dissolved (consigned to death) and as a
corpse inhabit the dark tombs of Hell where the true fruits of
its life will be revealed and receive retribution (κολάζειν is
in this type of literature the typical expression for punishment
in Hell, κόλασις).

Such a metaphor of the body as a seed is also to be found
in Paul's description of the resurrection body in 1 Cor. 15:
"Fool, what you sow will not come to life unless it die, and
what you sow is not the body that is to be, but a bare kernel,
perhaps of wheat, or something else." Again, a similar metaphor
closer to the meaning intended in *Thomas the Contender* is contained in Plato's *Phaedo*:

> For because it (the soul that considers visible
> things to be real) is of like opinion with the body
> and rejoices in the same things, it is compelled, it
> seems to me, to have the same habits and upbringing
> and never depart in purity to Hades, but always depart
> contaminated with the body, so that it immediately
> falls back into another body, like the sowing of a
> seed.[74]

The soul which, on the contrary, has avoided the deception
of the body:

> need not at all fear. . . that it will be torn assunder
> at its departure from the body, blown apart by the
> winds, and fluttering away vanish, and no longer be
> anywhere.[75]

Whatever may have inspired the composition of the metaphor
of the seed in *Thomas the Contender*, it is clear that although
Thomas receives no direct answer to his question, the answer to
it is ready at hand. Thomas may happen to have a body, but unless he is willing to undergo its fate, he had better disown it:
"Is it for yourself that you possess that which is visible?" No,
it is just an unfortunate accident. I do not possess it for my
benefit, but, unless I can come free of it, for my damnation.

142:18-26. With this response of Thomas to the Savior's conceit
on the body, we not only leave the block of material in which

Thomas is addressed as "thou" (141:25-142:18), but also encounter the formal end of the dialogue: "You have indeed persuaded us, Lord. We knew in our mind and it is obvious that this is so, and that your word is sufficient."[76]

The return to the use of the plural ("us," "we") in the conclusion to the dialogue itself (and to section A) may be a device of the author of section A to involve the readers in the conclusion: they, along with Thomas, are convinced.

We must, however, raise the question whether the return to the plural is a sign of redactional work. In this connection, it is interesting to note that the four "thou" blocks all belong to section A and respectively treat: the Thomas tradition (138:4-27); the metaphor of shooting arrows in the dark plus the confession of the Savior as "our light" (139:11-21); Thomas' confession that the Lord is "the one who is good for us" (140:5-8); and finally, the inexorable punishment of those bestial men who love the sweetness of the fire, the inexorability of which is demonstrated by the metaphor of the seed (141:25-142:18). Each of the four blocks appears to be "Christian" in the sense that in them Thomas is central, by virtue of being personally characterized (138:4-27), or directly confessing something about the Savior (139:11-21; 140:5-8), or being asked a direct personal question (142:6-9). It is very possible that these "thou" blocks may have originally formed an entire dialogue between Thomas and the Savior in which each addressed the other in the second person singular. Blocks of "you" material would have been inserted into the dialogue in order to expand the scope of the dialogue by introducing the themes: "visible" and "invisible" as well as "Perfection" (138:27-139:11); the light which shines to get the elect to abandon bestiality *versus* the bitter fire of lust (139:23-140:5); and of "Perfection" *versus* the fire which leads men astray as well as the subject of "visible" and "invisible" (140:8-141:18). That is, the material dealing with visible *versus* invisible and the light versus the fire of passion is largely confined to the plural sections, while the "thou" sections have much more to do with Thomas himself. Such a situation would be quite natural and not cause any suspicion at all if the dialogue ran smoothly, since it would be natural for the Savior to use "thou" when directing his attention to Thomas. But the fact that the "thou" sections always seem to change the subject, plus the fact that one of them

(140:5-8) is an absolute *non-sequitur*, give reason for suspect-
ing that the flow of the dialogue is not altogether "natural."
Indeed we have a section (139:25-31) which, since it is addressed
directly to Thomas (ⲱ ⲡⲙⲁⲕⲁⲣⲓⲟⲥ ⲑⲱⲙⲁⲥ) we would expect to be
cast in the second person singular, but, instead, it uses the
second person plural. All of this could be a sign of redactional
activity on the part of a redactor who combined section A with
section B. However, the contrasts between the singular and plural
blocks is not great enough to merit the conclusion that section A
is a conflation of two sets of material characterized by the singular (deriving from the redactor) and plural (deriving from the
original section A) forms of address respectively. Alternatively,
this irregularity we have noticed could be accounted for by assuming that originally the dialogue of section A was composed with a
wider audience in view, a situation which the vacillation between
singular and plural appears to convey, and that some of the questions and statements put to the Savior which receive answers cast
in the plural were asked by another group, for example, the disciples (i.e. for "his disciples said to the Lord" was substituted
"Thomas said to the Lord"). While there is not enough evidence
to draw any conclusion, whatever evidence of irregularity there
is should be brought to the attention of the reader.

To return to the passage at hand (142:18-26), we again note
that we have come to the formal end of the dialogue, since Thomas
(or rather "we") is convinced by the Savior and concludes that
his word is enough. It is also the material end of the dialogue,
since at this point Thomas disappears altogether from the tractate.

Yet the tractate continues on, as though nothing had ended,
by the addition of a new subject of discussion:

> But these words which you speak to us are laugh-
> ingstocks to the world and are sneered at, since they
> are not understood. So how can we go preach them,
> since we are reckoned as in the world? (142:21-26)

Thus, for all intents and purposes, the dialogue is picked
up again as though nothing had happened, except for the fact that
from here on to the end all we have is a long homiletical speech
by the Savior, linked together by continuation formulae (ⲁⲩⲟⲩⲱϩ
ⲉⲧⲟⲟⲧϥ̅ ⲛ̅ϭⲓ ⲡⲥⲱⲣ , or ⲓⲥ 143:8; 144:37). What has actually
happened is that a new subject has been introduced, since what

164

follows is an apocalyptic section in which the Savior condemns
to Hell (a Hell with different features from the Hell of section
A) those who mock his words. We are persuaded that the question
of the mockers which continues Thomas' concluding response is
redactional. It is designed to introduce a homily (section B)
of the Savior on subjects not greatly different from those
covered in the dialogue. In the comment on the *incipit* (138:
1-4) we have presented evidence to show that it derives from a
source other than the dialogue (section A), in particular from
the original title of the following homily or "sayings" document (section B).

142:26-143:7. The second (B) section of the tractate is a long
homily consisting of apocalyptic prediction and woes, delivered
by the Savior against those who mock his words, plus three beatitudes and a promise of (the) future rest for those who hear
them. The apocalyptic section, 142:26-143:7, is addressed to
those who reject his words. This oblique reference to his audience is prefaced by the Jesuanic formula ϨⲀⲘⲎⲚ ϯⲬⲱ ⲘⲘⲞⲤ ⲚⲎⲦⲚ̄
(ἀμὴν λέγω ὑμῖν):[77] "Truly I tell you (plural), as for the one
who (singular) will listen to your word and (at the same time)
turn away his face (=attention) or sneer at it or smirk ("curl
his lips") at these things, truly I tell you. . ."

Such a person "will be delivered over to the Archon above,
who rules over all the powers (ἐξουσίαι) as their king." No
further clue as to the identity of this Archon is given. As
the ensuing description of punishment progresses, we may have
to do with different sources, as is hinted at by two renderings
of the expression "deliver over," ⲤⲈⲚⲀⲦⲀⲀϤ ⲀⲦⲞⲞⲦϤ (142:30) and
ⲤⲈⲚⲀⲠⲀⲢⲀⲆⲒⲆⲞⲨ ⲘⲘⲞⲞⲨ, plus occasional changes from the singular
to the plural (142:38,42; and ⲦⲎⲚⲈ, "you," 142:40).

Apparently the Savior is referring to a punishment after
death, since this individual is handed over to the Archon who
is above, who rules over all the powers (ⲠⲀⲢⲬⲰⲚ ⲈⲦⲘ̄ⲠⲤⲀⲚⲦⲠⲈ
ⲠⲀⲒ̈ ⲈⲦⲀⲢⲬⲈⲒ ⲈⲝⲚ̄ ⲚⲈⲌⲞⲨⲤⲒⲀ ⲦⲎⲢⲞⲨ) and he will cast this soul
down to the abyss. This Archon is the same sort of being mentioned in Eph. 2:2:

    . . . once you conducted yourselves according to the
    era of this world, according to the Archon of the
    ἐξουσία of the air, the spirit controlling the sons
    of disobedience.

The Archon of *Thomas the Contender* is very similar to the highest demon of the Latin *Asclepius*, who is judge of souls. Tris-
megistos tells Asclepius that when the soul has left the body,
there will be held a trial of its merits:

> It (the soul) passes under the power of the highest
> demon. When he finds a soul to be godly and righteous,
> he allows it to abide in the region most suited to it;
> if, however, he sees it to be marred with the stains
> of sin and defiled by vice, hurling it down from
> above, he delivers it over to the tempests and whirl-
> winds of the (part of the) air frequently in conflict
> with fire and water, so that by eternal punishment it
> is continually swept and buffeted to and fro by
> streams of (cosmic) matter between heaven and earth.[78]

In *Thomas the Contender*, the soul of the mocker will be
turned about by the one who rules the ἐξουσίαι (=angels? cf. the
list in I En. 20) and cast from heaven down to the bottom of the
abyss (under the earth? ϪⲚ ⲚⲦⲠⲈ ⲱϣⲁⲡⲓⲧⲚ ⲁⲡⲚⲟⲩⲚ). This abyss is
further identified as a narrow dark place of imprisonment in
which it is impossible to turn or move "on account of the great
depth of Tartaros and the wide wall of Hades. The mention of
both Tartaros (τάρταρος) and Hades (ⲀⲘⲚⲦⲈ, "Hades," "the west-
ern place") is probably hendiadys, and has no special significance, for example, as evidence for a conflation of sources.
The remainder of the description of Hell is largely lost in a
lacuna. A possible restoration is:

```
142:35,  He can neither turn or move on account            [79]  ⲉ
    36,  of the great depth of Tartaros and ⲡⲓ[ⲭⲟⲓ]ⲉ
    37,  [ⲧⲡⲟⲣ]ⲱ ⲚⲦⲉ ⲀⲘⲚⲦⲈ ⲡⲁ̈ⲓ ⲉⲧⲧⲁⲭⲣⲏⲩ ⲁ[ⲣⲱⲩ ⲉ]ⲩ
    38,  [ⲱⲧⲡ] ⲘⲘⲟⲟⲩ ⲉϪⲟⲩⲚ ⲉⲣⲟⲩ ⲭⲉ[ⲕⲁ̈ⲁⲥ ⲚⲚⲉⲩ̄ⲣ̄]
    39,  [ⲡⲃⲟⲗ]ʹ ⲚⲤⲉⲚ[ⲁ]ⲕⲱ ⲀⲚ ⲉⲃⲟⲗ [Ⲙⲡⲟⲩ̄ⲁ̈ⲓ]ⲃⲉ[80]  [ⲁⲩ̄ⲱ]
    40,  [Ⲛⲓ ⲁ ⲣⲭⲱⲚ ⲉⲦⲚ]ⲁⲡⲱⲧ ⲚⲤⲁ ⲐⲎⲚⲉ[81]  ⲥ[ⲉⲚⲁⲡ]ⲁⲣⲁⲁⲓⲁ[ⲟⲩ]
    41,  [ⲘⲘⲟⲟⲩ ⲉϪⲣⲁ̈ⲓ ⲉⲡⲁⲣ]ⲅⲉⲗⲟⲥ ⲡⲧⲁⲣⲧ⳿ⲣⲟⲩⲭⲟⲥ[82]
    42,  [Ⲛⲩ̄ⲭ̄ⲓ Ⲛ̄ϩⲉⲚ̄ⲙⲁⲥⲧⲓⲍ Ⲛ̄ⲕ]ⲁⲧⲉ  ⲉⲩ̄ⲡⲏⲧ Ⲛ̄ⲥⲱⲟⲩ
143:1 ,  [Ⲛ̄]ϩⲉⲚ⳿ⲫⲁ̄ⲣⲉⲗⲗⲟⲩ (sic!) of fire casting a shower
         shower of sparks
    2 ,  into the face of the one pursued.
```

On the basis of this restoration, Tartaros appeared in
Thomas the Contender as a deep dark hole surrounded by broad
walls (or rivers?) which imprison the one who is punished, who
is then delivered over to Tartarouchos, the chief angel of Hell
for scourging with whips of fire. Furthermore we read that a
threatening, seething fire surrounds Hell on the West, South and
North, with the only exit towards the East (143:2-5). But the
one who is hemmed in by this fiery threat is unable to find the

way to the East and be saved, "for he did not find it in the day
he was in the body with the result that he might finally find it
in the day of judgment" (ϕοογ ⲛⲧⲕⲣⲓⲥⲓⲥ). Of course, at the
day of judgment, it will be too late to repent and be saved.

One of the earliest lengthy descriptions of Tartaros is
found in Hesiod's *Theogony*:

> And there, in all their order are the sources and
> ends of gloomy earth and misty Tartarus and the un-
> fruitful sea and starry heaven, loathsome and dark,
> which even the gods abhor. It is a great gulf, and
> if once a man were within the gates, he would not
> reach the floor until a whole year had reached its
> end, but cruel blast upon blast would carry him in
> this way and that.[83]

Such is the nature of "the great depth of Tartaros." In
the treatment of Tartaros, Plato refers (*Phaedo* 112A) to a similar description of Tartaros in Homer's *Iliad* 8.14. It occurs in
a speech to the gods: Zeus warns against giving aid to the Tro-
jans or Danaans, or else

> . . . I shall take and hurl him into the murky Tar-
> tarus, far, far away, where is the deepest gulf
> beneath the earth, the gates whereof are of iron and
> the threshold of bronze, as far beneath Hades as
> heaven is above earth.[84]

According to this, Hades is not only a deep gulf, but also has
iron gates and bronze thresholds. In the *Theogony* 807-812,[85]
where, after a literal repetition of a portion of the passage
just quoted from the *Theogony* (736-739=807-810), Hesiod says:

> And there are the shining gates and an immovable
> threshold of bronze having unending roots and is
> grown of itself.[86]

Owing to the lacuna in *Thomas the Contender*, we cannot tell
whether the feature of iron gates and bronze threshold was in
the text; there does not seem to be adequate space and clues to
allow it. Hesiod, however, does make mention of a wall which
confines the Titans in Tartaros (cf. *Thomas the Contender* 142:
39),

> . . . for Poseidon fixed gates of bronze upon it,
> and a wall runs all round it on every side.[87]

The descriptions of Tartaros in Plato's *Phaedo* (111c-113c;
cf. *Republic* 614ef) and in Vergil's *Aeneid*, 548-625, which are
very closely related in many details, are much more elaborate

than these earlier versions. In his edition of the Achmim fragment of the *Apocalypse of Peter*, Albrecht Dieterich[88] has argued forcefully that these descriptions of punishment in Tartarus ultimately derive "aus westgriechischen orphische-pythagoreischen Vorlagen" (p. 123), and that Plato's version (upon which Vergil's work is dependent?, cf. *ibid*. p. 150) was created from material known to him in Athens and later in Sicily as well as through Orphic mystics who had been in contact with the Pythagoreans of lower Italy, where there had occurred a conflation of the doctrine of the heavenly ascent of the soul with that of reward and punishment in the underworld (p. 125). Dieterich supposes that:

> Es muss ein grosses orphisches Buch gewesen sein,
> in dem Form des Berichtes über einen Hinabsteig zum
> Hades, ähnlich wie in der Republik auch, über alles
> das, was der Hinabsteigende gesehen, von diesem selbst
> berichtet wird: von den Totenrichtern, von dem Gericht,
> von den zu Bestrafenden und ihren Strafen, von den
> Flüssen der Qual und dem Tartaros, von den zu Belehn-
> enden und den Gebilden der Seligen, von der zweiten
> Wahl der Lebenslose, dazu auch von dem ersten Sünden-
> fall und der Busse, die dafür gesetzt sei.[89]

Whether or not Dieterich's theory can be sustained at all points, it is clear that the picture of punishment in Tartaros enjoyed wide currency in the Hellenistic world, and that its major purpose was minatory: to frighten men into leading a moral life. As it is applied in *Thomas the Contender*, it threatens with doom the man who mocks the Savior's words.

The chief agent of punishment is the angel Tartarouchos (ⲡⲁⲅⲅⲉⲗⲟⲥ ⲛ̅ⲧⲁⲣⲧⲁⲣⲟⲩⲭⲟⲥ), the "one in control of Tartaros."[90] According to I En. 20:2, it is Uriel who is over the world and over Tartaros. In the *Apocalypse of Peter* (c. 13) Tartirokos (=Tartarouchos) is the one who punishes with even greater torment those who have repented in Hell, where there is no more time for repentance.[91] According to the Greek *Apocalypse of Paul* (16), those who while living showed no mercy are to "be handed over to the angel Tartarouchos (or Temeluchos), who is appointed over punishments," and "he will send them into the outer darkness." The instrument of his punishment, according to *Thomas the Contender*, is a fiery instrument of scourging (probably whips) with which he pursues those to be tormented. Moreover this fiery threat hems him (note the change to the singular) in on all sides except the East, but his embodied state prevents him from taking this path to salvation, at least prior to Judgment Day.

Fire is the major instrument of punishment in the literature dealing with punishment in Hell. In *Thomas the Contender* it is the more ironical in that the instrument of punishment is analogous to that by which the tormented sinned in earthly life, the fire of passion. In the present section it is difficult to tell whether the fiery threat which hems in the tormented on three points of the compass is the fiery whip of Tartarouchos, or whether it is some kind of ring of fire, such as the Pyriphlegethon, one of the rivers of Hades (*Odyssey* 10.513; *Phaedo* 114a), which has become understood as an instrument of punishment.[92] Dieterich observes:

> Das Feuer als so recht eigentliches Element der unter-
> irdisches Pein findet sich verhältnismässig spät
> (z.B. deutlich Lukian vera. hist. II c. 27). Bei den
> Griechen wird nie ganz die Vorstellung seiner reinigen-
> den Kraft zurückgetreten sein; die "unheilbaren"
> z.B. bei Platon werden nie mit Feuer gestraft.
> Hinzugetreten sind dann freilich Lehren wie die von
> der ἐκπύρωσις, die durch die Stoiker überallhin
> drang. Für die Kreise, welche jüdischen Einflüssen
> zugänglich waren, ist dann das Wort des Jesaias von
> dem Worm, der nicht sterben, und das Feuer, das
> nicht verlöschen wird (Jes LXVI 24 Sept.), wirksam
> geworden und die durch fremde Einflüsse erst so
> entwickelte Anschauung von dem feuerigen Thal Ge-
> hinnom, Gehenna.[93]

The conception of the fire being met at every point of the compass occurs in the early second century *Apocalypse of Peter* (Ethiopic version), only the scene is not of punishment in Hell, but of the catastrophes of the day of judgment, where cataracts of fire plummet earthwards melting stars and earth:

> And as soon as the whole creation is dissolved,
> the men who are in the east shall flee to the west and
> those in the west to the east; those that are in the
> south shall flee to the north and those in the north
> to the south, and everywhere will the wrath of the
> fearful fire overtake them; and an unquenchable flame
> shall drive them and bring them to the judgment of
> wrath inthe stream of unquenchable fire which flows,
> flaming with fire.[94]

Here fire is both a feature of the eschatological holo-
caust, and at the same time an instrument of punishment which is inescapable. Now in the *Apocalypse of Peter* the fire is at all points of the compass; there is no escape whatsoever, since the

fire is a cosmic conflagration. In *Thomas the Contender*, however, the fire is not a cosmic conflagration, but is localized
in Tartaros, and whether it is a wall of fire or simply the
ubiquitous presence of the punishing angel Tartarouchos, it is
met at only three, not four points of the compass.

At this point, it is worthwhile to compare this description
of punishment in Hell with the one contained in section A (141:
32-142:2). According to the section A account, the miserable
mortals, who claim that they would not have known the fire if
they had not been begotten in the fire, are to be regarded as
beasts who propagate the lust of their fathers. They will be
1) thrown down to the abyss, 2) scourged so as to make them rush
headlong to the place which they do not know, and 3) becoming
utterly deranged and turned in upon themselves and the state and
actions of their bodies, they will be burnt by the fire.

The descriptions of punishment in the current section (B)
present the following schedule: he who mocks the Savior's words
will be 1) handed over to the highest Archon, ruling over all
the powers, who will cast the mocker down to the abyss, where
he will be 2) imprisoned in a narrow and dark place, called
Tartaros and Hades, and 3) be delivered over to Tartarouchos
who will pursue the mocker with fiery scourgings, such that
every path of escape is blocked by fire.

Clearly, while the two accounts share in common the motifs
of consignment to the abyss and subsequent scourging and burning by fire, they diverge in details. While in the former account the one to be punished is consigned to a place he does
not know, in the latter account the "place" is named Tartaros
and Hades. While in the former the one to be punished is beaten
by the ἀνάγκη of the bitterness of his evil nature, in the latter he is beaten by the fiery whips (?) of Tartarouchos. The
divergences in the two descriptions are in our view accounted
for by the separate origins of sections A and B, while the
similarities may have indeed arisen from an attempt on the part
of the redactor to harmonize section A with section B.

Finally, we should note that the problem of the individual's
future salvation is posed in terms of an eschatological tension
between the present and the future. Punishment in Hell goes on
until the day of judgment (cf. 2 Pet. 2:9f). He who undergoes
punishment in Hell does not find the eastern way to salvation,

because he did not find it when, being embodied, he still had a
chance. On the day of judgment, one can find the way to salvation only if he has already found it in the embodied state.
Present and future are thus linked together by an epistemological
bond; what one finds out now will determine his fate in the future. Once one has left the body behind, the possibility of
finding salvation is forfeited, since it cannot be discovered in
Hell. Thus there is a built-in device which operates against
those who mock the Savior's words; because they present the way
to salvation, one had better listen now, or soon it will be too
late. It is this minatory eschatology which sets the conditions
under which the reader must hear the woes and blessings that
follow.

143:8-144:36. The previous apocalyptic section functions as the
introduction to the Savior's concluding speech, which is homiletic
in style. The transition from apocalyptic prediction to the woes
is marked by an editorial seam; instead of passing smoothly from
the underworld scene to the woes, the latter are introduced by
the formula: ⲦⲞⲦⲈ ⲀⲩⲞⲨⲰⲍ ⲀⲦⲞⲞⲦⲨ Ⲛ̄ϬⲒ ⲠⲤⲰ̄Ⲣ ⲈⲨⲬⲰ Ⲙ̄ⲘⲞⲤ , "then the
Savior continued, saying:" (143:8f; cf. 144:36f; 139:31f).

     The present section consists of twelve woes (perhaps based
on the format of the twelve curses of Dt. 27:15-26): eleven woes
which are separated from a twelfth woe lying in the subsequent
section which is introduced by a repetition of the above formula:
ⲦⲞⲦⲈ ⲀⲩⲞⲨⲰⲍ ⲀⲦⲞⲞⲦⲨ Ⲛ̄ϬⲒ ⲠⲤⲰ̄Ⲣ ⲈⲨⲬⲰ Ⲙ̄ⲘⲞⲤ, "then Jesus (sic) continued and said:". The woes are as follows:

     1. Woe to those who hope in things which will not happen
(143:9f).

     2. Woe to those who hope in the imperishability of what
is perishable, i.e. the body and the world (143:10-15).

     3. Woe on account of the insatiable fire which burns with-
in (143:15f).

     4. Woe on account of the wheel that turns in your minds
(143:17f).

     5. Woe on account of the fire which destroys soul and
body (143:18-21).

     6. Woe on account of your captivity in caverns of darkness
which prevent you from recognizing your situation. Because of
this your minds are deranged, causing a reversal of values.

a) Your enemies' victory is a delight to you.

b) Darkness rises on you like the light.

c) You exchange freedom for servitude.

d) You make your thoughts into folly, filling your minds with smoke.

e) You hid your light in the cloud.

f) - h) lie in a lacuna

i) You baptized your souls in the water of darkness.

j) You behaved according to your own desires.

7. Woe to you for not noticing the light of the sun, which judges everything, and the moon, which sees your corpse-like bodies (144:2-8).

8. Woe to you for loving polluted intercourse with women (144:8-10).

9. Woe on account of the afflicting powers of your body (144:10-12).

10. Woe on account of the powers of the evil demons (144:12f).

11. Woe to you who beguile your members in the fire (144:14).

a) Who will extinguish this fire? (144:15-17) Who will give you the sun to shine and dissolve the darkness and the polluted water, and give a fragrance to you and all the natural elements? (144:17-21).

b) Here follows an extended metaphor on the sun, the grapevine and the weeds. What was probably originally intended to be a series of twelve woes is broken after this eleventh woe, the extreme length of whose agrarian metaphor probably caused the twelve-woe format to be forgotten, necessitating the insertion of the second formula "and Jesus continued, saying," after which the twelfth (obliterated) woe follows.

For the sake of convenience, we will refer to the woes according to the enumeration supplied above.

1. The first woe is against the godless (N̄ⲀⲦⲚⲞⲨⲦⲈ) who have no hope. The same style of curse occurs in Sir. 41:8, only the godless are those who despise God's law:

οὐαὶ ὑμῖν ἄνδρες ἀσεβεῖς

οἵτινες ἐγκατελείπετε νόμον θεοῦ ὑψίστου.

Thus, as regards style, we are within the biblical framework. In the New Testament the most famous examples of this woe-formula

are the woes against the Pharisees and scribes of Mt. 23 (cf.
Lk. 11). It consists of the exclamation "woe" plus a form of
direct address in the dative, followed by the charge and specification which gives rise to the woe. The charge and specification is introduced by a relative clause whose subject is the same
as the antecedent, or else by a causal particle such as ⲉⲃⲟⲗ
Ϩⲓⲧⲟⲟⲧϥ or ⲚⲦⲟⲟⲦϥ (corresponding to the ὅτι clauses in Matthew).

In this case the charge and specification is that the godless are those without hope. The phrase ⲚⲈⲦⲉ ⲘⲚ̄Ⲧⲉⲩ Ϩⲉⲗⲡⲓⲥ,
or ⲘⲚ̄Ⲧⲉⲩ Ϩⲉⲗⲡⲓⲥ, occurs three times in *Thomas the Contender*.
Aside from the present context it refers to those who persecute
the elect (145:5-7). In the present context it refers to those
"who rely on things which will not come to be" (143:10). The
phrase ⲚⲈⲦⲚⲀϢⲱⲡⲉ, "things which will come to be," usually has
an eschatological reference: according to section A, formless
ⲉⲓⲇⲱⲗⲁ "will come to be" (in this instance, "dwell") over en-
tombed corpses forever (141:15-18); a possibility of future existence is to "come to be" in the flesh (145:8f). Thus the
phrase "things which will not come to be" has an eschatological,
but pejorative, meaning. Its precise reference, however, seems
to be supplied by the next woe, which also treats the question
of hope, but more from the point of view of the object of one's
hope rather than the presence or absence of hope.

2. The second woe condemns those who hope (ἐλπίζειν) "in
the flesh and the prison that will perish."[95] This phrase is
probably hendiadys for the "perishable fleshly prison" (cf. the
σῶμα-σῆμα concept generally).[96] If we take this phrase as the
key to the interpretation of the first woe, then "to have no
hope," i.e. "to rely on things which will not come to be," is
to hope in the flesh which will perish. Our second woe goes on
to confirm this identification, and even broaden it to include
all material things. To hope in the fleshly, material things
of this world and this life is to cause one's soul to perish and
hence to be without hope. He who hopes in perishable things will
likewise perish.

The remainder of the second woe presents some extraordi-
narily perplexing grammatical problems.

ϢⲀⲚⲦⲉⲟⲩ Ϣⲱⲡⲉ ⲉⲦⲉⲦⲚ̄ⲟⲃⲱ̄ Ⲁⲩⲱ Ⲛ̄ⲀⲦⲦⲉⲕⲟ
ⲉⲦⲉⲦⲚ̄Ⲙⲉⲉⲩⲉ ⲉⲣⲟⲟⲩ ⲭⲉ ⲥⲉⲚⲀⲦⲀⲕⲟ ⲀⲚ ⲉⲦⲉⲦⲚϨⲉⲗⲡⲓⲥ
ⲦⲀⲬⲣⲏⲩ Ⲁⲭ̄Ⲛ ⲡⲕⲟⲥⲙⲟⲥ Ⲁⲩⲱ ⲡⲉⲦⲚ̄ⲚⲟⲩⲦⲉ ⲡⲉ
ⲡⲉⲉⲓⲃⲓⲟⲥ ⲉⲦⲉⲦⲚ̄ⲦⲀⲕⲟ Ⲛ̄ⲚⲉⲦⲚ̄ⲯⲩⲭⲟⲟⲩⲉ

a) In the phrase ϣⲁⲛⲧⲉⲟⲩ ϣⲱⲡⲉ ⲉⲧⲉⲧⲛ̄ⲟⲃϣ̄ⲅ̄ , ⲉⲧⲉⲧⲛ̄ⲟⲃϣ̄ⲅ̄ is probably a second tense with adverbial complement: "it is until when (ἕως πότε, Crum 573a) that you are oblivious?" = "*How long* will you be oblivious?"

b) ⲁⲩⲱ ⲛ̄ⲁⲧⲧⲉⲕⲟ ⲉⲧⲉⲧⲛ̄ⲙⲉⲉⲩⲉ ⲉⲣⲟⲟⲩ ⲇⲉ ⲥⲉⲛⲁⲧⲁⲕⲟ ⲁⲛ clearly begins a new sentence and can be translated a number of ways:

   α) "And (as for) the indestructible ones (or: things) which you think they will not perish" (no main clause).

   β) "And (as for) the indestructible ones, it is concerning them that you think they will not perish" (indicative, second present).

   γ) "And (as for) the indestructible ones, is it concerning them that you think they will not perish?" (interrogative, second present).

   δ) "And (as for) the indestructible ones, it is concerning them that you think they will also perish" (indicative, second present, ⲁⲛ is AA$_2$ for ⲟⲛ, "also").

   ε) "And (as for) the indestructible ones, is it concerning them that you think they will also perish?" (interrogative, second present, ⲁⲛ is AA$_2$ for ⲟⲛ, "also").

   Alternative α) is unsatisfactory since it does not yield a main clause. Alternatives β) and δ) are attractive in that they amount to emphatic (second tense) accusations, which harmonizes well with the "woe" form. Alternatives γ) and ε) are attractive because as interrogatives they are similar in mode to the immediately preceding question ("How long are you to be oblivious?"). On the whole, γ) and ε) seem most attractive for the reason given. Of these two, γ) has the difficulty of amounting to a tautology, since one would of course think that imperishable things will not perish. On the other hand, we could suppose the reference to ⲛ̄ⲁⲧⲧⲉⲕⲟ to be ironic: "And the (so-called) indestructible things, do you think that they will not perish?" But this interpretation has the disadvantage of straining the Coptic. Therefore, taking our cue from the AA$_2$ form ⲁⲛ

174

for S ⲟⲛ which occurs a few lines above (143:4), alternative ε) seems to be the best: "And as for the indestructible things, is it concerning them that you
think they will also perish?" = "Do you really think
that the imperishable things will also perish?" This
has the advantage of: being an interrogative following
another interrogative; being an example of forgetful
or oblivious thought (cf. ⲉⲧⲉⲧⲛ̄ⲟⲃⲱ̄, 143:12); and giving a positive meaning to ⲛ̄ⲁⲧⲧⲉⲕⲟ as distinct from
the perishable body. This alternative may be partially
confirmed by an apparent chiasmus which we shall point
out.

c) ⲉⲧⲉⲧⲛ̄ϩⲉⲗⲡⲓⲥ ⲧⲁϫⲣⲏⲩ ⲁϫⲛ̄ ⲡⲕⲟⲥⲙⲟⲥ is a proper indicative second present with adverbial complement.

d) ⲁⲩⲱ ⲡⲉⲧⲛ̄ⲛⲟⲩⲧⲉ ⲡⲉ ⲡⲉⲉⲓⲃⲓⲟⲥ (cf. Phil. 3:19) is a nominal
sentence which fits well in the woe context.

e) ⲉⲧⲉⲧⲛ̄ⲧⲁⲕⲟ ⲛ̄ⲛⲉⲧⲛ̄ⲯⲩⲭⲟⲟⲩⲉ is puzzling. It could be a
circumstantial phrase modifying the main clause d) "Your
god is this life," but we would rather expect the sub-
ordinating relationship to be reversed: "You are corrupting your souls since your god is this life." The
other possibility is to regard e) as an *emploi abusif*
of the second tense which results in an emphatic statement: "You are corrupting your souls!"[97]

Now taking the passage as a whole, we note an apparent
chiastic structure to the whole:

A b) "Do you really think that the imperishables (ⲛ̄ⲁⲧⲧⲉⲕⲟ)
       will also perish (ⲧⲁⲕⲟ)?"

B c) "It is upon the world that your hope is set."

B¹ d) "And your god is this life."

A¹ e) "You are corrupting (ⲧⲁⲕⲟ) your souls (= the imperish-
       able, as opposed to the destructible fleshly body)!"

The B, B¹ members are quite parallel in structure; their
object of hope is this world and their god is this life. The A,
A¹ members are not parallel in structure, but are reasonably
parallel in terminology: while they think that the imperishable
things will also perish, they fulfill their thought, since their
(imperishable) souls are perishing. The imperishable soul cannot hope in the perishable body.[98]

The net effect of the first two woes is to point out the
dire situation of those who hope in all that pertains to the

material world, things which "will not come to be" in the future, but will perish.

3. The third woe again brings in the theme of fire, which is the chief characteristic of the perishable body. This fire, which represents lust, is insatiable and therefore is likely to consume the body entirely.

4. It is difficult to understand what the fourth woe is about. To begin with, it seems to produce a pun when compared to the third woe. At least a portion of the third and fourth woes are parallel: "Woe to you in the fire which burns in you" and "woe to you for the wheel which turns in your minds." There appears to exist a homophony between the ⲕⲱϩⲧ (koh^{e}t) of "the fire which burns in you" and the ⲕⲱⲧⲉ (kot^e) of "the wheel (ⲕⲁⲧ) which turns (ⲕⲱⲧⲉ) in your minds." There is in addition a homophony within the third woe (ⲕⲱϩⲧ, ⲣⲱⲕϩ) as well as alliteration within the fourth woe (ⲕⲁⲧ ⲉⲧⲕⲱⲧⲉ). The metaphor of the fourth woe probably derives from Sir. 33:5:

> τροχὸς ἀμάξης σπλάγχνα μώρου
> καὶ ὡς ἄξων στρεφόμενος ὁ διαλογισμὸς αὐτοῦ.

If so, the effect is to condemn the addressees as idle-minded persons whose thought never leads anywhere. It is another way of saying that they are oblivious to their circumstances (143: 12; cf. 143:25).

5. The fifth woe returns again to the insatiable fire. The danger of the fire is not only that it will consume the flesh in a visible way (ϩⲛ ⲟⲩⲱⲛϩ ⲉⲃⲟⲗ) but, what is worse, it will at the same time secretly (ϩⲛ ⲟⲩϩⲱⲡ) rend the soul. The following sentence is completely obscure: ⲛ̄ϥⲥⲃ̄ⲧⲉ ⲑⲏⲛⲉ ϩⲣⲁ̈ⲓ ϩⲛ̄ ⲛⲉⲧⲛ̄ⲉⲣⲏⲩ "and it (the fire) will prepare you for your fel- lows."[99] It apparently has a bad sense, and is a future action which involves those who are besieged by the burning of the fire. Perhaps it means that destruction by the fire so effaces the body and soul that these individuals have no individual features left by which to recognize them. They all look the same, they and their fellows.

6. The sixth woe is very long compared to the first, third, fourth and fifth woes. It addresses the accused as captives, bound in caverns, who laugh and rejoice in mad laughter totally unaware of their precarious circumstances. They are unaware of the fact that they are perishing and exist in darkness and death.

Apparently the metaphor of being bound in caverns is interpreted
as existing in darkness and death, in a state where light and
life are totally obscured for them. The image reminds us of
Plato's picture of men dwelling in a cave at the beginning of
the seventh book of the *Republic*. They are held captive, unable
to move or turn their heads.[100] Above and to their rear is a
fire just in front of which real persons and objects pass, but
all the prisoners see is shadows cast by the light of the fire
onto the wall in front of them. By naming the shadows by the
names of the objects which cast them, the prisoners exhibit their
delusion, thinking that the shadows are real. So it is with the
condemned in *Thomas the Contender*. They are bound in caverns
unaware that they exist in darkness and death. They are drunk
with the fire (143:27) and full of bitterness (ⲘⲈⳘⲚⲤⲓϢⲈ, 143:
27f). Their minds are deranged on account of the burning within
them (143:28),[101] even laughing crazily (143:23f), totally unaware of their real situation (143:24f). Because of this they
become like the fool of whom it was said in section A (142:15f)
that the good and bad are one and the same for him; they confuse
and exchange good things for evil things: they delight in smiting
their enemies (literally ⲠⲔⲖⲟⲘ ⲚⲦⲠⲖⲎⲄⲎ ⲚⲚⲈⲦⲚⲬⲀϪⲈ, "the crown
of the smiting of your enemies") rather than granting them Christian forgiveness. Darkness rises for them like the light, they
exchange their freedom for servitude,[102] they darken their
hearts,[103] they make their thoughts into foolishness, they fill
their minds with the smoke of the fire which is in them, and
hide their light in the cloud. This list of absurdities continues with perhaps two more instances of crossed up thinking,
but they are lost in a lacuna. To judge from the remnants, the
sixth woe comes to a close with a question (ⲚⲒⲘ ⲠⲈⲚⲦ . . .,
143:39) mixed with some other declarative statements. The last
two statements of this lengthy woe are preserved at the top of
the next Coptic page (144:1f): "You baptized (ⲱⲙⲥ̄) your souls
in the water of darkness, and you behaved according to (lit.
"ran in," ⲠⲱⲦ ⳘⲚ̄) your own desires.[104]

Obviously, the sixth woe is a catch-all for every sort of
stupid inane thing that a person could do. As for the grammatical structure of the woe, a little less than half of it (143:
21-30) is cast in the present tense, using mostly the qualitative form of the verb to emphasize the state in which these

people currently exist, while the remainder (143:30-144:2) is
cast in the first perfect tense, emphasizing that they have already done these foolish things. Out of the eleven woes of this
section, only the fifth (143:18-21) and the ninth (144:10-12)
employ the future tense, which gives the impression that the
recipients of this homily indeed have no hope; they have commit-
ted all the mistakes they could and there is no turning back.
We shall see, however, in the final section of the tractate (144:
36-145:16) that there is yet a glimmer of hope.

7. The seventh woe accuses the addressees of existing in
error[105] since they have neither beheld the sun which judges the
All nor the moon which looks constantly on the bodies of their
corpses.[106]

The description of the sun looking down on the All is very
similar to Sir. 42:16a: ἥλιος φωτίζων κατὰ πᾶν ἐπέβλεψεν which
could have conceivably influenced the terminology.[107] The metaphor may have been further influenced by Jesus' discussion of
the treatment of enemies in the Sermon on the Mount, where the
Father's love is compared to the sun: τὸν ἥλιον αὐτοῦ ἀνατέλλει
ἔτι τοὺς πονηροὺς καὶ ἀγαθούς. (Matt. 5:45). We also find the
image of the sun revolving around all things in the Manichaean
Kephalaia 163 where, like the good (ἀγαθός) Father, the sun
daily passes very high over the whole earth, and thus is the key
to the mystery of the Light and Darkness. The sun as the second
φωστήρ is a type of the first and highest Father which daily reveals its goodness in the world, but the sects (δόγμα) do not
recognize this in their error (πλάνη). What the author of Thomas
the Contender meant by saying that the sun circles around all
things to enslave the enemies (ⲁⲧⲣⲉ︤ⲛ︦ⲭⲁⲁⲉ ⲡ̄ϫⲙ︥ϫⲁⲗ) remains to
be deduced from the metaphor of the sun, grapevine and weeds in
the eleventh woe (144:21-35). Suffice it to say here that the
sun which enslaves the enemies is a metaphor for the heavenly
light which makes the body wither away and causes the soul to
flourish (cf. the light which shines in order that the elect
shall abandon bestiality, 139:28f). Thus the idea of the sun
enslaving enemies seems to have to do with its destructive heat;
because of this it was identified with Seth-Typhon of the Isis-
Osiris myth:

> They (the Egyptians) think that Typhon is the
> solar world,. . . that the sun, by its untempered

and dry heat heats and burns up sprouting and
flourishing things and by its blazing heat makes
a large part of the earth uninhabitable.[108]

On the other hand, the moon gives no parching heat, but
rather γόνιον τὸ φῶς καὶ ὑγροποιὸν ἔχουσαν (de Is. et Os. 367d).
In *Thomas the Contender* it simply looks down night and day on
the bodies (σῶμα) of corpses (ϩⲉⲧⲃⲉ ; 144:6-8). Franz Cumont
conveys the following concerning the relation of the dissolution
of mind, soul and body to the action of the moon, drawn mainly
from the eschatological myths in Plutarch's dialogues *On the Face
of the Moon* and *On the Sign of Socrates*.

> The pagan theologians thus admitted that the
> souls which came down to the earth assumed in the
> sphere of the moon and in the atmosphere these aerial
> bodies which were regarded as the seat of the vital
> principle. Inversely, when they rose again to heaven,
> the function of the moon was to dissolve and to re-
> ceive these light envelopes, as on earth its damp
> rays provoked the corruption of the corpse. The soul,
> thus becoming pure reason (νοῦς) ascended to the sun,
> the source of all intelligence.[109]

This theory, according to Cumont, goes back to the teachings
of Oriental astrologers:

> Among the Greeks of the most ancient period Hecate was
> at one and the same time the goddess of the moon, the
> summoner of ghosts, and the queen of the infernal
> realm. In the East astrological ideas mingled with
> this mythology. It was taught that the moon's cold
> and damp rays corrupted the flesh of the dead and
> thus detached from it the soul which finally aban-
> doned the corpse.[110]

This description of the function of the moon seems to explain the image of the moon looking down upon corpses. Unfortunately, Cumont gives no documentation for the teaching of
these Oriental astrologers. However, a possible indication that
the moon has to do with the decay of bodies may be found in the
Hermetic *Asclepius*, if the parallelism of the following sentence
can be strictly maintained:

> Thus heaven, a god perceptible by sense, is the
> administrator of all bodies; their growth and decay
> fall under the charge of the Sun and Moon.[111]

Surely the sun has to do with growth, which leaves the moon in
charge of decay.

The image of the moon "looking down" (ⲟ̄ⲗⲩⲧ ⲉϩⲣⲁⲓ) should
probably be understood not only in terms of sending its rays

down, but also in the sense of governing. In the case of the
sun, its looking down is paralleled with judging or ruling (ⲧⲣⲏ
ⲡⲉⲧⲕⲣⲓⲛⲉ ⲙ̄ⲡⲧⲏⲣϥ ⲉⲧⲃⲁⲩⲧ ⲁⲝⲛ̄ ⲡⲧⲏⲣϥ); to look down means not only
to shine, but to have charge of what is looked down upon.

8. The eighth woe (144:8-10) changes from the concept of
the body as a corpse disposed of by the sun and moon to the concept of the body as a sexual entity. The sentence is difficult
to translate.

> ⲟⲩⲟⲉⲓ ⲛⲏⲧⲛ̄ ⲛⲉⲧⲙⲁⲉⲓⲉ ⲛ̄ⲧⲥⲩⲛⲏⲑⲉⲓⲁ ⲛ̄ⲧⲙⲛ̄ⲧⲥⲋⲓⲙⲉ
> ⲙⲛ̄ ⲡⲉⲥⲱⲡⲉ ⲛⲙ̄ⲙⲁⲥ ⲉⲧⲥⲟⲟⲩ

> Woe to you who love the intimacy (or: intercourse,
> συνήθεια) of womanhood (Crum 385a) and her being with
> her which is polluted.

I have translated the sentence: "Woe to you who love intimacy
with womankind and (who love) polluted intercourse with it (anything feminine)," taking the third feminine singular suffix pronoun of ⲡⲉⲥⲱⲡⲉ as referring to ⲥⲩⲛⲏⲑⲉⲓⲁ (i.e. as the intercourse pertaining to intimacy) and the like suffix of ⲙ̄ⲙⲁⲥ as
referring to ⲧⲙⲛ̄ⲧⲥⲋⲓⲙⲉ (intercourse with anything feminine).[112]
The meaning of the woe is perfectly clear from the general tenor
of the tractate and may derive from the author of section B
directly.

9. The ninth woe, as the seventh and eighth, again has to
do with the body, in this case with the ἐξουσίαι of the body
which afflict those persons who are addressed. These ἐξουσίαι
must be some sort of evil spiritual powers (cf. Eph. 2:2). In
this sense the term refers almost exclusively to heavenly powers
(so Bauer-Arndt-Gingrich 278a; Lampe's *Patristic Lexicon* 502a,b).
But the text seems to imply that these powers belong to the body
as such (ⲛ̄ⲉⲝⲟⲩⲥⲓⲁ ⲙ̄ⲡⲉⲧⲛ̄ⲥⲱⲙⲁ). Since the preceding woe deals
with sexual intercourse, we should naturally expect these ἐξουσίαι
to have to do with the sexual powers of the body, i.e. the passions. Such a meaning fits well with the general tenor of the
entire tractate. It may be, however, that these powers are related to the beings described in the next woe.

10. Here the woe arises on account of the "energies
(forces) of the evil demons (ⲛ̄ⲉⲛⲉⲣⲅⲉⲓⲁ ⲛ̄ⲛ̄ⲁⲓⲙⲱⲛ ⲙ̄ⲡⲟⲛⲏⲣⲟⲛ).
Interpreting this woe in the light of the previous woe, we are
led to think of some kind of spiritual forces which attack the
soul from without, but do so by the agency of the body. The

fourth Hermetic fragment from Stobaeus throws light on the subject:

> For forces, O Tat, themselves incorporeal, are in bodies and act through bodies. And so, O Tat, insofar as they are incorporeal, I say they are immortal, and insofar as they cannot act without bodies, I say they are always in bodies.[113]

Again:

> These forces are dependent on the bodies. On the one hand these forces which produce bodies descend from divine bodies into mortal bodies; on the other hand each of them acts either on the body or on the soul and also do not mingle with the soul apart from the body. There are always forces, but the soul is not always in a mortal body, since it can exist apart from the body. But the forces cannot exist apart from the bodies.[114]

These ἐνέργιαι of the Hermetic fragment are forces which account for bodily processes. Where in Aristotle ἐνέργεια means "actuality" as opposed to "potency" (δύναμις), the meaning of ἐνέργεια here is closer to δύναμις – it means "force," "effect," "influence." Even after the soul has left the body the process of decay is evidence of forces at work. The forces come down from the stars, lodge in bodies, and work only through bodies. On account of the forces of birth man is subject to εἱμαρμένη (CH Frg. VIII,3). In *Thomas the Contender*, it is said that these forces derive from (genitive of source?) the evil demons, which suggests that they are the forces of celestial beings, perhaps of the planets, upon the body. In the *Corpus Hermeticum* the ἐνέργειαι are astral influences emitted by celestial bodies and act on the mortal bodies of the sublunar world: "thus marshalled they (the demons) serve under the several planets. They are good and bad in their natures, that is, their forces. For the essence (οὐσία) of a demon is a force."[115] The seven planetary spheres were thought to be more or less connected with a series of seven vices, e.g. Agnoia, Authadia, Kakia, Zelos, Phthonos, Erinnys, Epithymia (Iren. I, 29,4). These vices were stripped off from the soul in its ascent and handed over to the planetary sphere responsible for them, e.g. the power of increase and decrease to the moon, guile to Mercury, deceitful lust to Venus, tyranny to the Sun, audacity to Mars, striving after wealth to Jupiter, and falsehood to Saturn (*Poimandres* 25-26).

The substance of the ninth and tenth woes, then, must be that man is under the dominion of evil spiritual forces which originate from without, perhaps from the celestial bodies, but which find their home and place of effect in the body. In view of the eighth woe directed against intercourse, we ought to assume that the sexual passions of the body are the ἐξουσίαι and ἐνέργειαι in question. The sexual nuance seems to be confirmed by the eleventh woe which follows.

11. The eleventh woe reintroduces the theme of fire present also in the second woe. Instead of saying woe to you "on account of the fire," the speech is more direct: "Woe to you who beguile their (=your) members with the fire." Here ϩⲙ ⲡⲕⲱϩⲧ seems to function as an instrumental complement to ⲥⲱⲕ (to "beguile"), such that the fire is that by which the addressee's members are deceived or led astray. Although the plural of μέλος generally means "body" (see note on 141:36), the precise nuance of the term "members" (μέλη) probably cannot be determined. In the main translation I have rendered it as "limbs." The term occurs three times in section A: 139:36 (the fire which scorches men's μέλη); 140:31 (the fire binds men's limbs in the bitterness of the bond of lust); and 141:36 ("they will not abandon (?) their limbs patiently). Clearly the μέλη are points of the body at which the fire of passion attacks men, and it seems logical to think of sexual members, i.e. the *genitalia*. If this is so, then the eleventh woe fits into the theme of woes directed against the body's sexual powers to which we have assigned woes eight through ten. We conclude, then, that the eighth through the eleventh woes seem to fit well together when given an anti-sexual nuance. When taken in this way, we see that the body was thought of as the seat of sexual passions which could be conceived as powers which perhaps originated outside the body, or were at least controlled from without by evil demons, and was led astray by them into the act of sexual intercourse which resulted in the affliction of the body. Thus the body, as bestial and lustful, was not a free agent, but was dominated and controlled by instinct or other beings, rather than being self-controlled.

The eleventh woe, however, as the longest woe of the twelve, has much more to say. The woe appears to be a composite, since the "woe" form is broken by a set of questions directed to the

recipients of the homily (144:15-19), followed by a promise that
they and the elements will receive a fragrance (144:19-21), and
concluded with another conceit or extended metaphor about the
sun, grapevine and weeds (144:21-36).

The first of the two rhetorical questions continues the
theme of fire with which the eleventh woe begins: "Who will rain
for (upon) you a dew of rest (ⲟⲩⲉⲓⲱⲧⲉ ⲛ̄ⲙⲧⲟⲛ) so as to extinguish[116] the great quantity of fire from you together with your
burning?" The metaphor of few extinguishing fire is very apt
as an expression of the hopeless situation of those besieged by
passion; who will save them from it? The understood answer is
probably the moon, which was thought to be the source of dew,
and such dew was a metaphor of salvation.[117]

The second rhetorical question, parallel in form to the
first, changes the image of salvation from "dew" to "the sun":
Who will give you the sun to shine upon you to disperse the darkness that is in you and to hide the darkness and polluted water?
The author of section B of the tractate has once before contrasted
light with darkness: the darkness rises like the sun for those
who are drunk with the fire (143:30). Darkness is apparently
synonymous (or at least forms a hendiadys) with death (ⲡⲙⲟⲩ[ ],
143:26) and is also connected with water ("You baptized your
souls in the water of darkness," 144:1). On the other hand, the
author of section A of the tractate considers darkness to be an
attribute of tombs (τάφος, 142:13) and as something which the
light (identified with the revealing Savior) comes and hides so
that everyone's deeds will appear (139:19). The present rhetorical question, due to its redundancy and lack of consistency,
may have resulted from an interpolation of the phrase "and to
hide the darkness and polluted water." The strange phrase "hide
the darkness," as we have indicated, occurs in section A. This
phrase creates an inconsistent redundancy since, once the sun
"disperses the darkness in you," it is hard to imagine what
"hiding the darkness and polluted water" might mean. Besides,
the sun does not really seem to be an apt agent for hiding polluted water. Thus it may be that the person who combined A and
B (if this thesis is correct) added the phrase "and to hide the
darkness and polluted water" to the question "Who will give you
the sun to disperse the darkness in you?" which originally stood
in B. A possible confirmation of this is that in the two

rhetorical questions, the first one about the dew of rest and the (original) first part of the second about dispersing the darkness either prefix the second person plural possessive adjective (ⲡⲉⲧⲛ̄ⲣⲱⲕ) or else append an equivalent second person plural phrase (ⲉⲃⲟⲗ ⲍ̄ⲛ ⲧⲏⲛⲉ , ⲉⲧⲍ̄ⲛ ⲧⲏⲛⲉ) to the noun naming what needs to be extinguished or dispersed, whereas the second (interpolated) part of the second question does not.

An apparent promise of salvation (144:19-21) follows the two rhetorical questions: "The sun and the moon will give a sweet fragrance to you, together with the air and the spirit and the water and the earth." If we assume that "spirit" (ⲡ̄ⲡⲛ̄ⲁ̄), due to the pejorative meaning of ⲕⲱⲍⲧ or ⲥⲁⲧⲉ (fire), refers to fire, the promise says that the addressee along with the four basic elements will receive a fragrance.[118]

The term fragrance is probably a metaphor for salvation. In the Manichaean *Psalm-Book*, it often has this nuance: Thomas, who evangelizes India, is called a sweet smell (194:13); according to 206:24,30, one awaits his fragrance just as one awaits his robe and enlightening Light. It is also a metaphor for the soul:

It is not possible that the glorious light should go to the land of the demons of the Darkness. Nor is it possible that the fragrant smell should remain in the land of the stink; it is not possible that the image of the living man should come to the dwelling places of the beasts. The Light shall go to the Light, the fragrance shall go to the fragrance"...[119]

It is possible that the metaphor of fragrance could have been influenced by this thanksgiving of Paul:

But thanks be to God who in Christ always leads us in triumph, manifesting through us the fragrance of knowledge of him everywhere. For we are the sweet smell of Christ to God among those being saved and among those who are perishing, for some a fragrance from death to death, for others a fragrance from life to life. (2 Cor. 2:14-16; cf. Phil. 4:18; Eph. 5:2).

To these passages which illustrate the use of the concept of fragrance should be compared one in the *Gospel of Truth*.

Thus the father loves his fragrance and he reveals it in every place (cf. 2 Cor. 2:14); and if it is mixed with matter, then he imparts his fragrance to the light, and in its light he elevates it above every form, every voice. For it is not the ears which perceive the fragrance but it is the spirit which possesses the

> sense of smell and it attracts it and is baptized into the fragrance of the father.[120]

While in Paul, "fragrance" refers to the life-giving knowledge of God in Christ, in the *Gospel of Truth* and Manichaean *Psalm-Book* it is related to the life-giving Spirit which dwells in man; while Paul applies it to Christians who bear the knowledge of Christ, for the Valentinian and Manichaean it is the soul of man. In *Thomas the Contender*, however, the fragrance seems to represent neither of these, but rather the notion of life-giving spiritual[121] energy which is lacking in the addressees and the elements until the sun and moon impart it. Plato (*Timaeus* 66e) witnesses to the conception of odors as exhalations of mist and vapor, thinner than water but denser than air. In the sense of a vapor, then, the "fragrance" could be related to the dew imparted by the moon (see on 144:15-19). The sun was understood by Mani to impart a fragrance to plant life:

> It (the sun) nourishes and gives power, taste and fragrance to the trees and fruits and vegetables and all the herbs and flowers and grass upon the whole earth.[122]

But Mani is not talking of just the world of nature, since within all living things there is entrapped a portion of the light which must eventually be restored in its source. Thus, part of the salvific function of the sun as the great φωστήρ is daily to nourish with light the particles of light entrapped in matter:

> It (the sun) gives power to the elements and also gives fragrance and taste to the entire cross of light.[123]

For Mani, the sun as illuminator gives power to the light which is entrapped within the elements, to the "light-cross" which is bound in all the living things upon the earth. The function of the sun and moon in *Thomas the Contender* is probably similar, as we shall see from the extended metaphor which follows.

The longest portion of the eleventh woe is the extended metaphor of the sun, grapevine and weeds (144:21-36). However, we are immediately beset with a textual problem. The text reads:

ⲠⲢⲎ ⲅⲁⲣ ⲉϥ[..]ⲡ̄ⲣ̄ⲣⲓⲉ ⲁⲝⲛ̄ ⲛⲓⲥⲱⲙⲁ ⲥⲉⲛⲁⲗⲟⲩⲗⲉϥ ⲛ̄ⲥⲉ[ⲧ]ⲁⲕⲟ
[ⲙ̄]ⲡⲣⲏⲧⲉ ϩⲱⲱϥ ⲛ̄ⲟⲩⲛ̄ⲧⲏⲃ ⲏ ⲟⲩⲭⲟⲣⲧⲟⲥ· ⲉⲩϣⲱⲡⲉ
[ⲙ̄]ⲉⲛ ⲉⲧⲡⲣⲏ ⲡ̄ⲣ̄ⲣⲓⲉ ⲁⲝⲱϥ ϣⲁⲩϭ̄ⲛϭⲁⲙ ⲛ̄ⲩⲱⲃⲧ
[ⲛ̄]ⲧⲃⲱ ⲛ̄ⲉⲗⲟⲟⲗⲉ· ⲉⲩϣⲱⲡⲉ ⲇⲉ...

If we restore the first line as ⲡⲣⲏ ⲅⲁⲣ ⲉϥ[ⲱⲁⲛ]ⲛⲣⲣⲓⲉ , "for if the sun shines on these bodies they will wither and perish just like a weed or grass" we contradict the following sentence which says that if the sun shines on the weed or grass (the antecedent of ⲁⲭⲱϥ), then they prevail. Obviously the sun cannot cause the weeds to both perish and flourish. Therefore we restore ⲡⲣⲏ ⲅⲁⲣ ⲉϥ[ⲧⲙ]ⲛⲣⲣⲓⲉ .

> For if the sun does not shine on these bodies they will wither and perish just like weeds or grass. If, now, the sun shines upon it (the weed), it prevails and chokes the grapevine; if, however, the grapevine prevails and shades those weeds and all that other brush growing up with it, and it spreads and broadens out, it alone inherits the land in which it grows, and it dominates[124] every place it shaded. So then when it grows up, it dominates all the land, and is bountiful for its master, and pleases him even more, for he would have suffered great pains on account of these weeds until he uprooted them. But the grapevine alone removed them and choked them and they died and became like the land.

The metaphor apparently has to do with the process of salvation, in which the sun (in its capacity as source of light) is the saving agent, the weeds are the body, and the grapevine represents the true inner man. If the body received the saving light, it would live on, thus keeping the soul or inner man imprisoned within it. If the soul receives the light, then it flourishes and overshadows the body and it alone inherits everything,[125] the cosmos in which it grows as well as its salvation. Even more, the soul thus enlightened dominates the entire cosmos to the degree that God (ⲡⲭⲟⲉⲓⲥ) has no need to destroy the body, since the soul all by itself removes the body which dies and returns to dust (ⲱⲱⲡⲉ ⲛⲑⲉ ⲙⲡⲕⲁⲍ).

The metaphor seems to consist of many biblical motifs, the sun which shines on the just and unjust, the vine which frequently represents Israel, the inheritance of the land (here, the earth) promised to Israel, and the uprooting of the weeds or tares. Since a great deal of this material occurs in the Matthean discourse sections (blessed are the meek for they shall inherit the earth, 5:5; his sun shines on the good and evil, 5:45; let the wheat and the weeds grow up together, 13:30) it may be that the author was inspired by the discourses of the *Gospel of Matthew*, or another similar collection of such discourse material. But there is no single locus from which the metaphor of *Thomas the*

Contender could have derived; rather we must accept its character as a *pastiche* of biblical motifs. The central imagery of the grapevine and weeds reminds one of the Matthean parable of the weeds (13:24-30), but there are significant differences. In *Thomas the Contender* it is the grapevine which is the "good seed" whereas in *Matthew* it is wheat. In *Matthew* the wheat and weeds grow up together at which time the master orders the harvesters to uproot and burn the weeds, whereas in *Thomas the Contender* the weeds and grapevine grow together to the point that the grapevine spreads out, overshadows and chokes the weeds all by itself; the master has no need to call the harvesters, since the grapevine has already separated the "bad seed" from itself. On the other hand, it is true that the master need not occupy himself with uprooting the weeds, just as in the Matthean parable no one needs to do this, at least until both wheat and weeds have matured.

The theme of vines (more properly the vineyard) and of inheritance is present in the parable of the wicked vinedressers (Mt. 21:33-41), esp. 21:38, κληρονομία). But here the story centers on the tenants and not the grapevines, which are never mentioned.

However, as *Thomas the Contender* also witnesses, the imagery of these two parables (plus the parable of the laborers in the vineyard in Mk. 20), was destined to be combined. An outstanding witness for this process of combination is to be found in the fifth similitude of the *Shepherd of Hermas* (Sim. V,ii,1-5),[126] written in the middle of the second century. Here is the parable about a fenced-in vineyard which grew up full of weeds which choke the vines. The keeper of the vineyard then digs the vineyard and pulls up the weeds, so that the vineyard becomes fertile with no weeds to choke it. Because of this, when the owner of the vineyard returns and sees the bountifulness of the vineyard, he makes the keeper a joint heir of his property along with his son. In the interpretation (Sim. V,v,1-5), the field is the world, the owner of the field is the Creator, the keeper is the Son of God,[127] the vines are "this people which he planted," the fences are protecting angels, and the weeds are the iniquities of the servants of God.

Although the *Shepherd* was widely enough read to have been used as a source, both parable and interpretation in Hermas are sufficiently different from the parable and tacit interpretation in *Thomas the Contender* to be sure that there is direct literary dependence. Nevertheless, the composite parable of the *Shepherd* does provide evidence of a tendency at work to produce a mosaic of such parabolic material. The similar phenomenon at work in *Thomas the Contender* is another example of this tendency to form a new mosaic out of the parabolic imagery of the Bible and more particularly of the teaching of Jesus, especially as it occurs in Matthew.

The parable probably was composed by the author of the second section (B) of *Thomas the Contender*. He has arranged the imagery in such a way as to draw a picturesque illustration of the eventual triumph of the soul over the body, providing it, rather than the body, receives the saving light. The interest-ing feature of this is that the soul needs, except for the saving light (the Savior's revelation?), no other help to overcome the body. Contrary to the Matthean concept, there is no need for a judge, either God or his representative, to make a final separa-tion between the good and the bad; with proper illumination, it happens automatically.

144:36-145:1. This short section, introduced by the formula: "Jesus continued and said," appears to contain the obliterated remains of a twelfth woe. The formula of continuation may have been used to reinstitute the format of twelve woes which the author (and the reader!) may have forgotten owing to the extreme length of the eleventh woe. It also has the peculiarity of be-ing the second place in the entire tractate, and the only one in section B, where the Savior is called Jesus (ⲓ̅ⲥ̅ , 144:37; cf. 139:21). Jesus is named in the first section (A) just after Thomas confesses the Savior as the Light, that is, after a "Christian" section. Similarly, the parabolic material in the eleventh woe is, as we have seen, at least intended to sound "Christian," and the Savior is called Jesus in the immediately following quotation formula. The collocation of the name Jesus with immediately preceding Christian material may be only a coincidence; if it indeed does have a peculiar significance, there seems to be no way of demonstrating it.

The formula appears to introduce a woe, judging from the appearance of the lacuna in 144:37f: ⲡⲁⲝⲉϥ ⲛⲁⲩ ϫⲉ ⲟⲩ[. . .]ⲏ / [. .]ϫⲉ ⲙ̄ⲡⲁⲧⲉⲧⲛ̄ϫⲓ ⲛ̄ⲧ- which obviously fits the pattern ⲟⲩ[ⲟⲉⲓ ⲛ]ⲏ[ⲧⲛ̄]

ⲭⲉ̅, repeated eleven times previously. The woe is directed to
those who have not received the doctrine. As a result someone
(perhaps the "ignorant," ⲛⲉⲧⲟ ⲛ̅ⲁⲧⲥⲟⲟⲩⲛ) will have to labor at
preaching in their stead (ⲥⲉⲛⲁ̇ϩⲓⲥⲉ ⲁⲧⲁϣⲉ ⲟⲉⲓϣ ⲉⲡⲙⲁ ⲛ̅ⲧⲉ ⲑⲏⲛⲉ, 144:39).
Apparently those who have not received the doctrine will flee
somewhere (remaining traces suggest "debauchery," 144:40, ⲁⲩⲱ
ⲧⲉⲧ[ⲛ̅]ⲡⲏⲧ ⲁϩ̇ⲟⲩⲛ ⲁ[ⲧⲙⲛ̅]ⲧϣⲛ[ⲁ]); certain ones have been sent down
(144:41, ⲧⲛ̅ⲛⲟⲟⲩⲟⲩ ⲁⲡⲓⲧⲛ̅) to "rescue" (?) those whom the ignorant have killed daily (144:42, ⲛ̅ⲛⲁϩ̇ⲙ ⲛⲉⲛⲧⲁⲧⲉ̇]ⲧⲛ̅ⲙⲟⲟⲩⲧⲟⲩ)
in order that they might arise from death (145:1, ⲭⲉⲕⲁⲁⲥ ⲉⲩⲛⲁⲧⲱⲟⲩⲛ
ϩ̇ⲙ̅ ⲡⲙⲟⲩ). If the proposed reconstructions be correct, these
final words of hope may act as a bridge to the following triad
of macarisms. The intact words remind one of Pauline phrases
found in I Cor. 15: "raise from the dead," vs. 20, and "I die
daily," vs. 31; (but *Thomas the Contender* reads "kill them
daily"). Such phrases leave us to wonder whether *Thomas the Contender* supported the doctrine of resurrection of the dead, and
just how the task of preaching was to be understood.

145:1-8. This short section of three beatitudes or macarisms
follows the long section of twelve woes. The first beatitude
is quite in keeping with the tenor of the woes and indeed the
whole tractate, and was probably freely composed in accordance
with the ascetic intention of the tractate: "Blessed are you who
are first to know about (to "have foreknowledge," "foreknow")[128]
the stumbling blocks (σκάνδαλον) and who flee alien things
(ἀλλότριον)." With the exception of the word σκάνδαλον, the
beatitude has no biblical ring to it. As the promise of 145:12ff
("For when you come forth from the suffering and reproach of the
body you will receive a rest. . .") shows, the "stumbling blocks"
and "alien things" are the bodies of those to whom the beatitudes
are addressed.

The second and third macarisms, however, show dependence
upon the beatitudes of Mt. 5:11 and Lk. 6:21b. The following
comparison between Horner's Sahidic text of Matthew and Luke
with *Thomas the Contender* 145:3-8 will prove illuminating:

ⲛⲁⲉⲓⲁⲧ ⲑⲏⲛⲉ	ⲛⲁⲓⲁⲧ ⲑⲩⲧⲛ̅
ⲛⲉⲧⲟⲩⲛⲟϭⲛⲉϭ ⲙ̅ⲙⲟⲟⲩ	ⲉⲩⲱϣⲁⲛⲛⲉϭⲛⲉϭ ⲑⲩⲧⲛ̅
ⲁⲩⲱ ⲉⲩⲱⲡ ⲙ̅ⲙⲟⲟⲩ ⲁⲛ	ⲛ̅ⲥⲉⲡⲱⲧ ⲛ̅ⲥⲱⲧⲛ̅
	ⲛ̅ⲥⲉⲭⲉ ϩ̇ⲱⲃ ⲛⲓⲙ ⲉⲑⲟⲟⲩ
	ⲉϩ̇ⲟⲩⲛ ⲉⲣⲱⲧⲛ̅

ⲉⲩⲁⲓϭⲟⲗ ⲉⲣⲱⲧⲛ̄
ⲉⲧⲃⲏⲏⲧ

ⲉⲧⲃⲉ ⲡⲙⲁⲉⲓⲉ ⲉⲧⲉⲩⲛⲧⲁϥϥ
ⲉϩⲟⲩⲛ ⲉⲣⲟⲟⲩ
ⲛ̄ϭⲓ ⲡⲟⲩⲁⲟⲉⲓⲥ

(145:3-5) (Mt. 5:11)

The close parallelism is noticeable. The vocabulary is
nearly identical: ⲛⲁ(ⲉ)ⲓⲁⲧ⸗, ⲧⲏⲩⲧⲛ̄/ⲧⲏⲛⲉ, ⲛⲟϭⲛⲉϭ/ⲛⲉϭⲛⲉϭ⸗, ⲉϩⲟⲩⲛ
ⲉⲣⲱⲧⲛ̄/ⲉϩⲟⲩⲛ ⲉⲣⲟⲟⲩ, ⲉⲧⲃⲉ⸗/ⲉⲧⲃⲏⲏⲧ   . Furthermore, where the
evangelist reads "and are persecuted," ⲛ̄ⲥⲉⲡⲱⲧ ⲛ̄ⲥⲱⲧⲛ̄ , *Thomas
the Contender* renders "and are not esteemed," ⲁⲩⲱ ⲉⲩⲱⲡ ⲙ̄ⲙⲟⲟⲩ
ⲁⲛ. The change from ⲡⲱⲧ to ⲱⲡ is phonically very close, and
may indicate that the author of section B of *Thomas the Contender*
is indeed rendering Mt. 5:11, but has deliberately altered the
macarism. In doing so he has omitted the phrase "and they persecute you and say every evil thing against you, lying to you,"
notions that would have been very congenial to the intention of
Thomas the Contender. The change from "on account of me" to "on
account of the love which their Lord has for them" is also strange.
Possibly both changes were deliberate, but it is hard to see what
was gained thereby. In any case the thrust of each version is
the same. The only other (and minor) difference between the two
is the general style: whereas the Sahidic version employs direct
address throughout the macarism (ⲧⲏⲩⲧⲛ̄, ⲧⲏⲩⲧⲛ̄, ⲛ̄ⲥⲱⲧⲛ̄, ⲉϩⲟⲩⲛ ⲉⲣⲱⲧⲛ),
the version in *Thomas the Contender* employs direct address in
the macarism formula, but third person plural (participial) expressions in the specification (ⲧⲏⲛⲉ, ⲙ̄ⲙⲟⲟⲩ, ⲙ̄ⲙⲟⲟⲩ, ⲉϩⲟⲩⲛ ⲉⲣⲟⲟⲩ).

The second blessing runs:

ⲛⲁⲉⲓⲁⲧ ⲧⲏⲛⲉ
ⲛⲉⲧⲣⲓⲙⲉ ⲁⲩⲱ
ⲉⲧⲟⲩⲑⲗⲓⲃⲉ ⲙ̄ⲙⲟⲟⲩ
ϩⲓⲧⲛ̄ ⲛⲉⲧⲉ ⲙⲛ̄ⲧⲉⲩ ϩⲉⲗⲡⲓⲥ
ϫⲉ ⲥⲉⲛⲁⲃⲱⲗ ⲧⲏⲛⲉ
ϩⲓⲧⲙ̄ ⲙ̄ⲡⲣⲉ ⲛⲓⲙ

ⲛⲁⲓⲁⲧ ⲧⲏⲩⲧⲛ̄
ⲛⲉⲧⲣⲓⲙⲉ ⲧⲉⲛⲟⲩ

ϫⲉ ⲧⲉⲧⲛⲁⲥⲱⲃⲉ

(145:5-8) (Lk. 6:21b)

Here there is exact parallelism between the first member
of the macarism in both *Thomas the Contender* and the *Gospel of
Luke*. However, the second member of *Thomas the Contender* shows
a tendentious change, since in place of the promise "you will

190

laugh," it substitutes the ascetic promise of a future release
from the restraints of the body and world for those oppressed
by the hopeless. It is peculiar that the addressees of the
concluding homily (section B) can on the one hand be accused as
"godless ones who have no hope" (143:9), and yet on the other
hand be "oppressed by those who have no hope." This contradiction can be resolved by supposing that within section B, the
woes and beatitudes respectively were composed with two separate
audiences in view. The same phenomenon occurs elsewhere in homiletical literature of the Bible, (Dt. 27-28; Luke 6:20-26), where
macarisms and woes or even blessings and curses are addressed to
the same general audience, as if to single out the cursed from
the blessed among the recipients.

We conclude that while the content of the woes of section B
does not derive from biblical literature, the content and, to a
certain degree, the form of the last two beatitudes do; on purely
formal grounds we further conclude that the collocation of woes
and macarisms in *Thomas the Contender* shows an awareness of the
tradition of woe and macarism in the biblical literature.

145:8-17. The final admonition of *Thomas the Contender* is introduced by the words with which Jesus admonishes Peter to avoid
temptation: γρηγορεῖτε καὶ προσεύχεσθε (Mk. 14:38; cf. Mk. 13:33).
In this case, however, the same tendentious completion which was
added to the third beatitude is added also to the "watch and
pray" section: "You shall come forth from the bonds of the oblivion of this life." Thus it is very likely that both the beatitudes and the admonition have been consciously drawn by a
single author from the synoptic tradition and given a unified
application: final escape from the body. Indeed the admonition
continues with a promise that having left behind the suffering
and mocking which derive from bodily existence, the addressees
will receive a repose, or rest (Ⲙ̄ⲧⲟⲛ). This promise is even
further spelled out in the final version of the promise which
concludes the tractate:

> For when you come forth from the sufferings and
> passions of the body, you will receive rest (ἀνάπαυσις)
> from the Good One (ⲡⲁⲅⲁⲑⲟⲥ), and you will reign with
> the king, united with him and he with you, from now
> on, forever and ever. Amen.

The idea of rest as a resultant state of coming forth from the sufferings (ϩⲓⲥⲉ; also means "labor," "toil") of the body recalls Jesus' invitation to the weary:

> Come to me all who labor and are heavy-laden, and I shall give you rest. Take my yoke upon you and learn from me, for I am meek and humble in heart, and you will find rest for your souls. (Mt. 11:28f).

This rest (ἀνάπαυσις) is a refreshment from the labors of life (cf. Mk. 6:31; 14:41; Lk. 12:19). The term "rest" (κατάπαυσις) also occurs in Heb. 4 referring to God's rest on the seventh day from the work of creation (v. 4) and of Joshua's bringing the people to rest in the promised land. Yet God's people were not given that rest in the land owing to their disobedience, so that they had to await it in the future. Thus the promise of rest yet remains (Heb. 4:1) and could even be offered "today," if the people are not disobedient (Ps. 95:7-11; Heb. 3:7-15), that is, without faith (Heb. 3:19). This "sabbath rest" is therefore an eschatological gift, by which one "ceases from his labors as God did from his" (Heb. 4:9).

One ought also to note that this "rest" involves a resting place, such as the promised land of the Old Testament. Similarly in *Thomas the Contender* one can speak of the soul as the grape-vine (144:21-36) inheriting the whole earth (or: "land," ⲕⲁϩ). Thus both the eschatological motifs of salvation, rest from the sufferings or labors of the body, as well as inheriting the land, form together a part of the eschatology of *Thomas the Contender*. In this sense, the eschatology of *Thomas the Contender* is a descendant of biblical eschatology, although it differs in stressing the necessity to escape the lust-ridden body.

Moreover, it is to be noted that this "rest" is given "by the Good One" (ⲛ̄ⲧⲟⲟⲧϥ̄ ⲙ̄ⲡⲁⲅⲁⲑⲟⲥ, hardly legible in the manuscript). This agentive phrase suggests that there is a being, called "the Good One" by whom this rest is given. For the source of such a term, one thinks immediately of Philo of Alexandria, for whom God is the supreme good. For Philo, God is both ὁ ἀγαθός (*Leg. all.* I,47; *De som.* I,149) and τὸ ἀγαθόν (*De gig.* 45). God is also called "good" in the New Testament: οὐδεις ἀγαθὸς εἰ μὴ εἷς ὁ θεός (Mk. 10:18; Lk. 18:19); εἷς ἐστιν ὁ θεός (Mt. 19:17). This usage also persisted into late antiquity: ὁ οὖν θεος τὸ ἀγαθόν, καὶ τὸ ἀγαθον ὁ θεός (CH II,16);

God is even called ἀγαθῶν ἀγαθώτατος (Eus. *Praep. evan.* I, 10:52); both are Platonic theolegumena.

Finally, we must note that the promise of rest for him who escapes the body is also consonant with the promise of reigning forever in union with the King. The collocation of the motifs of "resting" with "reigning" is to be found in Clement of Alexandria, *Stromateis* II 9,45.5 (cf. V 14,96.1); "he who seeks will not cease till he find; having found he will wonder, having wondered he will reign, and having reigned he will rest (ὁ Βασιλεύσας ἐπαναπαύσεται)." Another version of this saying, attributed to Jesus, is found in the *Gospel of Thomas*, Logion 2, but here the promise of rest is omitted, and an intermediate stage of being troubled (ⲯⲧⲟⲣⲧⲣ̄) is inserted (cf. 140:41f: [Blessed] is the wise man who sought after [the truth and] when he found it, he rested on it forever, and was not afraid of those who wanted to disturb him").

In the phrase: "you will receive rest from the Good One, and you will reign with the King," "Good One" and "King" probably designate the same being, God. This God grants salvation to men when they have left the body, and not before (ⲉⲧⲉⲧⲛ̄ϣⲁⲛⲉⲓ ⲉⲃⲟⲗ ϩⲛ̄ ⲛ̄ϩⲓⲥⲉ ⲙⲛ̄ ⲙ̄ⲡⲁⲑⲟⲥ ⲛ̄ⲧⲉ ⲡⲥⲱⲙⲁ). However, the discovery of the way to salvation while one is still in the body is a precondition of future salvation (143:5-7).

Salvation is not only a rest from and outside of the body, but it is also an eternal union with the God-King: ⲉ[ⲧⲉⲧⲛ̄]ⲧⲏⲧ ⲛⲙ̄ⲙⲁⲩ ⲉⲩⲧⲏⲧ ⲛ̄ⲙⲙⲏⲧⲛ̄ ϫⲓⲛ ⲧⲉⲛⲟⲩ ϣⲁⲉⲛⲉϩ ⲛ̄ⲁⲛⲉϩ . This apparently means, not a consubstantiality of the saved with the Savior, but rather an eschatological union. From the present version of *Thomas the Contender* we cannot tell whether this is a future once-for-all union with the divine, or a reunion. In view of the future orientation of this final passage, we should prefer to regard it as the former; it is a union with the divine which can only take place out of the body and its bondage. While one's salvation is actually *determined* while in the body (143:5-7), one's salvation actually *occurs* outside the body.

The question naturally arises whether the Good One/King is to be construed as the Savior who conducts the dialogue, i.e. Jesus. Since we tend to regard this final paragraph as belonging to a homiletic work (B) not originally a part of the dialogue proper (A), it is extremely difficult to answer this question.

Unfortunately, the intention of the present passage is not re-
coverable in terms of the rest of the homily (B) which, outside
the two continuation formulae (143:8; 144:35f), makes no reference to the Savior. In short, there seems to be no warrant contained in section B (the homily) to identify the Good One/King
with Jesus the Savior.

In terms of the larger context created by the combination
of the dialogue (A) with the homily (B), producing the current
tractate, we still cannot be certain whether the person(s) responsible for the current work intended the reader to identify
the Savior, Jesus, with the Good One/King. In view of the fact
that the Christology of section A (the identification of the
Savior with the light, 139:20) understands the Savior more as a
revealer figure than as one who directly works salvation, we
should be inclined to doubt that the Good One/King is to be
identified with the Savior.

Before we proceed on to the title and scribal note appended
to the tractate, a general remark concerning the general structure of the homiletic (B) section of the tractate is in order.

The collocation of macarism, woe and promise which charac-
terizes the second (B; 143:8-end) section of *Thomas the Contender*
is typical of a certain class of homiletical literature whose
chief representative is Deut. 27:11-28:15. Here we find curses
(27:15-26), blessings (28:1-6) and conditional promises for the
future (28:7-15). This section belongs to the concluding section of Moses' farewell address. The Priestly (P) concept regards the material in Dt. 1:1-34:4 as happening on the day of
Moses' death (Dt. 1:3; 27:11-14; 32:48-52), such that the
material through Chapter 30 constitutes his farewell speech.
This is followed by a descriptionof Moses' testamentary dispo-
sitions and finally by his death. Thus the whole of Deuteronomy
seems to be in the form of a testament of a person who faces
death or the termination of his office and must put things in
order and insure their bequeathal to his successors.[129]

The other representative of the homiletical style of section B of *Thomas the Contender* is the introduction to the sermon
on the plain of Luke 6. Here, however, we have only woes and
macarisms, while the promises for the future are incorporated
into the beatitudes. Again, the woes and macarisms of Luke 6:
20-26 are not part of Jesus' testamentary activities, or a

farewell speech, but rather the introduction to a sermon delivered to his disciples.

In terms of the total structure of section B of *Thomas the
Contender* it seems as though the structure conforms to the conclusion of Moses' farewell address insofar as it consists of
woes (curses)[130] and blessings in that order. The language of
two of the last two beatitudes of *Thomas the Contender* corresponds to that of the ninth Matthean and the third Lucan beatitudes respectively, while the content of the curses does not
correspond to that of the Lucan (or Deuteronomistic) curses at
all. Thus we can only speak in vague terms such as "inspired
by" and "echo of" when we characterize the relationship between
the woes and macarisms of *Thomas the Contender* and the major
loci of woes and blessings in the biblical literature. There
seems to be some dependence, but it is rather remote except for
the language of the last two beatitudes. We can say, however,
that in section B we are clearly dealing with discourse or homiletical material, since the biblical material similar to it is
traditionally homiletical. If we were to take Deuteronomy as the
model, we might even go further by characterizing this concluding section of *Thomas the Contender* as a farewell address, or at
least a genre of literature designed to hand on a tradition to
one's successors. It is even possible that the redactor of A
and B may have thus viewed the function of section B in his completed product. We thus characterize the genre and intention of
section B of *Thomas the Contender* as a farewell address of the
Savior in which he delivers over to his successors (in terms of
the total document A plus B, to Thomas) the ascetic tradition
defined by its content.

147:17-19. The subscript title of *Thomas the Contender* claims
that it is Thomas the Contender (ἀθλητής) who is writing to the
Perfect Ones. We have already observed that this subscript title
is contradicted by the *incipit* title of the tractate naming
Mathaias as scribe. For reasons already given we have suspected
that the *incipit* title of the tractate naming Mathaias as scribe
is secondary to the composition of sections A and B of the tractate; the name of Mathaias would presumably derive from the earlier title of section B by itself, whereas we supposed the present subscript title to have been the original subscript title of
section A, the dialogue between Thomas and the Savior. Thus we

should interpret the current subscript title of *Thomas the Contender* mainly in accordance with section A, but at the same time realize that this title was important enough to the redactor who combined A and B for him to have appended it to the entire tractate; the intention is that the entire tractate be ascribed to Thomas the Contender, writing to the Perfect.

The salient feature of the subscript title is that Thomas receives the epithet ἀθλητής, which I have translated "Contender." It derives from ἀθλεῖν, "to engage in competition or conflict," and is applied often to martyrs (LXX, N.T.), who, as leaders of the community, must undergo persecution for the faith.[131] The specific meaning in *Thomas the Contender* is that Thomas is designated as one who must contend against the fiery passions of the body which consume men's souls by preaching the message of sexual abstinence. It is in the face of this task that Thomas is characterized as extremely anxious (μεριμνᾶν, 142:4f) over the fate of those who are blinded by the fire of passion to the extent that they are but beasts and are bound for Hell.

In his capacity as contender, Thomas writes to the 'perfect' (τέλειος). In section A, in the midst of a passage employing the metaphor of wings to express the wise man's flight from the fire of lust, there are inserted the following words spoken by the Savior:

> Therefore it is necessary for us to speak to you, for this is the doctrine of the perfect (τέλειος). If, then, you desire to become perfect (τέλειος), you shall observe these things.

That is, "the perfect" are those who heed the doctrine of the perfect: flee the fiery passions of lust. Thus the perfect one is also the true athlete, he who heeds the message of the Athlete (Thomas). By virtue of the fact that it is the Savior who counsels Thomas to preach this doctrine of abstinence, the Savior also is implicitly a true athlete. Indeed he is so invoked in another example of the Thomas literature, the *Acts of Thomas*.

> O Jesus Christ. . . O peace and quiet. . . O hidden rest. . . preserving us and giving us rest in alien bodies,. . . the defender and helper of thy servants in the fight, who dost turn aside the enemy (passion). . . who in many battles dost fight for us, and make us conquer in them all, our true and invincible champion (ἀθλητής).[132]

That this implication ought to be drawn by the reader is also
suggested by the fact that the Savior is the twin of Thomas, and
thus, they are both ascetic athletes. The connection between
Thomas, the ἀθλητής, the τέλειοι, and the Savior is clear. The
central thread connecting them all is the demand for asceticism,
the denial of the body, and abstinence from its pleasures, especially the sexual.

One must take note that according to the subscript title
Thomas is writing to the Perfect (plural). Even though the
recipients (of the original section A, and now those of A + B)
are implied by the title to be perfect, the text nevertheless
informs us that they, insofar as they are represented by Thomas,
have not yet received the majesty of the perfection (ⲘⲠⲀⲧⲉⲧⲚ̄Ⲭⲓ
ⲘⲠⲘⲉⲅⲉⲑⲟⲥ Ⲛ̄ⲧⲘⲚ̄ⲧⲧⲉⲗⲉⲓⲟⲥ 138:35). Right now they are only
disciples (ⲍⲉⲚⲥⲃⲟⲩⲉⲓ , 138:35), babes (ⲍⲉⲚⲕⲟⲩⲉⲓ , 139:11),
and only on their way to becoming laborers or missionaries.

We have, therefore, identified three distinguishing features that pertain to the term "perfect": 1) The term occurs
only in the plural portions of section A and in the subscript
title (which was probably the original title to section A) and
therefore must refer to the recipients of the original section A;
2) the "doctrine of the perfect" involves becoming a wise man who
makes himself wings to flee from the visible realm, i.e. the
world of the body together with its lust; and 3) the recipients
have not yet received "the majesty of the perfection" nor are
they yet laborers for the ascetic cause, but are still only babes
and disciples. All of this tends to suggest that the addressees
of the original section A were non-ascetic Christians, who, in
order to attain perfection, had to adopt the ascetic style of
life, at which time they could be called τέλειοι. Thus to address the recipients of section A (and now sections A and B) as
"the perfect" was to address them in a proleptic fashion: "those
who are (potentially) perfect."

Certainly one component of this perfection is to receive and
observe the doctrine taught by the Savior and so to come to know
themselves (cf. 138:17f). The way to perfection in the Hermetica
is similar: "Those who observe the proclamation (κήρυγμα) and
have baptized themselves with Nous, these men have participated
in *gnosis*, and have become perfect men (τέλειοι ἄνθρωποι, CH IV,
4). Such men as have not observed the call to the knowledge of

God only pay attention to their bodily desires (IV,5), or as
Plato in his discussion of the wings of the philosopher's mind
puts it, have not separated themselves from human interest
(*Phaedrus* 249d). The perfect man is the wise man who has consulted wisdom (142:1-5) and has thus surpassed ordinary everyday knowledge:

> For the real wealth, the perfect virtues, are the
> possessions of the perfect (τέλειοι) and true-born
> alone, while the secondary things of daily duties
> are fitting to the imperfect (ἀτελές) having arrived
> only at the primary learning of the schools.[133]

Hence "perfection" involves knowing a higher doctrine whose
source is the divine, but also a doctrine having to do with one's
behavior and moral conduct, with respect to the degree to which
he shuns the ordinary everyday cares of this life and looks beyond them. Again consulting Philo, we find no one may enter the
sanctuary of the tabernacle except he who has a perfect nature
(τελειοτάτη φύσις) and having shunned all passions (πάθος) yearns
for the incorporeal and imperishable (*De ebr.* 135f). The perfect man has excluded anger (θυμός) from his soul; the exemplar
is ὁ μὲν σοφὸς τέλειος ἡδονας ἀπορρυπτόμενος καὶ ἀποσειόμενος
Μωυσῆς (*Leg. all.* 140; cf. 144:147). In short, the perfect man
always makes perfect freedom from passion his study (ὁ τέλειος
τελείαν ἀπάθειαν αἰεὶ μελετᾶ, *Leg. all.* 131). This, then, is
the meaning of the "perfect" in *Thomas the Contender* as well,
provided that we bear in mind that, for *Thomas the Contender*,
this *apatheia* involves a fierce denial of the body as the seat
of bestial lust and passion.

Before we leave this subject of perfection, one further
observation is in order. We have suggested that the recipients
of the original section A of the tractate were perhaps ordinary
Christians with good intentions ("we came to do good, and not
to curse," 141:22f) but who had to do much more than this (i.e.
deny their body) in order to become perfect. Until then, they
are only babes and disciples. Such a demand on Christians to
exceed the ordinary in order to be perfect has well-known prece-
dent in the *Gospel of Matthew*.

> For I say to you that unless your righteousness
> exceed that of the scribes and Pharisees, you will
> never enter the Kingdom of heaven (5:20).

> If you want to enter life, keep the commandments
> . . . if you want to be perfect (cf. 5:48), go sell
> your belongings and give to the poor, and you will
> have treasure in heaven. . .

Distinctions[134] of this sort have been taken by some commentators
to imply that Matthew envisioned a two-level ethic, one for the
mass of Christians, and one of supererogation for a smaller group
of τέλειοι. Whether or not this be Matthew's intention, the fact
that commentators have taken it to imply such means that others
in late antiquity could have taken it to be such. The fact that
Paul in his Corinthian correspondence wages battle against a
group of self-styled "apostles" who claimed to be superior to
him in spiritual capability should alert us that very early on
there was a tendency in the Church to make a distinction between
ordinary Christians and superior Christians. This, it seems to
me, is a distinction presupposed in the addressing of section A
of *Thomas the Contender* to "the perfect." And now, although
section B seems to be addressed to a more general audience, apparently of whom is presupposed a lesser degree of self-awareness
and desire for perfection, the combination of B with A tends to
convey this distinction in degree of perfection to the readers
of the entire *Book of Thomas the Contender*: if you would attain
the Majesty of the perfection, if you would be perfect rather
than mere disciples and babes, deny the body, and you will escape its sufferings, and you will receive rest.

Finally, attention should be drawn to the designation of
the entire tractate as a "book" (ⲡϪⲱⲘⲉ). The other occurrence
of this designation in the Nag Hammadi Corpus is CG III,2, *The
Egyptian Gospel*. (*The Holy Book of the Great Invisible Spirit*,
69:16f; *The Divine Holy Book that is Hidden*, 69:7f; cf. CG IV,2).
The contents of *Thomas the Contender*, and particularly of section
A, with which we have originally connected the subscript title,
gives no help in explaining the significance of this designation.
During the first three centuries A.D. in which *Thomas the Contender* must have been written, βιβλίον or βίβλος could refer to
a codex, roll of papyrus, library, archive or chronicle.[135] If
the subscript title originally went with section A, we might expect the designation διάλογος, "conversation," as it is found in
the subscript title of the *Dialogue of the Savior* in Codex III
(CG III,5), but we have in Nag Hammadi other tractates written in
the dialogue style which do not bear the designation διάλογος,

but rather "Sophia of Jesus Christ," "Gospel of Mary," etc. Perhaps the reason for naming *Thomas the Contender* as a "book" was
to distinguish it from another work belonging to the Thomas tradition, *The Gospel according to Thomas*. In both cases the desig-
nations ("book" and "gospel" respectively) are not entirely descriptive of the contents. Another possibility, which seems unlikely, is that when the two sections of *Thomas the Contender* were
combined, an hypothetical original title of section A (e.g. διάλογος, or λόγος, etc.) was suppressed because of the designation
of the material in section B, which was of a different nature
(λόγοι; cf. commentary on 138:1-4), and supplanted by the more
neutral term "book" (ϪⲱⲘⲈ), as a designation for dialogue plus
logia. It seems no conclusion can be drawn on this matter.

145:20-23. Since the scribal colophon is not a part of this
tractate, no extended comment is necessary. It is an admonition
that the scribe be remembered by his brethren in their prayers.
This is done by the common formula ⲀⲢⲓ ⲠⲀⲘⲈⲈⲨⲈ (Ⲍⲱ) ⲚⲀⲤⲚⲎⲨ (ⲌⲚ̄
ⲚⲈⲦⲚ̄ⲠⲣⲟⲤⲈⲨⲭⲎ) followed by a prayer, in this case "Peace to the
saints and to the spiritual," which is written entirely in Greek
except for the last line which was apparently written in Coptic.
The latter may have been added to what appears to be a standard
prayer (εἰρήνη τοῖς ἁγίοις) because the scribe of Codex II
wished to refer to himself as a "spiritual one" (ⲈⲓⲢⲎⲚⲎ ⲦⲟⲓⲤ
ⲀⲄⲓⲟⲓⲤ ⲘⲚ̄ ⲚⲓⲠⲚⲈⲨⲘⲀⲦⲓⲕⲟⲤ . If this be the case, we can wonder whether the scribe of Codex II knew how to write Greek,
since he apparently completed the Greek prayer with a Coptic
(ⲘⲚ̄ ⲚⲓⲠⲚⲈⲨⲘⲀⲦⲓⲕⲟⲤ) rather than a Greek (καὶ τοῖς πνευματικοῖς)
expression.

We should call attention once more to the form of the rein-
forcing particle Ⲍⲱ used by the scribe himself, because we
cited this as evidence that the person who composed the *incipit*
of the tractate (which uses the form ⲌⲱⲱⲦ) was someone other
than the individual who wrote the colophon, the scribe of Codex
II.

NOTES

[1]cf. P. Oxy. 654: ΟΙΤΟΙ ΟΙ ΛΟΓΟΙ ΟΙ [ⲀⲠⲞⲔⲢⲨϤⲞⲒ ⲞⲨⲤ ⲈⲖⲀ]
ⲀⲎⲤⲈⲚ ⲒⲎ̄Ⲥ̄ Ⲟ ⲌⲰⲚ Ⲕ[ⲀⲒ ⲈⲢⲠⲀⲨⲈⲚ ⲒⲞⲨⲆⲀⲤ Ⲟ]
ⲔⲀⲒ ⲐⲰⲘⲀⲤ

[2]See on this James M. Robinson, "ΛΟΓΟΙ ΣΟΦΩΝ": Zur Gattung
der Sprachquelle Q," *Zeit und Geschichte: Dankesgabe an Rudolf
Bultmann zum 80. Geburtstag*, ed. E. Dinkler (Tübingen: J.C.B.
Mohr, 1964), pp. 77-96.

[3]Eusebius, *Hist. Eccl.* III,39,16. text in K. Aland, *Synopsis
Quattuor Evangeliorum* (Stuttgart: Würtemburgische Bibelanstalt,
1964), p. 531.

[4]*Hippolytus Werke*, Vol. III: *Refutatio Omnium Haeresium*,
ed. P. Wendland (Die griechischen christlichen Schriftsteller der
ersten drei Jahrhunderte #26; Leipzig: Hinrichs, 1916), p. 195.

[5]Titi Flaui Clementis Alexandrini, *Opera Omnia*, ed. Rein-
holdus Klotz (4 vols.; Lipsiae: Schwickert, 1831), II, p. 226.
H.-C. Puech ("Les nouveaux écrits gnostiques," in *Coptic Studies
in Honor of Walter Ewing Crum* (Boston: Byzantine Institute, 1950),
p. 119f) wondered whether these *Traditions of Mathias* might be
identical with a lost work entitled the *Gospel of Mathias*, which
might in turn be identical with our *Thomas the Contender*. He
later abandoned this hypothesis in E. Hennecke, *New Testament
Apocrypha*, ed. W. Schneemelcher (Philadelphia: Westminster, 1963),
p. 312f.

[6]*Ev. Th.* has "Twin Judas Thomas" but not "brother of the
Lord"; here Koester must have intended to refer either to *Thomas
the Contender* or to the *Acts of Thomas*.

[7]H. Koester, "ΓΝΩΜΑΙ ΔΙΑΦΟΡΟΙ," *HTR* 58 (1965), 297f.

[8]*Chronicon Edessenum*, ed. Ignatius Guidi (Corpus Scrip-
torum Christianorum Orientalium [hereafter abbreviated CSCO],
Ser. III, Tom. IV; Louvain: Secrétariat du Corpus SCO, 1903),
Lat. p. 5, Syr. p. 4.

[9]Noted by Koester, *art. cit.*, p. 292, n. 30.

[10]W. Bauer in Hennecke-Schneemelcher, *op. cit.*, Vol. 1, p.
438.

[11]A.F.J. Klijn: *The Acts of Thomas* (Leiden: Brill, 1962),
p. 13.

[12]cf. especially the Paraclete's claim to have been incar-
nated and to have gone to India (15:25), Persia (15:29), Mesene
(15:30 and Parthia (16:1).

[13]In *Thomas the Contender*, twin is ⲤⲞⲈⲒⲰ ; but cf. ⲰϢⲢ̄
Ⲙ̄ⲘⲎⲈ , 138:8.

[14]G. Bornkamm in Hennecke-Schneemelcher, *op. cit.*, Vol. 2,
p. 440f.

[15]R.A. Lipsius & M. Bonnet, *Acta Apostolorum Apocrypha* (3
vols.; Hildesheim: Olms, 1959), II, pt. 2, p. 156.

[16]B.P. Grenfell & A.S. Hunt, ΛΟΓΙΑ ΙΗΣΟΥ, *Sayings of Our Lord from an Early Greek Papyrus* (New York, 1897), p. 6.

[17]H.-C. Puech in Hennecke-Schneemelcher, *op. cit.*, Vol. 1, p. 287.

[18]Marcionite Christianity probably began in the late third century, to judge from the fact that the orthodox as late as 400 had to call themselves Palutians, since the Marcionites had pre-empted the name Christian (Ephraem, 22nd Midrash against the Heretics, 5f; cited in W. Bauer, *Rechtgläubigkeit und Ketzerei im ältesten Christentum* (Tübingen: Mohr, 1963), p. 26. The inception of orthodox Christianity occurred around A.D. 200 under Palut; Bauer, *ibid.*, p. 26.

[19]The *Excerpta ex Theodoto of Clement of Alexandria*, ed. R.P. Casey (*Studies and Documents*, Vol. 1, ed. K. & S. Lake; London: Christophers, 1934). Cf. also the Marcosian password ἐγὼ οἶδα ἐμαυτὸν καὶ γινώσκω ὅθεν εἰμί, Irenaeus I, 14,4 in W. Harvey, ed. *Libros quinque adverus haereses* (Ridgewood: Gregg, 1965); the password of the Levite Gnostics in their Gospel of Phillip: ἐπέγνων ἐμαυτήν, Epiphanius, *Panarion* 26,13,2, in Karl Holl, ed. *Epiphanius* (Die griechischen christlichen Schriftsteller der ersten drei Jahrhunderte, Vol. II; Leipzig: Hinrichs, 1915); and the first *Apocalypse of James* CG V,2,33:15f: ⲚⲦⲔ ⲚⲒⲘ Ⲏ ⲚⲦⲔ ⲈⲂⲞⲖ ⲦⲰⲚ ("who are you or whence are you?") 34:16: ⲈⲔⲚⲀⲂⲰⲔ ⲈⲦⲰⲚ ... ⲀⲠⲘⲀ ⲈⲦⲀⲒⲈⲒ ⲈⲂⲞⲖ ⲘⲘⲀⲨ ⲈⲒⲚⲀⲂⲰⲔ ⲞⲚ ⲈⲘⲀⲨ ("whither are you going?...it is to the place whence I came that I shall return.")

[20]Cf. e.g. the *Second Apocalypse of James* (CG V,4,33:15,19f; 34:16).

[21]Lipsius & Bonnet, *op. cit.*, p. 121.

[22]A. Guillaumont, H.-C. Puech, G. Quispel, W. Till and Yassah 'Abd al Massah, *The Gospel According to Thomas* (New York: Harper & Row, 1959), p. 39. To be compared is Logion 3, (33:26-34:5) which gives basically the same idea, but in different words: ⲒⲞⲦⲀⲚ ⲈⲦⲈⲦⲚⲨⲀⲚⲤⲞⲨⲰⲚ ⲦⲎⲨⲦⲚ ⲦⲞⲦⲈ ⲤⲈⲚⲀⲤⲞⲨⲰⲚ ⲦⲎⲚⲈ ⲀⲨⲰ ⲦⲈⲦⲚⲀⲈⲒⲘⲈ ⲬⲈ ⲚⲦⲰⲦⲚ ⲠⲈ ⲚⲨⲎⲢⲈ ⲘⲠⲈⲒⲰⲦ ⲈⲦⲞⲚⲌ ⲈⲨⲰⲠⲈ ⲆⲈ ⲦⲈⲦⲚⲀⲤⲞⲨⲰⲚ ⲦⲎⲚⲈ ⲀⲚ ⲈⲈⲒⲈ ⲦⲈⲦⲚⲨⲞⲞⲠ ⲌⲚ ⲞⲨⲘⲚⲦⲌⲎⲔⲈ ⲀⲨⲰ ⲚⲦⲰⲦⲚ ⲠⲈ ⲦⲘⲚⲦⲌⲎⲔⲈ ("When you know yourselves, then you will be known, and you will know that you are sons of the living Father. But if you do not know yourselves, then you exist in poverty and you are poverty.")

[23]G.W.H. Lampe, *A Patristic Greek Lexicon* (Oxford: Clarendon, 1961), *ad. loc.*

[24]Hermetic citations from A.D. Nock & A.-J. Festugière, *Corpus Hermeticum* (4 vols.; Paris: Les Belle Lettres, 1960).

[25]So Bultmann in *Theological Dictionary of the New Testament* (= TDNT), ed. by G. Kittel (in progress; Grand Rapids: Eerdmans, 1965), vol. 1, pp. 689-695.

[26]The term "walking with" the Savior, who is later identified as the "light" means that Thomas, as long as he is with the Savior, is potentially enlightened, and must actualize this enlightenment before the Savior's ascension (138:23). Cf. John 12:35: "For a while you still have the light. *Walk* while you have the light, lest the darkness engulf you."

[27]There remains the possibility that the conflation could have been a deliberate attempt at obfuscation, perhaps a gnostic device to conceal the true significance of the "secret words" whose true significance the initiate may have been instructed to sort out. However, the prominence of the theme of preaching tends to give one the impression that the text intends to edify, rather than to confuse, the reader.

[28]Irenaeus, *Adv. Haer.* II,40,2 (Harvey, *op. cit.*) in abscondo haec eandem Salvatorem docuisse non omnes sed aliquos (alios quosdam?) discipulorum, qui possunt capere, et per argumenta, et aenigmater, et parabolas ab eo significata intelligentibus.; cf. *Exc. ex Theod.* 66: ὁ σωτὴρ τοὺς ἀποστόλους ἐδίδασκεν, τὰ μὲν πρῶτα τυπικῶς καὶ μυστικῶς, τὰ δὲ ὕστερα παραβωλικῶς καὶ ἠνιγμένως, τὰ δὲ τρίτα σαφῶς καὶ γυμνῶς κατὰ μόνας. (Casey, *op. cit.*); cf. Lk. 18:34.

[29]Resurrection is alluded to only in section B, and even here it does not appear to refer to the Savior (145:1).

[30]To be assigned to this class are the following Gnostic works: *The Gospel of Mary* and the *Sophia Jesu Christi* of BG 8502, the *First Apocalypse of James*, plus the material in the *Apocryphon of James*, and the *Letter of Peter to Philip*, all in the Nag Hammadi Library.

[31]Cf. *A.Th.* 37: "If, then, you cannot see me who am like you unless you raise yourselves a little from the earth, how can you see him who spends his time in the height and now is found in the depth?" Cf. also *Ev.Th.*, Log. 5 (33:10–14); "Jesus said: 'Know what is in front of you and what is hidden from you will be revealed; for nothing is hidden which will not be revealed.'" Cf. Manichaean *Kephalaia* 163:28.

[32]Lampe, *op. cit.*, *ad. loc.*

[33]D. Georgi, *Die Gegner des Paulus im 2. Korintherbrief* (Wissenschaftliche Monographien z. A. und N. Testament, vol. II; Neukirchen-Vluyn: Neukirchener, 1964), p. 50.

[34]This motif enjoyed use in the world of Christian orthodoxy as well. *On Christian Behavior: Ms. Pierpont Morgan 604* ed. K.H. Kuhn (*CSCO* 29; Louvain: Secrétariat du Corpus SCO, 1960) contains a rather ascetic homily entitled *On Christian Behavior*, which says: "A man...is like irrational beasts, and he is like them because the beasts are ignorant. Therefore he has been reckoned with them in Hell. It was said: Death shepherds them, summoning them into the fire and every anguish. For Solomon said: What is the state of man and beast? Who knows the spirit of man that it goes up to heaven, and the spirit of the beast, that it goes down to Hell? Just as the death of the one, so also the death of the other? He said this when he saw that man has the nature of a beast."

[35]G. Quispel, "Makarius und das Lied von der Perle," in *Le Origini dello Gnosticismo: Colloquio di Messina 13-18 Aprile 1966*, ed. Ugo Biarchi (Leiden: Brill, 1967), p. 643.

[36]CH. IV, 5.

[37]Cf. CH Frg. IIa, 16: "and everything upon earth the providence of truth overcomes by decay, and encompasses and shall encompass it. For without decay generation cannot be sustained. Upon every generation there follows corruption, in order that there might again be generation. For things that are generated must be generated from that which is decaying, and the things that are generated must undergo decay, lest the generation of beings should cease."

[38]In H.N. Fowler, trans. *Plato, Euthyphro, Apology, Crito, Phaedo, Phaedrus*. (Loeb Classical Library; Cambridge: Harvard University, 1966), *ad. loc.*

[39]ϫⲱⲁⲕ ⲛ̄ⲛⲉⲩⲥⲟⲧⲉ is a difficult expression, since commonly means to stretch a bow (ⲡⲓⲧⲉ) or extend a chain or, intransitively, "to reach" (Crum, 766bff). In his index to *A Manichaean Psalm-Book* (Stuttgart: Kohlhammer, 1938, p. 41), C. Allbery lists the meaning of ϫⲁⲗⲕ as "to shoot." The metaphor could also be rendered: "They are like those who extend fires for signalling in the night; to be sure they extend their fires like anyone else, since they are extended for signalling, but it (the signal) is not visible."

[40]ⲉⲕⲣ̄ⲟⲩⲟⲉⲓⲛ can also be taken as a second present "emphatic" tense, and would thus fall under the "emplois abusif" category discussed by Polotsky in his *Études de syntaxe copte*: "You truly shine, Lord!" I have decided, however, to render it as a circumstantial: "You are our light, since you enlighten, Lord," even though this loses some of the force of the direct confession.

[42]*Die Pseudoklementinen*, Vol. II: *Recognitionen in Rufins Übersetzung*, ed. Bernhard Rehm (Die griechischen christlichen Schriftsteller der drei ersten Jahrhunderte #51; Berlin: Akademie Verlag, 1965), p. 219.

[43]The Odes of Solomon 15:1f: "As the sun is a joy to those who seek its daybreak, so is my joy the Lord, because he is my sun and his rays have lifted me up, and his light has dispelled all darkness from my face." *Die Oden Salomos*, ed. W. Bauer (Kleine Texte für Vorlesungen u. Übungen #65; Berlin: de Gruyter, 1933), p. 31. Cf. also the Pseudo Clementine Homilies, 17, 10, 4 (*Die Pseudoklementinen*, Vol. I: *Homilien*, ed. Bernhard Rehm (Die griechischen christlichen Schriftsteller der ersten Jahrhunderte #42; Berlin: Akademie Verlag, 1953), p. 235. "Souls...though they be separated from the body and be found with a thirst for him, they are borne immortal to his breast as in wintertime the mists of the mountains, attracted by the beams of the sun, are borne to it."

[44]Compiled from Shahrastani, En-Nadim, and Hegemonius by Hans Jonas in *The Gnostic Religion* (Boston: Beacon, 1958), p. 233. For an earlier treatment of the theme of the waxing and waning of the moon due to transference of light, cf. I Enoch 78.

[45]For the exclamatory style, see the *Acts of Thomas* 44, and the Pseudo-Titus Epistle in Hennecke-Schneemelcher, *op. cit.*, vol. 2, p. 149.

[46]Cicero, *De natura deorum II*, 10,28. The idea may have originated with Empedocles: "Come now, hear how the fire, as it was separated, caused to spring up the night-born scions of men and of tearful women. . . First sprang up from the earth whole-natured forms (οὐλοφυεῖς, without distinction) having a share of both water and fire; these the fire sent forth, desiring to join its like, showing forth as yet neither the lovely form of the limbs, nor the voice nor the organ proper to men." (Fr. 62, Simplicius, *Phys.* 381,31, in G.S. Kirk & C.E. Raven, *The Presocratic Philosophers* (Cambridge: University Press, 1966), p. 338.

[47]Makarios, Homily 15,50 in *Die 50 geistlicher Homilien des Makarios*, ed. A. Dorries, E. Klostermann, M. Kroeger (Patristische Texte und Studien #4; Berlin: de Gruyter, 1964), p. 155. Cf. Philo, *Leg. all.* III, 248-9.

[48]Cf. *Thomas the Contender* 144:15-17: "who is the one who will rain upon you a dew of rest so as to extinguish the multitude of fire from you?"

[49]Pseudo-Clementine *Recognitions*, op. cit., IX,5,4f. Cf. Pseudo-Clementine *Homilies*, op. cit., XI,26,4; *Exc. ex Theod.*, op. cit., 81.

[50]*Elenchos* V, 8,16 in *Hippolytus Werke*, Band III, *Refutatio Omnium Haeresium*, ed. Paul Wendland (Die griechischen christlichen Schriftsteller der ersten Jahrhunderte #26; Leipzig: Hinrichs, 1916), p. 92.

[51]For the Hermetics, the fire is generally good; as the most penetrating of the elements, it is destined to clothe the equally penetrating *Nous* when it leaves the body (CH X,18).

[52]Quoted in C.G. Montefiore & H. Loewe, *A Rabbinic Anthology* (New York: Meridian, 1963), p. 298.

[53]Pseudo-Cyprian, "On the Discipline and Advantage of Chastity 9, 10 in *The Writings of the Ante-Nicene Fathers*, 10 vols. (Grand Rapids: Eerdmans, 1965), V, p. 590. Phrases like this are frequent in the wisdom literature; cf. Job 31:9ff; Sir. 9:9; 23:16, etc.

[54]In Hennecke-Schneemelcher, op. cit., vol. 2, pp. 150, 152, 156.

[55]Cf. the adage: δι᾿ ὧν τις ἁμαρτάνει, διὰ τούτων κολάζεται (*Wisd. Sol.* 11:16).

[56]ⲚⲦⲈⲞⲨⲣⲘⲚ̄ⲌⲎⲦⲞⲨⲱⲌⲘⲚ̄ⲞⲨ᾿ can be read either ⲞⲨⲰⲌ ⲘⲚ̄ ⲞⲨ᾿ ("dwell with a. . ." or ⲞⲨⲰⲌⲘ Ⲛ̄ⲞⲨ᾿ ("answer to a. . ."). Neither rendering is *prima facie* more suitable than the other, although the fact that we would expect a supralinear stroke or other punctuation after Ⲙ in ⲞⲨⲰⲌⲘ Ⲛ̄᾿ balances the scales slightly in favor of ⲞⲨⲰⲌⲘⲚ̄᾿. But the punctuation in *Thomas the Contender* is too irregular to serve as final criterion.

[57]*Leg. all.* III,16-17.

[58]*De. som.* I, 139.

[59]The phrase ⲚⲞⲨϤⲀⲚⲦⲀⲤⲒⲀ ⲘⲘⲎⲈ means literally "a true illusion," since ⲘⲘⲎⲈ is in adjectival position. We would expect ⲞⲨϤⲀⲚⲦⲀⲤⲒⲀ ⲚⲦⲘⲎⲈ , "an illusion of *the* truth." Although the text lacks the definite article, we can obtain a meaning close to the latter by interpreting ⲘⲎⲈ as an indefinite abstract noun with zero article, and translate "an illusion of truth." Another possibility is to regard ⲚⲞⲨϤⲀⲚⲦⲀⲤⲒⲀ ⲘⲘⲎⲈ as a case of reversed position of the attributive (Till, KG 117) and translate "an illusory truth." A third alternative is to regard the Ⲙ of ⲘⲘⲎⲈ as the Ⲛ of equivalence and translate "an illusion as truth." In any case, the intent is clear.

[60]Note the use of good epithets for bad things = parody of a bedroom scene.

[61]The fire is like a stake which they can never shake off (ⲈⲘⲚϢϬⲞⲘ ⲘⲘⲞⲞⲨ ⲚⲚⲀϪⲌ ⲈⲚⲈϪ 140:28). For Plato, the situation is not so hopeless, because παραλαβοῦσα ἡ φιλοσοφία ἔχουσαν αὐτῶν τὴν ψυχὴν ἠρέμα παραμυθεῖται καὶ λύειν ἐπιχειρεῖ. (*Phaedo*, 83a).

[62]The following sentence is difficult to understand: "It (the fire) bound all their members in the bitterness of the bond of the lust for these visible things (or person?) which will decay and change and turn according to impulse. They have always dragged from heaven to earth, slaughtered, dragged upon all the unclean beasts of the corruption" (140:31-37). We do not know whether it is persons or things which perish and change and turn. Is the bond of lust (ⲦⲘⲢⲢⲈ ⲚⲦⲈⲠⲒⲐⲨⲘⲈⲒⲀ ⲚⲚⲀⲈⲒ ⲈⲦ´...) a "bond of lust of these persons who" . . . or a "bond of lust for these things which. . .," i.e. subjective or objective genitive? The fact that these things or persons will "perish and change" seems to favor the "objective" genitive, and thus refers to "things," but when it continues: "which turn according to impulse," it seems as though persons are in view. Nevertheless, we have decided to understand it as referring to things. The phrase "being dragged over (ϨⲒⲬⲚ) all the beasts of the corruption" seems to mean that the soul is dragged down from heaven (ⲚⲦⲠⲈ) to the visible body or corpse (under the metaphor of a beast, cf. 140:39-141:11) on earth (ⲀⲠⲒⲦⲚ). Cf. the *Kore Kosmou* (CH Frg. XXIII, 39): "But if you be found guilty of any greater sins. . . having quit the body you shall not dwell in heaven nor in human bodies. but shall thenceforth not cease wandering from one beast to the next."

[63]*Phaedo* 81C,D; for the imagery of souls frequenting tombs, cf. 141:14-18; 142:13.

[64]"Rest" is used in Heb. 3:7-4:11 and Rev. 14:13 with reference to the anticipated state of the blessed. On "rest" in Gnostic texts, see F.M. Sagnard, *La gnose Valentinienne et le temoignage de Saint Irenée* (Études de Philosophie Médievale, Directeur Etienne Gilson, XXXVI; Paris: J. Vrin, 1947), p. 655 and P. Vielhauer in *Apophoreta* (Beihefte ZNW, 30, 1964), pp. 281ff. See comment on 145:8-17.

[65]For the translation "yes" for γάρ, see Liddell, Scott, and Jones, *A Greek-English Lexicon* (Oxford: Clarendon, 1961), p. 338b, 3a: "In Tragic dialogue and Plato, where 'yes' or 'no' may be supplied from the context."

[66]In *Laws* 959a,b, Plato calls the body "an attendant semblance of the self" and uses the term εἴδωλα of corpses. On the other hand, Plutarch calls the soul an εἴδωλον, since "the soul receives the impression of its shape through being moulded by the mind and moulding in turn and enfolding the body on all sides, so that, even if it be separated from either one for a long time, since it preserves the likeness (ὁμοιότητα) and the imprint (τύπον) it is correctly called an image (εἴδωλον)." *De facie in orbe lunae*, 945a in H. Cherniss & W.C. Helmbold, trans., *Plutarch's Moralia*, vol. XII (Loeb Classical Library; Cambridge: Harvard University Press, 1957).

[67]*Phaedo* 81 D,E.

[68]*Asclepius* 22.

[69]The phrase is ⲥⲉⲍⲟⲩⲣⲟⲉⲓⲧ ⲛ̄ⲧⲙⲛ̄ⲧ[ⲉⲓⲁ]. ⲍⲟⲩⲣⲟⲉⲓⲧ is the hitherto unwitnessed qualitative of ⲍⲟⲟⲩⲣ(ⲉ) (Crum 737; in view of the qualitative in -ⲟⲉⲓⲧ, the int. may be ⲍⲟⲟⲩⲣⲟ). The restoration ⲙ̄ⲛ̄ⲧⲱⲛ̄ⲍ "vitality", is a guess, and was chosen as the only form I could locate of an abstract noun with no more than six letters, so as to restore the lacuna.

[70]CG VII,4, 105:6-11. Note the pun on the word ⲥⲟⲧⲉ , which can mean either "fire" or "arrow." Thus one can speak either of the "fire" or "darts" of fornication. Apparently the theme of Cupid's arrow is in view.

[71]*Kephalaia* 93:2-5.

[72]The text reads ⲥⲉⲛ|..]ⲟ ⲛ̄ⲛⲉⲩⲙⲉⲗⲟⲥ (141:37). The only restorations I can think of are, assuming the expression is in the future tense in parallel with ⲥⲉⲛⲁⲫⲣ̄ⲁⲅⲉⲗⲗⲟⲩ (141:35), ⲥⲉⲛⲁⲕⲟ , they will "place" or "leave" their members, or ⲥⲉⲛⲁⲗⲟ , they will "leave" their members. Either alternative gives the sense of "abandoning members (μέλος)" in despair. Apparently this image is meant to convey the fact that these wretched men will not strip off the earthly body in patient expectation of salvation, but will shuck them off in utter despair, since their limbs have become vehicles of torture for their souls, undergoing scourging and burning. The plural, τα μέλη, occurs in burial inscriptions of the first and second centuries A.D. meaning "body": πνεῦμα μελῶν ἀπέλυε and ψυχῆς ἐκ μελέων αποπταθείσης (TDNT, IV [1967], p. 556).

[73]In the Sahidic versions of Mk. 14:54//Lk. 22:56 and Acts 16:29, ⲕⲱⲍⲧ ("fire") translates φῶς, "light," in the sense of some kind of lamp or torch which gives both light and heat. This is an apt metaphor for the heat and light of the sun necessary for the germination of a seed (cf. ⲡⲟⲩⲟⲉⲓⲛ ⲉⲧⲣ̄ⲟⲩⲟⲉⲓⲛ ⲙ̄ⲡⲥⲁⲛⲍⲡⲉ , 142:18).

[74]*Phaedo* 83 D,E.

[75]*Phaedo* 84 B.

208

[76]Cf. the end of the farewell discourse in John where the disciples say: "Look, now you are speaking plainly, and not at all in parables. Now we know that you know everything and have no need of being questioned. Accordingly we know you came from God." (Jn. 16:29f).

[77]It should be noted that this formula (142:27,29f) in this section uses the Greek word ἀμήν and perhaps derives from a different source than the same formula in 141:25, which uses the Coptic ϩⲛ ⲟⲩⲙⲏⲉ.

[78]*Asclepius* 28.

[79]The only "furniture" of Hell that is both masculine in gender and fits the lacuna ⲡⲓ[...]ⲉ seems to be ϫⲟⲉ , "wall" or ⲓⲟⲟⲣⲉ , "canal." The adjective which modifies it, ⲉ/[. . . .]ⲱ̄, is in all probability either ⲉⲧⲟⲣ ⲱ , "which is heavy," or ⲉⲧⲡⲟⲣⲱ , "which is wide." The thing which is heavy or wide is also ⲉⲧⲧⲁⲭⲣⲏⲩ ⲁ[, probably set against (ⲁⲣⲱ·), which seems to apply to a wall rather than a canal. The prepositional complement (ⲙ̄ⲙⲟⲟⲩ ⲉϩⲟⲩⲛ ⲉⲣⲟⲩ , "them (D.O.) into it" seems to require the idea of constraint, thus ⲱⲧⲡ "to imprison."

[80]Requires a direct object (ⲙ̄ⲙⲟⲟⲩ) as in 142:42. This leaves two letters before]ⲃⲉ[, which is probably ⲗⲓⲃⲉ .

[81]The direct object changes from "them" to "you" (plural). But since the direct object continues as "them" (ⲛ̄ⲥⲱⲟⲩ, 142:42, and thereafter), "you" is not the direct object of the description, but is probably the object of a verb which is used to illustrate some feature of the description. Because "you" is not a subject under discussion we restore ...ⲉⲧⲛⲁⲡⲱⲧ ⲛ̄ⲥⲁ ⲧⲏⲛⲉ "who will pursue you." This allows something like ⲁⲩⲱ ⲛⲓⲁⲣⲭⲱⲛ, "and the archons" to fill out the sentence: "They will not be forgiven their madness. And the archons who will pursue you...." The "archons," however, is only a guess (cf. 142:31-32).

[82]The sneerers are then delivered (παραδιδόναι) over to the angel (ἄγγελος) Tartarouchos, who pursues (ⲡⲱⲧ ⲛ̄ⲥⲁ·) them with fiery scourges (ⲫⲣⲁⲅⲉⲗⲗⲟⲩ must be for φραγέλλιον) which cast sparks into the face of the one who is pursued. Thus I restore 142:42 with words denoting some kind of fiery instrument of scourging such as chains, swords or whips. In this case I have chosen whips (μάστιξ): [ⲛ̄ⲩϫⲓ ⲛ̄ϩⲉⲛⲙⲁⲥⲧⲓ̅ⲝ̅ ⲛ̄ⲥⲁⲧⲉ , "and he will take fiery whips."

[83]*Theogony* 735-744. This is the translation of H.G. Evelyn-White, *Hesiod, The Homeric Poems and Homerica* (The Loeb Classical Library; Cambridge: Harvard, 1967).

[84]*Iliad* VIII 13-16. This is the translation of A.T. Murray, *Homer, The Iliad* (The Loeb Classical Library; Cambridge: Harvard, 1965).

[85]Cf. also 749f.

[86]The translation of H.G. Evelyn-White, *op. cit.*

[87]*Ibid.*

[88]*Nekyia* (Leipzig: B.G. Teubner, 1893).

[89]*Ibid.*, pp. 125-127. He adds: "Wir wissen dass es ein solches Gedicht gegeben hat mit dem Titel Ὀρφέως εἰς ᾍιδου κατάβασις (p. 128).

[90]Tartarouchos is derived from the roots τάρταρο plus ἔχ(ειν) = ταρταροῦχος.

[91]According to the Ethiopic version, English translation in Hennecke-Schneemelcher, *op. cit.*, Vol. 2, pp. 668-683. This work is to be distinguished from a work of the same title discovered in the Nag Hammadi Corpus.

[92]For the classical references, see Dieterich, *op. cit.*, pp. 197f.

[93]*Ibid.*, p. 199f.

[94]Text in Hennecke-Schneemelcher, *op. cit.*, vol. 2, p. 671.

[95]The text reads ⲛⲉⲧⲣϩⲉⲗⲡⲓⲍⲉ ⲁⲧⲥⲁⲣⲝ ⲁⲩⲱ ⲡⲱⲧⲉⲕⲟ ⲉⲧⲛⲁⲧⲉⲕⲟ . In such phrases, I have observed that usually has the function of joining nouns which lie in the same syntactical position so that in a compound oblique object as hope "in the flesh and in the prison which will perish" the preposition does not need to be repeated: ⲁⲧⲥⲁⲣⲝ ⲙⲛ ⲡⲱⲧⲉⲕⲟ . . . On the other hand, ⲁⲩⲱ generally has a consecutive function so that such a phrase would read ⲁⲧⲥⲁⲣⲝ ⲁⲩⲱ ⲁⲡⲱⲧⲉⲕⲟ . However, in the phrase under consideration, the preposition ⲁ , functioning as *nota accusativi*, was probably not felt to have prepositional force, so that either ⲁⲩⲱ or ⲙⲛ could be used. Cf. Latin *et* and *-que*.

[96]Plato, *Gorgias* 493A; *Cratylus* 400C.

[97]Such a usage has been recorded by H.J. Polotsky (*Études de syntaxe copte* (Le Caire: Société d'Archéologie Copte, 1944), p. 53) as an *emploi abusif* of the second tense: "L'emphase avec laquelle le verbe est prononce s'exprime 'abusivement' par l'emploi des Temps Seconds, dans des exclamations comme 'tu es fou!' p.ex. ⲉⲣⲉⲗⲟⲃⲉ: ⲁⲣⲉⲗⲟⲃⲉ - μαίνη Actes XII,15."

[98]Cf. *Gospel of Thomas* Log. 87: "Miserable is the body which depends on a body and miserable is the soul which depends on these two," and Log. 112: "Woe to the flesh which depends on the soul, woe to the soul which depends on the flesh."

[99]Crum lists no entry for ⲥⲱⲃⲧⲉ ϩⲣⲁⲓ ϩⲛ᾽. ϩⲣⲁⲓ ϩⲛ᾽ usually means ἐν, but can also mean εἰς. Thus we get something like ἐτοιμάξειν εἰς, "prepare for." We may have a scribal error, but have no emendation to suggest.

[100]Very much like those cast down to Tartaros; cf. 142:35f.

[101]We have here what appears to be another Coptic pun. They are full (ⲙⲉϩ) of bitterness and their minds are deranged by the

burning (ⲙⲟⲩⲍ) within them. (Some form of ⲙⲟⲩⲍ [to be full of]
is required in the lacuna; the qualitative is the only form used
in 143:27-29).

[102]This is a New Testament concept; cf. Gal. 2:4; 5:1;
2 Pet. 2:19.

[103]This too is a New Testament concept; cf. Rom. 1:21;
Eph. 4:18.

[104]These two phrases are also echoes of N.T. ideas. The
one is a perverse application of the frequent expression "to be
baptized with water" and the other is found in the later writings; Eph. 2:3; 2 Pet. 2:10; 3:3; Jude 16,18.

[105]A metaphor for ignorance; cf. CH I,28: μετανοήσατε οἱ
συνοδεύσαντες τῇ πλάνῃ καὶ (hendiadys) συνκοινωνήσαντες τῇ
ἀγνοίᾳ.

[106]Cf. CH XI,7: "(See) the sun, the begetter of all good,
the ruler of all order, the governor of the seven worlds. And
(see) the moon who runs before all (the planets), the instrument
of nature (φύσις), transforming matter here below."

[107]Cf. the description in CH Frg. IIa,14: "The sun alone
is real, unlike all else it is unchanging, remaining as it is.
Thus it alone has been entrusted with the making of all things
in the cosmos, ruling all things, making all things."

[108]Plutarch, De Iside et Osiride 367d, trans. by F. C.
Babbitt, Plutarch's Moralia, Vol. 5 (Loeb Classical Library;
Cambridge: Harvard, 1962).

[109]F. Cumont, After Life in Roman Paganism (New York:
Dover, 1959), p. 103. Here he no doubt refers to Sulla's elaborate myth in Plutarch, De facie in orbe lunae, 942-945. Cf.
also Diogenes Laertius VIII 1.31.

[110]Ibid., p. 92. Cf. Cumont, Lux Perpetua (Paris:
Libraire orientaliste Paul Guenther, 1949), p. 171f.

[111]Asclepius 3; cf. Plutarch, De genio Socratis, 591b,
where generation and decay are linked by Nature in the moon.
Cf. also the fourth century astrologer Firmicus Maternus
(Mathesis 4.1): "having obtained the entire substance of the
compound product from a blending of opposites and from various
elements, and having conceived all animal bodies it (the moon)
both begets them, and, having been engendered, it dissolves
them."

[112]For references to the use of ⲩⲱⲡⲉ ⲙⲛ̄ (=συνουσία) as a
synonym for intercourse, see Crum, 578b.

[113]CH Frg. IV,6.

[114]CH Frg. IV,9.

[115]CH XVI,13. Cf. XVI,16: "Thus they (the demons) govern
this entire earthly realm using our bodies as instruments, and
this government Hermes called εἱμαρμένη."

[116] ⲍⲱⲧⲙ̄ ⲛ̄ⲍⲁⲍ ⲛ̄ⲕⲱⲍⲧ ⲉⲃⲟⲗ ⲍⲛ̄ ⲧⲏⲛⲉ. ⲍⲱⲧⲙ̄ ⲉⲃⲟⲗ ⲍⲛ̄´ is unattested in Crum, but is listed in R. Kasser's *Compléments au dictionnaire Copte de Crum* (Le Caire: Inst. Français, 1964), p. 103a as occurring in his edition of the Bodmer VI papyrus of the Book of Proverbs, 10:7; 13:9, where it renders the present passive indicative of σβέσαι, "to quench."

[117] W.H. Roscher, *Ausführliches Lexikon der griechischen und römischen Mythologie*, 7 vols (Hildesheim: Georg Olms, reprint 1965), art. "Mondgöttin", Vol. II, pt. 2, cols. 3147-9.

[118] In view of the anti-hylic attitude of the tractate, it is difficult to see why this saving fragrance should be granted to the four elements.

[119] Manichaean *Psalm-Book* 214:28-215:4.

[120] CG I,2, 35:3-14.

[121] For the common relationship between fragrance and the spiritual, cf. the references in Lampe's *Patristic Greek Lexicon* under εὐωδία, p. 585a.

[122] Manichaean *Kephalaia* 160:1-3. Cf. Job 14:9 where it is said of a withered tree that ἀπὸ ὀσμῆς ὕδατος ἀνθήσει.

[123] *Ibid.*, 162:11f.

[124] (ⲣ̄)ⲛⲁⲡ, ⲛⲉⲡ is attested in R. Kasser, *op. cit.*, p. 36 as A² for Bo. ⲛⲏⲃ, "lord." In the Manichaean *Psalm-Book* 201:21 ⲁⲥⲣ̄ⲛⲉⲡ ⲁ´ is translated "be mistress over."

[125] "Everything" is an abstraction. Actually the soul inherits the land in which it grows. This motif of inheriting the land goes back to the Old Testament, where it means not only inheriting the land of Canaan, but also refers to inheriting the promise of future salvation, eternal life, etc. (Gen. 12:7; Ex. 19:5; 32:13; Ez. 20:5f; 36:12; 37:25; Is. 60:1,21; cf. Ps. Sol. 14:10; I En. 40:9; Mt. 5:5; 21:43; Mk. 12:1-12, etc.).

[126] I use the edition of K. Lake, *The Apostolic Fathers*, 2 vols. (Loeb Classical Library: Cambridge: Harvard, 1965).

[127] The son in the parable remains unexplained.

[128] ⲣ̄ⲩⲟⲣⲡ ⲛ̄ⲙ̄ⲙⲉ apparently carries the same nuance as ⲩⲡ̄ⲥⲟⲟⲩⲛ, πρόγνωσις (Crum 380b; cf. 1 Pt. 1:2). ⲣ̄ⲩⲟⲣⲡ renders the particle πρό, and thus "be first to know" should be translated "to foreknow" (προγινώσκειν).

[129] For this observation, I am dependent upon a private communication by Professor Rolf Knierim, of the Southern California School of Theology at Claremont.

[130] Though Dt. 27:15-26 are not literally woes, they nevertheless correspond to the pattern of twelve woes in *Thomas the Contender*: twelve "curses" composed of the passive participle ארור followed by an active participle indicating the perpetrator of the action which calls forth the woe. In *Thomas the Contender* we have the explicative ⲟⲩⲟⲉⲓ followed four times by the second person plural indirect object "epexegeted" by a following active participle.

[131]So E. Stauffer, TDNT I (1965), p. 167.

[132]*Acts of Thomas* 39.

[133]Philo, *De sacr.* 43.

[134]e.g. B.W. Bacon, "Jesus and the Law," *Journal of Biblical Literature* 47 (1928), p. 225. However, see the convincing argument that the demand for perfection is aimed at all the Church, by G. Barth in G. Bornkamm, G. Barth, H.J. Held, *Tradition and Interpretation in Matthew* (Philadelphia: Westminster, 1963), pp. 95-99.

[135]So G. Schrenk, TDNT I (1965), pp. 615ff.

CHAPTER III

CHAPTER III

CONCLUSIONS

We shall conclude this analysis of *Thomas the Contender* by offering a summary of its literary composition, its teaching and some observations concerning its position within the history of religion.

A. The Literary Composition of *Thomas the Contender*

In the commentary we have offered reasons for considering *Thomas the Contender* to be the sum of two originally separate works. One work, section A, was a dialogue between Thomas and the Savior, perhaps entitled "The Book of Thomas the Contender writing to the Perfect." The other work, section B, was a collection of the Savior's sayings gathered into a homiletical discourse (introductory apocalypse, woes, blessings, final admonition), perhaps entitled "The Hidden Words which the Savior spoke, which I wrote down, even I, Mathaias." A redactor has prefixed section A to section B, and prefaced the whole with an *incipit* title composed on analogy with the original title to section B, and designating Mathaias as the scribe of the whole. The subscript title, designating Thomas as the scribe of the whole, was borrowed from the original title to section A, and suffixed to the newly-formed whole. Because of the fact that Thomas figures prominently in section A as participant in the dialogue, but is mentioned nowhere in section B, it is likely that his name was originally at home in section A, but not in section B. Because Mathaias' name is never mentioned outside the *incipit*, it seems likely that it derived from the original title to section B; it probably would not have derived from section A in which Thomas is dominant, nor would it have derived from the body of section B, which provides no occasion for the mention of names. The likelihood of Mathaias' name having derived from the title to section B receives some confirmation when we recall that various traditions of some antiquity (mentioned by Eusebius' Papias, Hippolytus and Clement of Alexandria; cf. references in comment on 140:1-4) connect the name of a certain Matthew

215

(variously spelled Matthaios, Matthias) with the collection and transmission of sayings (λόγια, λόγοι ἀπόκρυφοι) of Jesus.

In turn, each of the two sections of *Thomas the Contender* presents us with a profile of its own.

We call section A a "dialogue," but by doing so we speak, not of a dramatic dialogue with co-equal participants, but rather of a much more colorless and fictitious literary device. Moreover, as Kurt Rudolf has pointed out,[1] the dialogue of section A cannot even be classified along with the literary device of the Platonic dialogues. There a central figure (e.g. Socrates) presents the thesis of the dialogue almost as one would expound it in an essay, but is occasionally interrupted by participants who by their questions and objections interact with the central figure in such a way that they arrive at the truth, or at least come to recognize their ignorance. Rudolph would rather seek the *genre* of literature like section A in a class of literature known as *erotapokrisis*, in which dialogue functions not as *maeutic*, as a dialectical process of discovering a philosophical truth by statement (thesis), objection (antithesis) and clarification (synthesis), but rather as a vehicle to expound revelation of salvific knowledge in the form of catechetical question (topic) and answer (commentary). While Plato's dialogues are the prime example of the philosophical dialogue, the tractates of the *Corpus Hermeticum* are a prime example of *erotapokriseis*, where a disciple, within a dialogue framework, elicits revelation of supernatural knowledge in philosophical dress. Thus while section A of *Thomas the Contender* presents the formal structure of a dialogue, its material structure is that of the *erotapokriseis*, in which a noted apostle, Thomas, elicits from the Savior salvific knowledge for the instruction of the mature ("The Book of Thomas the Contender writing to the Perfect").

This characterization of the literary *genre* of section A corresponds to the general flavor of its contents: it is written to men who, like Thomas, at least know that the Savior is the knowledge of the truth (138:13), but are presently ignorant of the real truth, "that which is hidden" (138:11f,14,20). As a result of knowing about that which is hidden (the truth about oneself) they shall come to know themselves as well as the "depth of the All" (138:17f). We thus get the impression that section A was originally addressed to a group of ascetic,

syncretistic Christians (in view of the Christian framework) who
were familiar with some knowledge about the Savior, but needed
to have this interpreted in a strongly ascetic direction. They
had the best of intentions to do good, but even so betray that
they have known the fire of passion (141:22-25). They were
people who evidently revered the figure of Thomas, and who valued his direct contact with the resurrected Savior. The intended
effect of the document upon them would have been to exhort them
to observe the teachings of the Savior and preach them to other
mortals who burned with the fire of lust.

Furthermore, the figure of Thomas in section A is a crucial
factor in obtaining this intended effect upon the readers. While
it is true that, literarily speaking, Thomas functions mostly as
an interlocutor who provides topics for the Savior's commentary,
the fact that he assumes this function as an apostle, the twin
brother of the Savior, who interviews the presumably resurrected
Savior just prior to his ascension, means that any progress in
understanding made by Thomas is absolutely crucial to the reader.
This is emplicit in the analogy presupposed between Thomas and
the recipients of the document. Thomas, although he knows that
the Savior is the knowledge of the truth, is nevertheless ignorant of the "real truth" (that which is hidden); but as a result
of the Savior's impending revelation, he is about to know the
"real truth" (about himself). Likewise, the reader of section
A, while currently ignorant, will, as a result of reading section A, come to know the "real truth" about himself. Thus
Thomas' progression from ignorance to true knowledge is crucial
to the reader.

Furthermore, not only is the figure of Thomas crucial, but
so also is the setting of the dialogue; it occurs just prior to
the Savior's ascension, and thus presumably with the resurrected
One. The dialogue takes place with the Savior at just the point
where the "real truth" about him is most evident, when his exalted
nature is most truly exposed, in his resurrected condition. What
had formerly been obscured by the bonds of the Savior's flesh is
now revealed in his pre-ascension condition. Simultaneously,
Thomas initiates the ensuing dialogue:

> Therefore I beg you to tell me the things about
> which I ask you before your Ascension. And whenever I
> hear from you about that which is hidden (or: "the
> hidden one"), then I can speak about them. (138:22-26)

That is, the point at which the hidden nature of the Savior
is disclosed corresponds to the point at which the things about
which Thomas wants to know, but are now hidden, become manifest.
When the Savior tells Thomas that in order to be perfect, he
must first know the visible in order to know the hidden, Thomas
presses straight to the point of the dialogue: "Tell us about
these things which you said are not visible, but are hidden from
us" (138:37-39). All of this points to the conclusion that there
is presupposed a shift from "unintelligible" knowledge (Thomas
knows the Savior is the knowledge of the truth, but is nevertheless ignorant), acquired before the ascension (e.g. from the
earthly Jesus), to a higher plane of revealed or "enlightened"
knowledge that takes place with the Ascension. What is hidden
becomes revealed.

James M. Robinson[2] in commenting on this phenomenon, points
out that the Markan messianic secret involves a similar shift,
except that the transition from hidden to manifest occurs at
the first prediction of the passion and resurrection: "and he
spoke the word clearly" (παρρησία Mk. 8:32). In the Gospel of
John the transition occurs at the end of the farewell discourses
before Jesus' elevation to the Cross (Jn. 16:29), and in the
Pistis Sophia, after the Ascension. In *Thomas the Contender*,
the point of higher revelation begins just prior to the Ascension. In Justin's *Apology* (I,50) the disciples, just like
Thomas in *Thomas the Contender*, can teach the Christian message
only after they witness the Ascension. That the shift from "unintelligible" knowledge about man's situation to "enlightened"
knowledge takes place with the disclosure of the Savior's exalted
reality is further confirmed by a passage in section A which provides the hermeneutical key to the whole section:

> And Thomas answered: "Therefore I say to you,
> Lord, that those who speak about things that are not
> visible and which are difficult to explain are like
> those who shoot their arrows at a target at night.
> Indeed they shoot their arrows like anyone else, since
> they shoot at the target; however, it is not visible.
> But when the light comes forth and hides the darkness,
> then the work of each one will appear. And you are
> our light, because you enlighten, Lord.

That is, illumination by the Savior will make the hidden things
visible and the things that are difficult to explain plain.
Thus confrontation with the exalted Savior before his Ascension

is the source of the real truth. Thomas has experienced this, and has thereby achieved true knowledge. If now the reader can identify himself with Thomas, he too will pass from a veiled knowledge of the truth into a state of full revelation. He will know the truth about himself (e.g. that his bestial body will perish) and escaping the passion of the body, will receive the exaltation of the Perfection.

In our characterization of the profile of section A, we hope to have shown how its literary form (dialogue), its setting in the life of the Savior (prior to the Ascension), and its hermeneutical foil (Thomas, with whom the reader is to identify) and movement (from unintelligible to enlightened knowledge) each contribute to informing and convincing the reader of its ascetic message. By identifying with Thomas and participating in his enlightenment by the Savior, the reader can achieve perfection and can himself become a 'contender,' a missionary for abstinence from the flesh.

Now section B is also a document which preaches asceticism, but instead of using a dialogue between the Savior and a revered apostle as a vehicle to impress the Savior's ascetic teaching upon the readers, section B relies on a collection of the Savior's sayings employing the devices of threat (scene of punishment in Hell, woes) and promise of salvation (beatitudes, direct admonition) to get the ascetic message across. Where the readers of section A are to become perfect by identifying with Thomas who directly receives the ascetic message from the exalted Savior, the readers of section B are to be jolted out of their current life and look forward to salvation freed from the flesh.

Since the ultimate goal of each section is the same, it is not difficult to see why they have been combined.

A material motivation behind their combination, beside their obvious similarity in content, can be gleaned from the frequent mention in section A of the necessity to preach the ascetic message to those whose lives are ridden with lust. Thomas, like the reader, is supposed to speak about that which is hidden (the true self hidden by the fleshly body); he must speak to miserable mortals beset with the fire of lust (141:19-25) and warn them of their terrible fate. Thus when the dialogue ends, ("we are persuaded, Lord," etc., 142:19), what is there that remains to be done other than to go forth and preach

the Savior's words to these miserable men? Accordingly, it would
be most relevant to prefix section A to section B, an already-
existing example of the Savior's words on the ascetic life, thus
illustrating the type of preaching that the readers of section A
were expected to perform. In doing this, the redactor of A and
B simply spelled out the fitting response of the reader of section A, by attaching it to a homiletic, hortatory document on
the same theme. At the same time, section B would intensify the
message of section A by spelling out a fearful fate for those who
mocked the Savior's words (142:27-143:7).

This material motivation, however, while it may have been a
factor in the redactor's decision to prefix A to B, must be
supplemented with another, in this case formal, motivation for
the combination of A with B. This formal motivation is much
broader in scope than the material motivation just suggested,
and indeed may have operated upon the redactor's mind in a quite
unconscious fashion.

We begin with a few observations about the general drift of
literary *genres* in early Christianity. If we take our start with
collections of the sayings of Jesus, such as lay behind the mid-
first century Matthean-Lukan source Q, and such as have found
their way into the mid-second century *Gospel of Thomas*, we see
that, as time passes, these sayings collections develop from
relatively isolated sayings received from an oral tradition into
larger and larger collections. There comes a point, however,
when they are taken up into a more comprehensive *genre*. For
example, in the first century, sayings of Jesus were assembled
into a larger framework including a passion story, as in the
Gospel of Mark. The collection of sayings represented by Q are
assembled into the larger frameworks of the gospels of Matthew
and Luke. So in the church traditions represented by Mark,
Matthew and Luke, which were eventually accepted as orthodox
writings, the sayings of Jesus are arranged into a life of Jesus
beginning with an account of his baptism or even of his birth,
and ending with an account of his passion and resurrection. The
net result and also the intention of this movement from sayings
to gospel (εὐαγγέλιον) is to produce an authoritative interpretation of the sayings (and miracles and other traditions as well)
of Jesus; his sayings are interpreted by his passion, his resurrection, etc.

At a later date, in the *Gospel of Thomas*, we see another
phase in the trend towards providing an authoritative interpretation of the words of Jesus. Here the tendency is much more to
interpret the sayings by expanding the individual saying with
interpretation, rather than to provide the interpretation by including them in a larger (passion-ressurection) framework.
Whereas in the Gospels, interpretation was provided by a life-
of-Jesus framework, and, especially in John, by appending interpretations to Jesus' words and to stories of his deeds, in the
Gospel of Thomas interpretation is provided mostly by expanding
the original saying with Gnostic theology.

Something similar to the process displayed in the *Gospel of
Thomas* can also be seen in *Thomas the Contender*. We have posited
that section B was an originally separate document, consisting
of an introductory apocalypse, woes, blessings and a final admonition to watch and pray. In each of these subsections, we
have what purport to be sayings of Jesus ("truly I say to you,"
"woe to you," "blessed are you who," "watch and pray"). But
they can only be the end-product of a process in which the original sayings have been so expanded with (ascetic) interpretations
that whatever may have been the original saying has been all but
obliterated by the accretion of (ascetic) interpretation. The
interpretation of the saying, by expanding it with ascetic comment, has proceded to the point that all that is left of the
saying is at most a variant of a beatitude, and at the least a
Jesuanic formula, "truly I tell you," "woe to you," "blessed are
you," etc. The interpretation so predominates over the saying
that the "saying" portion has become a mere vestige. In fact
this process has gone so far since the stage of "saying expanded
with interpretation," which we find in the *Gospel of Thomas*, that
one might say that section B was written as an interpretation
before and aside from the saying; the Jesuanic formulae are only
an atavism designed to legitimatize the message of the interpretation by designating Jesus the Savior as its source.

If this characterization of section B is correct, it is
clear that the tendency to mix an interpretation of a saying
with the saying itself has reached the point where the saying
has disappeared and all that remains is the interpretation. The
suitability of the "sayings collection" as a vehicle for presenting gnostic or ascetic theology, anthropology, etc. has come

to an end, since it can no longer be creatively developed. It
is on the verge of becoming an essay or treatise, a *genre* of
literature which even the syncretistic Christian would credit
with little traditional value as an authentic record of what
the Savior said. The Savior presented his message in the form
of sayings, parables, etc., not in the form of an essay. To
continue the use of the "saying plus interpretation" model when
the saying has become a mere atavism has severely limited the
possibility of its further creative development; a new and more
suitable and creative vehicle for presenting the Savior's teaching had to be found.

It is the feeling of this author that the only possibility
open for the creative theologian to expand further the "exploded"
form of the "saying plus interpretation" model of the Savior's
teaching which we find in section B of *Thomas the Contender*, was
to embed it within a fresh, new literary *genre* which still possessed the capacity for further creative expansion. For the
mid-third century gnostic (and ascetic) theologian, this *genre*
was the dialogue between the Resurrected One and his disciples.
Instead of trying to bring out the hidden truth of the teaching
of the earthly Savior by expanding his sayings with gnosticizing
interpretation (as is done in the *Gospel of Thomas* and to a gross
extent in section B of *Thomas the Contender*), one could bring out
the hidden truth of the Savior's teaching by having him directly
teach the disciples between his Resurrection and Ascension. That
is, what the Savior taught during the time he could actually be
confronted in his exalted and hidden nature would truly have a
claim to being direct open revelation. With the Savior in his
exalted state, nothing about him, neither his true exalted nature
nor the true hidden meaning of his words, could remain hidden;
the stark truth was there to behold.

A similar but much earlier attempt at this device seems, to
some extent, to lie behind the composition of the "farewell discourse" of the Gospel of John (14:1-16:33). Here the hour for
Jesus' glorification has come (17:1); after the crucifixion (his
ὕψωσις) he is to return to his father (14:12,20,28; 16:10,28).
As in *Thomas the Contender*, in the Gospel of John Jesus speaks
plainly (παρρησίᾳ, 16:29) with the disciples just prior to the
"hour" of his elevation, and he does it in the form of a dialogue
with his disciples. They ask him questions to which he responds

"clearly and not in figures," and when the dialogue is over, the disciples believe that he has come from God; they are convinced (cf. *Thomas the Contender*, 142:19-21). For the author of the Gospel of John, the point where Jesus speaks most clearly is made to occur in the form of a farewell dialogue (cf. the eschatological discourses in the Synoptics, which are not "farewells"), prior to the Savior's exaltation. It is certainly not too far-fetched to see how the farewell dialogue in the Gospel of John, written probably just before the turn of the first century, could have provided a model for the dialogue of section A of *Thomas the Contender*, probably written near the turn of the second century. In this regard, the main difference, besides date, between these two works is that in John, although the saying has been altered and enlarged in comparison to the sayings in the Synoptics, this process of expansion and alteration has not yet reached the gross proportions we find witnessed to in *Thomas the Contender*. As we have said, by the time section A of *Thomas the Contender* was composed, the "sayings of Jesus" tradition as represented in section B had become so expanded and thereby altered as to demand inclusion in a new, more liberal form, the dialogue.

Therefore, the no longer creatively useful "sayings" type of teaching, as we find it in section B, could quite naturally have found its way into the framework of the potentially very creative dialogue form of section A. The sayings in section B, having been "interpreted to death," find a fresh possibility of interpretation by virtue of being spoken by the resurrected Savior himself directly to a revered apostle. The sayings of section B, just as the content of the dialogue of section A, are guaranteed as being of the highest revelatory significance. At the same time the redactor of *Thomas the Contender* had achieved a way to advance his speculative interpretation beyond the range of possibilities offered by the traditional sayings collection of which section B represents a "*fin-de-siècle*." From now (ca. A.D. 225?) on, as one can judge from the large number of dialogues of the Resurrected with his disciples to be found in the Nag Hammadi gnostic corpus, the literary future of the teachings of the Savior is to be found in the *genre* of dialogue. To be sure, as one can see from the *Pistis Sophia*, traditional sayings plus their interpretive expansion would be provided, but their

unwieldiness would cause them to appear more as discourse than
saying. The fact that even here the interpretive expansion was
no longer regarded as satisfactory is demonstrated by the con-
stant addition of a disciple's comment or analysis at the end
of each speech of the Savior. To quote James M. Robinson:

> . . . we are carried step by step through the final
> stage in the procedure that one can only sense from
> the introduction to the Gospel of Thomas to have begun
> in some sayings already there. For in the Gospel of
> Thomas the "secret sayings" of Jesus that the gnostic
> is to "interpret" have in some instances already re-
> ceived a gnosticizing interpretive reformulation, which
> would then be carried a step further when the gnosti-
> cizing interpretation is again interpreted for a still
> deeper meaning. Yet the saying and its interpretation
> are not kept distinct, side by side, as in Pistis
> Sophia, but are rather presented in fusion with each
> other, as a single statement. In Pistis Sophia, the
> speech of Jesus that the disciples proceed to resolve
> is already gnosticized; yet the side-by-side presenta-
> tion in Pistis Sophia of two advanced stages in the
> process illustrates what was less visibly happening in
> the earlier stages as well. . . We thus arrive in
> Pistis Sophia at the point in the trajectory of the
> sayings collection where it is absorbed into and finally
> replaced by the *Gattung* which had no doubt all along
> been most typical of Christian Gnosticism, namely the
> dialogue of the resurrected Christ with his disciples.[3]

Thus *Thomas the Contender* occupies a point with Robinson's
Gattungsgeschichte midway between the *Gospel of Thomas* and *Pistis
Sophia*: the sayings collection (section B) has been absorbed into, but not yet replaced by, the dialogue *genre*. The process is
similar to, but not simultaneous with, the *Gattungsgeschichte* of
the sayings of Jesus in the orthodox sphere: there the isolated
saying was included within small collections of sayings (such as
Mk. 4), or were assembled into larger collections (e.g. Q). The
evangelists then included these collections plus other materials
into a life-of-Jesus framework (εὐαγγέλιον) concluded by passion-
resurrection narratives. Finally, the episodes of the life of
Jesus gain prominence and interest with the addition of birth
narratives, and eventually in the construction of separate in-
fancy stories, etc. In both orthodox and syncretistic Christianity the tendency is towards the embedding (and eventual dif-
fusion) of the saying into even larger interpretive frameworks,
whether they be gospels (εὐαγγέλια) or dialogues of the Resurrected with his disciples. *Thomas the Contender* is most significant as a representative of a late stage of this process in

the sphere of syncretistic (ascetic, mildly gnosticizing) Christianity; the vestiges of the sayings collection (section B) are still quite clear, but have been embedded in the interpretive framework of the dialogue, eventually destined to replace the "sayings" form altogether.

B.   The Doctrine of *Thomas the Contender*

Since *Thomas the Contender* stands in a Codex which contains definitely Gnostic writings, such as the *Apocryphon of John*, the *Gospel of Philip*, *On the Origin of the World*, and the *Hypostasis of the Archons*, it is legitimate to ask if *Thomas the Contender* is itself a Gnostic document. We shall comment on this question by reviewing *Thomas the Contender* under various headings: theology, anthropology, cosmology, eschatology, soteriology, Christology, and morality.

1. *Theology*. "The cardinal thought of gnostic theology is the radical dualism that governs the relation of God and the world and correspondingly that of man and the world.[4] The asceticism of *Thomas the Contender* certainly implies a dualism in the relation of man and the world, but it is difficult to identify the corresponding dualism in the relation of God and the world.

There are several divine beings or entities mentioned in the tractate: the essence (οὐσία) of light (139:30), the true wise one (ⲧⲥⲁⲃⲏ ⲙ̄ⲙⲏⲉ fem., 140:2), the Archon who is above, ruling over all the powers (ἐξουσίαι) as their king (142:31f), and the Good One (ⲡⲁⲅⲁⲑⲟⲥ, 145:14), who is the king (145:14). In addition, there are lesser powers, such as the powers (142:32) and the angel, the chief of Tartaros (ταρταροῦχος, 142:31). Finally of course, there is "the Savior," who is "the knowledge of the Truth" (138:13), the "light" (139:20), "the one who is good for us" (140:8), and "the Lord," twice called Jesus.

Of the first group, the divine entities or beings, it seems clear that the most transcendent is the essence of the light, to which the Savior, the light of men, ascends whenever men abandon bestiality (life in the body). The next entity in our list is the true wise one, a (feminine?) being who is the source of the wise man's truth, the truth which allows him to evade the clutches of the lustful spirit of men. In the commentary we have tentatively identified this with the hypostatized wisdom

of God, a sort of metaphysical intermediary between God and man.
"The Archon who is above" seems to represent a being similar to
the "prince (ἄρχων) of the powers of the air" mentioned in Eph.
2:2 under his aspect as judge, and occupying a position lower
in the levels of being than the light-essence. The being identified as "the Good One" seems in the present tractate to refer
to the Savior as "the one who is good for us" (140:8), but in
its original context, section B, it appears to refer to the
highest God. Such is probably also the case with the being referred to as "the King."

     It appears that we do have a hierarchy of divine beings or
hypostases, at least in section A of *Thomas the Contender*, and
that there is a gulf between these beings and man. On the other
hand, even though the body and matter are derogated, there is no
claim to the effect that the world is the creation of inferior
powers, or that the beings intermediate in the scale of divine
beings obstruct God's relation to man and *vice-versa*. Moreover,
in section B of *Thomas the Contender* there appears to be no
hierarchy of divine beings. Thus we conclude that while a dualism is created by the derogation of matter, this dualism is not
as omnipresent and perverse as it is in so many Gnostic systems.

     2. *Anthropology*. As already stated, both sections of
Thomas the Contender claim quite explicitly that the spirit of
man is entrapped in a lustful material body, which blinds the
spirit in such a way that it is not aware of its immersion in
the lustful flesh. This theme is typically Gnostic, except that,
whereas most gnostic systems are at great pains to recite the
chain of events by which this immersion came to be, *Thomas the
Contender* is only concerned to point out man's present predicament, and the way out of it. There is no attempt to tell the
tragic history of the soul. At the same time, there is no attempt to point out the consubstantiality of man's spirit with
the divine substance above, a feature of much gnostic thought.[5]
Thus we should classify the anthropology of *Thomas the Contender*
as ascetic and dualistic, rather than specifically Gnostic. I
say "not specifically gnostic" because there are enough points
of contact with gnostic thought so as not to exclude completely
the gnostic classification. Thus, so far as anthropology is
concerned, section A has fewer gnostic features than section B.
Section A views man in somewhat Platonic fashion, as composed

of a self imprisoned in a bestial, lustful body. But this body
is scorched by the flames of its natural (in its nature as
bestial) drive for sex. This drive enslaves the body, which in
turn deludes the self as to its true estate. Even though the
lustful body will perish, excessive attachment to it will cause
the soul to share the body's fate. Section B, however, represents man as possessing a lust-ridden body, but whose lust results not fron an inner drive, but apparently from the influence
of celestial powers, the forces of the evil demons (144:12f).
The way to escape these forces is to open oneself to the influence of other more beneficent celestial powers, the sun and the
moon, which impart a sweet fragrance to men and hide their darkness and pollution (144:19ff). Thus section A regards the sexual
lust of men as resulting primarily from an inner drive of their
bestial body, while section B regards this lust as resulting primarily from the body's domination by hostile celestial powers.
In this regard, section B appears to be more "gnostic" than section A.

    3. *Cosmology*. Gnostic cosmology views the universe as a
vast system of concentric shells at whose center lies the impri-
soning earth, with each shell or heavenly sphere occupied by a
hostile celestial being (Archon, etc.) who prevents the passage
of souls out of the world in their attempt to return to the
world of light beyond the spheres. These Archons collectively
rule over the world *via* "fate" expressed in terms of natural law.
The world is the product of an inferior being, often the chief
Archon or the demiurge, and as such, matter, particularly in the
form of the body, is the chief point of contact at which the
Archon's power impinges upon and imprisons the human soul.[6]

    Thomas the Contender exhibits some of these features, but
to a far less degree than most gnostic documents. Whereas most
gnostic documents relate an elaborate myth about the creation
of the world through deception and ignorance on the part of divine beings inferior to the highest God, *Thomas the Contender*
relates no such myth, and even though it regards matter as evil,
does not even seem to presuppose such a myth. *Thomas the Contender* is, indeed, anti-hylic, particularly in regard to the
sexuality of the human body, but it does not ascribe the creation of the world to an inferior being. By the same token, it
does not affirm the world's creation by the highest being, but

simply takes the existence of the material world as a given fact
which necessitates, not an explanation of its origin, but an
escape from it. All that is required is that one know *that* it
is evil, not *how* it became evil.

Furthermore, *Thomas the Contender* admits the existence of
celestial beings, but is not concerned to describe their nature,
or even elaborate tactics to escape their clutches in the ascent
through the spheres. In section B there are celestial forces
(ἐνέργειαι) which control the body through its sexual lust, and
there is an Archon who prevents the lustful from entering heaven.
But the ascent of the soul does not require an elaborate system
of passwords to conceal its identity from, or frighten, the
celestial Archons; it only requires that one abandon the life
of the body while on earth, or as section B⁹ puts it, that one
pray that one not be found in the body. Having accomplished
this, according to section B, one is virtually guaranteed of
being granted an eternal rest from the Good One, and of reigning
forever with the King (145:13ff). Thus the creation and habita-
tion of the earth and the planetary spheres by hostile Archons,
even if envisaged by the author of section A or section B, or by
the redactor of the whole, is not a substantive issue for *Thomas
the Contender*. On this account then, *Thomas the Contender*
should be regarded as ascetic rather than gnostic.

4. *Eschatology*. The eschatology of both section A and
section B is quite similar: the decision one makes about his
loyalties in this life conditions and even determines his future
fate (143:6ff). Excessive attachment to the body means sharing
its fate at death; both soul and body dissolve and perish (cf.
139:4ff). To abandon the body in this life means escaping its
fate at death; the body dissolves and perishes, but the soul,
perfected independently of the body, and fleeing every visible
spirit (140:4f), will come forth from the bonds of this life
and inherit eternal rest (145:12ff). Apparently, at least in
section B, this "rest" is found in the future, on the Day of
Judgment (143:8). When one dies, if he has not abandoned the
flesh, he is punished in Hell with no escape, until the Day of
Judgment. If one abandons the flesh, presumably when he dies,
he escapes this punishment and finds salvation on the Day of
Judgment. Beyond that time, the saved soul reigns with the
King in eternal rest, but of the fate of the soul sullied with

the body we hear nothing further. Thus, while spelled out in more elaborate and traditional terms in section B, the entire tractate views salvation and damnation as an eschatological process, worked out by one's loyalties during his embodied life. Therefore, one needs only to be concerned with the present and the future, but not with the past: "inquire and be aware of who you are, in what way you exist, and in what manner you will come to be" (138:8f).

5. *Soteriology*. For both sections A and B, salvation is escape from the body and from the prison of the material world. Furthermore, salvation is a future event, dependent on one's detachment from the body during this earthly life. This detachment is achieved by a *gnosis*, a knowledge or awareness of the power of the lustful body to beguile the soul or spirit of man by deluding him that he is to serve the needs of the body, particularly its sex drive. The *gnosis* in *Thomas the Contender* consists of knowing not only the true estate of the soul imprisoned in the body, but also that this estate will surely result in the soul's demise at the time of the body's death. Thus the soteriology is minatory, based on the threat of future peril, and this peril is spelled out in terms of future punishment in Hell. The actual process of salvation is to act upon this *gnosis*, and to deny the world and bodily life within it. But what makes this *gnosis*, and therefore salvation, possible is its revelation by a revealer figure, in this case the "Savior," who is "the knowledge of the truth," "the light," "the one who is good for us."

In section A the Savior functions as revealer, who must get the recipient of the revelation to know himself, his true estate, and thus his destiny: "the one who knew himself has already obtained knowledge of the depth of the All" (138:17f). In order to know oneself, one must at least know this much of the nature of the revealer, that "he is good for us" (140:7), and that he is "the knowledge of the truth." The revealer's authority is actually established when the recipient of his word recognizes his nature (You are our light!", 139:20) and his origin, the οὐσία of light (139:29f); he is the representative of that light-world to which the prospective recipient of the *gnosis* aspires. The Savior then explains that in order to perform the things of the Pleroma, which are invisible, one must first recognize "that which is visible" for what it is, that is, the lustful body which is destined to perish because it is bestial (138:27-139:12).

In section B, the Savior also functions as the revealer of man's true estate and destiny depending on whether 1) he remains attached to the body, or 2) he abandons the body. The main difference between the two sections is that in section A we have a much more philosophical rationale built up for understanding man's true situation: the Platonic distinction between the visible and invisible, the wise man who flees every visible spirit and thus avoids sexual lust *versus* others who flee to the visible things wherein burns the fire of lust, which in turn blinds them to their true estate. But in section B all we have is outright expression of doom for those who submit to the body's lust, concluded by a promise of a future rest with the King for those who watch and pray that they do not come to be (progressively identify with) in the flesh.

Again, while in section A the saving *gnosis* is mainly philosophical, in section B the *gnosis* is interpreted in a much more metaphorical way. For in section B, just as bodily lust is not just an inner drive, but results from, or at least is compounded by, the influence of hostile celestial powers, so also celestial powers (in this case beneficent) intervene in the process of salvation:

> Who is the one who will give you the sun to shine upon you so as to dissolve the darkness which is in you and hide the darkness together with the polluted water? The sun and the moon will give you a fragrance, etc. (145:17-20)

It seems that here the sun and moon are conceived as divine agents who attack the body and exalt and illumine the soul. Here the *gnosis* is conceived under the metaphor of the illumination of the sun, rather than under the philosophical guise of visible and invisible, etc.

While it is true that the details of the salvation process differ in sections A and B, it is pertinent to note that both sections regard a saving *gnosis* as prerequisite to salvation, and that they both understand this *gnosis* as related to illumination. In section A, it is the Savior who is the light that descends from his οὐσία of light to illumine the soul with *gnosis*. In section B, it is the light of the sun and moon which

dissolve the darkness of bodily life and cause the soul to out-
strip the body. Once the soul (like the grapevine) receives
the sun's light, it prospers and branches out, thus overshadow-
ing the body (the weeds) and chokes it out and kills it (144:
21-36). Thus in section B, the Savior is not directly identified
with the revealing illuminator, but is only loosely linked with
the saving illumination. That is, he and his mission are compared with the lifegiving light of the sun, without actually
naming him the illuminator, perhaps because it would be objec-
tionable to identify him explicitly as the source of illumination (like the sun) rather than the mediator of illumination.
This leads us to the question of Christology.

6. *Christology*. Christology is an issue in *Thomas the
Contender* because the revealer figure, mostly called "Savior,"
and addressed as "Lord," is twice called "Jesus," and sustains
relationships with the Christ of the New Testament and other
Christian literature. He sustains a relationship with a well-
known Christian apostle, Judas Thomas; he is to undergo an ascension; he calls his hearers "disciples" (138:35); he is the
"light"; and he speaks in formulae attributed elsewhere to
Christ: "Truly I tell you" (142:27,29f; cf. 141:25, "woe to
you," "blessed are you," and "watch and pray" (145:8).

In all of these respects, however, the Savior acts only as
revealer and exhorter, and no other salvific functions, such as
are found in the New Testament, are attributed to him. There
seems to be no hint of the Pauline "being in Christ," or the
understanding of Christ as a "ransom"; there is no mention of
Christ's life or of his incarnation, cross, and Resurrection.
All that is mentioned of his life is that he walks with Thomas
prior to his ascension, that he is the twin brother of Judas
Thomas, and that he is addressed as "Lord" and named "Jesus,"
and "Savior."

Thus the Christology of *Thomas the Contender* is freely-
floating, anchored to the traditional scheme of Jesus' life
only at a point just prior to the Ascension, with no concern
expressed for the problem of his death, nor for the fact that
his life has become past history, nor for the question about
his present accessibility, nor his relation to the future salvation (or punishment). Jesus is only a revealer of man's current situation in the light of his proclamation of a future

punishment and for salvation. The only feature of the Savior that is significant for the reader of *Thomas the Contender* is his pre-Ascension nature; his hidden nature is his exalted nature. As a glorified being, as "our light," he can illumine the darkness covering the meaning of his earthly teaching (cf. 138:13-20).

7. *Morality*. Little need be said of the moral teaching of *Thomas the Contender* save to emphasize its ascetic character. In order to avoid perishing along with one's lustful, perishable body, one is obliged to avoid contamination by matter, i.e. the world and one's body. According to *Thomas the Contender* the most prominent feature of the body is the point which it shares in common with the beasts: its sexual, lustful nature. The body's propensity for sexual lust defines the point at which the individual inhabiting a body is most susceptible to the contamination of the world. It is because of this that it can be said that the sexual drive is a fire which burns the spirits (140:3) and souls (140:26) of men. Unless one denies the body, one will share its fate in the fires of Hell. Whoever takes delight in the pleasures of this life, especially in satisfying the fires of passion, is like an insect attracted to a blazing candle; he is drunk, his mind is deranged, "but it is the fire which will burn them" (142:2).

Therefore, at least according to section A, one has the obligation to proclaim this condition to other miserable mortals who have the misfortune to be "begotten in the flesh" (141:19-25). This seems to be the extent of any positive ethical action prescribed in section A. In section B, the only action of any sort that is prescribed can scarcely be called ethical or moral: "Watch and pray that you shall not come to be in the flesh, but rather that you shall come forth from the bondage of the oblivion of this life" (145:8-10). The net result is that one must primarily avoid sexual intercourse 1) as a deceiving pleasure that attaches one to the body and 2) as a means of eventually producing another body with which to entrap another human soul (cf. 139:8-11). As a corollary, it even appears that one also ought to refrain from eating meat, since one is only using the flesh of one lustful body to satisfy and nourish his own lustful body (139:2-6). Thus there appears to be no significant difference between the morality of *Thomas the Contender* and the

morality prescribed by specifically gnostic sects, e.g. the
Manichaeans.

C. The Position of *Thomas the Contender* within the History of Religions

The position of *Thomas the Contender* in the history of
religions, specifically of Christianity, is complicated by the
hybrid nature of the tractate.

We have characterized section B of *Thomas the Contender* as
a collection of sayings expanded with (ascetic) interpretation,
in which the interpretation has outgrown the sayings far more
than has the gnosticizing interpretation of the *Gospel of Thomas*
outgrown the sayings therein. We have further placed section B
within the arena of certain collections of sayings traditionally
ascribed to an individual named Matthew (Matthaios, Matthias,
Mathaias). The fact that the witnesses to the existence of these
collections lived roughly from the middle of the second century
A.D. through the first half of the third century A.D. (Papias,
fl. ca. 130; Clement of Alexandria, fl. ca. 160-214; Hippolytus,
fl. ca. 160-235), suggests that these Matthean traditions flour-
ished from 150 to 250 A.D. Since the interpretation so prepon-
derates over the saying that the latter has become (except for
the beatitudes of section B) an atavistic formula, we would tend
to place the sayings collection of section B toward the end of
this period, say around 225 to 250 A.D.

We have characterized section A as a dialogue of the Resurrected with his disciple(s), in this case the disciple-apostle
Judas Thomas. We have located the provenance of the Thomas-
tradition in the Syrian Osrhoëne, in particular, the city of
Edessa. These traditions probably antedate[7] the inception of
both Marcionite (ca. 275 A.D.?) and orthodox Christianity (ca.
200 A.D.?) in that area as well as the work of Mani (ca. 240
A.D.), who himself made mention of Thomas and may have regarded
him as the "Living Paraclete." The fact that the history of the
Thomas tradition seems to be established at two points, the
Gospel of Thomas (ca. 130-150) and the *Acts of Thomas* (ca. 200-
250), both of which (since the latter seems to presuppose the
former) have been attributed to pre-Manichaean Syrian Gnosis,
provides us with a chronological/geographical framework in which
to locate section A of *Thomas the Contender*. In fact, we have

already pointed out several parallels between section A of
Thomas the Contender and the *Gospel* and *Acts of Thomas* respectively. All three contain the ascetic theme, possess a dualistic
anthropology, and regard Judas Thomas as the twin (δίδυμος) of
the Savior and recipient of his most secret revelations. In
both section A of *Thomas the Contender* and the *Acts of Thomas*,
Thomas has the mission to exhort men to abandon filthy intercourse and passion. In view of these common themes and particularly of the Thomas-tradition central to all three works, we
believe section A of *Thomas the Contender* occupies a median
position in the stream of the ascetic Syrian Thomas-tradition
as we move from the *Gospel of Thomas* to the *Acts of Thomas*.

First of all, section A of *Thomas the Contender* occupies a
median position in terms of the relative dominance of Thomas as
a character in the literature bearing his name. In the *Gospel
of Thomas*, Thomas appears as the scribe of Jesus' secret words,
and only in one episode, Logion 13, does he appear as a genuine
character. On the other hand, in the *Acts of Thomas*, Thomas is
always and everywhere the central character: apostle to India,
recipient of secret words, proclaimer and counselor of abstinence from what is carnal, and, finally, martyr. A median
position is now expressed in section A of *Thomas the Contender*.
Although Thomas is not here the central character owing to the
presence of the Savior as teacher, he is nevertheless the one
who through his questions and comments moves the dialogue ahead.
In addition, although no activity of his is reported, by the
nature of his questions he does in fact contemplate a mission
of teaching and exhortation to abstinence. Conversely, where
Thomas dominates a work, the Savior's role is reduced: in the
Gospel of Thomas he is ostensible author of and central character of every episode; in the *Acts* he only occasionally appears
to comfort and instruct Thomas in times of crisis, and in fact
appears to others in Thomas' likeness. Section A of *Thomas the
Contender* strikes a happy medium by presenting the Savior as
merely the dominant participant in a dialogue.

Furthermore, the increasing dominance of the figure of
Thomas and the corresponding attenuation of that of the Savior
bears a noticeable relationship to the kinds of materials used
in the composition of each work. In the *Gospel of Thomas*, a
long catena of logia of the living Jesus cause him to dominate

the work utterly. In section A of *Thomas the Contender*, a large
amount of discourse material uttered by the Savior has been
structured into a dialogue which takes place for the benefit of
Thomas, who keeps it moving by his questions. Finally, in the
Acts of Thomas, large blocks of legendary narrative material
concerning the exploits of the apostle Thomas (some of which,
judging by the varying lengths of the separate rescensions of
the *Acts*, had separate histories of transmission) have been
combined with prayers and other discursive and hymnic material
to yield a document whose intent is to present the life of its
dominant figure, Thomas.

Lastly, there is a relationship between these documents
exhibited by the theme most clearly common to them other than
the Thomas tradition, namely, the negative attitude toward embodied life in the world, particularly the sexual life. Thus
in the *Gospel of Thomas*, out of thirteen logia clearly having
to do with rejection of the world (22,27,37,42,48,68,69,78,79,
81,110,114), only four center on a rejection of the sexual life:
the sexual abstinence motif is present, but not dominant; nor
is it explicit, but rather conveyed in enigmatic, metaphorical
sayings. In section A of *Thomas the Contender*, the sexual abstinence motif is much more central, portrayed under the metaphor of a burning flame which must be extinguished, and is de-
nigrated as common bestiality pertaining to perishable bodies.
In the *Acts of Thomas*, however, the sexual abstinence motif
clearly predominates, no longer conveyed in enigmatic metaphors,
but explicitly in the form of erotic tales in which lovers are
enjoined to continence. As another aspect in the thematic relationship between these documents, one ought further to recall
the similarity in the order, noted in the comment on 140:27-141:
12, in which similar themes are treated in *Thomas the Contender*
and in the *Gospel of Thomas*, respectively.

In view of these comparisons, and at the risk of repetition, I should postulate the existence of a tradition centered
on the apostle Thomas, the twin of Jesus and recipient of his
secret words, which increasingly regards Thomas as champion and
contender in the cause of abstinence from all that is worldly,
especially sex. The association of Thomas with the sexual abstinence motif appears to be a growing tradition whose growth
parallels the increasing interest in the character of Thomas as

apostle and missionary. Section A of *Thomas the Contender* looks
like a product deriving from this stream of ascetic Thomas tradition at a point somewhere between its expression in the *Gospel
of Thomas* and in the *Acts of Thomas* respectively. As the provenance of the latter two works seems to be the Gnostic Christianity of East Syria (between Edessa and Mesene), we have
assigned section A of the *Book of Thomas the Contender* to the
same milieu. A Syrian provenance would have been a suitable
host to the sexual abstinence motif of our *Book of Thomas the
Contender* since, with the exception of Bardesanes, the great
figures of Syrian Christianity (Tatian, Marcion, Mani), as well
as its chief literary products under the name of Judas Thomas,
strongly contend for such abstinence.

Moreover, it seems quite certain that the tradition naming
the apostle Judas, the brother of James (Jude 1), and thus
Jesus' brother as "Thomas" (an Aramaic term whose Greek equivalent is "Didymus") meaning "twin," is of Edessene provenance
(cf. Syr[C]. rdg. "Judas Thomas" for "Judas not Iscariot" of Jn.
14:22; the Edessan Abgar legend of Eus. H.E. 1,13,4). Since
on the one hand, the *Gospel of Thomas* contains logia which re-
cur in the Manichaean *Kephalaia*, Manichaean *Psalm-Book*, Mani's
Epistula Fundamenta (Aug.) as well as in the Turfan fragments,
and on the other hand, the use of the *Acts of Thomas* by the
Manichees is witnessed by Augustine, it is conjectured that
these works are likely of Edessan origin.[8] Thus the Didymus
Judas Thomas tradition contained in them is also likely to have
been originally Edessan. Judging from the great age of the
Gospel of Thomas, perhaps as early as the first half of the
second century, since it was known in Egypt at the beginning of
the third century in the Oxyrhynchus Papyri, the Thomas tradition was, to quote Helmut Koester again: "the oldest form of
Christianity in Edessa."[9] On the other hand, the date now proposed for the origin of the *Acts of Thomas* is, due to evidences
of Manichaean redaction (the wedding hymn, epiclesis of c. 7,
hymn of the pearl)[10] placed between the times of Bardesanes and
Mani, or in the first half of the third century. As for section
A of *Thomas the Contender*, we can at least say that it is later
than the *Gospel of Thomas*, but, because of its intermediate
position in terms of the dominance of roles of the Savior and
Thomas respectively, and because of its less elaborate structure,

probably earlier than the *Acts of Thomas*. However, its asceticism more nearly approaches that of the *Acts* than that of the
Gospel of Thomas; indeed the abstinence motif seems to become
more prominent in Syria as we move from Tatian to Mani.

We thus date the composition of the original section A at
ca. 200 A.D.

It now remains to deal with the redaction of sections A and
B which yielded the completed work, *The Book of Thomas the Contender*, in its present form.

Because the Coptic style of the *incipit* differs from that
of the rest of the document, and because the *incipit* carries
forward from section B its designation as "words" of the Savior,
the combination of A with B must have occurred in the Coptic
stage of their transmission, not at some point during their
existence in Greek dress. Since the Coptic style of sections
A and B is very similar, they were present to the scribal redactor of A and B perhaps in the same document, or at least in
documents copied, maybe even translated from Greek to Coptic,
by the same scribe. At this point the redactor of A and B prefixed A to B, placed the original title of A at the end of the
whole, and composed a fresh *incipit* title to the whole using
the original title of section B as his model. This activity
must have occurred at a time and place where both A and B would
have been translated into Coptic and in close proximity to one
another. It is probable that the redaction was accomplished
in Egypt, and most probably upper-Egypt, to judge from the Coptic style of the freshly-composed *incipit*; it is written, with
the exception of one word-form (ⲙ̄ⲙⲁⲩ for ⲙ̄ⲙⲟⲟⲩ) in standard
Sahidic, the dialect of upper-Egypt.

Judging from the Subachmimically-influenced Sahidic dialect
of the body of the tractate (sections A and B), these were translated into Coptic slightly north of the area of their final redaction.

Finally, the completed tractate was included, perhaps by
yet another scribe, at the end of Codex II of the Nag Hammadi
corpus. Thus we obtain the following family tree of the *Book
of Thomas the Contender*.

238

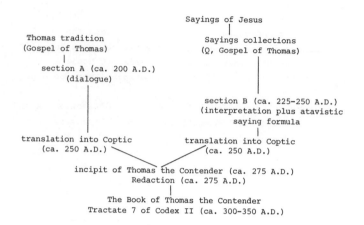

Sayings of Jesus
|
Thomas tradition   Sayings collections
(Gospel of Thomas)   (Q, Gospel of Thomas)
    |
    section A (ca. 200 A.D.)
        (dialogue)

                                    section B (ca. 225-250 A.D.)
                                    (interpretation plus atavistic
                                          saying formula
                                             |
translation into Coptic   translation into Coptic
   (ca. 250 A.D.)   (ca. 250 A.D.)

        incipit of Thomas the Contender (ca. 275 A.D.)
              Redaction (ca. 275 A.D.)
                         |
           The Book of Thomas the Contender
        Tractate 7 of Codex II (ca. 300-350 A.D.)

We have now reached the end of a study of what seems to be
a most valuable document, valuable as a representative of the
Thomas-tradition, and as evidence which it provides for characterizing the development of literary *genres* in early Christianity as vehicles for conveying and interpreting the teachings of
Jesus. It is also of value, though less strikingly, as a representative of a brand of Christian ascetic teaching with gnostic
features, but which cannot be called gnostic in the same sense
as the teaching of other dialogues of the Resurrected with his
disciples. In these ways, *Thomas the Contender*, in its capacity
as a representative of an intermediate stage of the development
of the Thomas tradition, the gnostic dialogue and gnostic asceticism, makes a contribution to an understanding of the syncretistic Christianity of the first three centuries. While an attempt has been made at completeness, there has been no attempt
on the part of the author to be final. It is hoped that this
study of the *Book of Thomas the Contender* will, both by its
successes and failures, make a real contribution to the ongoing
study of Gnosticism and early Christianity.

NOTES

[1]Kurt Rudolph, 'Der gnostische "Dialog" als literarisches Genus,' *Probleme der koptischen Literatur* (Wissenschaftliche Beiträge der Martin-Luther-Universität; Halle-Wittenberg, 1968).

[2]In an unpublished paper "On the Gattung of Mark (and John)," p. 19.

[3]*Logoi Sophon: On the Gattung of Q*, expanded E. T. of "ΛΟΓΟΙ ΣΟΦΩΝ," *Zeit und Geschichte: Dankesgabe an Rudolf Bultmann zum 80. Geburtstag*, ed. Erich Dinkler (Tübingen: J.C.B. Mohr, 1964), pp. 77-96.

[4]Hans Jonas, *The Gnostic Religion* (Boston: Beacon Press, 1958), p. 42.

[5]Cf. the definition of *gnosis* in the proposal of the Messina Colloquium on Gnosticism in *Le Origini dello Gnosticismo: Colloquio di Messina, 13-18 aprile 1966.*, Testi e Discussioni, Pubblicati a Cura di Ugo Bianchi (Leiden: E.J. Brill, 1967), p. xxvii: "The *gnosis* of Gnosticism involves the divine identity of the knower (the Gnostic), the known (the divine substance of one's transcendent self) and the means by which one knows (*gnosis* as an implicit divine faculty is to be awakened and actualized)."

[6]Thus, Jonas, *op. cit.*, p. 43.

[7]See the comment on 138:7-21.

[8]See H.-C. Puech in Hennecke-Schneemelcher, *op. cit.*, vol. 1, p. 283, 299 and G. Bornkamm, *ibid.*, vol. 2, p. 427.

[9]HTR 58, 1965, p. 293.

[10]So Bornkamm, Hennecke-Schneemelcher, *op. cit.*, vol. 2, p. 441.

SELECT BIBLIOGRAPHY

Grammar and Lexicography

Arndt, W. F., and Gingrich, F. W. *A Greek-English Lexicon of the New Testament and Other Early Christian Literature* (translation and adaptation of W. Bauer's *Wörterbuch*) Chicago: University of Chicago Press, 1960.

Crum, W. E. *A Coptic Dictionary*. Oxford: Clarendon, 1962.

Kahle, P. E. *Bala'izah: Coptic texts from Deir el Bala'izah in Upper Egypt*, 2 vols. Oxford: University Press, 1954.

Kasser, R. *Compléments au dictionnaire Copte de Crum*. Le Caire: Institut Français d'Archéologie Orientale, 1964.

Lampe, G. W. H. *A Patristic Greek Lexicon*. Oxford: Clarendon, 1961.

Lidell, H. G., and Scott, R. A. *A Greek-English Lexicon*. Revised and augmented throughout by H. S. Jones and R. McKenzie, with a supplement. Oxford: Clarendon, 1968.

Polotsky, H. J. *Études de syntaxe Copte*. Le Caire: Institut Francais d'Archéologie Orientale, 1964.

_____. "The Coptic Conjugation System," *Orientalia* (1960), pp. 392-422.

Spiegelberg, W. *Koptisches Handwörterbuch*. Heidelberg, 1921.

Steindorf, G. *Lehrbuch der koptischen Grammatik*. Chicago: University of Chicago Press, 1951.

Stern, L. *Koptische Grammatik*. Leipzig: T. O. Weigel, 1880.

Till, W. C. *Koptische Dialectgrammatik mit Lesestücke und Wörterbuch*. München: C. H. Beck, 1961.

_____. *Koptische Grammatik (saidischer Dialect) mit Bibliographie, Lesestücken und Wörterverzeichnissen*. Leipzig: VEB, 1966.

_____. "Die Satzarten in Koptischen," *Mitteilungen der Deutsche Akademie der Wissenschaften zu Berlin*, Band II, Heft 3 (1954), p. 379-402.

Text Editions Cited[1]

Aland, K. *Synopsis Quattuor Evangeliorum.* Stuttgart: Württem-
bergische Bibelanstalt, 1964.

Allberry, C. R. C. *A Manichaean Psalm-Book,* Part II (Manichaean
Manuscripts in the Chester Beatty Collection, II) Stuttgart:
W. Kohlhammer, 1938.

Babbitt, F. C. *et. al. Plutarch, Moralia,* 15 vols. (Loeb
Classical Library) Cambridge: Harvard University Press,
1927 - .

Bauer, W. *Die Oden Salamos.* (Kleine Texte für Vorlesungen und
Übungen, 64) Berlin: de Gruyter, 1933.

Casey, R. P. *The Excerpta ex Theodoto of Clement of Alexandria.*
(Studies and Documents I) London: Christophers, 1934.

Charles, R. H. ed. *Apocrypha and Pseudepigrapha of the Old
Testament,* 2 vols. Oxford: University Press, 1913.

Colson, F. H. *et. al. Philo,* 12 vols. (Loeb Classical Library)
Cambridge: Harvard University Press, 1929-1953.

Dorries, A., Klostermann, E., Kroeger, M. *Die 50 geistlicher
Homilien des Makarios.* (Patristische Texte und Studien, 4)
Berlin: de Gruyter, 1964.

Evelyn-White, H. G. *Hesiod, the Homeric Poems and Homerica.*
(Loeb Classical Library) Cambridge: Harvard University
Press, 1914).

Fowler, H. N. *Plato*: *Euthyphro, Apology, Crito, Phaedo, Phaedrus.*
(Loeb Classical Library) Cambridge: Harvard University
Press, 1914.

Grenfell, B. P. and Hunt, A. S. ΛΟΓΙΑ ΙΗΣΟΥ, *Sayings of Our
Lord from an Early Greek Papyrus.* New York: H. Frowde,
1897.

Guidi, I. *Chronicon Edessenum.* (Corpus Scriptorum Christianorum
Orientalium, III, Tome IV) Louvain: Secretariat du Corpus
SCO, 1903.

Guillaumont, A., Puech, H.-C., Quispel, G., Till, W., al Massah,
Y.A. *The Gospel According to Thomas.* New York: Harper and
Row, 1959.

Harvey, W. W. *Sancti Irenaei, Libros Quinque Adversus Haereses.*
2 vols. Ridgewood: Gregg, (reprint) 1965.

---

[1] All citations, except as noted, of texts contained in the
Coptic Gnostic Library from Nag Hammadi are taken from their
respective transcriptions located at the Coptic Gnostic Project
of the Institute for Antiquity and Christianity, Claremont,
California.

Holl, K. *Epiphanius, Ancoratus und Panarion*, 3 Bände. Leipzig: Hinrich's, 1915.

Horner, G. *The Coptic Version of the New Testament in the Southern Dialect, otherwise called Sahidic and Thebaic*, 7 vols. Oxford: University Press, 1911-1924.

Klotz, R. *Titi Flaui Clementis Alexandrini, Opera Omnia*, 4 vols. Lipsiae: Schwickert, 1831.

Kroll, W., Skutsch, F., Ziegler, K. *Firmicus Maternus, Mathesis.* (Bibliotheca scriptorum graecorum et romanorum Teubneriana) Stuttgart: B. G. Teubner, 1968.

Kuhn, K. H. *On Christian Behavior, Ms. Pierpont Morgan 604.* (Corpus Scriptorum Christianorum Orientalum, 29) Louvain: Secrétariat du Corpus SCO, 1960.

Lake, L. *The Apostolic Fathers*, 2 vols. (Loeb Classical Library) Cambridge: Harvard University Press, 1912.

Lipsius, R. A. and Bonnet, M. *Acta Apostolorum Apocrypha*, 3 vols. Hildesheim: G. Olms, (reprint) 1959.

Nock, A. D., and Festugière, A.-J. *Corpus Hermeticum*, 4 Tomes. Paris: Société d'Édition "Les belles Lettres," 1960.

Polotsky, H. J. *Manichäische Homilien.* (Handschriften der Sammlung A. Chester Beatty, I) Stuttgart: W. Kohlhammer, 1934.

Polotsky, H. J. and Bohlig, A. *Kephalaia*, 1. Hälfte. (Handschriften der Sammlung A. Chester Beatty, III) Stuttgart: W. Kohlhammer, 1940.

Rackham, H. *Cicero, De Natura Deorum.* (Loeb Classical Library) Cambridge: Harvard University Press, 1933.

Rehm, B. *Die Pseudoklementinen, Homilien, Recognitionen in Rufins Übersetzung*, 2 vols. (Die griechischen christlichen Schriftsteller der drei ersten Jahrhunderte, 42,51) Berlin: Akademie, 1965.

Roberts, A. and Donaldson, J. eds. *The Writings of the Ante-Nicene Fathers*, 10 vols. Grand Rapids: Eerdmans, (reprint) 1965.

Swete, H. B. *The Old Testament in Greek according to the Septuagint*, 3 vols. Cambridge: Harvard University Press, 1891.

Wendland, P. *Hippolytus Werke*, Band III: *Refutatio Omnium Haeresium* (Die griechischen christlichen Schriftsteller der ersten drei Jahrhunderte) Leipzig: Hinrich's, 1916.

246

Secondary Works

Books:

Bauer, W. *Rechtgläubigkeit und Ketzerei im Ältesten Christentum*,
2 Aufl. mit einem Nachtrag von G. Strecker. (Beiträge zur
historischen Theologie, 10) Tübingen: J. C. B. Mohr, 1964.

Bianchi, H. *Le Origini dello Gnosticismo, Colloquio di Messina,
13-18 Aprile 1966*. (Supplements to Numen, XII) Leiden:
E. J. Brill, 1967.

Bornkamm, G., Barth, G., Held, H. J. *Tradition and Interpretation
in Matthew*. Philadelphia: Westminster, 1963.

Cumont, F. *After Life in Roman Paganism*. New York: Dover,
(reprint) 1959.

_____. *Lux Perpetua*. Paris: Librairie Orientaliste Paul
Guenther, 1949.

Doresse, J. *Les livres secrets des Gnostiques d'Égypte*. Paris:
Librairie Plon, 1959.

_____. *The Secret Books of the Egyptian Gnostics*, trans.
P. Mairet. New York: Viking, 1960.

Georgi, D. *Die Gegner des Paulus im 2. Korintherbrief*. (Wissen-
schaftlichen Monographien zum Alten und Neuen Testament,
11) Neukirchen-Vluyn: Neukirchener, 1964.

Giversen, S. *Apocryphon Johannis: the Coptic Text of the Apocryphon Johannis in the Nag Hammadi Codex II with Translation, Introduction and Commentary*. (Acta Theologica Danica,
V) Copenhagen: Prostant Apud Munksgaard, 1963.

Hennecke, E. *New Testament Apocrypha*, 2 vols. ed. W. Schneemelcher, trans. R. McL. Wilson. Philadelphia: Westminster
Press, 1964.

Jonas, H. *The Gnostic Religion*. Boston: Beacon Press, 1958.

Kirk, G. S., and Raven, C. E. *The Presocratic Philosophers*.
Cambridge: University Press, 1966.

Kittel, G., and Friedrich, G. *Theologisches Wörterbuch zum
Neuen Testament*. (in progress) Stuttgart: W. Kohlhammer,
1933 - .

_____. *Theological Dictionary of the New Testament*, ed.
and trans. G. W. Bromiley (in progress). Grand Rapids:
Eerdmans, 1965 - .

Klijn, A. F. J. *The Acts of Thomas, Introduction - Text -
Commentary*. (Supplements to Novum Testamentum, V) Leiden:
E. J. Brill, 1962.

Krause, Martin. *Die drei Versionen des Apokryphon des Johannes im Koptischen Museum zu Alt-Kairo.* (Mitteilungen des Deutschen Archäologischen Instituts Abteilung Kairo, XIX) Wiesbaden, 1962.

Montefiore, C. G. and Loewe, H. *A Rabbinic Anthology*. New York: Meridian, 1963.

Roscher, W. H. *Ausführliches Lexikon der griechischen und römischen Mythologie*, 7 vols. Hildesheim: G. Olms, (reprint) 1965.

Sagnard, F. M. *La Gnose Valentinienne et le témoinage de Saint Irenée.* (Études de Philosophie Médievale, XXXVI) Paris: J. Vrin, 1947.

Articles:

Bacon, B. W. "Jesus and the Law," *Journal of Biblical Literature* 47 (1928), pp. 95-99.

Doresse, J. "Nouveaux textes gnostiques découverts en Haute-Égypte: La bibliothèque de Chenoboskion," *Vigiliae Christianae* III (1949), pp. 129-141.

Koester, H. ΓΝΩΜΑΙ ΔΙΑΦΟΡΟΙ, *Harvard Theological Review* 58 (1965), pp. 279-318.

Muller, C. D. G. "Buch von Thomas dem Athleten," *Kindlers Literatur Lexikon* I, Zürich: Kindler, 1965, p. 1936f.

Puech, H.-C. "Les nouveaux écrits gnostiques," *Coptic Studies in Honor of Walter Ewing Crum*. Boston: Byzantine Institute, 1950, pp. 105-120.

Robinson, J. M. ΛΟΓΟΙ ΣΟΦΩΝ, *Zeit und Geschichte: Dankesgab an Rudolf Bultman zum 80. Geburtstag*, ed. E. Dinkler. Tübingen: J. C. B. Mohr, 1964, pp. 77-96.

Rudolph, K. "Der gnostische 'Dialogue' als literarisches Genus," *Probleme der Koptischen Literatur.* (Wissenschaftliche Beiträge der Martin-Luther-Universität) Halle-Wittenberg, 1968.

94